ACCOMMODATION AND CLEANING SERVICES

Volume 1: Operations

By the same author

ACCOMMODATION AND CLEANING SERVICES
Volume 2: Management

ACCOMMODATION AND CLEANING SERVICES

Volume 1: Operations

David M. Allen

Principal Lecturer in Applied Science
Doncaster Metropolitan Institute of Higher Education

HUTCHINSON

London   Melbourne   Sydney   Auckland   Johannesburg

Hutchinson Education

An imprint of Century Hutchinson Ltd
62-65 Chandos Place, London WC2N 4NW

Century Hutchinson Australia Pty Ltd
PO Box 496, 16-22 Church Street, Hawthorn,
Victoria 3122, Australia

Century Hutchinson New Zealand Limited
PO Box 40-086, Glenfield, Auckland 10, New Zealand

Century Hutchinson South Africa (Pty) Limited
PO Box 337, Bergvlei 2012, South Africa

First published 1983
Reprinted 1984, 1985, 1986

Set in Times

Printed and bound in Great Britain by
Anchor Brendon Ltd, Tiptree, Essex

British Library Cataloguing in Publication Data
Allen, David
  Accommodation and cleaning services.
  Vol. 1: Operations
  1. Hotel management 2. Hotels, taverns, etc. –
  Great Britain 3. Buildings – Cleaning
  I. Title
  647'.9441'068   TX910.G7

ISBN 0 09 150991 2

Contents

Foreword

By Lord Parry of Neyland

David Allen is a leader among a small group of academics who, earlier than so many of their colleagues in teaching, have realised that Britain earns its living as much from the so-called 'service sector' of the economy as from manufacturing goods.

Working in an area where heavy industry created so much of the social structure and founded and funded so much of the further education system he has, nevertheless, associated himself and his courses with the less popular but vital areas of research. In consequence he has become an important student of Britain's cleaning industry. His book carries the authority of its author's experience.

As chairman of the Wales Tourist Board and a member of the British Tourist Authority, President of the British Institute of Cleaning Science and, temporarily, Chairman of the emerging Council of the cleaning industry, I have worked with David Allen on the obviously related interests that make tourism on the one hand and cleaning on the other vital contributors to Britain's rapidly changing economy.

Cleanliness is not only next to Godliness, but it is, in fact, the key to a better living for Britain. We have deluded ourselves for too long that our heavy industrial economy would continue to pay our country's way. It has failed to do that for more years than we have been prepared to admit. The service sector of the economy has long been responsible for closing the gap and, on occasions, has actually created a balance of payments surplus for Britain in its overseas markets. For example, the tourism industry and the cleaning industry earn similar sums of money for Britain overseas and save similar sums of money for Britain at home, circulating it moreover through the home financial system. Together, they earned more money than the offshore oil industry did for Britain last year.

This book and its companion volume recognize that the considerable level of technical and management skills required by supervisors and managers in the accommodation service sector of the hospitality industry and in the cleaning industry are the key to Britain's economic survival. These technical skills are basic to the industry's efficiency and to its growing confidence.

It is vital that not only industry, but those servicing it, be seen to be the key workers of the future. Qualifications and competence will be essential in achieving this.

David Allen's book has come out at exactly the right time to achieve it.

Preface

This book and its companion volume were written to meet the requirements of students studying accommodation and cleaning services and who are enrolled on the following courses:

TEC Diploma in Hotei Catering and Institutional Operations
HND and TEC Higher Diplomas in Hotel Catering and Institutional Management
HCIMA Parts A and B
CGLI 764 Cleaning Science
CGLI 708 Accommodation Services

The books will also be of particular value to supervisors and managers involved in the provision of accommodation and cleaning services in the following areas:

Hospital Domestic Services Departments
Contract Cleaning Companies
Housekeeping Departments in Hotels and Residential Establishments
Public Authority Buildings

Taken as a whole the various organizations, companies, establishments and institutions involved in the provision and supply of accommodation and cleaning services form one of the largest industries in the UK with an annual turnover of several billion pounds. The supervisor or manager in any of the various sectors of the industry must have a depth and spread of technical knowledge and be conversant with and be able to exercise a wide range of general and particular supervisory and management techniques in order to deal with the often complex interelating factors involved in determining the services required in a particular situation and in providing these services. The student must acquire that knowledge and become conversant with these techniques and skills.

Only within recent years has it been recognized that the supervisor or manager of accommodation services requires an extraordinary range of knowledge, skills, techniques and abilities. This is reflected in the very limited information available dealing objectively and critically with technical matters and with the supervisory and management techniques particular to accommodation and cleaning services. This book and its companion volume were written in response to that lack of information.

In preparing both volumes of this work it has been the intention to provide students of accommodation services and in post supervisors and managers with the necessary knowledge of technical matters relevant to the various services, with the necessary practical details relevant to each service, with a knowledge of the factors determining the types and standard of service to be provided and with a knowledge of particular supervisory and management techniques relevant to accommodation services. Only with a comprehensive understanding of all aspects of accommodation services is it possible to objectively determine, plan and control the types and standard of services required in any particular situation.

It is inevitable that some points in the text will be controversial and that there are some broad generalizations. However, wherever possible the validity of factors judged to be controversial have been tested under laboratory or working conditions and broad generalizations have been used where a detailed treatment would have rendered the subject all but incomprehensible to other than the most experienced manager.

The preparation of this book would not have been possible without the support of my wife Mary. For her help and for putting up with more than one might reasonably expect, I express my gratitude. I also thank Mrs Doreen Evans and her colleagues for their help in the preparation of the text and my colleagues and students without whose help and criticism it would not have been possible.

Separately I wish to extend my thanks to Mrs G. M. Hayes for her contribution in the preparation of the sections dealing with Bedding and Linen, Interior Design, Hygiene and Pest Control in this volume and for her contribution in the initial drafting of the various chapters in Volume 2.

Acknowledgements

I wish to thank the following organizations for permission to reproduce or make use of copyright material: British Standards Institution for permission to quote details from a variety of standards, in particular BS 1129, BS 1139, BS 1397, BS 2037, BS 2747, BS 3913, BS 5720, BS 5845, Chapter 1 of CP3 (Part 2) 1973 and CP97 (Parts 1, 2 and 3) 1967, and which are listed at the end of each section; Chartered Institution of Building Services for permission to quote standard service illuminances from The CIBS *Code for Interior Lighting;* BAS Management Services for permission to reproduce diagrams from the manual *Construction Safety.*

I also wish to thank the following organizations and companies for permission to reproduce photographs: BMM Weston Ltd; G.N. Burgess & Co. Ltd; Clarke-Gravely Ltd; Cimex Ltd; Contico Manufacturing Ltd; Danum Hotel, Doncaster; Doncaster Metropolitan Institute of Higher Education; Dowding & Plummer Ltd; K.E.W. Sales Ltd; H. Morris & Co. Ltd; Nilfisk Ltd; Pritchard Services Group Plc; Reckitt Industrial Ltd; Rentokil Ltd; Von Schrader (UK) Ltd.

Finally, I thank Mrs E. Johnson for her assistance in the preparation of photographs for inclusion in this work.

1 Introduction

Accommodation and cleaning services require the supervisor or manager to have a wide range of knowledge and skills at his/her fingertips. To be able to provide the services required in any given situation, the necessary knowledge and skills will include:

- Knowledge of the materials and finishes used in the construction of a building.
- Knowledge of furniture, fixtures and fittings installed in a building.
- Ability to select the most appropriate finishes, furniture, fittings and fixtures in relation to their use and the methods of cleaning and maintenance to be employed.
- Knowledge and understanding of the types of services which can be provided, e.g. cleaning, room, linen, laundry.
- Knowledge of the practical aspects involved in providing these services.
- Knowledge of the factors determining the services to be provided, their extent and the standards to be met.
- Knowledge of the types and standards of services required in specified situations.
- Awareness of the resources available to the supervisor or manager, i.e. equipment, materials, labour.
- Knowledge of relevant technical information concerning equipment, chemicals and other materials.
- Ability to select equipment, chemicals and other materials.
- Knowledge of health and safety requirements and procedures.
- Ability to determine the types of service required, the standards to be met, the extent of the services to be provided and the methods to be employed in a given situation.

- Knowledge of and the ability to apply the methods of work planning.
- Knowledge of and the ability to apply the methods of costing and budgeting.
- Knowledge of and the ability to apply methods of control in relation to work standards, stock, purchasing and costs.
- Knowledge of the duties of staff employed in the various sectors of the industry.
- Knowledge of the techniques and skills employed in the supervision and management of personnel.

This first volume is largely concerned with all but the last five of these areas of knowledge and skill.

A knowledge of the range of materials and finishes used and of the furniture, fixtures and fittings installed in a building, together with their respective physical and chemical characteristics, is essential. Without such knowledge the process of selecting the most appropriate finishes and furniture for use in a particular situation will frequently be less than successful and the methods of cleaning and maintenance selected may have a deleterious effect. The selection of finishes and furniture will be made with reference to a clearly defined set of criteria, a specification, which will be drawn up with reference to, for example, wear and tear expected and the activities carried out within the building. The actual finish or item of furniture selected will be that which most nearly matches the criteria set.

Within the range of services that can be defined as accommodation services, cleaning will be the one all establishments will require. The necessity to provide other services, e.g. laundry, linen, food and beverage, and the extent to which that service is provided will depend on the establishment concerned. Nevertheless, where they are required a thorough understanding of what is required and how that requirement can most effectively be met is essential. The extent to which cleaning services are provided will depend on the standards of hygiene and appearance required, which in turn will depend on the establishment or part of the establishment concerned. A clear understanding of the standards required and of the factors influencing these standards is essential since they will determine the frequency of cleaning and the methods which can be employed.

An enormous range of cleaning equipment and chemicals is available for use. An understanding of the characteristics of the equipment, the physical and chemical properties of the chemicals, the criteria upon which selection is made for a particular use and the correct methods of use will affect the ability to achieve the standard of service required at the most economic cost.

For any building, a knowledge of the characteristics of the materials, finishes, furniture, fixtures and fittings used, of the activities carried out, of the services provided within it and of the standards of hygiene and appearance required and the ways in which they can be achieved will make it possible to define what must be done to provide the required types, extent and standards of accommodation services. The supervisor or manager with a thorough understanding of the resources at her/his disposal will be able to provide these services in the most cost-effective way by correctly selecting the most appropriate combination of types and amount of equipment and materials, working methods and procedures, frequency of carrying out tasks and the number of staff to carry out the work.

The particular techniques involved in planning, costing and controlling accommodation services in order that these services are cost-effective are described in Volume 2.

2 Materials and finishes

This chapter describes the materials and finishes used in the construction of a building and its fittings and furnishings. The components that make up the fabric of a building and the range of fittings and furnishings available are then described with particular reference to characteristics relevant to their selection for use in certain situations.

Plastics

Plastics are simple organic molecules (monomers) combined together to form polymers. For example, polyethylene (more commonly known by the trade name, Polythene) is a polymer of the molecule ethylene.

monomers   polymer

Figure 1 *Polymers*

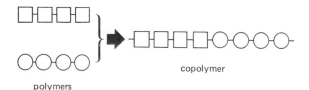

polymers

copolymer

Figure 2 *Copolymers*

In some cases a particular plastic will be a copolymer. These are polymers consisting of two or more different monomers. For example, ABS is a copolymer of acrylonitrile, butadiene and styrene.

Types of plastics

There are three major classes of plastics:

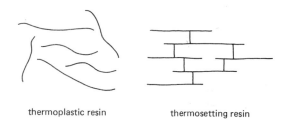

thermoplastic resin   thermosetting resin

Figure 3 *Thermoplastic and thermosetting resins*

thermoplastic, thermosetting and elastomeric. Table 1 shows the types of plastic within each class.

Thermoplastics consist of individual polymer chains. When heated they will soften and can be moulded into new shapes.

Thermosetting plastics consist of polymer chains linked to form three-dimensional lattices. When heated they will char rather than soften.

Elastomers consist of polymers with elastic properties. When subjected to tension or compression they will expand or contract, but will return to their original shape when the tension or compression is removed.

Properties and uses

The properties of a plastic will depend on the constituent polymers. They can, however, be modified by the addition of other chemicals: *plasticizers* to improve flexibility; *reinforcing agents* to improve strength; *fillers* to increase the body; *pigments* to give colour.

Thermoplastics and thermosetting plastics have their own characteristic properties (as shown in Table 2) and together with the elastomeric

Table 1   *Types of plastics, their properties and uses*

Type	Properties	Uses
(a) Thermoplastics		
Polypropylene (PP)	Fair abrasion resistance; deterioration in sunlight; attacked by hot solvents; burns if subjected to abrasion	Curtains, pipes, buckets, carpets
Polyethylene (PE)	Flexible; good impact resistance; limited abrasion resistance; poor resistance to solvents other than alchohols	Buckets, containers, polishes
Polystyrene (PS)	Very rigid but brittle; softens at $100^{\circ}C$ and distorts at $75^{\circ}C$; burns with a dense smoke	Expanded foams, cups, wall tiles, adhesives
Acrylonitrile-butadiene-styrene (ABS)	Good impact resistance; low abrasion resistance; poor resistance to solvents and sulphuric and nitric acids	Pipes, window tracks, sliding doors, containers
Cellulose derivatives	Fair impact and abrasion resistance; poor resistance to solvents and strong acids	Light fittings and shades, toilets seats, telephone housings, soft furnishings, paints
Polymethyl acrylates (PMA)	Softens and whitens at $100^{\circ}C$; unsuitable at working temperatures much above $65^{\circ}C$; good impact resistance; limited abrasion resistance; very poor solvent resistance	Baths and sinks, lampshades, light fittings. Perspex (a clear acrylic) is used for shelves and tap handles. Paints, polishes
Polyester	Either formed in slabs or reinforced with glass fibre (glass-reinforced plastic—GRP); good impact and abrasion resistance; limited resistance to acids and alkalis; poor resistance to solvents; can be thermosetting	Baths and sinks, containers, wall panels or sheets, flooring, soft furnishings, paints
Nylon (various types)	Can be reinforced; good impact and reasonable abrasion resistance; can soften at $60-80^{\circ}C$; either resistant to solvents or acids and alkalis depending upon type	Door fixtures, cleaning materials, carpets, soft furnishings
Polyvinyl chloride (PVC)	Rigid or flexible depending on whether plasticizer added; softens at $70^{\circ}C$; good impact and reasonable abrasion resistance; excellent resistance to acids and alkalis; resistance to solvents depends on other ingredients, fair in general and poor if plasticized	Cable insulation, containers, pipes, floorings, soft furnishings
Polyvinyl acetate (PVA)	Flexible; good resistance to acids, alkalis and solvents	Surface coatings, fabric finishes

Table 1 — *continued*

Type	Properties	Uses
(b) Thermosetting		
Epoxy resins (EP)	Can be used in slabs or reinforced with glass fibre (GRP); good impact and abrasion resistance; excellent resistance to alkalis; fair to poor resistance to acids and solvents	Laminated sheet, wall panels, adhesives, flooring, surface coatings
Phenol formaldehyde, e.g. Bakelite (PF)	Physical properties depend on other additives; impact resistance can be poor; good abrasion resistance; very hard; poor resistance to acids and alkalis; good resistance to solvents	Kitchen ware, telephone covers, toilet seats, furniture fittings, electrical fittings, surface coatings
Melamine formaldehyde, 'Melamine' (MF)	Very hard — excellent scratch and abrasion resistance; impact resistance can be poor if not plasticized; resistance to alkalis, acids and solvents good but only fair if inorganic fillers used.	Laminated sheets, wall panels, appliance housings, tableware, surface coatings
Urea formaldehyde, e.g. Carbamide (UF)	Properties similar to melamine formaldehyde	Electrical fittings, food containers, adhesives, surface coatings
Polycarbonates (PC)	Very hard; abrasion resistance good; excellent impact resistance but affected by exposure to solvents and adhesives	Appliance housings
Polyurethane	Not normally used for moulded products; excellent abrasion resistance; good resistance to acids and fair resistance to some solvents	Expanded foams, surface coatings
(c) Elastomeric		
Rubber and synthetic rubbers	Properties depend very much on type, fillers and other factors; rubber is prone to oxidation leading to breakdown of surface	Flooring, foams

Table 2

Property	Thermoplastic	Thermosetting
Organic solvents	Dissolve	—
Acids/alkalis	—	Attacked
Hardness	Soft	Hard
Heat	Soften	—

plastics, are used in a variety of materials: moulded products, surface coatings, carpets, soft furnishings, polishes and seals, floorings and adhesives.

Table 1 shows the use of the common plastics and their properties relevant to moulded products.

Metallic surfaces and finishes

The principal metallic surfaces and finishes are given in Table 3.

Textiles

The characteristics of soft furnishings and carpets depend on the type of fibres used and their properties, type of yarn, the method of construction, dye fastness and the type of finish applied

Characteristics of soft furnishings and carpets

The possible characteristics required and the principal factors influencing them are shown in Table 4.

Types of fibre and their properties

There are three principal groups of fibres:

1 *Natural:* animal (hair, wool, silk) and vegetable (cotton, linen, jute, coir).
2 *Regenerated:* rayon, cellulose acetate and cellulose triacetate (the latter two being thermoplastics).
3 *Synthetic:* polyamides, polyesters, acrylics, modacrylics, chlorofibres, polypropylene and polyurethane, all except the last being thermoplastics.

Wool Natural outgrowth of animal skin. A typical fibre consists of an outer scaly cuticle enclosing a cortex and medulla largely composed of the elastic protein, keratin. The outer scales are the cause of the shrinkage of wool when washed.

Hair and jute will be referred to when discussing carpets (see page 44).

Silk is a continuous filament formed by silk worms and composed of the protein, fibroin.

Cotton fibres are separated from the seed heads of the cotton plant. They are 1–3 cm in length and composed of long cellulose molecules packed tightly together, and for the most part parallel to each other. The fibres are spun together to form a staple yarn.

Linen fibres are separated from the stems of the flax plant. They are composed of cellulose and other polymers and are produced in three grades. The fibres are spun together to form a staple yarn.

Rayon is composed of cellulose. It is made by treating wood pulp or cotton linters with caustic soda and carbon disulphide to form a viscose solution from which the cellulose is regenerated as long filaments by spinning the viscose into a bath of sulphuric acid. The properties of rayon can be altered to produce modified rayons such as Evlan by altering the spinning bath and stretching the filaments during spinning.

Cellulose acetate is a polymer of cellulose which has been altered by the addition of chemical groups called acetyl groups to the molecules. It is made by treating wood pulp or cotton linters with acetic acid and acetic anhydride. The cellulose acetate formed is dissolved in acetone and then dry-spun into hot air to form long filaments.

Cellulose triacetate is similar to cellulose acetate but possesses more acetyl groups.

Polyamides, or nylons, are polymers composed of monomers from a class of chemicals called amines. There are various types of nylon which are numbered according to the number of carbon atoms in the molecules of the starting chemicals. Nylon 66 is formed from adipic acid (6 carbon atoms) and hexamethylene diamine (6 carbons) and Nylon 6 from caprolactam (6 carbons). The starting chemicals are mixed together to form a nylon salt which is them melted and forced through a spinneret to form long filaments as it cools.

Polyesters are polymers of ethylene glycol terephthalate or similar compounds. The filaments are formed in a similar way to nylon.

Table 3 *Metallic surfaces and finishes*

Metal	Properties	Uses
Aluminium	Resistant to corrosion. It forms a surface layer of aluminium oxide which resists further attack. Attacked by strong alkalis	Kitchen ware, window frames, doors, decorative finishes
Anodised aluminium	A protective layer of aluminium is deposited on the surface during manufacture. If abrasives are used the protective layer is removed and white, powdery spots will be produced	
Brass	An alloy of copper and zinc. May be solid or plate applied to mild steel. Corroded by acids. Tarnishing occurs as a result of oxidation in a moist atmosphere to form green verdigris. Abrasive will scratch or wear away surface	Ornaments, object d'art, decorative finishes, furniture finishes
Bronze	An alloy of tin and copper with properties similar to brass. Can be lacquered	As for brass
Copper	Properties similar to brass. Can be lacquered	Kitchen ware, decorative furniture, ornaments
Chrominium	A thin layer of plate on mild steel or brass. Surface oxidation can result in formation of white spots. Reacts with alkalis causing surface discolouration. Abrasives will wear away plate	Furniture, taps, handles
EPNS (electroplated nickel silver)	A layer of nickel and silver plate applied electrically to mild steel or brass. Good resistance to abrasion, acids and alkalis, but metal polishes should be avoided	Cutlery, tableware, ornaments
Galvanize	A coating of zinc applied to mild steel. Good abrasion and alkali resistance. Attacked by acids	Buckets, bins, tanks, cooker hoods, ducting
Gold	May be solid, plate or leaf. Resistant to acids, alkalis and tarnishing. Corrodes if exposed to mercury	Ornaments, jewellery, tableware, decorative finishes
Pewter	An alloy of tin, copper and antimony. Tarnishes and has little resistance to alkalis, acids and abrasives	Ornaments, tableware
Silver	May be solid, plate or sterling. A soft metal which will be worn away by abrasion. Sterling is harder. Tarnishes relatively easily, reacting with sulphides in the air to form black silver sulphide or with oxygen in a moist atmosphere to form green discolourations. Resistant to acids and alkalis. Can be lacquered	Cutlery, ornaments, tableware
Stainless steel	An alloy of iron, chromium and nickel. 18/8 steel consists of 18% chromium and 8% nickel. Good resistance to corrosion, acids and alkalis. Silver dips, bleach, salt/vinegar mixtures will attack surface and cause discolouration. Black deposits will occur if left in contact with moist aluminium or galvanized surfaces	Work surfaces, kitchen ware, sinks, bowls, furniture, decorative finishes
Tin	A layer of plate on mild steel, brass or copper. Good resistance to acids and alkalis	Food containers, baking sheets

Table 4   *Textile characteristics*

Characteristic	Influencing factors
Abrasion resistance	Hard fibres, dense construction
Tear resistance	Strong fibres, extensible fibres, loose knit or weave
Flame resistance	Non-flammable fibres, flame resistant finish
Resilience	Elastic fibres, dense construction
Static	Antistatic fibres, antistatic finish
Drape	Weight of fabric, fibre flexibility, finish
Feel	Hard or soft fibres, type of finish
Moth and mildew resistance	Resistant fibres, resistant finishes
Light deterioration	Resistant fibres, resistant dyes
Stain and soil resistance	Antistatic fibres, less absorbent fibres, resistant finishes
Ease of cleaning	Less absorbent fibres, soil-resistant finish
Resistance to alkalis, acids and solvents	Type of fibre
Wetting	Less absorbent fibres, waterproof finish
Insulation	Absorbent fibres, open knit or weave, cellular or bulk construction, density and depth of pile
Crease retention	Type of fibre, type of finish

Acrylics are polymers of acrylonitrile. When formed the polymer is dissolved in solvent and then either dry-spun into hot air or wet-spun into water to form long filaments.

Modacrylics are copolymers of acrylonitrile and other polymers.

Chlorofibres are polymers of either vinyl chloride [poly (vinyl chloride)]or vinylidene chloride.

Polypropylene is a polymer of propylene. Filaments are formed in a similar way to nylon.

The properties of the major fibres are shown in Table 5.

Identification of fibres

Fibre identification can be difficult. The principle methods involve chemical tests, observation of physical appearance and burning.

Chemical tests   Various tests can be applied. The tests described are specific for the major types of fibre.

- *Wool* dissolves in 1% sodium hydroxide and when 2 or 3 drops of lead acetate are added a brown colour results.
- *Silk*, similar to wool, but a white colour results.
- *Linen* dissolves in cuprammonium hydroxide.
- *Cotton,* as linen.
- *Acetate* dissolves in 70% acetone, but not methylene dichloride.
- *Triacetate* dissolves in methylene dichloride but not 70% acetone.
- *Polyester* is insoluble in 75% sulphuric acid.
- *Acrylics* are soluble in dimethyl formamide.
- *Polyamides* are soluble in *m*-cresol.

Burning   Whether a fibre burns or melts, the smell from the fumes and the nature of the ash can be used to identify the fibres – see Table 6.

Physical appearance of fibres   The microscopic

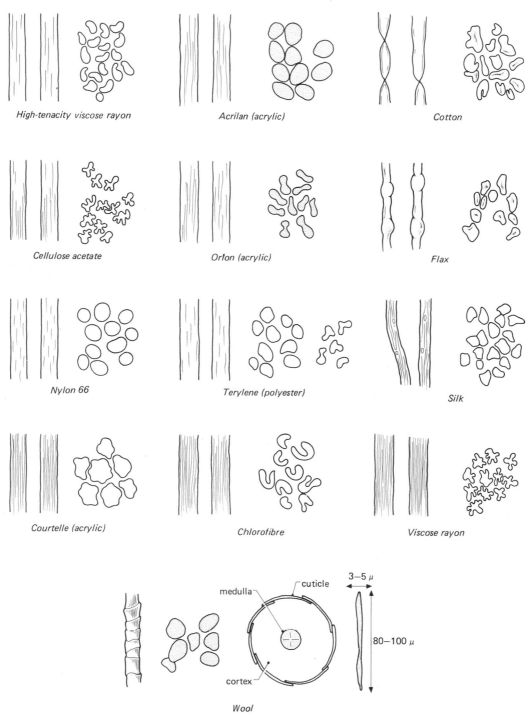

High-tenacity viscose rayon

Acrilan (acrylic)

Cotton

Cellulose acetate

Orlon (acrylic)

Flax

Nylon 66

Terylene (polyester)

Silk

Courtelle (acrylic)

Chlorofibre

Viscose rayon

medulla   cuticle   3—5 µ

cortex   80—100 µ

Wool

Figure 4 *Microscopic appearance of some textile fibres*

Table 5 *Properties of the major textile fibres*

Characteristic	Wool	Silk	Cotton	Linen	Rayon	Acetate
Examples	—	—	—	—	Sarille Evlan Vincel	Dicel Celafibre
Strength	Poor	Moderate	Moderate	Moderate	Poor to Moderate	Moderate
Elasticity	Good	Moderate	Poor	Poor	Poor to Moderate	Moderate
Absorbancy	High	High	High	High	High	Moderate
Weak acid resistance	Good	Fair	Good	Good	Good	Fair
Weak alkali resistance	Fair	Poor	Good	Good	Good	Fair
Bleach resistance	Poor	Poor	Fair	Fair	Fair	Good
Solvent resistance	Good	Good	Good	Good	Good	Poor
Wet strength, % of dry	75-95%	70%	110%	110-120%	60-70%	60-80%
Abrasion resistance	Good	Fair	Fair	Good	Fair	Good
Moth resistance	Poor	Poor	Good	Good	Good	Good
Mildew resistance	Good	Good	Poor	Poor	Poor	Good
Static resistance	Good	Good	Good	Good	Good	Fair
Shrink resistance	Poor	Good	Fair	Good	Good	Good
Soil resistance	Good	Good	Fair	Fair	Fair	Poor
Resilience	Good	Fair	Poor	Poor	Poor to Fair	Poor
Tear resistance	Good	Fair	Poor	Fair	Fair	Fair
Ease of cleaning	Fair	Fair	Good	Good	Good	Good
Light resistance	Fair	Poor	Good	Good	Good	Good
Wetting resistance	Poor	Poor	Poor	Poor	Poor	Fair
Flame resistance	Fair	Fair	Poor	Fair	Poor	Fair
Insulation	Good	Fair	Fair	Fair	Fair	Poor
Crease resistance	Good	Fair	Poor	Poor	Poor to Fair	Poor
Crease retention	Poor	Fair	Poor	Fair	Poor to Fair	Good
Safe ironing temperature	150°C	150°C	200°C	200°C	200°C	110°C

Note: Polypropylene burns if subject to excessive abrasion.

Triacetate	Polyamide Nylon	Polyester	Acrylic	Mod-acrylic	Chloro-fibre	Polypro-pylene
Tricel	Brinylon Enkalon Celon	Terylene Dacron	Acrilan Courtelle Orlon Dralon	Teklan	Dynel Saran	Courlene
Poor	Good	Good	Moderate	Moderate	Poor	Good
Poor	Good	Poor to Good	Good	Moderate	Good	Poor
Low	Low	Low	Low	Low	Low	Low
Fair	Poor to Good	Good	Good	Good	Good	Good
Fair	Good	Fair	Good	Good	Good	Good
Good	Fair	Good	Good	Good	Good	Good
Poor	Fair to Good	Poor to Fair	Poor	Fair	Poor to Good	Good
65-70%	80-90%	100%	80-90%	80-90%	100%	100%
Good	Good	Good	Good	Good	Good	Good
Good	Good	Good	Good	Good	Good	Good
Good	Good	Good	Good	Good	Good	Good
Fair	Poor	Poor	Poor	Poor	Poor	Poor
Good	Good	Good	Good	Good	Good	Good
Poor	Poor	Poor	Poor	Poor	Poor	Poor
Poor	Good	Poor	Poor	Poor	Good	Poor
Fair	Good	Good	Good	Good	Good	Good
Good	Good	Good	Good	Good	Good	Good
Good	Poor	Fair	Good	Good	Good	Poor
Fair	Fair	Fair	Fair	Fair	Good	Fair
Fair	Fair	Fair	Fair	Good	Good	Fair
Poor	Poor	Poor	Poor	Poor	Poor	Poor
Poor	Fair	Good	Good	Good	Good	N/A
Good	Fair	Good	Good	Good	Fair	N/A
110°C	110°C	110-150°C	110°C	110°C	100°C	150°C

Table 6 *Identification of textile fibres by burning*

Fibres	Burning/melting	Smell of fumes	Ash
Cotton, linen, rayon	Burn in and out of flame	Burning paper, acid fumes	Little grey or white powder
Wool, silk, hairs	Burn in and not out of flame	Burning feathers, alkaline fumes	Black bead, crushes when cold
Acetate, triacetate	Burn in and out of flame	Vinegar, acid fumes	Black bead, does not crush when cold
Nylon	Melt and shrink from flame	Boiling celery	Hard, light-coloured round bead
Polyester	Melt and shrink from flame	Sweet smell	Hard, light-coloured round bead
Acrylics	Burn and melt in and out of flame	Burnt meat	Hard, irregular black bead
Modacrylics, modified rayons	Does not burn or melt		

appearance and physical characteristics of the common fibres are shown in Figure 4.

Yarns and methods of fabric construction

The construction of carpets is dealt with on pages 43-44.

Yarns Fibres or filaments which are spun by pulling and twisting them together:

- *Monofilament* Yarns of a single filament.
- *Multifilament* Yarns of several continuous filaments spun together.
- *Staple yarns* Numerous short fibres, staples, are spun together. The staples may be natural fibres or filaments of synthetic and regenerated fibres cut into short lengths. Short staples are used to form bulky yarns and long ones to form fine yarns with smooth appearances.
- *Plyyarns* Several yarns spun together.
- *Textured* Bulked or stretched yarns.

Construction Frequently one fibre will not have all the properties required by a fabric; accordingly it will be made of a number of different fibres. The principle methods of construction are:

- *Knitted* Rows of loops which are held together by subsequent rows of loops. A variety of stitches are possible and by using them and different types and colours of yarn a variety of textures and patterns are possible (see Figure 5).
- *Woven* Fabrics consist of two sets of yarns, warps and wefts. Warps run vertically and are generally strung tightly across a loom. Wefts

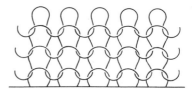

Figure 5 *Fabric construction, knitted*

run horizontally and are carried across the warps by a shuttle. The **weft** yarns pass under and over the warps and the way in which they do determines the type of weave. The warp and weft may be the same, of different **thicknesses or of different fibres.**

Plain – weft passes over and under alternate warps.

Twill – similar to plain, but the weave is reversed at regular intervals to give a herring-bone effect.

Satin – some warps are left floating as a result of several adjacent wefts passing under the same warp.

Damask – similar to satin, but both warps and wefts float.

Pile – warp or weft yarns are pulled through to produce a pile which may be cut or uncut. This is similar to woven carpets. A pile can also be made by tufting.

Figured – patterns are introduced.

● *Bonded* Two different types of fabric are glued together by adhesive, e.g. PVA or urea formaldehyde.

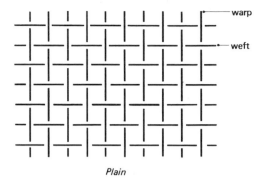

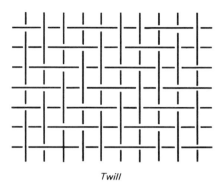

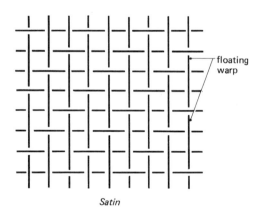

Figure 7 *Fabric construction, woven*

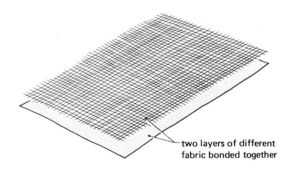

Figure 6 *Fabric construction, bonded*

Dye fastness

Dyes should be fast both to light and laundering processes and must suit both the fibres and finishes used. Fastness to light can be reduced by oxides of nitrogen in the air, chemical softeners and crease-resistant finishes. Fastness to laundering will depend upon the tenacity with which a dye is held by the fibres. Dyes that are strongly held physically or chemically will have greater fastness.

Types of finishing and finishes

A wide range of finishes can be used to give a

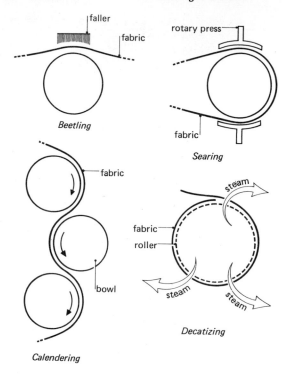

Figure 8 *Textile finishes, mechanical*

fabric particular characteristics. They can be achieved mechanically or chemically.

Lustre can be improved by:
- *Mercerization* The twist in cotton fibres removed by treating cotton with strong alkali and subjecting it to tension.
- *Beetling* Linen struck several hundred times a minute with fine hammers called fallers.
- *Searing* Heat used to remove surface fibres from wool. Typically the fabric is passed through a rotary press which acts like a hot iron.

Softening can be achieved by:

- *Calendering* Fabric passed through a series of rotating cylinders (bowls) and subjected to compression. Running one bowl faster than another will also increase lustre.
- *Beetling and searing.*
- *Decatizing* Fabric, usually wool, passed

over a hollow perforated cylinder through which steam is passed.
- *Cationic surfactants* These act as lubricants, but are not fast to washing.
- *Polyethylene and polyacrylates* act as fibre lubricants and are wash-fast.

Raising A brushed or suede finish is achieved by gently scratching or plucking the surface of a fabric.

Antishrink characteristics can be imparted:

- *Mechanically* In the Sanforize and Evaset processes, wool and cellulosic fabrics are subjected to compressive shrinkage so that when washed they neither shrink nor expand too much.
- *Chemically* The scales of wool fibres are softened by treatment with various chemicals, e.g. a mixture of sodium hypochlorite and potassium permanganate. Fabrics can be treated with dimethylol ethylene which, when cured, polymerizes and cross-links.

Crease resistance Treatment of fabrics with dimenthylol ethylene urea will give wet and dry crease resistance.

Crease retention Thermoplastic fibres can be heat-set to form a crease. Fabric can be steeped in dimethylol, dihydroxy ethylene urea which, when cured, cross-links to set a crease. The keratin molecules of wool possess chemical groups called sulphydryl groups. These can be oxidized to form a cross-link which will set a crease (see Figure 10). The finish is fast to light washing.

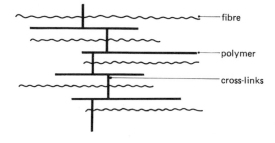

Figure 9 *Antishrink finish*

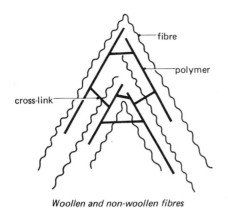

Woollen and non-woollen fibres

Woollen fibres only

Figure 10 *Crease-retention finish*

Wear resistance This can be improved by impregnating fabric with polyacrylate resin.

Stiffness The body of a fabric can be improved by:

- Filling with gums or starches which are not wash fast
- Regenerating cellulose within the fabric. The cellulose is wash fast.

Water-repellancy can be achieved in a number of ways:

- *Phobotex* Wax and thermosetting resins fixed at 140°C for 5 min to give a waterproof finish.

- *Silicones* Fabric stepped in polymethyl siloxane which, when cured, gives a water-repellant finish.
- *Ventile* Fabric woven so that the fibres swell immediately on wetting, creating a non-porous surface.
- *Scotchguard* A complex fluorocarbon which, when applied to a fabric, gives it both water-repellancy and oil and stain resistance. The molecules possess both hydrophobic and hydrophilic chemical groups. The former repels water and the latter oils and staining.

Flameproofing can be achieved in one of several ways:

- *Boric acid* Fabrics steeped in derivatives of boric acid have a flameproof finish which is not wash-fast.
- *Pyrovatex* Involves the use of a cyanomide phosphorous compound which produces a wash-fast finish.
- *Proban* Fabric steeped in THPC (tetrakis-hydroxy phosphonium chloride) and urea has a wash-fast, flameproof finish when cured.
- *Post-dry-cleaning treatments* Involve the use of titanium chloride or a mixture of THPC and vinylchloride copolymers.

Moth and mildew proofing Fabrics can be proofed by treating them with copper compounds, bactericides and fungicides. Chemical methods of shrink proofing or giving crease resistance or retention characteristics will also proof against moths and mildew.

British Standards

BS 5523: 1977, *Glossary of Terms for Textiles – Weaves – Definitions of General Terms and Basic Weaves.*
DD 40: 1974, *Definitions of Some Commonly Used Terms Applied to Textiles.*

Surface coatings

Surface coatings are solutions or dispersions of

film-forming resins that form a hard protective film as a result of either solvent evaporation or a chemical reaction. There are two possible classes of coating: obliterating coatings such as paints, or transparent coatings such as varnishes and lacquers. They differ in that paints contain pigments.

Composition

Coatings are formulated from a range of chemicals:

Vehicle/binder/film former   A resinous material which will form a continuous film when applied to a surface. This type of binder will effect the hardness and toughness of a paint or varnish. There are two types:

1   Binders forming a film as a result of stoving (application of heat), atmospheric oxidation, reacting with a water vapour in the atmosphere or the action of a catalyst. The film consists of long polymers which may be cross-linked. Resins used include polyurethane, epoxy resin, urea formaldehyde, melamine formaldehyde, alkyd resin and drying oils.
2   Binders forming a film simply as a result of evaporation of a solvent. Resins used include acrylic, alkyd, PVA, shellac and copal.

Solvent   The binder is dissolved or dispersed in a solvent. Typical solvents include white spirit and water.

Pigments   Organic or inorganic materials that give a paint opacity and colour.

Extenders   Materials that increase the body of a paint.

Plasticizers   Materials that soften a resin. The coating will be tougher and more resistant to knocks.

Catalysts, driers, accelerators, hardners and initiators   Metals, salts, acids and other chemicals that promote drying and film formation as a result of resin polymerization and cross-linking. Two-pack or catalysed coatings require the addition of a catalyst or other chemicals to a base material just before application to a surface. Other coatings, sometimes referred to as one-pot or precatalysed coatings, form a film without the addition of further chemicals before application.

Fungicides, bactericides and fire-retardent chemicals are included in many coatings.

Types of varnish or lacquer

Varnishes and lacquers consist of film-forming resins dissolved in an organic solvent.

French polish   Shellac resin dissolved in methylated spirit. Film is formed by solvent evaporation. Resistance to alcohol and heat is poor.

Oleoresinous   Lacquer is a mixture of drying oils, other resins and white spirit which dries as a result of atmospheric oxidation of the oils. Durability, adhesion and resistance to humidity are good. Resistance to acids, alkalis and solvents is limited.

Alkyd resin   A mixture of resins modified by linseed oil which dry as a result of atmospheric oxidation of the oil. The film is tough and durable with good resistance to acids, alkalis, solvents and humidity.

Epoxy resin   A two-pack coating which consists of a base to which an initiating chemical is added just before application. The film is tough, durable with excellent resistance to alkalis and humidity. Resistance to solvents and acids is fair.

Melamine and urea formaldehyde resins   Acid-catalysed lacquers consisting of a base material to which an acid is added just before application. The film is tough and durable with good resistance to solvents, acids, alkalis and humidity.

Polyurethane resins   There are three types,

differing in the way in which drying and film formation takes place.

1 One-pack, moisture-cured, involving a chemical reaction with water vapour in the atmosphere.
2 One-pack, oil-modified, involving atmospheric oxidation of the oils in the laquer.
3 Two-pack, consisting of a base to which a hardner or accelerator of isocyanate is added just before application.

The film is hard, with excellent resistance to acids. Resistance to alkalis and solvents is fair. Adhesion, particularly of the one-pot types, can be poor.

Types of paint

Paints may be either solvent-based or water-based emulsions. Depending on the actual formulation, either type can have a matt, gloss or semi-gloss finish when dry.

Paints either have a liquid consistency or they can be modified to give them thixotropic properties. A thixotropic paint has a jelly-like consistency before application. When stirred or applied to a surface, the gel breaks down to form a free-flowing paint. Such paints are formulated to eliminate drips and enable thicker coats to be applied.

Solvent-based paints are not unlike varnishes and lacquers. Resins, pigments and other ingredients are dissolved in an organic solvent, usually white spirit. Drying and film formation usually involves a chemical reaction. The principal resins used are alkyd, melamine and epoxy. The properties and methods of drying and film formation are similar to those described for varnishes and lacquers employing the same resins.

Epoxy and melamine resins are also stoved to promote film formation and drying. Stoved finishes are frequently described as enamels.

Emulsions consist of film-forming resins, oils and pigments dispersed in water. The principal resins used are polyvinyl acetate (PVA), alkyds and acrylics. Drying and film formation takes place as a result of evaporation of the water and does not involve a chemical reaction. Durability and resistance to acids, alkalis, solvents and humidity is generally good, but usually not as good as solvent-based paints.

Textured and multicolour emulsions are formulated for heavy-duty use where a solvent-based paint might be considered appropriate or to cover poor surfaces. Textured emulsions are heavy bodied and usually applied by a spray. Multicolour emulsions include fine coloured drops of cellulose which when applied to a surface give a speckled effect.

Anti-graffiti paints are coatings formulated to give a very hard finish, resistant to most chemicals.

British standards

BS 2015: 1965(1979), *Glossary of Paint Terms.*

Ceramic products

Ceramic products include bricks, roof tiles, floor tiles, sanitary ware, table ware and wall tiles.

Composition

Ceramics are mixture of clays, quartz or flint and feldspar.

Clays are oxides of aluminium and silicon, the actual composition determining the type. The main types are:

- *China clay (kaolin)* Relatively pure.
- *Ballclays* Appreciable percentage of organic matter.
- *Terracota* Appreciable percentage of iron compounds which will pigment products made from them.
- *Fire clay* A small percentage of organic matter together with iron compounds and other pigmenting compounds.

Quartz or flint are crystalline forms of silica, quartz being purer than flint.

Feldspars are aluminium silicates of potassium and sodium.

China stone a type of clay containing significant quantities of feldspar.

The ingredients appropriate to the product being made are mixed with water, moulded or shaped and then heated (fired) to temperatures of between 1,000° and 1,400°C to fuse them together. The properties of the product formed depend upon the ingredients and the firing temperature. The higher the temperature, the greater the degree of vitrification. Vitrification is the process of fusing the ingredients together to give them glass-like properties. The greater the vitrication the less porous will be the clay body.

A glaze, which is non-porous with good resistance to chemicals and abrasion, is applied to many products.

Decoration can be applied before or after glazing.

Types of ceramic product

Bricks and roof tiles are mixtures of terracota clays and pigments. The porosity and hardness depend upon the actual type. Bricks intended for external use will be relatively non-porous. A glaze may be applied to decorative bricks.

Earthenware table and sanitary ware Mixtures of ball and china clays, china stone and flint. The body is opaque, porous and durable.

Fireclay sanitary ware A mixture of fire, ball and china clays, china stone and flint. The body is opaque, off white, porous and very durable.

Stoneware, table and sanitary ware Similar in composition to earthenware but with a higher percentage of china stone (feldspar). The body is opaque, non-porous and extremely durable.

Vitreous china sanitary ware A mixture of china clay, china stone and quartz. The body is non-porous and less durable than earthenware, but with a higher standard of appearance.

Porcelain tableware A mixture of china clay, china stone and quartz. The body is non-porous, translucent, very hard and rather fragile.

Bone china tableware Similar in composition to porcelain, but includes an appreciable percentage of bone ash. It is non-porous, translucent, hard and less fragile than porcelain.

Floor tiles There are various types and grades to suit particular situations but all are mixtures of clays, feldspar and flint. They may be glazed or unglazed, decorated or plain.

Wall tiles Mixtures of ball, china and fire clays, feldspar and flint. The body is opaque, porous and not unlike earthenware. They are usually glazed and may or may not be decorated.

Glass products

Glass products include sheet and plate glass, tableware, bricks, vitreous enamels and ceramic glazes.

Composition

Glass is a mixture of complex silicates formed at high temperature which, when cooled, is translucent. A mixture of sand, sodium or potassium carbonate, calcium carbonate, feldspar, dolomite and cullet (broken glass) is heated to temperatures of 1300 to 1600°C. The formulation will determine the type of glass formed – see Table 7.

Types of glass product

Products can be formed by blowing, casting in a mould or as sheet or plates. Patterns are formed in the mould, cut with an abrasive tool, etched, or hand engraved, or they can be impressed during the manufacturing of sheet or plate glass.

Sheet glass is made from soda glass and is used for windows, doors, and mirrors. Sheets are manufactured in one of two ways, either as polished plate or float glass.

Safety glass is made from soda glass. There are three principal types.

- *Wire-filled*   Plate glass including a fine wire mesh.
- *Laminated*   A sheet of plastic is sandwiched between sheets of glass.
- *Toughened*   Glass sheets heated to just below softening temperature and then cooled quickly.

Tableware is made from soda, hard, crystal or borosilicate glass. The product is shaped by moulding or blowing.

Ceramic glazes   Ceramic bodies are usually dipped into a glaze bath and then fired at high temperatures to vitrify the glaze. The composition of the glaze is similar to that for other types of glass, but it includes various metal oxides.

Table 7   *Types of glass*

Type	Formulation	Uses
Soda glass	Sodium carbonate rather than potassium carbonate	Sheet and plate glass, tableware
Hard glass	Potassium carbonate rather than sodium carbonate	Cheap tableware
Crystal	Oxides of lead added	Expensive tableware with lustre and ring
Borosilicate	Borax added	Heat-resistant ware
Vitaglass	Almost pure silica	Glass transmits almost all UV light

Vitreous enamel consists of a layer of glass fused to a metal surface, usually iron or mild steel. The enamel is extremely durable although it will chip and its resistance to strong alkalis and to fluorides is limited.

Wood

Natural timbers

There are two principal types of wood:

Soft wood   The timber cut from pine, red cedar and Douglas fir. They tend to be resinous, have little colour or grain and in many respects are less durable than hard woods. Soft woods are used for floor and ceiling joists, window frames, floor boards and less expensive furniture.

Hard woods   Timber cut from oak, walnut, ash, mahogany, elm, teak, yew and afromosia. They have colour and grain, are extremely durable and are less likely to warp than soft woods. They are used for window frames, exterior doors and furniture. When used in the construction of furniture the wood is used as solid pieces or as veneers applied to chipboard, or a less expensive hard wood. A veneer is a thin sheet of timber cut from larger pieces.

Although wood is an extremely useful product it has a number of natural disadvantages. Unless the water content is less than 16% it will rot; there are exceptions, e.g. teak. Wood is subject to attack by fungi and insects and may require protection. Weathering causes alternate shrinkage and expansion which will cause deterioration and warping. It therefore requires protection.

Processed timber products

Wood is an expensive commodity and a number of less expensive timber products have been developed with many of the properties of more expensive natural timbers.

Plywood   Sheets or veneers of timber, 1 to 2 mm thick, laid at right angles to each other and glued together. There are various grades and plys (the number of veneers in a sheet of plywood) suitable for interior use, exterior use and the construction of furniture.

Insulation board A low-density open board about 10 mm thick with good insulation properties. It is formed from pulped timber and other materials.

Hardboard A hard, dense board, approximately 2 to 3 mm thick, formed from pulped timber.

Chipboard A hard, dense board formed from wood chips bound together by urea formaldhyde or phenolic resins.

Blockboard Blocks of softwood sandwiched between two sheets of hardwood.

Exterior fabric

The exterior fabric of a building includes forecourts, walls, roofs, windows and doors.

Forecourts

Forecourts include pavement and car parks which will generally be constructed of concrete, tarmac or gravel.

Walls

Walls may be constructed from a range of materials. The following are representative examples:

Wood Hard and soft woods are used, finished with paints, lacquers or oils.

Brick, used for exterior walls, can be formed from a variety of materials. Typical examples are ceramic, concrete and glass. They are hard and relatively non-porous, but the binding mortar is less abrasion-resistant and subject to attacks by acids.

Limestone and marble, used in blocks or slabs, are essentially calcium and magnesium carbonate. They are attacked by acids and tend to absorb soot.

Sandstone, used in blocks, is essentially sand particles bound by alumina, calcium carbonate and other materials. It is relatively soft and tends to absorb soot.

Granite, used in slabs and blocks, is a mixture of feldspar, quartzite and mica. It is extremely hard and impervious.

Prefabricated units are preformed units of cement, filler and reinforcing materials used in preference to convential building materials. They are hard with good resistance to weathering.

Exterior walls are subject to four main types of attack:

1   Graffiti, which may penetrate the surface.
2   Acid gases, notably sulphur dioxide, which will have a corrosive effect.
3   Soot produced as a result of combustion which will stain and may penetrate the surface.
4   Abrasion by wind and sand which will erode the surface.

Roofs

Roofs may be flat or pitched (slope exceeds 10^0 from horizontal) and can be formed from a variety of materials which include, slates, ceramic tiles, concrete which is weather-sealed and corrugated sheet, frequently of asbestos, which is extremely fragile.

Windows

Windows are usually made from sheet glass which may be toughened or laminated and secured in hard wood or in anodized aluminium frames by putty or other means. They may be double or triple glazed and, where a building is air-conditioned, will not usually open. The exterior surface becomes soiled relatively quickly with a mixture of particulate soil, grease and rubber dust which requires regular removal if windows are to transmit as much light as possible to the interior of the building. The height of many buildings requires the use of a cradle and platform for cleaning and in many cases building design is inadequate to permit completely safe cleaning to take place.

Doors

External doors can be constructed of hard woods or anodized aluminium, which may be glazed, and of plate glass.

British Standards

CP 152: 1972, *Glazing and Fixing of Glass for Buildings.*

Interior fabric

The interior fabric of a building includes walls, floors, windows, doors, ceilings and their respective finishes.

Construction

Walls can be constructed of brick, breeze blocks, timber frames to which plaster or fibre board is fixed, or preformed partitions, e.g. laminate sheets supported by metallic frames. Brick, breeze blocks and plaster board are usually finished with a layer of hard plaster, although brick walls can be wood-panelled. Where abuse is likely, walls constructed of laminates, plaster or fibre board will be more easily damaged and will therefore involve greater maintenance costs than brick or breeze block.

Ceilings There are three major types (see Figure 11):

● *Sheets of plaster board* fixed to timber joists or battens and covered with a thin layer of hard plaster. Paint, paper or tiles with thermal or acoustic insulation properties are applied to the surface. Services, notably light fittings, will be suspended below the ceiling, the space between ceiling and the floor above only being

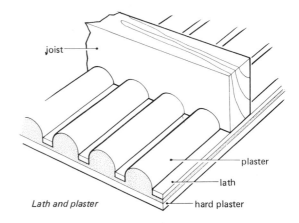

Lath and plaster

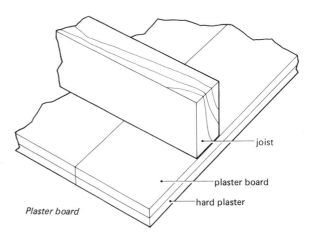

Plaster board

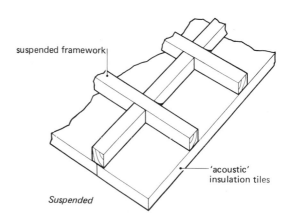

Suspended

Figure 11 *Types of ceiling*

sufficient to allow the passage of water pipes and electric cables.

- *Lath and plaster* where plaster is applied and keys to thin laths fixed to joists.
- *Suspended ceilings* in the form of insulation board tiles with acoustic insulation, thermal insulation and fire-resistant properties supported by a framework suspended some distance below the floor above. The intervening space is deep enough to accommodate pipes, cables, ventilation ducts and other services. Light fittings will be fixed into the ceiling rather than suspended from it, making cleaning easier. In areas where the highest standards of hygiene are required there must be no possibility of dust entering the air from the space above the ceiling. In older buildings suspended ceilings can be used to lower the height of the ceiling and to introduce decorative and lighting effects.

Doors and door frames are most frequently constructed of hard woods finished with paints or lacquers. Doors may be solid, panelled, include panes of safety glass or consist of a frame covered with plywood or hard board sheets.

Floors   See page 38.

Finishes

The type of finish selected for doors, walls and ceilings will depend on the relative importance of a number of criteria:

- *Contribution to decor*   The colour texture and pattern will influence the apparent warmth and dimensions of a room and the level and . type of illumination used. The use of different finishes in the same room will add interest and create focal points. The type of room, its size and existing decoration must be considered.
- *Ease of cleaning*   Smooth, hard impervious surfaces, preferably light in colour, are most easily cleaned and are required where high

standards of hygiene are required. Textured surfaces tend to attract and hold dust.

- *State of existing surfaces*   Textured or patterned finishes can be used to mask poor surfaces.
- *Resistance to abrasion and knocks*   Hard surfaces will be most resistant to abrasion. Damage caused by knocks will be minimal if the surface is hard, resilient, firm and well supported.
- *Stain resistance*   A non-porous surface has greater stain resistance than a porous one. Resistance to abrasion and wet cleaning methods will enable stains to be removed more easily and will reduce the possibility of damaging the surface during stain removal procedures or recourse to restorative procedures.
- *Durability*   Surfaces subject to abuse, graffiti, knocks and abrasion require finishes that are resistant to stains, abrasion and knocks and which can be cleaned easily or inexpensively restored or repaired if required.
- *Life expectancy*   Where it is intended to change the decor of a room relatively frequently, more expensive finishes designed to last several years may be inappropriate if less expensive finishes are available which will meet all other requirements.
- *Insulation*   Where possible, finishes with good sound and insulation properties should be selected.
- *Cost*   When comparing the costs of different finishes, not only the cost of the material and its application must be considered, but also the likely incidence and cost of damage requiring restoration and the expected frequency of complete redecoration.

Paints and lacquers can be applied to almost any surface providing it is free from water, grease or dust and is of sound construction. For example, plaster must be smooth, hard and not flaking from the underlying plaster or brickwork.

Paints, either solvent-based or emulsion, can be applied to walls, ceilings, skirting boards, doors, door frames and window frames, to give a matt or gloss finish depending on the formulation of the paint. A gloss finish, unlike a matt one, will show up surface blemishes and produce a harsher decorative effect contributing to glare and uneven levels of illumination.

Solvent-based paints form a more durable film with better stain, water and abrasion resistance than emulsion giving a similar thickness of film. Emulsions, however, are easier to apply, dry more quickly, have no offensive odour and are cheaper. Solvent-based paints are most suitable where resistance to soiling, abrasion and water is necessary and where regular washing will be required, e.g. skirting boards, doors, window frames, walls of kitchens and sanitary accommodation. Emulsions are usually suitable for walls and ceilings not subject to heavy soiling or requiring regular washing. They are preferred where there is a possibility of dampness arising beneath the paint and are applied to freshly plastered walls to allow the plaster to dry out.

Antigraffiti paints and multicolour emulsions can be applied to walls in corridors, sanitary accommodation and similar areas to give a stain- and abrasion-resistant finish which can be washed and cleaned regularly. Multicolours produce a matt finish patterned by numerous coloured spots, the overall effect depending on the number of colours, contrast, density and size of the spots.

Lacquers of the precatalysed one-pot type or of the two-pot acid-catalysed type can be applied to doors and skirting boards. Both types have good resistance to soiling and abrasion, although the adhesion of the latter is better.

Textured finishes can be applied to walls and ceilings to mask surface defects or as a decorative effect. The relief finish can be achieved in one of two ways. A plaster-based material is applied to the surface which is then worked with trowel and combs, or a heavy emulsion is sprayed onto it. This type of finish, because of the numerous ledges and crevises, tends to become more heavily soiled than a smooth one and is less easily cleaned.

Paint has a number of advantages and disadvantages when compared to other finishes, particularly papers.

Advantages of paint:

1   Wide range of decorative uses: the range of colours together with texture, gloss and matt finishes enables decorative effects to be achieved even where a finish must be principally functional.
2   Relatively inexpensive.
3   Good durability: depending on degree of soilage, abuse and cleaning, redecorating may be required only every five years or more.
4   Good stain resistance: the degree of resistance will depend upon the type of paint.
5   Washable: some paints are more tolerant of regular washing than others.
6   Ease of restoration: surface damage and stains may be removed by further application of paint.
7   Good resistance to abrasion, solvents and alkalis: the degree of resistance will depend on the type of paint.

Disadvantages of paint:

1   Requires a good surface: paints have only a limited ability to mask poor surfaces.
2   Soiling of textured surfaces: textured coatings tend to hold soil which can be difficult to remove.

Wallpaper can be applied to almost any wall and ceiling providing it is dry and reasonably firm. It is unsuitable in very moist atmospheres, where regular washing is required and where heavy soilage and abuse is likely. A range of paper types are available, the properties of each, to some extent, governing their particular uses.

● *Surface-printed papers*   A pattern is applied to the surface of the paper by one of several methods, e.g. hand printing or screen printing. A wide range of colours and designs are produced. The surface finish is usually smooth. The cost is related to the design and the method of reproduction. The paper is not washable and damp wiping must be undertaken with great care. It can be easily soiled or stained.

- *Spongeable papers* Similar in most respects to surface-printed papers, but finished with a surface coating that provides some stain resistance and the ability to be damp wiped.
- *Washable papers* Similar to surface-printed papers, but finished with a plastic coating giving them good stain resistance and enabling them to withstand washing.
- *Anaglypta* An embossed paper that is relatively inexpensive. After hanging, it is normally painted. It is frequently used to cover poor surfaces. Its stain resistance and washability depends on the type of paint applied, but if badly stained it can be repainted.
- *Lincrusta* A heavily embossed paper which may have a plastic coating. It is expensive but has good stain resistance, is washable and has excellent durability. It is frequently used to cover very poor wall surfaces. When applied it can be painted and, if badly stained or soiled, repainted.
- *Wood chip* Wood flour, wood chips or straw are sandwiched between two layers of paper. In other respects it is similar to anaglypta.
- *Flock* A raised, patterned pile is fixed by adhesive to a paper backing. The pile (which is electrostatically applied) may be cotton, silk, wool or synthetic. It is expensive but is intended to give a luxurious feel to a room. It attracts and holds dust, detracting from its appearance and making cleaning more difficult. Ease of staining depends upon the type of fibre, synthetic fibres having more resistance than natural fibres. The surface of paper may be damp wiped.
- *Silk* Paper finished with or including silk or silk-like strands. It is expensive, is easily stained, cannot be cleaned by wet methods and is easily damaged by abrasion. It has a soft sheen producing a luxurious appearance.
- *Hessian* Strands of hessian fixed to a paper backing to give the appearance of a hessian covering. It is not washable but the surafce can be damp wiped. It is easily stained and damaged by abrasion.
- *Grass* Pieces of grass fixed by adhesive to a

backing of paper. In other respects similar to silk.
- *Wood grain* A photographic reproduction of a wood surface printed on to a paper which is finished with a wax coating. In other respects it is similar to a spongeable paper.
- *Wood or cork veneer* Paper to which a very thin veneer of wood or cork is applied. It is expensive but when finished with a suitable lacquer has good stain resistance, is washable and is extremely durable.

Wallpapers have a number of advantages and disadvantages which will govern their use.

Advantages of wallpaper:

1   Contribution to decor: this is the principle reason for using wallpapers. The use of different textures, patterns and colours will influence the apparent warmth, dimension and luxury of a room. Among the factors to be considered are type of pattern (floral, pictorial, striped or geometric); colour (the actual colours and the number of colours); design (advancing or receding, horizontal or vertical); size of the pattern in relation to the size of the room; compatibility of new and existing decoration.
2   Ability to cover poor surfaces: patterned, textured or embossed papers can be used.
3   Insulation: heavier papers, particularly flock and cork veneer, contribute to sound and thermal insulation requirements.

Disadvantages of wallpaper:

1   Cost: both the paper and its application can be more expensive than paint.
2   Use limitation: paper cannot be used in very moist atmospheres or in situations where high levels of hygiene are required. In moist atmospheres the adhesive may fail, and mildew, mould and bacteria may develop. Where high levels of hygiene are required few papers will withstand regular washing, even those classed as washable.
3   Abrasion: most papers have only limited

resistance to abrasion and knocking, becoming scratched or torn and consequently requiring restoration.

4   Staining: although differences exist in the ease with which different papers can be stained, most types have limited resistance to staining.

5   Cleaning: unless specifically designed to be washable, most papers will not tolerate wet cleaning methods, cleaning being limited to suction cleaning, dusting or damp wiping. The limited abrasion resistance of most paper makes the use of any method involving other than the mildest form of abrasion inappropriate for removing stains or soil.

6   Restoration: where paper has been torn, it may be possible to stick it back into place or to cut out the damaged paper and replace it. If paper has been stained it may be possible to use cleaning agents, but there is always a danger that removal of the stains may destroy the area of paper affected. It can be preferable not to attempt removal. Badly stained papers which are painted may be repainted. Alternatively if the paper is patterned the affected area can be cut out and replaced with a new piece of paper, success being dependent on the location of the affected area and pattern.

7   Durability: paper is unsuitable where abuse or damage is likely to occur with any degree of regularity.

PVC cloths   Woven cotton finished with a layer of PVC is used to form decorative panels on walls or doors. It may be plain or quilted, involving the use of a foam stuffing, and fixed by adhesive or metal studs. It produces a luxurious effect, improves sound and thermal insulation but is expensive and difficult to repair satisfactorily.

Leather is used in similar ways to PVC cloth.

Fabrics used as wall covering can be divided into two groups: woven fabrics, e.g. hessian, used in a similar way to wallpaper, and hangings, e.g. tapestries, oriental carpets and drapes.

Hessian produces an attractive finish, is relatively expensive, tends to attract and hold soil, stains easily, is reasonably abrasion-resistant and can be cleaned by damp wiping using an absolute minimum of water.

Hangings are used to produce a luxurious appearance to hide poor surfaces and to contribute to thermal and sound insulation. They are, however, expensive to purchase, can be expensive to maintain, are not suitable where high standards of hygiene are required and are subject to attack by moths and mildews.

Laminates are produced in a wide range of surface finishes which, when fixed by adhesive to plywood, are used as an alternative to ceramic tiles, wood panelling or to form internal walls. They are durable, stain-resistant and easily cleaned, but unless adequately supported they will fracture when knocked.

Wood panelling   This is usually made from hardwood, e.g. oak, mahogany, or teak, and consists of solid wood or a veneer fixed to a less expensive hardwood. It can be finished with a wax polish, french polish and wax, or a lacquer. Panelling may be fitted on staircases, in foyers, in board rooms and in restaurants, although it is most usually encountered in older buildings.

Cork   Tiles or sheets are used to form a decorative wall covering. It assists sound and thermal insulation. If sealed, cork is reasonably durable, stain-resistant and easily cleaned.

Glass can be fixed to whole walls or parts of a wall as sheets or tiles in the form of coloured opaque glass, a mosaic, or mirrors. The latter may be of the conventional type, plate glass coated on the back with silver, or be of a non-glass reflecting surface which is shatter-proof and a fraction of the weight of a glass mirror.

Metals   Tiles or sheets of copper, brass, anodized aluminium or stainless steel are used as wall coverings. Foils may also be used as a cheap alternative. Copper and brass are usually lacquered and, although durable and easily maintained, their use is largely decorative. In kitchens, stainless steel is used as an alternative to ceramic tiles to cover the lower parts of walls. It is more resistant to knocks and the absence of grouting makes it possible to maintain a higher standard of appearance and hygiene.

Ceramic tiles   Plain coloured or patterned tiles can be used for decorative effects and where high standards of hygiene are required, e.g. bathroom and kitchen. They are durable, stain-resistant and easily cleaned. However, where soilage is heavy, the grouting can become discoloured and they will fracture if subjected to severe knocks. The replacement of broken tiles is relatively expensive.

Bricks and stone similar to those used for exterior walls can be left unplastered to give a decorative finish to walls, fireplaces and chimney breasts. The surface will be durable. Stain resistance will depend on the porosity of the brick or stone but, in general, it will be good. The formation of dust particles, particularly from the mortar, and the accumulation of soil on ledges or in crevices makes them unsuitable when high standards of hygiene are required.

Marble and terrazzo slabs or tiles are hard, non-porous, easily cleaned and have an attractive appearance. These properties at one time recommended terrazzo for use in areas where high standards of hygiene were required, e.g. toilets, and both for use in the public rooms of hotels, and civic buildings. Their use is now limited by their cost.

Protection

The life expectancy of a wall covering or finish can be increased and the cost of cleaning, maintenance and restoration reduced in several ways:

1   Selection of a finish or covering suitable for the degree of soilage, abuse and damage expected.
2   Selection of a covering that does not hold and

attract dust and is easily cleaned or restored if damaged or stained.
3   Use of a more durable, easily cleaned and maintained covering or finish for the lower part of a wall. This is called a dado.
4   Use of plastic sheets, e.g. Perspex, to cover less durable surfaces subjected to staining and knocks.
5   Fitting of finger plates to doors, light switches and other places where hands will constantly come into contact with the surface.
6   Use of door stops to prevent damage to surfaces behind a door.
7   Use of kick plates to protect the lower part of a door.
8   Treatment of porous surfaces with a soil-retardent finish.

British Standards

PAS 32: 1980, *Specification for a Paint System Comprising an Undercoat and Gloss Finish.*
CP 290: 1973, *Suspended Ceilings and Linings of Dry Construction Using Metal Fixing Systems.*

Hard and semi-hard floors

Hard and semi-hard floors can be classified in five groups: stone, wood, seamless resin, resilient and antistatic. Suitable uses of these floors and the methods of maintenance will depend on their hardness, abrasion resistance, resilience, noise, porosity, slip resistance, resistance to various chemicals and the requirement for antistatic properties.

Stone floors

Concrete   A filler of aggregate bound with cement and water. It is hard, abrasion-resistant, noisy, slip-resistant, moderately porous, stained by mineral oils and grease, attacked by strong acids and prone to dusting unless sealed. Most suitable for sub-floors, workshops and basements.

Granolithic   Granite chips bound with cement

Dado

and water. It is hard, abrasion-resistant, noisy, slip-resistant when dry, non-porous, fairly resistant to oils and grease and attacked by strong acids. Suitable for stairs, reception areas and traffic isles.

Terrazzo   Marble chips bound with cement and water; can be precast or laid *in situ*. It is hard, abrasion-resistant, noisy, slip-resistant when dry, non-porous, stained by oils and grease, and attacked by strong acids. The regular use of strong alkali will render the floor porous. Suitable for stairs, reception areas and traffic isles.

Marble   Limestone metamorphosed by heat and pressure. Cut blocks are laid on mortar. In most respects its properties and uses are similar to terrazzo; however, cost generally prohibits its use in new buildings.

Stone   Various types have been used in churches, markets, dairies and similar buildings and include granite, limestone, sandstone, quartzite and slate. Granite, quartzite and slate are hard, abrasion-resistant, noisy, slip resistant, non-porous, stain-resistant and resistant to most chemicals. Limestone and sandstone are hard, noisy and slip-resistant but are less abrasion-resistant than other stone floors. They are stained by oils and grease and attacked by strong alkalis. Limestone is attacked by acids.

Quarry tiles   A mixture of clays and water, compressed and baked at temperatures in excess of 1,000°C. They can be decorated and grades are available for use in domestic, commercial and industrial situations in various colours. They are hard, abrasion-resistant, slip-resistant only when dry (unless they are designed for use in wet areas), non-porous, resistant to oils and grease. Harsh alkaline powders render them porous. Suitable for kitchens, toilets, washrooms, dairies, breweries and other situations requiring high levels of hygiene.

Brick   A mixture of clays and water baked to a high temperature. In many respects similar to quarry tiles but are much more porous.

Resilient floors

Asphalt   Mineral aggregate bound with bitumen and mineral oils (mastic asphalt) or coaltar pitch (pitchmastic). Light, medium and heavy grades in various colours are available for use in offices, institutions and factories. It is fairly hard, abrasion-resistant, fairly noisy, slip resistant, non-porous, damaged by grease and oil, attacked by strong acids and alkalis, and softened by high temperatures and organic solvents. Suitable for corridors and situations where the standard of finish is secondary to other factors.

Thermoplastic   Tiles of mineral filler bound with asphalt or synthetic resin laid on a screed concrete sub-floor. It is semi-hard, prone to fracture, fairly noisy, abrasion-resistant, damaged by grease and oil, attacked by strong acids and alkalis, softened by heat and bleached by alcohol. White spirit and other solvents will cause pigments to bleed and render the floor porous. Water can seap between the edges of adjoining tiles and affect the adhesive. Suitable for general use in offices and institutions. They have frequently been used incorrectly in toilets and kitchens.

PVC asbestos   Tiles of asbestos fibre filler bound with PVC resin. Physical and chemical properties and uses are similar to those for thermoplastic floors. Asbestos tiles are less prone to fracture and some grades are resistant to grease and oils. Solvents may cause the floor to swell.

PVC   Tiles or sheet consist of PVC and other resins and mineral fillers depending on the characteristics required. PVC floorings are available which have a backing of needleloom felt or cellular PVC which resembles a dense foam. In general PVC floors are resilient and reasonably quiet. Properties, uses and misuses are in many respects similar to those of thermoplastic and PVC asbestos floors. However, depending on the actual composition, some types have significantly better abrasion resistance, slip resistance and resistance to solvents, grease and oils than other types of PVC flooring, thermoplastic or PVC asbestos. Welded PVC sheet is suitable for use in areas where high levels of hygiene are required and wet cleaning methods will be used routinely. It is frequently used in hospital wards.

Linoleum   Fine granules of cork bound by synthetic resin and fixed to a hessian or poly-propylene backing. It is resilient, quiet, reasonably abrasion-resistant, slip-resistant, damaged by grease and oils, attacked by strong acids and alkalis and it has good solvent resistance. Alkalis will cause colour changes. The regular use of excessive quantities of water for cleaning can, in some circumstances, damage linoleum. Various

grades are available for general use in offices, institutions and other commercial establishments.

Rubber   Sheet or tiles of natural and/or synthetic rubber resins. It is resilient, quiet, reasonably

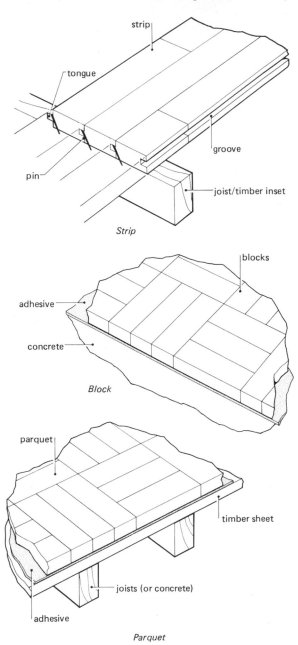

Figure 12   *Laying of wood floors*

abrasion-resistant, slip-resistant, attacked by strong acids and alkalis and the greater the proportion of natural rubber the more likely it is to be damaged by solvents, oils and grease. Rubber floorings may also be subject to oxidation which will damage the surface. Water can seap between the edges of adjoining tiles and affect the adhesive. Rubber flooring is suitable where quietness is a major consideration.

Wood floors

Softwood boards Lengths of softwood fixed to joists or timber insets in concrete. Although they can be sealed and polished, softwood floors are more normally used as a sub-floor and covered with, for example, carpet or linoleum.

Strip Narrow strips of hardwood, e.g. maple, fixed to joists or timber insets in concrete. Suitable in situations where a high standard of finish is required. Typical uses include boardrooms and gymnasia.

Block Rectangular blocks of hardwood of various dimensions, 25–50 mm thick, 150–300 mm long and 50–100 mm wide. They are laid on a sand and cement screed or concrete sub-floor and secured by adhesive. Herringbone or square basket designs are most frequently used (see Figure 13). Suitable where a high standard of appearance is required, typically reception areas and lounges.

Parquet Rectangular lengths of selected kiln-dried oak, teak, walnut or mahogany, 6–10 mm thick and of three types. Paquet sections are of similar dimensions to wood block and are laid individually or as panel 300–600 mm square. Parquet strip is similar in appearance to hardwood strip, 50–75 mm in width and of various lengths. Mosaic sections are 113 mm in length and 25 mm wide and are laid as panels. All types are fixed by adhesive or panel pins to a wooden sub-floor. Suitable uses are similar to those of wood block.

End grain paving Blocks of softwood, normally

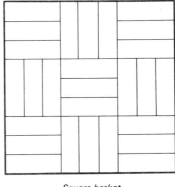

Square basket

Herringbone

Figure 13 *Wood block and parquet floor patterns*

75 mm wide, 225 mm in length and 63–113 mm thick laid so that the end grain of the wood is vertical. They are secured to a concrete sub-floor and used in factories and workshops where heavy traffic conditions prevail.

Granwood Tiles of wood flour and sand filler bound with Portland cement, laid usually on a concrete sub-floor in basket or herringbone design. They are used as a cheaper alternative to hardwoods in corridors, foyers, offices and gymnasia.

Magnesite Wood flour and other fillers mixed with burnt magnesite. It can be laid *in situ* or as small tiles. It is suitable for general use in commercial, industrial and institutional premises, but must be sealed if there is any likelihood of wetting.

Cork Tiles or carpet made from granules of cork bonded together by natural and added resin when subject to pressure and heat. Suitable for use in offices, corridors, bathrooms where quietness and a high standard of appearance are required.

Hardwood floors are resilient, hard, noisy, slip-resistant and, unless sealed, extremely porous, easily stained, affected by alkalis and bleaches and will swell or distort if wetted excessively. If well maintained they are extremely attractive. Parquet floors cannot be sanded.

Other floors within the wood group have similar properties but differ in the following respects. Softwood is less resilient. Granwood and magnesite unless sealed are attacked by acids. Cork has poor resistance to indentations but has good sound and thermal insulation properties.

Antistatic floors

Antistatic floor are floors specifically designed to conduct static electricity to earth and thus prevent a build up of static charge. Terrazzo floors with antistatic properties have metal strips and possibly wire netting placed in the floor during construction. PVC and rubber floors with antistatic properties contain carbon fibres.

No form of maintenance should be carried out that will leave a film on the floor so affecting the conductivity. Frequent cleaning with a minimum of water and cleaning agents and a relative humidity of 65% if appropriate will minimize static. It is essential that conductivity is tested regularly. They are used in computer rooms, operating theatres and in any situation where static electricity can interfere with electrical equipment or electrostatic sparking may result in an explosion.

Seamless resin

These floors consist of epoxy, polyester or polyurethane resins, hardners, pigments and fillers of silica, quartz, bauxite and aggregate. They can be laid on any sub-floor of sound construction. There are three principle types:

1 *Screed* in which the ingredients are mixed to a cement-like consistancy and spread with a steel trowel.
2 *Self-levelling* in which the ingredients are mixed to a semi-liquid consistency and allowed to flow over the floor to give a smooth, glossy surface.
3 *Decorative* in which the ingredients are mixed to a liquid consistency, poured on to the floor and coloured plastic, marble or granite chips scattered in it. After sanding, one or two coats of glaze are applied.

All types are extremely durable, hard, slip-resistant, non-porous, relatively noisy and abrasion-resistant. The thickness of screed or self-levelling floors is normally related to the type of wear expected. They are all resistant to mild acids and alkalis, oils, fats and grease. Epoxy floors will resist strong alkalis. Polyester can be damaged by some organic acids, e.g. citric and acetic acid, and chlorinated solvents, e.g. perchlorethylene. Polyurethane will resist strong acids, but can be affected by acetone.

Self-levelling and screed floors are used in factories, hospitals, offices, hotels and public buildings. Decorative floors are specifically used in shops, offices, foyers and corridors.

British Standards

BS 1286: 1974, *Clay Tiles for Flooring.*
BS 1711: 1975, *Solid Rubber Flooring.*
BS 2592: 1973, *Thermoplastic Flooring Tiles.*
BS 3187: 1978, *Specification for Electrically Conducting Rubber Flooring.*
BS 3260: 1969, *PVC (Vinyl) Asbestos Floor Tiles.*
BS 3261: 1973, *Unbacked Flexible PVC Flooring: Part 1: Homogenous flooring.*
BS 5085: 1974, *Backed Flexible PVC Flooring: Part 1: Needle-loom felt-backed flooring.*
BS 5085: 1976, *Part 2: Cellular PVC backing.*
CP 201: Part 2: 1972, *Wood Flooring (Board, Strip, Block and Mosaic).*
CP 202: Part 2: 1972, *Tile Flooring.*
CP 203: Part 3: 1972, *Sheet and Tile Flooring (Cork,*

Linoleum, Plastics and Rubber).
CP 204: Part 2: 1970, *In situ Floor Finishes.*

Carpets

Carpets generally consist of a surface pile fixed to
a backing material. The pile and backing may be
formed together or the pile applied to the backing.
In some types a secondary backing will be applied.
They are produced as broadlooms, 2–5 m in width,
strip which is laid in lengths and joined at edges to
form wall-to-wall carpeting, stair carpet and
carpet tiles and squares.

Types

Woven The backing and pile are formed together
during weaving.

- *Wilton* Pile yarns are woven into the backing
  and pulled through at intervals to form the
  pile and pattern if appropriate (see Figure 14).
  The backing generally consists of warp yarns
  of cotton, weft yarns of jute and pile yarns not
  pulled through. In plain carpets, additional
  stuffer yarns will be included in the backing.
  Wilton is characterized by a cut pile, firm
  backing, a relatively smooth reverse side,
  streaks of colour on reverse side, limited
  number of colours in patterned carpets and
  generally a very dense pile.
- *Brussels and Cord* These are essentially
  similar to Wilton but the pile is uncut (see
  Figure 14). They are harder wearing, but
  harder and less resilient.
- *Axminster* The pile is inserted as tufts into
  the backing (see Figure 15). The backing
  consists of warp yarns of cotton, weft yarns of

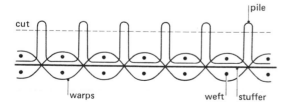

Figure 14 *Wilton and Brussels carpets (simplified)*

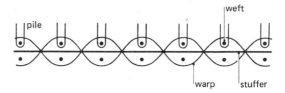

Figure 15 *Axminster carpet (simplified)*

jute and additional stuffer warp yarns. The
pile yarns contribute little to the backing.
Axminster is characterized by a cut pile and a
firm backing with distinct ribs on the reverse
side. The pattern may be visible on the reverse
side. Numerous colours are used in patterned
carpets and the pile is not as dense as Wilton.

- *Oriental and knotted* The pile of wool or silk
  is knotted to the warp yarns of a woven
  backing, the warp and weft yarns being of
  cotton. The type of knot and design is
  characteristic of the place of origin. The
  principal types are Persian, Turkish, Indian
  and Chinese. They are generally expensive
  and any cleaning and maintenance other than
  vacuuming must be undertaken by trained
  personnel.

Tufted A cut or uncut pile (see Figure 16) is
formed by inserting the pile yarns into a prewoven

Figure 16 *Tufted carpet*

base and securing them with latex, PVC or other
adhesive resin. A secondary backing, usually of
jute or foam rubber, is applied.

Bonded pile A pile composed of natural or
synthetic yarns is formed by direct bonding of the
pile yarns with a layer of adhesive onto a backing,
frequently of PVC or jute (see Figure 17). The pile
may be cut or uncut.

Flocked An impervious PVC sheet to which is

Figure 17   *Bonded-pile carpet*

Figure 18   *Flocked carpet*

Figure 19   *Needle-pile carpet*

anchored a dense short pile of nylon (see Figure 18). It combines the appearance of a carpet with the advantages of sheet PVC.

Needle-punch/fibre-bonded carpet with a pile   Also known as *needle-pile carpet (see Figure 19)*. Needling of a layer of fibres is employed to entangle a layer of fibres and form a pile . The fibres are bonded with an adhesive resin and/or heat.

Needle-punch/fibre-bonded carpet without a pile   A carpet with a felt-like appearance (see Figure 20) is formed by overlaying a support fabric with a batt of fibres and needling the fibres to entangle them into the support material. A backing may be applied.

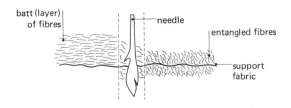

Figure 20   *Needle-bonded/fibre-bonded carpet*

Carpet fibres

One or more different fibres will be used in the manufacture of a carpet, the type of fibre used influencing the cost and properties. The properties of fibres used in carpet manufacture are shown in Table 5. In general, abrasion resistance will increase the durability of a carpet by increasing its wear resistance. Resilience will permit pile to recover from crushing, thus increasing appearance retention. The fibres used are wool, silk, nylon, polypropylene, acrylics, cotton, rayon, high-tenacity rayon, modacrylic, metallic and animal hair. Animal hair is abrasion-resistant, reasonably resilient, less prone to static build up, stain-resistant and easily cleaned, but hard, expensive and requires regular maintenance. Modacrylic is included to increase fire resistance. Metallic is included to reduce build up of static.

Blends of fibres include:

100% wool, nylon, polypropylene or animal hair.
80% wool and 20% nylon
Various combinations of wool, rayon, acrylics, nylon, polyester and polypropylene.

The actual properties and cost of a particular carpet will depend on the method of construction, i.e type, the depth and density of the pile, and the blend of fibres.

Carpet backing

A variety of backing materials are used including jute, cotton, PVC, polypropylene, nylon and foam rubber. The essential requirement is strength, although the resilience of a secondary backing will contribute to durability. Synthetic materials have the advantage of not being subject to attack by animal pests or mildew and, being relatively impervious to water, will not rot.

Laying

The life of a carpet is greatly influenced by the method of laying.

Sub-floor must be dry, smooth and level, free from cracks and nails. Where the sub-floor is poor it may be covered with timber sheeting, correctly laid and secured or a suitable seamless resin can be applied. If carpet is to be stuck down with adhesive, the floor must be free from dust, oil, grease and wax. Carpets must not be permanently fixed to a sub-floor that is damp or where there is inadequate underfloor ventilation, particularly if the backing is impervious to water.

Underlay must be used where the carpet is not stuck down. It will increase the life of a carpet by reducing uneven wear as a result of slight unevenness in floor, by improving resilience and by preventing creeping. The feel of the carpet will also be improved. Typical underlays are needle-punch felt and synthetic foam or foam rubber. There is a tendency for some felts to flatten in use and, therefore, lose their resilence. Underlays must be the same size as the carpet and, in the case of stair carpet, individual pieces should overlap the edges of each tread. Rubber underlays, because of their high resilience, may not be suitable for strip carpets.

Fixing (see Figure 21) Carpet tiles can be permanently fixed or laid loose. The latter is generally preferable so that they can be moved round as tiles in areas more subject to heavy traffic become worn.

Strip carpet should be secured to adjacent strips and the whole carpet secured at the edges. Normally strips should be laid with the pile running in the same direction.

Broadloom carpets should be secured at the edges.

Joints between adjoining lengths of carpet, either strip or broad loom, should be strong enough to permit the complete carpet to be stretched without the seams breaking. Methods of seaming include the use of machine or hand sewing, hessian tape and an adhesive, or heat-bonded tape.

Carpet should be installed such that it is flat and taut. Methods of fixing include:

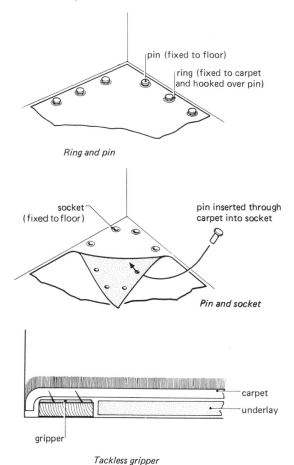

Ring and pin

Pin and socket

Tackless gripper

Figure 21   *Methods of fixing carpets*

1   Tackless grippers consisting of metallic or plastic strips bearing steel pins which enter the underside of the carpet.
2   Turn and tack in which the edge of the carpet is turned and tacked through the turned edge. It is not suitable for foam-backed or fibre-bonded carpet.
3   Full adhesion in which the carpet is bonded to the floor with an adhesive.
4   Ring and pin or pin and socket which can be used when the carpet requires regular lifting.

Carpet selection

The properties of a carpet depend upon colour and

pattern, density of pile, type of fibres, method of construction and length of pile. These properties are abrasion resistance, chemical resistance, resilience, light resistance, anchorage of pile, moth and mildew resistance, moisture absorbancy, resistance to static build up and stain and soil resistance. When selecting a carpet for a particular situation these properties must be evaluated in relation to the following criteria.

Appearance and appearance retention   Plain carpets will make a room look larger, but will show stains and flattening of the pile. Patterns reduce the apparent size of a room but will not show stains or flatten as easily.

The ability to recover from crushing is an important component of appearance retention and therefore life expectancy. It will be enhanced by resilient fibres and a dense pile. Long pile carpets are not generally suitable for heavy traffic areas.

Resistance to soiling and effective maintenance of surface appearance is generally better in carpets made from wool rather than synthetic fibres and in carpets with a dense pile.

Soil and stain resistance is enhanced by the application of compounds based on silicone or fluorinated hydrocarbons. These coat the fibres and prevent the entry of soil or stains.

Durability will require good abrasion resistance, resilience and firm anchorage of the pile. Generally the greater the density of the pile, the greater the abrasion resistance and resilience. Abrasion resistance is generally greater where synthetic fibres, nylon in particular, are used and resilience greater when more resilient fibres are used.

Contract grades of carpet should be used, grades being available for light, medium or heavy duty use.

Water resistance   Carpets manufactured from synthetic fibres are generally unaffected by water. The more absorbent animal and vegetable fibres will rot if allowed to remain moist.

Ease of cleaning   The removal of soil from within the pile by suction cleaning is less effective where carpets have a dense pile, have an impervious backing or are stuck down. This is not necessarily a problem. Synthetic fibres being less absorbent can be more easily cleaned by wet methods. Conversely, wool will tend to absorb water resulting in longer drying times. Carpet dyes should show no significant change in shade and not be prone to bleeding when normal wet or dry cleaning methods are used. Soil and stain retardent finishes can make cleaning easier.

Chemical resistance   Synthetic fibres are generally more resistant to chemicals. Wool and silk are affected by alkalis and bleach.

Sunlight resistance   Most fibres will be affected by light to some extent. Silk is notable in that its deterioration can be relatively rapid. The principal problem associated with sunlight is the fading of dye although the dyes used in good quality carpeting should be light fast.

Pests   Synthetic fibres are unaffected, but wool will be affected by carpet beetles and moths whilst cotton or rayon can be affected by mildews. Carpets manufactured from natural fibres should be treated with suitable repellents and fungicides.

Static   Synthetic fibres are particularly prone to accumulation of static charge. Non-static carpeting can include metallic fibres which act as an earth.

Testing   It is essential that carpet is tested to ensure that it meets the required specification; in particular.

Preventive maintenance

In addition to cleaning procedures, a number of other maintenance operations are undertaken to deal with particular carpet problems.

Wear significantly shortens the life of a carpet.

Regular vacuuming will only remove grit in part. It is therefore essential that barrier matting be used to prevent soil reaching a carpet.

Furniture legs and castors should be covered with suitable cups.

Druggets of canvas, linen or plastic can be placed on heavy traffic or heavily soiled areas.

A rubber foam or net underlay may be fixed to rugs to prevent movement.

Carpet tiles should be moved round, stair carpets jogged and broadloom carpet turned, if possible, to prevent uneven wear.

Edges of carpet must be firmly secured to prevent shifting.

Sprouting caused by loops of loop-pile carpet being pulled up, can be cut off or pulled back using a crochet hook. Shooting caused by pile yarn being pulled up can be cut off. Fluffing caused by loose fibres in new carpets can be removed by brushing or gentle vacuuming.

Shading This is caused by light striking pile lying at different angles and may be removed by vacuuming to produce an erect pile. If this is unsuccessful the position of furniture can be altered judiciously or the carpet turned round.

Shading may also be the result of dyes fading after exposure to light. Careful placing of furniture or regular turning of the carpet may disguise the problem. Shading caused by ingrained dust can be removed by cleaning.

Static Charge is caused by the transfer of electrons from one surface to another as a result of abrasion. Unless there is some means by which the charge can leak to earth it will accumulate. When a statically charged surface is touched the accumulated charge can be conducted through the person touching it to earth and they will experience an electric shock. Synthetic fibre carpets are particularly susceptible to this problem. A dry atmosphere will further contribute to it. The problem can be solved in a number of ways:

1 The use of carpets which include conducting metal fibres.

2 Maintenance of an atmospheric humidity of 60–75%.

3 The application of an antistatic finish by means of a spray. When dry, the finish attracts and holds moisture which can then conduct any static charge to earth. They tend to lose their effect eventually or are removed by shampooing or hot water extraction.

Wet cleaning methods will temporarily remove the charge. Wool fibres contain 10–15% moisture and, therefore, are not usually affected, as they leak the charge to earth naturally.

Deterioration by natural agencies Wet carpets, particularly if made of natural fibres, must be allowed to dry and lifted to complete drying if necessary. Carpets and backings of natural fibres will rot if allowed to remain moist.

Moths, carpet beetles and mildews can be controlled by regular vacuuming of all parts, particularly edges, regular lifting and inspections, application of suitable repellents and fungicides.

Oriental carpets, particularly those of silk, must be protected from natural light.

British Standards

BS 1006: 1978, *Methods of Test for Colour Fastness of Textiles and Leather.*
BS 4052: 1972, *Method for Determination of Thickness Loss of Textile Floor Coverings under Dynamic Loading.*
BS 4939: 1980, *Method for Determination of Thickness Loss of Textile Floor Coverings after Prolonged Heavy Static Loading.*
BS 5352: 1976, *Code of Practice for the Installation of Textile Floor Coverings.*
BS 5557: 1978, *Textile Floor Coverings: Classification and Terminology.*
PAS 24: 1977, *Specification for Woven Carpets.*

Selection of floors and floor coverings

The selection of a floor must take account of a number of factors and will normally be made at the planning stage of a building. In an existing building it may be required either when alterations are to be made in the use of particular areas or when carpeting is to be introduced.

Appearance

Hard and semi-hard floors are more utilitarian. Carpets will enhance the decor of a room and give an appearance of luxury.

Shiny and pale surfaces give an impression of coolness. Matt surfaces and intense colours are warmer.

Plain floors will increase the apparent size of a room. Patterns will reduce it. Patterns will disguise soil and the flattening of carpets, plain surfaces will not.

Comfort

Hard floors are less comfortable to stand on, noisy and cold but are less tiring to walk upon. Semi-hard floors, and carpets in particular, are more comfortable to stand on, quiet and warm, but are more tiring to walk upon.

Ease of cleaning

Non-porous or sealed floors can be more effectively cleaned than porous or carpeted floors. Routine and periodic maintenance of many carpets may only remove 50 to 60% of the total soil in them. Carpets of the flock type are notable exceptions. The surface appearance of a carpet can, however, be more easily maintained than that of hard floors and maintenance will therefore be less expensive.

Safety and hygiene

Most floors have good slip resistance, although smooth floors will become slippery when wet. Slip-resistant surfaces and carpeting should be used where slip resistance is of particular importance.

Non-porous floors, e.g. terrazzo, quarry tiles and PVC sheet, are used in situations where high standards of soil and bacteria removal are required. With the exception of carpets of the flock type, carpets are generally unsuitable in this respect although bacteriastatic finishes can be applied.

Durability

The resistance to wear and tear required by a floor will depend upon the amount of traffic, operations involving equipment, the amount and type of soil introduced, exposure to grease, oils, acids, alkalis and solvents, amount of wetting likely to be experienced and the possibility of cigarette and other burns. When the likely influence of these factors has been evaluated, a floor with suitable abrasion resistance, resilience and resistance to water or chemicals can be selected. Selection should also consider the actual life expectancy of the floor. For example, the floors of kitchens and hospitals wards might be expected to last the life of the building whilst carpets, e.g. in lounge areas, may be changed in response to fashion or decoration. Carpets are also notable, in that, although they can be extremely durable, it may be necessary to change them before they are worn simply because it is no longer possible to restore their surface appearance to an acceptable standard.

Insulation

Carpets, particularly those with a deep pile have better sound and thermal insulation properties than carpets with a short pile or hard and semi-hard floors.

Static

Antistatic floors are used where the control of static is essential, e.g. computer rooms and operating theatres.

Fire risk and smoking

The resilient floors, notably PVC and linoleum, are damaged and the standard of appearance reduced relatively reasily by extinguishing cigarette ends on them. The hard floors and some types of carpet, e.g. those made from wool, are more suitable where smoking is permitted.

Cost

Cost should be considered when one or more floors have been selected which meet all other criteria. It must include not only the cost of the floor but the costs of regular cleaning and maintenance.

Sanitary accommodation

Requirements

To achieve high standards of hygiene the accommodation and its furniture must meet the following requirements:

- All surfaces and furniture must be smooth, non-porous, free of cracks and crevices as far as possible and easily cleaned.
- A supply of hot and cold water must be made to each appliance and to storage tanks to meet the regulations relevant to each appliance, the number of appliances in a building and the number of persons likely to use them. The appropriate standards are described in BS Codes of Practice CP 310 and CP 342. The number of appliances installed must conform with BS Code of Practice CP 305.
- The water supply must be free of contamination.
- Taps should be designed to discharge above the flood point of a basin or bowl to prevent back siphonage of foul water into the main water supply.
- The fouling area of appliances should be reduced to a minimum.
- Sanitary accommodation must not open directly into any room used for sleeping or dressing, a kitchen or food storage area, or a room used habitually for manufacture or trade. In these cases a ventilated lobby must be provided between the sanitary accommodation and the room, with doors opening to the room and the sanitary area.
- Ventilation may be natural or mechanical. If natural, the amount of window opening must exceed one twentieth of the floor area. If mechanical, three complete changes of air are

required per hour which should discharge to the outside.
- WC cistern, taps and similar fittings should preferably be foot-operated.
- A supply of soap and hand driers will be required.

Floor and walls

Floors will ideally be constructed of seamless resin or quarry tile. PVC sheet is a satisfactory alternative where usage and soiling is light. Tiles of PVC or thermoplastic are unsuitable in that regular wetting will result in them lifting. Terrazzo has formerly been used but heavy usage coupled with an increase in porosity tends to result in the accumulation of stains that are difficult to remove without causing further damage to the floor.

Coving between walls and floors will facilitate cleaning. Structural walls should be of hard plaster finished with a solvent-based paint. Half or full tiling with ceramic tiles is attractive but less easy to maintain. Partition walls may be similar to structural walls or may be constructed of preformed sheets.

Furniture construction materials

Ceramics A range of ceramic materials are employed, differing largely in the porosity of the clay body, strength and resistance to knocks. The glaze of all types is non-porous with excellent soil, stain, alkali, acid, and organic solvent resistance. Abrasion resistance is good, although the use of abrasive powders will scratch the glaze.

Glazed earthenware is cheap, porous if the glaze is chipped and has fair resistance to knocks. It is used mainly for sinks and WC pans.

Glazed fireclay is more expensive than earthenware, porous if glaze is chipped, but has good resistance to knocks. It is used for sinks, WC pans and urinals installed in schools and factories.

Glazed stoneware is non-porous when chipped and has excellent resistance to knocks. It is used for drains, gullies and urinal stalls.

Vitreous china is non-porous but not as strong as fireclay. It is unsuitable where heavy wear is expected. However, its high standard of finish makes it suitable for all types of appliance installed in hotels.

Cast iron is usually finished with a white or coloured vitreous enamel. At one time it was used extensively in the manufacture of larger appliances, e.g. baths. It is strong with good resistance to knocks, heavy and has good resistance to stain, acids, alkalis, solvents and bleaches. Abrasive powders will scratch the enamel.

Pressed steel Mild steel is moulded in a press to form a range of one-piece units, e.g. sinks and baths, which can be finished either with a vitreous or stoved enamel. Unlike ceramic materials it will not crack when subject to a heavy knock. The finish has, in general, good resistance to mild acids and alkalis, solvents, bleaches and stains, although the stoved finishes tend to be less abrasion-resistant than the vitreous ones.

Stainless steel is moulded and pressed to form one-piece units, e.g. sinks, urinals and wash basins. It is particularly resistant to hard wear, but strong oxidizing bleaches and salt/vinegar mixtures will attack the surface. Abrasive powders will leave fine scratch marks.

Chrome is used as a finish for taps, towel rails and similar fittings. Strong alkalis will blacken the surface. Abrasives, in particular powders, will gradually remove the plate to reveal the metal beneath.

Plastics A range of plastics are used to form baths, sinks, urinals, shelves and bins. They include opaque acrylics, clear acrylics (Perspex), polyethylene and polypropylene. They are generally strong, durable, cheap, available in a range of colours and resistant to mild alkalis and acids, but in most cases organic solvents and bleaches will remove the surface gloss finish leaving it rough and dull. Strong abrasives and the regular use of mild abrasives will score and roughen the surface. Very hot water will cause surface discolouration of acrylic baths.

Glass-fibre reinforced plastics (GRP) Epoxy or polyester resins reinforced with glass fibre and with a hard gloss finish are used to form a variety of moulded products including sinks, baths, urinals and cisterns. They are strong, relatively cheap and resistant to mild acids and alkalis and bleaches, but abrasives and some organic solvents will remove the surface gloss.

Laminates are used for work surfaces and splash backs. They have excellent resistance to most chemicals, but strong abrasives should be avoided.

Appliances

WC Consists of a pan containing water, a device for providing flushed water, the cistern and a seat. The cistern and pan may be separate or coupled together. The pan will generally be constructed of a ceramic material. There are two principal types, wash down and siphons (see Figure 22). Wash downs are cheap, simple and rarely block. The siphon type is more positive in action but more prone to blockage.

The area around and behind the pan is usually difficult to clean. Corbelled pans, fixed to the wall, are available giving access beneath them. When selecting a pan, particular attention should be paid to the flush being powerful enough to completely discharge the contents and to scour all inner surfaces, the surface area of water being large enough to ensure all excrement falls into the water, and the back of the pan being vertical to prevent fouling. Seats are generally plastic although wood finished with an acid-catalysed laquer is equally hygienic. An open front is desirable. Alternatively the ceramic may be moulded to eliminate need for a seat.

Slop hoppers are often installed in hospital sanitary annexe areas and less frequently in hotels and other buildings for the disposal of waste material. They consist of a pan similar to the WC pan, a hinged brass grating which is raised or lowered over the pan on which buckets can be stood, a high-level cistern for flushing the pan and bib taps to supply hot and cold water for filling

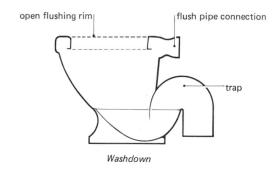

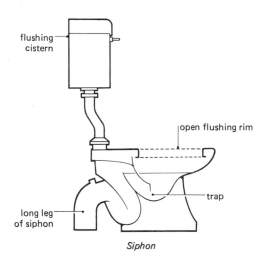

Figure 22   *Types of WC pan*

buckets. The pan has a large diameter outlet to prevent blockages. The system may be combined with a sink.

Generally in hotels and other buildings a simpler system consisting of a Belfast sink, grating and bib taps is installed in the cleaners' cupboards.

Urinals are most usually installed in male communal lavatories. There are three types: slab, stall and bowl. They are generally made of ceramic materials although the slab type may be made from plastics or stainless steel. Automatic flushing is usual at the rate of 4.5 litres per unit every 15 to 20 min.

A number of factors must be considered when installing urinals. Because flushing is at intervals, the flow of urine from urinals is relatively concentrated and the face of a stall wetted by urine

will not be washed immediately. This can result in a build up of deposits of urine salts and the generation of unpleasant odours. Leakages at the joints of slabs and stalls can occur, resulting in the need for major maintenance work.

A grating is required to catch litter deposited in the channel. A raised ceramic or glass panel should be erected to prevent splashing.

Urinals are generally easier to clean than WC pans, at least in terms of accessibility.

Bowls should be installed where abuse is unlikely. They are cheaper, have smaller surface areas for cleaning, have no cement joints and the absence of joints and accessible pipework makes maintenance easier.

Cisterns are installed to flush pans and urinals with clean water. Manually operated cisterns are positioned at a high or low level above the pan or are coupled to it. They are usually of the piston or bell type (see Figure 23). When the handle is depressed the piston rises, displacing water over the siphon into the flush pipe. Water passing down the pipe carries air with it creating a partial vacuum in the siphon, thus setting up a siphoning action. The cistern continues to empty until air is able to enter beneath the piston, thus breaking the siphon action. A ball valve regulates the filling of the cistern. When full, elevation of the float causes the valve to be closed. A warning pipe (overflow) fitted to the cistern will indicate a faulty ball valve.

Bell-type cisterns include a bell which is raised by the action of pulling the handle. When the handle is released the bell falls and forces water over the siphon to create a siphoning action.

Dual-flush cisterns which deliver 4.5 or 9 litres of water, depending on whether solid or liquid matter is to be flushed from the pan, can also be installed.

Automatic flushing cisterns are installed to flush urinals. As the cistern fills air trapped in the cistern compresses. When full, the increased air pressure is sufficient to displace water from the cistern into a siphon to set up a siphoning action.

Flushing troughs are used as an alternative to separate cisterns for each WC pan. They consist of

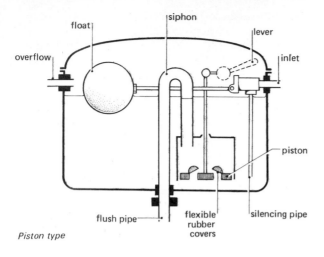

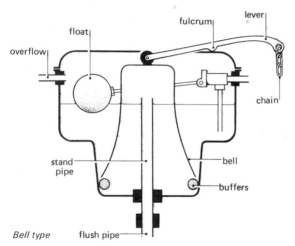

Figure 23 *Types of cistern*

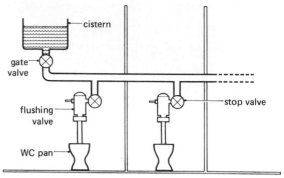

Figure 24 *Flushing valves*

of scalding. Hot water should also be supplied to the rim of the bowl.

Wash/lavatory basins are available in a variety of shapes and sizes and can be supported by brackets, pedestals or corbelled. Figure 26 shows a section through a typical basin. Water supply will be via separate hot and cold taps or via a 'mixer' tap. Water is contained by a simple plug and chain or pop-up waste. Where communal washing facilities are required a long trough served by several spray taps or a circular wash fountain will be more economic to install and more easily cleaned and maintained than a number of individual sinks.

Baths are constructed of cast iron, pressed steel, GRP, acrylic plastic, and occasionally terrazzo.

a single trough with a siphon and chain for each pan.

Flushing valves A fixed amount of water is delivered to a pan via a manually operated valve. Several pans can be served by the same cistern.

Bidets (see Figure 25) are used for perineal washing (or as a foot bath) and consist of a bowl either floor-mounted or corbelled. A pop-up water trap is generally preferable. Hot and cold water are supplied to an ascending spray, preferably via a thermostatic valve to prevent risk

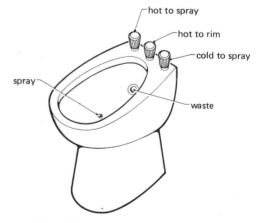

Figure 25 *Bidet*

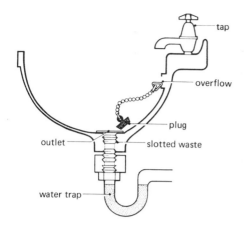

Figure 26 *Section through wash basin*

There are a number of types (see Figure 27) which include:

1 Traditional, with roll edge, free standing.
2 Magna type, with flat top and straight edges.
3 Sitz bath, which is short, deep and has a seat. Suitable for old people and confined spaces.

The water supply will be via separate hot and cold taps or a mixer tap which may incorporate a shower fitting.

Showers, where they are independent of a bath, will consist of a 1 metre square tray of plastic, pressed steel or ceramic material in a tiled compartment. Water is supplied either by an overhead rose spray or an adjustable umbrella spray fitted at chest height. The latter uses less water. The water supply can be controlled by one of two means:

1 Valves fitted to both the hot and cold supply and independently adjusted to give the required water temperature. With this method there is a risk of scalding if variation in water pressure occurs as a result of water being used elsewhere in the building.
2 Alternatively a mixer valve is fitted which adjusts the supply of both hot and cold water to give the required water temperature. The valve may be thermostatically controlled or will include an antiscald device which will cut off the hot water if the cold supply fails.

Soap dispensers

Soap bars are subject to pilferage. Small bars are, however, provided in hotel rooms. In accommodation to be used by the general public, liquid soap is generally provided and will involve the use of a suitable dispenser. Top-up dispensers are generally wasteful and tend to dry up at the nozzle. Dispensers delivering pre-proportioned amounts of soap are preferable, a positive piston action preventing blockage. Dispensers supplied from a central reservoir of soap are particularly suitable where several sinks are provided.

Hand driers

These can take the form of hand towels, cabinet towels, paper towels or hot air driers.

Hand towels are only suitable when they are to be used by one or two individuals and where they can be removed for laundering as soon as they are

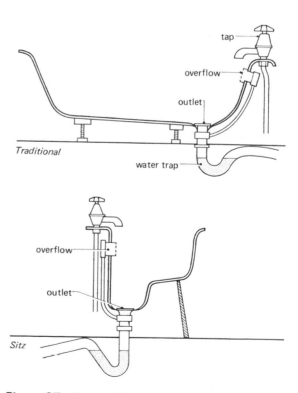

Figure 27 *Types of bath*

soiled, e.g. hotel guest rooms or private bathrooms.

Cabinet towels are normally supplied and serviced by a hire company. They are suitable where usage of the accommodation is relatively light. The towel dispenser will provide a fresh area of clean towel each time it is used but, if usage exceeds the amount of clean towel available, between service times, then only soiled towel is available.

Paper towels are suitable in most situations, but particularly where usage of the accommodation is heavy. They ensure that each user is provided with a clean hygienic towel. They can however prove expensive in that large numbers may be used and overuse is likely, each user using two or three rather than one. Careless use can result in the accommodation becoming unsightly, the towels either being dropped on the floor or spilling over from the litter bin provided.

Hot air driers represent the most suitable means of ensuring a hygienic method of hand drying. Where use of the accommodation is light their installation may be uneconomic but, where use is heavy, they represent a more economic alternative to paper towels, despite the initial cost of installation. They are, however, subject to breakdown and vandalism.

British Standards

CP 305:1974, *Sanitary Appliances. Part I: Selection, installation and special requirements.*

CP 310: 1965, *Water Supply.*

CP 342: 1974, *Centrallized Hot Water Supply. Part 2: Buildings other than individual dwellings.*

Kitchens

The *Food Hygiene (General) Regulations 1970,* specify the broad requirements for a kitchen. In practical terms, the following are required.

General

The premises must be clean and in good condition so that no contamination of food is possible by soil, odours or pests.

Fabric

Floors should be even and impervious, with no cracks or open points, and non-slippery. Junctions with walls should be coved to facilitate cleaning. Where gulleys are present the floor should slope towards them. The most suitable flooring materials are quarry tiles and seamless resins. Walls should be hard, impervious and easily cleaned. Suitable materials include hard plaster finished either with a washable paint or ceramic tiles. The latter are less easy to maintain and clean.

Ceilings should be underdrawn and finished with an impervious washable paint. If possible light fittings should not be suspended from the ceiling. Suspended fittings are dust traps, tend to become greasy and are difficult to clean. Service pipes should be encased, chased into walls or pass through service ducts to prevent accumulation of soil.

Ventilation and lighting

Adequate ventilation and lighting must be provided. Complete air changes 20 to 40 times per hour are required. This will require the installation of canopies and extractor fans which should be fitted with accessible filters and grease drip trays.

Work surfaces and equipment

Work surfaces should be hard, impervious, easily cleaned and non-reactive with foodstuffs. Stainless steel is ideal although laminates are quite suitable. Equipment should be designed and positioned to allow ease of cleaning. In order to clean walls and floors, non-movable equipment should stand 0.3 m from walls or from other equipment and have legs if possible.

Water supply and washing facilities

A supply of clean water is required. Separate sinks must be provided for:

1 Washing of equipment and should be supplied with hot and cold water.
2 Hand washing and should be supplied with hot and cold water.
3 Washing of food and should be supplied with cold water.

Sinks for washing food and equipment should ideally be made from stainless steel. Wash hand basins must be situated in food-handling areas and adjacent to sanitary accommodation. Soap, scrubbing brush and paper towels, or hot air driers, must be provided.

Sanitary accommodation

Must be provided to comply with the *Offices, Shops and Railway Premises Act 1963,* and must display a notice 'Now Wash Your Hands'. They must not open directly onto, or be situated, where odours can penetrate into food areas.

Changing rooms

Provision must be made for food handlers to change into protective overalls and to securely store their outdoor clothing.

Drainage

Must be adequate.

Food storage

All food should be covered. Provision must be made for the storage of perishable foods in the form of cold stores, refrigerators and freezers and for the storage of dry goods. Stores should be cool, well ventilated and not permit access to pests.

Foods should not be stored less than 50 cm from the ground if unprotected and not less than 15 cm if protected, to allow air to circulate and facilitate cleaning.

Waste

All waste should be placed in impervious sacks in bins with a tightly fitting lid. When sacks are full they should be sealed and transferred to a clean dry waste storage area which is cool, well ventilated and denies access to pests.

Food handling

Clean and dirty processes must be isolated from each other. For example, staff handling dirty crockery should not also be involved in food preparation. Tasks involving raw and cooked food must be kept separate from each other. All high risk foods, namely protein foods, must be stored either below 10°C or above 62.7°C. If such food is to be reheated, the internal temperature must exceed 62.7°C.

Furniture

The term furniture is traditionally applied to all those movable, fitted and built-in structures which furnish bedrooms, lounges, offices, foyers and similar areas. It can be more broadly applied to a wide range of other surfaces, for example, door frames, door furniture, notice boards, light switches and mirrors, and to the fixtures and fittings found in bedrooms, toilets, kitchens and other areas.

In this section we consider traditional furniture together with a number of the more notable exceptions to which the term can be applied and which are not considered elsewhere.

Construction materials

Wood is used in the manufacture of table tops, cupboards, wardrobe panels, doors, legs, arms and the frames of upholstered furniture. Solid wood, laminated wood, chipboard, blockboard, veneers and whicker are used.

Solid wood includes the hardwoods, oak, mahogany teak, aframosia, and the softwood, pine. It is generally durable and resistant to warping, but furniture constructed exclusively of solid woods will be expensive.

Plywood constructed of hardwoods is strong, durable and resistant to warping. Laminated wood is similar to plywood but the sheet grains run in the same direction. It can be shaped to form arms and legs.

The durability and resistance of chipboard to warping depends on its density.

Veneers of teak, mahogany and yew give furniture the appearance of having been made from expensive solid wood.

Wicker reeds or canes are woven to form seats, backings of chairs, headboards, baskets and most types of furniture. It is prone to warping, not very durable and, because pieces may protrude, it may tear other materials.

Wood finishes   Wood is extremely porous and will require surface protection. Wax of the solvent-based type can be rubbed into the wood to leave a surface film of wax. The protection is limited and requires more maintenance.

Oil mixed with white spirit can be rubbed into wood. It tends to darken wood and accentuate the grain but will attract and hold dust.

French polish was the traditional method of finishing high-quality woods. It is expensive and has poor resistance to alcohol, water and heat, and scratches easily. Shellac resin dissolved in ethanol is applied to the surface and by rubbing successive applications the resin dries and hardens to give a high-gloss film.

Paints and laquers of the polyurethane, epoxy resin or melamine type form a hard impervious film resistant to water, heat and most chemicals. Other paints are less resistant but are used on cheaper furniture.

Metals are used to form legs, arms, framework and anti-knock strips of wooden furniture. Those most commonly used are iron, steel, aluminium, chrome, brass and copper, In general they are easily maintained, durable and resistant to most chemicals, but may be subject to tarnishing.

Plastics   Expanded polyurethane and rubber foams are used as filling for upholstered furniture.

Glass-fibre reinforced plastics (GRP) and high-density polypropylene are moulded to form lightweight seating, tables and the framework of some upholstered furniture. They are easily maintained but scratch easily and are affected by stains and some solvents.

Laminates are durable, water- and stain-resistant and resistant to most chemicals. They are particularly suitable for the tops of dressing tables, work surfaces, draw bottoms and as a general alternative to the use of wood veneers.

Glass and tiles may be used to form decorative table tops, but tiles will fracture and become unsightly while glass will break unless toughened and shatter-proof.

Upholstery fabrics are woven from one or more textile fibres, the type and method of weaving determining the properties of the fabric.

Wool will contribute to recovery from stretching, tear and crease resistance and has good resistance to general soiling. Wet cleaning methods may cause shrinkage.

Cotton and viscose rayon are reasonably abrasion- and tear-resistant and have reasonable resistance to general soiling. But they have more limited stretch recovery and crease resistance. Cotton fabrics may shrink when wet cleaning methods are used.

High tenacity rayons, nylon and polyester will contribute to the abrasion resistance and crease resistance of a fabric.

Nylon and crepe high-tenacity rayons will increase the tear resistance and stretch recovery.

Acrylics are reasonably abrasion resistant, have good stretch recovery, and are resistant to tearing.

Textured fabrics with a pile, cut or uncut, are attractive but tend to hold dust and may show shading and flattening of the pile, particularly in cheaper fabrics.

A number of fabrics are commonly used:
- *Brocade*   A multi-coloured jacquard pattern woven from cotton, silk, wool or nylon, additional wefts appear on the surface to form the pattern.

Metal-framed and moulded-plastic furniture

- *Brocatelle* A heavy fabric with raised pattern, the pattern being formed by warp satin weaves on a plain weave background.
- *Chintz* A patterned cotton fabric possibly having a glazed finish which may be lost as a result of heavy usage.
- *Corduroy* A weft pile fabric usually made from cotton, cut pile forming lines or cords in the warp direction.
- *Cretonne* A printed cotton or rayon fabric, heavier than chintz in a plain or twill weave.
- *Damask* Fabric of characteristic appearance woven from cotton, linen, silk, rayon, nylon or polyester, a design being formed by weft satin weaves on a background of warp satin weaves or by warp satin weaves on a plain weave background.
- *Denim* A plain weave fabric of cotton or rayon which is very hard wearing.
- *Moquette* A cut or uncut pile fabric; the pile is formed from wool or cotton on cotton.
- *Plush* A cut warp pile fabric with a deep pile, but less closely woven than velvet, and made from cotton, silk or synthetic fibre.

- *Ratine* A plain or twill weave, but the warp being of spiral threads or having knob like irregularities gives it a rough texture.
- *Repp* A plain weave with a rib running from selvedge to selvedge and woven from silk, cotton or synthetic fibre.
- *Satin* A lustrous warp-faced satin weave fabric, originally made of silk but now from cotton, rayon, or synthetics. It is frequently used on antique furniture.
- *Sateen* Similar to satin, but weft-faced.
- *Tapestry* A closely woven, plain weave fabric, the pattern being formed by the weft, and woven from cotton, rayon or wool.
- *Tweed* A heavy woollen fabric in plain or twill weaves.
- *Velvet* A cut warp pile fabric originally made from silk but now from cotton or rayon. It has a dense pile but is expensive and has a tendancy to crush.
- *Dralon velvet* Similar to velvet but made from dralon acrylic fibres, overcoming many of the problems associated with real velvet.
- *Velour* Similar to velvet but the pile tends to

lie down and be smooth-faced. It may be woven from cotton, rayon, silk or synthetic fibres.

- *Simulated leather* is formed from woven or knitted cotton to which in bonded PVC or polyurethane resin. Unless made specifically porous it will be non-porous and feel rather uncomfortable. PVC-coated fabrics must be of contract grade; breakdown of the plasticizer in cheaper grades will leave the coating brittle.
- *Hide* is durable and easily cleaned, but it is essential that it is kept supple.

Upholstered furniture

The method of construction of chairs, armchairs and settees (see Figure 28) may take a number of

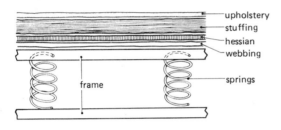

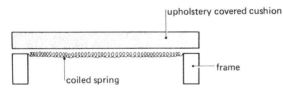

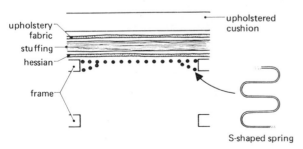

Figure 28   *Construction of upholstered furniture*

forms, such as:

1 A cover stretched over a padded panel.
2 A framework across which is stretched webbing overlaid with hessian and then padding. Upholstery material fixed to the frame covers the webbing hessian and padding. Coiled springs situated between the webbing and cross-members of the frame increase the resilience of the seating.
3 An upholstery-covered, foam-filled cushion placed on a framework across which is fixed a number of S-shaped springs overlaid with stuffing. The framework and stuffing are covered with upholstery fabric.
4 A framework across which is stretched or fixed webbing, springs, wooden slats, a sheet of synthetic rubber or a wooden panel supporting a foam-filled cushion.

In older furniture tow, sisal and horse hair were used as stuffing. These have been replaced by expanded polyurethane foams or rubber. No-sag springing can be incorporated into the foam which counteracts compression of the foam through usage, preventing puddling.

Foam should be covered with a fire-resistant covering in addition to upholstery fabric.

Beds

These generally consist of a base, headboard and mattress.

Base   This can take a number of forms (see Figure 29).

1 A metal frame supporting coiled springs across which is stretched a wire mesh.
2 A metal frame across which is stretched a wire mesh held by stretched springs.
3 A wood frame with a number of wooden slats. Frames of this type with a raised edge are suitable for hostels, reducing damage to the edge of the mattress as a result of people frequently sitting on the edge of it.
4 Divans consisting of a wooden frame and padded springs covered by upholstery fabric.
5 A metal frame with a rigid, flat, mattress-

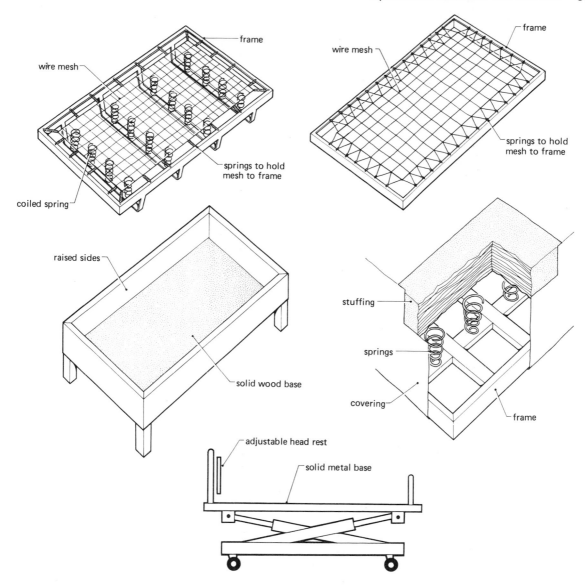

Figure 29 *Construction of bed frames*

support panel. The frame will be attached to legs of fixed height or be mounted on a central trolley with lockable castors, the height of which is adjustable. This type is used in hospitals.

For convenience bases should have lockable castors. The inclusion of drawers for additional storage in the base is useful in hostels. For bases other than divans or hospital beds, a hessian, canvas or cotton blanket should be placed under the mattress.

Headboards may be fixed to the bed or wall to protect the wall and support people lying in bed. They may be made from wood, plastic or metal and be veneered, laminated, quilted or painted as appropriate. Hospital beds have an adjustable back support.

Mattresses are generally of two types (see Figure 30):

1 Interior spring mattresses consist of independent coiled springs, pocket springs (mattresses for heavy-duty use) or interlocking springs (posture springing) padded with a layer of cotton linters, cotton felt and/or foam and covered with a fabric casing. The padding is normally held in position by quilting. A reinforced edge increases the strength of the mattress. Generally interior sprung mattresses have two sleeping surfaces although those used in hospitals have only one. Venting holes in the edge allow air to circulate through them. The thickness will range from about 12 to 22 cm. Regular inspection, airing and, where relevant, turning will help to prevent attack by pests.
2 Foam mattresses are formed from expanded latex or polyurethane foams. They may have one or two sleeping surfaces depending on the actual mattress. They recover their shape easily, are less heavy than interior spring mattresses and are not attacked by pests. The thickness will vary from about 10 to 15 cm.

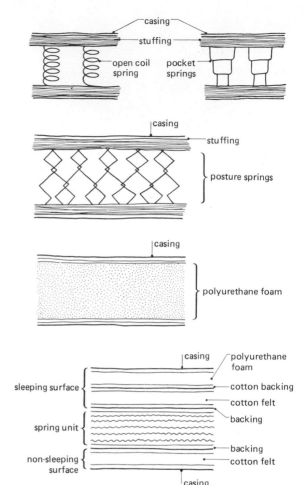

Figure 30 *Types of mattress construction*

Selection

Consideration should be given to the following:

Style must be in keeping with existing furniture or style of room.

Comfort will depend upon the shape and size of seats, back of chairs and the relative heights of tables and chairs.

Space available may influence whether free standing, fitted or built-in furniture is preferred.

In hostels or residential homes residents should be allowed some choice in how furniture is arranged. Built-in furniture may be fitted into alcoves, permits floor to ceiling storage space and can be used to hide wash basins when not in use.

Free-standing furniture will allow standardization of furniture throughout an establishment. Built-in and fitted furniture must be tailored to suit a particular room. Mirrors should be wall-mounted.

Dimensions Most types of furniture are manufactured within a fairly wide range of dimensions. The dimensions listed in Table 8 are based on the British Standards listed at the end of this section. Where British Standards are

Table 8   *Furniture dimensions*

Furniture	Part	Dimension	Furniture	Part	Dimension
Restaurant and office chairs	Seat height	40-45 cm	Wardrobes (depends on length of stay)	Space per hanger	8 cm
	Seat depth	37-43 cm		Depth	60 cm
	Seat width	Not less than 40 cm		Height:	
				ladies	175 cm
	Back rest height:			mens, hanging	150 cm
	lower edge from seat	16-17 cm		mens, hat shelf	25 cm
	upper edge from seat	33-36 cm		Rail distance from roof	10 cm
	Back rest width	36-40 cm		Hanging space:	
	Angle between seat and back rest	95-100°		single	50-120 cm
				double	90-180 cm
	Slope of seat towards back rest	0-5°	Beds	Approximate height of top of mattress above floor	56-64 cm
Coffee table	Height	40-50 cm		Single:	
				general	90 x 190 cm
Restaurant or writing tables	Height	71-73 cm			100 x 200 cm
	Gap between seat and underside of table	22 cm		hospital	96.5 x 208 cm
				Double	135 x 190 cm
	Allowance per person:				150 x 200 cm
	depth	65-70 cm		Headboard height	30-40 cm
	width (rectangular table)	50-55 cm			
	width (circular table)	48 cm			
Storage space (depends on length of stay)	Single room	1.3-1.5 m²			
	Double room	1.8-2.3 m²			
	Minimum draw dimensions	12 x 33 x 42 cm			
	The space to be comprised of drawers and shelves as appropriate				

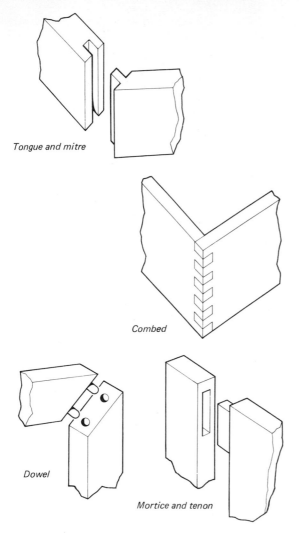

Tongue and mitre

Combed

Dowel

Mortice and tenon

Figure 31   *Types of joint used in the construction of furniture*

unavailable they are based on standard sizes available or on dimensions that are generally found to be acceptable.

Construction   The following points should be borne in mind:

- Timber frames should be of hardwood.
- Legs and arms of chairs, if not upholstered, should be of metal or hardwood, with no rough or unfinished edges.

- Joints (see Figure 31) should be tight fitting, well finished and show no trace of glue. Suitable joints will be tongue and mitre, combed, dowel or mortice and tenon, drilled and pegged at points of stress. Dovetail joints will be suitable for drawers.
- Drawers and shelves should be strong enough to support the weight of contents. Sides of drawers should be constructed of hardwood with a base of plywood or, alternatively, suitably constructed plastics. Drawers should run smoothly and be fitted with stops and should not be slack.
- Doors should be balanced, fit well and have strong hinges. Stays should be fitted.
- Sliding doors should run smoothly.
- Handles should be attached securely and in the correct position.
- Locks if fitted should work and be strong.
- Wood veneers should have no exposed edges (see Figure 32), rather a solid wood lip.
- Laminates should have no exposed edges, rather GRP moulded edge or rounded edge.
- Wood beneath veneers or laminates should be either high-density chipboard or solid hardwood.
- Moulded furniture should be GRP, toughened polypropylene or similar plastic.
- Castors should have no sharp edges, be free running and lockable if necessary.
- Surface finishes should be either a catalysed lacquer, metallic or a laminate as most appropriate. If clear lacquer is used on hardwood then the wood must be stained before the lacquer is applied.
- Hanging rails should be metal and properly fixed, including the centre.
- Free standing furniture should be firm and rigid with the legs well attached.
- Cupboards should be stable when empty, full or when drawers are open.
- Cantilevered furniture should be securely fixed (see Figure 33).
- Stackability and stability when stacked of tables and chairs should be considered when this is likely to be required.
- When tested for structural strength, furniture

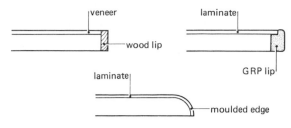

Figure 32 *Types of edge suitable for laminated furniture*

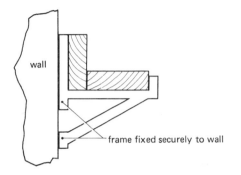

Figure 33 *Cantilevered furniture*

should exhibit no fracturing, no loosening of joints, no free movement other than that required, no permanent deformation and no damage to feet.

Upholstery Desirable characteristics will include:

● Abrasion resistance
● Crease resistance
● Resilience – stretch recovery
● Soil resistance
● Non-flammability
● Tear resistance
● Resistance to fading
● Pest-proof
● Easily cleaned
● Non-shading

The extent to which these are achieved will depend on the constituent fibres and method of construction of the upholstery. Particular points to be considered are:

1   Pile should run downwards or wear will be rapid.
2   Wood or metal parts should be available to pick the furniture up by.
3   Covering should be securely fixed.
4   A minimum of trim is desirable.

Mattresses The advantages of foam-filled mattresses must be considered. If interior spring mattresses are preferred then quality will be governed by depth, type, gauge and number of springs, type of padding and nature of upholstery covering. For all types of mattress a well reinforced edge is required. Mattresses used in hospitals may be required to be capable of withstanding regular disinfection.

Ease of cleaning All furniture on legs, particularly if large or if there are no castors, should be 20–30 cm above the ground, providing reasonable access for cleaning. A simple design with no nooks or crannies that will harbour soil and which are difficult to clean is preferred.

Testing Where furniture of the same type is being bought in quantity it is essential that a test piece is subjected to rigorous testing to ensure that it meets the desired requirements. Testing services are available.

Blinds

These are designed to limit the amount of light entering a room and are of four main types:

1   Venetian blinds consisting of horizontal slats, occasionally of wood, but more usually of lightweight alloy finished with stoved enamel paint.
2   Vertical blinds consisting of vertical (usually plastic) slats.
3   Roller blinds consisting of a vinyl or similar coated fabric.
4   Roman blinds consisting of a shaped fabric, exactly fitting a recess, and battened every 15 to 20 cm. Cords enable the blind to be adjusted.

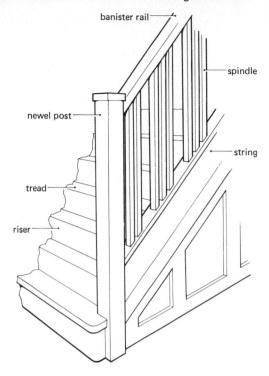

Figure 34 *Parts of a staircase*

Venetian and vertical blinds may be appropriate where it is necessary to protect fabrics, paintings and objets d'art from the effects of sunlight. They do, however, have a large surface area that can attract and hold dust and can therefore involve significant amounts of time in cleaning and maintenance. Roller blinds can offer an alternative to conventional curtaining.

Lighting

Lighting includes ceiling, wall and table lights. Fittings and bases can include plastics, alloy metals finished with stoved enamel paint, china, glass, wood, iron, brass and anodized aluminium. Shades and diffusers include plastics, glass, textile fabrics, parchment derived from animal skins and glass fibre. The type of construction material will influence the method of cleaning and maintenance.

Telephones

Telephones are frequently the property of British Telecom who lay down specific guidelines for their care and maintenance. Because of the intimate nature of their use, periodic or routine disinfection is necessary.

Staircases

In addition to the treads, staircases include banister rails (see Figure 34) with a variety of finishes, e.g. wax polished wood, brass, plastics and various paints, and may include stair rods of brass or wood. All cleaning and maintenance must be undertaken with particular care for the safety of users.

British Standards

BS 4875: 1972, *Strength and Stability of Domestic and Contract Furniture. Part 1: Seating.*
BS 4875: 1977, *Part 2: Tables and trolleys.*
BS 4875: 1978, *Part 3: Cabinet furniture.*
BS 4886: 1973, *Hospital Bedsteads. Part 1: Bedsteads of variable height. Part 2: Bedsteads of fixed height.*
BS 5223: 1975, *Hospital Bedding. Part 1: Adult size spring interior mattresses.*
BS 5223: 1979, *Part 2: Flexible polyurethane mattresses.*
BS 5223: 1976, *Part 4: Mattress covers of polyurethane-coated nylon.*
BS 5790: 1979, *Coated Fabrics for Upholstery. Part 1: Specification for PVC-coated knitted fabrics. Part 2: Specification for PVC-coated woven fabrics.*
BS 5852: 1979, *Part 1: Methods of test for the ignitability of smokers material on upholstered composites for seating.*
BS 5873: 1980, *Part 1: Specification for functional dimensions, identification and finish of chairs and tables for educational institutions. Part 2: Specification for strength and stability of chairs for educational institutions.*
BS 5940: 1980, *Part 1: Specification for design and*

dimensions of office workstation desks, tables and chair..

PAS 26: 1978, *Specification for Office Furniture and Accessories.*

Bedding and linen

Bedding

Pillows, eiderdowns, duvets and comforters contain a variety of fillings:

a *Down* is the undercoating of water fowl (duck, goose, swan) and consists substantially of clusters of light fluffy filaments but without any quill shaft. It must include up to 15%, by weight, of small fine feathers. It is expensive, attacked by moths and comfortable.

b *Feathers* are the outercoating of various fowl. They are less expensive than down.

c *Down and feathers* is a mixture containing not less than 51% by weight of down.

d *Feathers and down* is a mixture containing not less than 15% by weight of down.

e *Rubber or expanded polyurethane foam* is non-absorbent, light, not attacked by pests and inexpensive, but can be too resilient for comfort.

f *Terylene fibres* have the advantages of foam but are less resilient and are therefore more comfortable.

New curled hair (horse or cow), curled woollen flock, kapok and new curled fibre (coir, Cochin or Mexican) are also used as fillings.

Pillows consist of a filling covered with a closely woven fabric, known as ticking. Typical dimensions are 48 × 73, 46 × 69 and 40 × 66 cm. Quality depends largely upon the type of filling.

Bolsters are similar in construction to pillows. The dimensions are normally 48 × 145 cm.

Blankets Normal requirements are one under-blanket and one, two or three overblankets per bed. In British hotels it is normal to provide two overblankets for European guests and three for American guests. Typical dimensions are 180 × 230 cm and 230 × 250 cm, respectively, for single and double beds. Essential requirements are good insulation, ease of cleaning and non flammability. White or off-white blankets are used by many organizations because they are cheaper than coloured ones and residents or guests can inspect their standard of cleanliness.

Underblankets are used to provide extra warmth and mattress protection.

Wool blankets have good thermal insulation properties. Those with a shrink-resistant finish will withstand regular laundering. Those without such a finish shrink, felt and become hard if laundered regularly.

Cotton or synthetic cellular blankets are light, easily laundered, withstand regular laundering and have good thermal insulation properties. Synthetic blankets are generally made from nylon or acrylic yarns.

Blankets are also made with mixtures of fibres, e.g. wool and cotton, rayon or nylon.

Bedspreads are used to cover beds during the day and may be of the throw-over or fitted type. Desirable characteristics will include abrasion resistance, ease of cleaning and ability to withstand regular laundering, tear, crease, flame and soil resistance and good drape. Fabrics most commonly used are brocade, satin, tapestry, chintz, candlewick and taffeta (see page 56). Candlewick is a plain weave fabric with thick tufted yarns inserted into it. Taffeta is a plain weave fabric with slightly thicker weft than warp yarns.

Sheets are required to protect the blankets and to increase comfort. They may be fitted or flat. Fitted bottom sheets fit the mattress at four corners, top sheets fit only at the bottom two corners. Fitted sheets tend to speed up bed-making, but are less easily stored and sorted. The top and bottom where applicable, should be the same, making the sheet completely reversible. Typical dimensions are 230 × 275, 150 × 215, 135 × 185 and 65 × 90 cm.

Essential characteristics will be abrasion resistance, ease of cleaning, non-flammability,

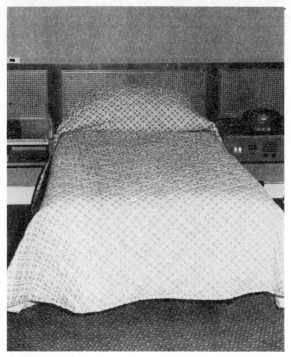

Made-up bed

reasonable crease resistance, shrink resistance and resistance to oxidizing bleaches. Their expected life is at least 250 washes.

Sheets are generally classified by the type of fibre used in their construction:

- *Standard cotton* has a close, well balanced weave and meets most of the essential requirements but will shrink a little.
- *Percale* is light in weight, made of cotton or polyester and cotton and has a smooth silky feel, but is stronger than standard cotton sheets.
- *Flannelette* is a cotton sheet with a brushed finish. It is warmer than other cotton sheets, but does not have the same crisp finish.
- *Linen* is the traditional type of sheeting. It is expensive, has a high standard of appearance, is extremely hard wearing and does not shrink.
- *Nylon or terylene* sheeting is usually thinner than cotton or linen. It is hard wearing, withstands regular laundering, will not

shrink, does not require ironing and is cheaper and dries faster than cotton or linen. However, it tends to feel hot in Summer and cool in Winter and is therefore less comfortable than cotton or linen.
- *Cotton and polyester unions* combine the advantages of cotton and terylene with few of the disadvantages.
- *Cotton and linen unions* combine the advantages of the two types of fibre.

Bolsters and pillow slips are made from the same materials as sheets and are therefore similar in most respects. Typical dimensions are 50×76 cm for pillows and 50×150 cm for bolsters. They should either have a flap to close over the pillows at the open end or be at least 5 cm longer.

Sleeping quilts or duvets consist of a filling held between two layers of cloth stitched together in channels. Fillings will be natural, e.g. down, down and feathers or feathers, or synthetic, i.e. polyester. The casing for natural fillings is made from cotton cambric, and for synthetics cotton or cotton and synthetic blends. BS 5335 recommends a minimum length of 198 cm for an adult bed. Typical dimensions are:

Single	135×198 cm
Small double	180×198 cm
Double	200×198 cm
King size	230×220 cm
Extra long (single)	135×220 cm
Extra long (double)	200×220 cm

Quilts are designed to be used in place of blankets and as such should have good thermal insulation properties. The warmth (thermal insulation) of quilts is measured in togs. The higher the tog value the warmer will be the quilt. There are four categories: 7.5, 8.5, 9.5 and 10.5 togs minimum.

The essential characteristics of a quilt should be good abrasion resistance, good crease resistance and good thermal insulation, good drape and a down-proof casing. Polyester fillings should not cause allergic reactions.

Consumer acceptance of quilts must be considered before purchasing them. Many people prefer them for their lightweight, warmth and the ease of bedmaking. Others dislike them because of tradition, and because some have a tendency to slip.

A quilt is used in conjunction with a protective cover. The cover will be made from cotton, polyester and cotton, or nylon and will be similar in construction to a pillow slip. The opening may be closed by press studs or ties and should be placed at the bottom of the bed.

A set of bedding for a single bed, when a quilt is used, will consist of a bottom sheet, two pillows and slips and a cover. In some hotels the covered quilt is used with a bottom and top sheet and covered with a bedspread.

Polyester-filled quilts can be washed or dry cleaned. Natural fillings must be dry cleaned.

Eiderdowns provide a warm, light covering, used in conjunction with sheets and blankets. They consist of a cover made from down-proof cotton, cotton and polyester, or nylon, enclosing a filling of down, down and feathers, feathers or polyester. The underside of the eiderdown should be of non-slip material, e.g. brushed nylon, so that it will not slip from the bed. Typical dimensions of eiderdowns are: single, 84×127 cm, and double, 144×127 cm.

Comforters are another form of quilt constructed of similar materials to duvets but are larger and have less filling. The casing is coloured and patterned. They are designed to be used with sheets and do not require a cover. In winter blankets will also be required. Typical dimensions are: single, 175×250 cm, and double, 228×250 cm.

Mattress covers are used to completely cover mattresses and protect them. They are made from linen, cotton, nylon or polyurethane-coated nylon, are shaped to fit all surfaces of the mattress and usually close with ties or a slide fastener.

Towels

Towels are broadly classified according to their size and use. The dimensions of each type can vary, but typical dimensions are 46×91, 56×111, 61×121, 69×137 and 91×152 cm. Types in order of increasing size are, face, guest, hand, bath and bath sheet. They are most frequently made of cotton or cotton and terylene in a turkish (terry) weave with a pile on both sides. Less commonly they may be in a plain or huck 'a' back weave.

Cabinet towels mounted in a dispenser and serviced by a hire company are usually cotton or linen in a plain or huck 'a' back weave. Essential requirements are abrasion resistance, high water absorbancy (up to 125% of own weight), ease of laundering and the ability to withstand regular laundering. Generally the closer the weave the greater the durability and absorbancy.

This type of towel is not to be confused with the traditional roller towel which consists of a loop of towelling hung from a horizontal rail.

Lavatory towels are small towels provided for the wiping of toilet seats and should be used for no other purpose. These, and razor towels have been largely replaced by disposables.

Bath mats are generally candlewick or terry towelling but are being superceded by disposables. Mats of cork or rubber are also used.

Table linen

Table linen includes table cloths, napkins, table slip covers, tray cloths and waiters cloths. Traditionally they are made in a plain linen weave or a damask weave of cotton or linen. Linen is more expensive than cotton, but cotton can be finished to give a comparable product.

For the traditional types of table linen the desirable characteristics are that they have a high sheen and are crisp and smooth.

Linen made from polyester and cotton, linen and polyester and from nylon is replacing the more traditional types in many organizations. It is cheaper, has better stain resistance and can be laundered more easily.

Table cloths, slip covers and tray cloths are available in a number of sizes.

Table cloths should overhang the table by 30–45 cm and be about 30 cm from the ground. Napkins are traditionally 45–60 cm square.

Glass cloths

These are intended only for the polishing of glassware. The essential requirement is that they are lint free.

Table 9 *Advantages and disadvantages of linen hire*

Advantages	Disadvantages
No capital outlay resulting in financial benefits	May not meet the requirements of a particular establishment
Capital may be employed elsewhere more effectively and profitably	Choice may be limited
	Quality may be variable
Revenue expenditure resulting in financial benefits	Rags and articles made from otherwise worn out items will have to be purchased
Less operative and supervisory staff required	
Less storage and other space required	
Short loans are available to meet infrequent but greater requirements	
Laundering facilities not required	
No repairs service required	
Reduction in administrative functions	

Tea towels

These are made of cotton or linen and must be strong and absorbent. Their use for drying crockery should be discouraged.

Selection and purchasing of linen

Linen should only be purchased once it has been determined that the use of a hire service or the use of disposables is not appropriate. All types must be tested to ensure that they meet the desired performance characteristics described earlier. Samples provided by a number of manufacturers should be compared for price, size and the extent to which they meet the desired characteristics. General points which must be considered are:

- Selvedges and hems firm and secure.
- Colours fast to light, dry and wet rubbing, perspiration, washing and bleach.
- Shrink-resistant, or shrinkage to be within specified limits, e.g. 5%.
- Need for mothproofing.
- Table linen and sheets free of fillers which improve the apparent quality.
- Sheets to have similar hems top and bottom.
- Towels to have a soft feel and a strong weave to prevent loops being pulled out.
- Purchase to be made from a reliable supplier.
- Contribution to decor.

Linen hire

To determine whether hire will be appropriate the following points must be considered:

1 The costs involved in purchasing, repairing, storing and maintaining your own linen stocks compared with linen hire can be analysed using a technique known as discounted cash flow analysis. In principal the financial analysis will include: the financial implications of capital expenditure involved in purchasing, the financial implications of revenue expenditure involved in hiring, operating expenditure including labour,

materials, heat, light, indirect and other costs.

2 Particular requirements not met by hiring. These include: frequency of exchange, reliability, standard of hygiene and appearance required and the nature of the establishment, e.g. linen in hospitals will include infected linen.

3 Capital involved in purchasing may be employed more effectively or profitably elsewhere.

4 Storage and other space requirements will be greater where linen is purchased.

5 Supervisory, management and administrative functions should be reduced by linen hire.

The comparable disadvantages and advantages of linen hire are summarized in Table 9.

Disposables

To determine whether the use of disposables will be more appropriate, an analysis similar to that described for linen should be carried out.

Amount of linen

This will depend on a number of factors including:

- The type of establishment.
- The number of rooms.
- The number of beds.
- The number of restaurant tables.
- The occupancy rate of rooms.
- The number of changes of occupiers.
- The number of meals served.
- The number of times bed linen, towels and table linen are to be changed.
- Frequency of laundry collection and turn-round time.

British Standards

BS 1899: 1963, *Pillows (Excluding Cellular Rubber Pillows) for Hospitals, Institutions, and Government Departments.*

BS 2005: 1966, *Glossary of Terms for Fillings of Bedding, Upholstery and Other Domestic Articles.*

BS 4984: 1973, *Cotton Cellular Blankets.*

BS 5129: 1974, *Dimensions of Bed Blankets (EN 14).*

BS 5223: 1976, *Hospital Bedding. Part 3: Flexible polyurethane pillows.*

BS 5335: 1976, *Continental Quilts.*

BS 5815: 1979, *Specification for Cotton and Man-made Fibre Blend Sheets, Pillowslips, Towels and Napkins for Use in the Public Sector.*

BS 5866: 1980, *Part 1: Specification for wool and wool/nylon blankets (for use in the public sector). Part 2: Specification for cotton leno cellular blankets.*

PAS 17: 1974, *Sheeting Sheets and Pillow Slips.*

PAS 19: 1975, *Towels and Napkins.*

See also standards listed after Laundry Services, page 273.

Curtains

Curtains are required to provide privacy, hide unacceptable views, enhance decor, hide poor surfaces, and act as means of insulation, reducing heat losses and noise levels. They can also reduce the amount of light entering a room, so contributing to personal comfort and controlling the amount of ultra-violet light which may otherwise damage other furnishings. Curtains can be used as a room divider, e.g. a sleeping area may be cut off from the rest of a large room.

Characteristics of curtains

When purchasing curtains the relative merits of the following must be evaluated and, when any quantity is being purchased, testing is recommended.

Contribution to decor   The quality, colour, type and size of pattern must be related to the type of room, existing and planned decor, position in room and general character of room.

Appearance in natural and artificial light   Fabrics may appear quite different when viewed in natural and then artificial light.

Appearance viewed from front and back If unlined, curtains should look acceptable when viewed from either side.

Room type Different rooms will require different qualities and types of curtain fabric. Public rooms usually require heavy fabrics and will generally be lined, e.g. brocades, satins, tweeds, velvets, corduroys, tapestry. Bedrooms require lighter fabrics and may not necessarily be lined, e.g. chintz, cretonne, folk weave, repp. Bonded fabrics that include an inbuilt lining are a satisfactory compromise. Bathrooms require curtains that will withstand regular laundering, e.g. gingham, net, plastic sheet, towelling, glass fibre.

Abrasion resistance This requirement will be greater when wear or regular washing is expected. Closely woven, heavier fabrics are more abrasion-resistant than light and loosely woven fabrics. Polyamides and polyesters are inherently more abrasion-resistant than many other fabrics.

Curtains being suction-cleaned

Insulation properties Heavy, lined curtains help to reduce heat losses, exclude draughts and deaden noise. The more absorbent fabrics, including cotton, rayon and particularly wool, have good heat and sound insulation properties.

Linings made from milium, a metallic fabric, or sateen, which has a lustrous finish, reflect infra-red radiation and therefore contribute significantly to the heat insulation properties of a curtain. Some net curtains are made from polyester fibre to which aluminium particles are bonded. The effect is similar to that for milium and sateen.

Soil resistance must be considered where heavy soilage is likely or where there is significant air pollution. Synthetic fibres are generally more resistant to soiling than other fibres. Silk, cotton, linen, rayon and nylon will all be affected to some extent by acid gases in the atmosphere.

Soil-resistant finishes may be applied to the fibre before or after washing. Those based on silicones and fluorocarbons have good wash-fastness. There are others which are less wash-fast.

Fire resistance will also be desirable and will be required for curtains hung in public rooms. If the fire resistance is an applied finish it should be wash-fast.

Fabric blends containing fibres based on polyvinylidene chloride (e.g. saran), modacrylics (e.g. teklan) or glass fibre have a high degree of fire resistance. Cotton and rayon are highly flammable, wool and the synthetic fibres less so.

A close-weave fabric will burn less easily than an open one.

Flame resistance can be enhanced by chemical treatment, e.g. with Proban, before or after weaving. Some finishes, however, tend to affect the draping qualities, making the fabric hard and stiff. Other finishes have limited wash-fastness and require renewal after cleaning.

Light-induced deterioration must be considered for any drape to be hung in a window. Most fibres, but particularly nylon and silk, are to some extent affected by light. Reaction between dyes and light can sometimes result in the formation of chemical products that can cause deterioration of fabric fibres.

Cotton, linen and rayon are subject to yellowing when exposed to light for any length of time.

Dye-fastness Dyes should be light-fast and wash-fast if cleaning involves washing. Sunlight can cause many dyes to fade. The process is accelerated by the presence of oxides of nitrogen in the air (pollution) and by some of the finishes which provide crease resistance.

Washing will progressively remove the dye from a fabric unless it is strongly held either physically or chemically by the fibres. Surface printed fabrics in particular can have poor wash fastness. If a curtain is to be dry cleaned colours must be fast in the solvents to be used.

Dimensional stability involves two elements, shrink resistance and resistance to deformation.

A curtain should not shrink when hung or cleaned. An allowance of up to 3% should be made for pre-shrunk or shrink-proofed fabrics and up to 5% for untreated fabrics. Fabrics may shrink when hung as the yarns recover from stretch imposed during weaving. Wool, cotton and rayon will shrink when washed unless the fabric has been chemically or mechanically treated. Synthetic and acetate fibres will not shrink when washed. In fabric blends that include wool, cotton or rayon, vertical shrinkage may be prevented by the use of synthetic or acetate yarns for the warp.

Deformation can occur as a result of pulling. Resistance to deformation depends on the extensibility and elastic recovery of the constituent fibres. Fabrics made from normal viscose rayon, which has considerable extensibility but limited elastic recovery, will distort more easily than fabrics that include cotton, which is less extensible, or wool, which is extensible but has good elastic recovery.

Crease resistance When crushed creases should drop out. Wool, silk and the synthetic fibres have good crease resistance although the crease resistance of fabrics made from other fibres can be enhanced by application of a crease-resistant finish.

Drape includes all those factors associated with hanging qualities. It will include dimensional stability and crease resistance and will depend upon the weight of the curtain and its fullness. In general, the heavier a curtain and the fuller it is, the better it will hang.

Ease of cleaning Fabrics finished with soil-resistant finishes or made from the less absorbent fibres will be most easily cleaned. In practice, however, ease of cleaning may be less important than other factors. Ideally a curtain should be capable of being washed, but for a variety of reasons, e.g. possibility of shrinkage and dye-fastness, they are frequently dry cleaned. When regular washing is required, the important criteria will be shrink resistance, colour-fastness of any finishes applied and the ability to withstand high temperatures.

Types of curtain fabric

Fabrics will generally be a blend of fibres. Most fabrics can be used for curtains including brocade, brocatelle, bump, chintz, corduroy, cretonne, damask, glass fibre, folkweave, gingham, milium, net, plush, ratine, repp, sateene, tapestry, towelling, tweed, velour, velvet, velveteen and wild silk.

- *Bump* A thick fabric used for interlining curtains.
- *Folkweave* A loosely woven fabric, formed from course-coloured cotton yarns, with a simple pattern.
- *Gingham* A plain weave cotton fabric with check or striped pattern.
- *Net* An open-mesh fabric, the yarns being woven or knotted together and made from polyester or acrylic fibres.
- *Wild silk* Fabrics woven from natural silk filaments.

The characteristics of the other fabrics are described on page 56.

Construction and hanging

The following points should be considered:

- Curtains made from fabrics with large patterns will be more expensive than those made from fabrics of similar quality, but with small patterns, since the matching of patterns will involve a greater wastage of material during manufacture.
- Pile fabrics should be hung so that their pile runs downwards.
- Hems and edges should be hand sewn.
- High-quality curtains will be lined with milium, satin or sateen and be interlined with bump.
- Detachable linings can overcome some of the problems encountered in laundering, e.g. different shrinkage rates for lining and curtains.
- Drape can be improved by including weights in the hem of the curtain and the lining.
- Headings can be of various types including plain, pleated or gathered.
- The minimum width should be one and a half times the width of the rod or tracks and up to three times the width for light fabrics.
- A minimum turning of 15 cm is usually required and it should be greater if shrinkage is expected.
- The length of curtains will be governed by their position: full-length curtains should hang within 15 to 25 mm of the floor; curtains to hang outside a window reveal may hang to the sill or about 15 cm below the sill; curtains to be hung inside a window reveal should hang to within 10 mm of the sill.
- Opening curtains or decorative drapes are usually suspended by one of four methods: fixed to a rail by runners and hooks; fixed to a track by concealed runners; suspended from a rod by rings; cartridge loading in which the curtain is first loaded onto a cartridge device which in turn is then fitted to a track.
- Draw cords are preferred for opening curtains.
- Net curtains are held by a rod or plastic-coated wire fastened across the top of the

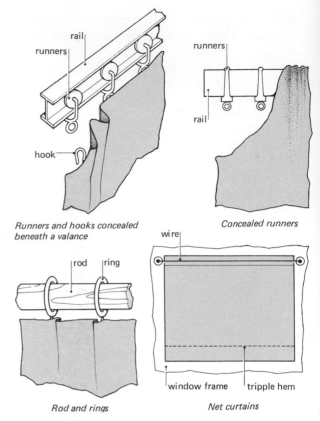

Runners and hooks concealed beneath a valance · Concealed runners · Rod and rings · Net curtains

Figure 35 *Methods of hanging curtains*

window reveal. Drape is improved by either treble hems or by holding the curtain at the bottom by means of another rod or wire.
- Pelmets and valances may be used to hide curtain rails and as a contribution to decor. Both are decorative headings. A pelmet is a shaped piece of wood painted or covered with fabric or wall covering. A valance is a shaped or gathered piece of fabric hung from a supporting rail. Where either is used it is usual for the curtain track or rail to overlap in the middle so permitting the curtains to overlap when drawn. Curtains suspended from tracks by concealed runners or suspended from rods by rings do not require pelmets or valances.

British Standards

BS 5867: 1980, *Specifications for Fabrics for*

*Curtains and Drapes. Part 1: General require-
ments. Part 2: Flammability requirements.
See also standards listed after Laundry Services,
page 273.*

Loose covers

Detachable covers may be fitted to upholstered
furniture, principally to cover shabbiness. They
may also be used to protect upholstery and to
change the appearance of furniture.

Covers of suitable quality are expensive. The
most important feature is that they fit well. If they
do not fit well, problems may be experienced in
maintaining their overall appearance. They are
usually secured by zips, ties or touch-and-close
fasteners to allow easy removal and refitting.

Most fabrics suitable for upholstery can also be
used for covers. The particular characteristics
required will be abrasion resistance, crease
resistance and good stretch recovery.

Glass, crockery and cutlery

Glassware

Types and materials Glassware is made by
blowing or in moulds from soda, hard, crystal or
borosilicate glass. Patterns will be formed either in
the mould, by cutting with an abrasive wheel, or
by engraving or etching. The cost is related to the
type of glass used, the method of making and the
method of making a pattern.

Borosilicate glass is used to make heat-resistant
glassware and is relatively expensive. Moulded
glassware is considerably cheaper to produce than
blown and the quality is suitable for most
situations. Glassware with patterns formed in a
mould is generally no dearer than plain ware made
in a similar way. Cutting, engraving or etching
significantly increases the cost.

The various types of glass are used to make a
variety of shapes and sizes of ware including cups,
saucers, bowls and drinking glasses. In the case of
drinking glasses there are a number of distinct
shapes and sizes the uses of which are governed by
custom, e.g. brandy, claret, champagne.

Selection and purchasing will depend on the
following criteria:

- The type of drinking glasses required will
depend on the type of establishment. Where a
variety of different shapes and sizes are
required some duplication of function should
be considered.
- In hostels and institutions where water glasses
are the principal requirement, other types
should be purchased in small quantities and
hired when large numbers are required.
- Some traditional designs are particularly
fragile. If less traditional designs are
acceptable, glassware with thicker stems and
heavier bases is preferred. Glassware made
from soda glass is suitable for most situations.
- Glassware made from hard glass will be
suitable where appearance is less important
and breakages are frequent.
- Traditional or commonly produced shapes
have the advantage that they can be easily
replaced.
- Where dishwashers are installed, glassware
selected should not require manual washing.
Crystal must be washed by hand.
- Ware should be marked to indicate the
establishment.
- The number of drinking glasses of any one
type depends on the type of establishment, the
number and frequency of breakages and the
time taken to obtain replacements. In general
it will be between 1.5 and 2.5 times the
maximum number in use at any time.

Crockery

Types and materials Crockery is made of one of
four types of material: earthenware, stoneware,
bone china or porcelain, all of which are glazed.
Patterns and decorations can be applied to the
glaze or before glazing.

- Earthenware is durable, relatively inexpensive
and can be used to make crockery with a high
standard of appearance and finish.
- Stoneware is strong, durable but prone to
staining.

- Bone china is strong, expensive and used to make crockery with a very high standard of appearance and finish with a translucent quality. It breaks more easily than earthenware or stoneware if knocked.
- Porcelain is used to make crockery of the highest standard of appearance and finish. It is too expensive and not sufficiently durable for use in hotels, institutions or similar situations.

Selection and purchasing will depend on the following criteria.

- Crockery must be durable in that it will not chip easily when knocked and it will not break when knocked.
- The standard of appearance and finish required will depend on the type of establishment.
- Earthenware meets the requirements of most establishments, being manufactured in a variety of shapes, sizes and standards of appearance and finish. Hotel ware is a heavy, thick type of earthernware with excellent durability and a reasonable standard of appearance and finish.
- Handles and spouts must be firmly attached.
- Glaze must be sound and resistant to scratching.
- On-glaze decoration will wear away with use and will not withstand machine washing with detergent.
- Decoration should be simple.
- Ware should be marked to indicate the establishment.
- Cups and other hollow ware should be designed to allow effective washing to take place, particularly when passed through a dishwasher.
- Must not be prone to stain build up.
- Where possible, crockery should have a dual function, e.g. cereal and soup bowls the same.
- Cups, plates and saucers should be stackable and stable when stacked. The bases of saucers and plates should not touch the one beneath. Cups should be broad and shallow with straight edges.

- To reduce the possibility of chipping, plates and saucers should have rolled edges and cups should have edges just incurving at the top.
- Ease of replacement should be considered because breakages will occur. Traditional, simple shapes with limited decoration typified by hotel ware are most suitable in this respect.
- Stainless steel or possibly EPNS food-service dishes, e.g. teapot and vegetable dishes, should be used in preference to ones made from earthenware.
- The number of pieces of crockery of each type, e.g. plates and cups, will depend on the type of establishment, number of breakages and time to replace. In hospitals or institutions where there may be sufficient time to collect all soiled crockery, wash and dry them before the next period of food service, the number will probably be 1.5 times the maximum number in use at one time. In hotels it may be 2.5 times that number.

Cutlery

Types and material Cutlery includes knives, forks and spoons, each of which can be of several types, each type designed for a specific purpose, e.g.

Knives: table, steak, fish, cheese, butter.
Forks: table, dessert, fish, fruit, pastry.
Spoons: table, dessert, tea, coffee, ladles.

Handles can be made of the same or different materials to the rest of the tool, e.g. stainless steel (usually 18/8), EPNS (electroplated nickel silver), silver, wood, bone or plastic. The rest of the tool is usually made from stainless steel, EPNS or silver.

Selection and purchasing will depend on the following criteria:

- Knives should have a good cutting edge.
- Stainless steel is more durable than other materials.
- Handles glued to the rest of the tool can become detached as a result of routine washing.
- Can be marked to identify establishment, but this has limited effect on pilferage.

- To reduce the number of different items in stock, some dual function is preferred, e.g. tea or coffee spoons should be the same.
- The number of items of each type required will depend on the type of establishment, the type of item, time to replace and particularly on losses. It will range from two to three times the maximum number in use at any time.

Interior design

The interior environment affects to some extent every person who enters a building, e.g. some positively like it, some dislike it, whilst others may feel rebellious or aggressive towards it. Consequently, if an interior can be created that fulfills the requirements of most of the users of a building it will contribute positively to the successful use of that building. For example, a lounge area that is restful, comfortable and relaxing will encourage more guests to use that area and may lead to increased sales of light refreshments etc.

Interior design is the area of study that will help to achieve the interior most suitable for any area of the building. In most large organizations, i.e. large hotel and restaurant groups, interior design consultants are employed to advise on and plan all aspects of interior design, whilst in small organizations this work is often one of the duties of the housekeeper or accommodation manager.

Ideally the interior design of the building should correlate to its architecture. The scope of the design will be limited by:

1 The purpose of the building or area.
2 The structure of the building or area.
3 Finance – both capital and revenue consequences.
4 The siting of the building or area.
5 The time available to accomplish the design.
6 Individual taste.

Successfully designed interiors generally seem easy to use and attract use, and in order to achieve such good planning, it is necessary to try to forget preconceived ideas and look at the area for which the design is to be prepared with an open mind. It is also important to remember that the interior environment includes not only appearance, but also sounds, aromas, patterns, shapes and often inconveniences, all of which will affect users of that area. Designs therefore should link these factors to achieve the required end result.

Before planning a design for any area, it is important that the accommodation manager has a knowledge of the following points.

Textures

The materials used in interior design are available in a wide range of textures. Rough textures promote a feeling of warmth, whilst smooth surfaces seem to recede and to be cool, e.g. high-glare ceramic tiles often appear 'cold and clinical'. Some textures are warm to the touch, e.g. cork. Rough textures are often in the colour group yellow/red, e.g. tree bark, whilst smooth textures are often in the blue group, e.g. slate.

Colour

Colour plays an important part in all aspects of life and is used as a means of expression, and as such, is able to arouse emotion. Historically, red has been considered the colour of activity and energy, whilst green has been considered the restful colour, and within one group of colours, e.g. greens, one shade may be stimulating whilst another is subdued.

Choice of colour in interior design has been affected greatly throughout history by the availability of dyes, the fashion of the time, the traditions of the age and national preferences. Today, designers have far greater freedom of choice and combinations of colours and may use many traditionally 'unconventional' colour combinations to great effect. In general:

- Light colours reflect light, promoting a feeling of spaciousness.
- Dark colours absorb light, appearing to reduce space.
- Reds, yellows and oranges are considered warm colours and appear to reduce space.

- North-facing rooms appear warmer when warm shades are used.
- South facing rooms can be apparently cooled by cool colours, e.g. blues.
- Dark colours on a ceiling appear to reduce height.
- Light colours on a ceiling, particularly with dark walls, appear to increase height.
- A long room can appear shorter if the end wall is decorated with a strong colour.
- Colour is greatly affected by lighting conditions and the effect of daylight and artificial lighting should be considered.

The following terms are used when discussing colours:

Value is the lightness or darkness of a colour. In the Munsell colour system colours are graded from 1 to 9:

Increasingly darker ◄———   ———► Increasingly lighter

1	2	3	4	5	6	7	8	9 White

Shades   Middle tone   Tints

High-value colours appear to increase light in dark areas which receive little light.

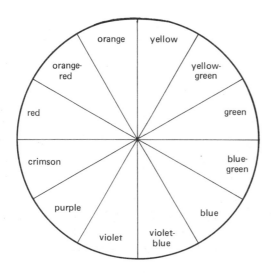

Figure 36 *Traditional colour circle*

Weight is a subjective term for lightness.

Chroma is the intensity or purity of a colour, e.g. a bright yellow which has no other colour quality is as full of yellow as possible and is called full chroma. A full-chroma colour used in interior design will reflect strongly on other colours and may distort them and so should be used with care. Strong chroma colours can look most effective when chosen for their own decorative effect and can appear to great advantage against white or may look more luminous when shaded or darker than their surroundings.

Greyness is the estimated grey content of a colour. BS 5252 defines five groups of greyness:

Group	A	B	C	D	E
	Grey	Nearly grey	Grey/ clear	Nearly clear	Clear

Increasing purity of colour ➝

Hue is the colour itself, e.g. yellow, purple, blue-green. When choosing colour it is important to be aware of the effect of light, shade and reflections on a colour in a particular setting.

Colour systems

The traditional colour circle is based on the three primary colours, red, blue and yellow, and their secondary colours, green, orange and purple. The centre of the circle is grey, i.e. neutral. Complementary colours are those which are exactly opposite each other.

Munsell and British Standard colour ranges The Munsell* system defines a range of colours in terms of their hue, value and chroma. In the British Standard colour range colours are defined in terms of hue, greyness and weight. In both ranges specific colours are identified by a coding system.

The two ranges can be used to identify, match,

*See *Munsell Book of Colour,* Munsell Colour Inc., Baltimore, Maryland, USA.

specify and order particular colours. However, in Britain, the Munsell reference numbers should not be used when specifying or ordering colours.

Colour schemes

Monochromatic Composed of shades of the same colour, e.g. pale green, grass green, olive green, holly green. The success of this type of scheme depends upon the degree of contrast and texture.

Complementary The combination of opposites on the traditional colour circle. Success with this type of scheme will usually be achieved if one colour is dominant, e.g. blue with pale tones of orange and grey orange.

Double complementary A scheme composed of a pair of adjacent colours and a pair of opposite adjacent colours. This scheme will be most successful where one pair dominates and the other pair is used as an accent. For example, walls, floors and ceilings of greens and blue-greens will be complemented by soft furnishings in red and red orange.

Black and white All-white colour schemes, depending on texture for contrast, can appear luxurious and sophisticated, but can be more effective if accented by small areas of black or full chroma colours.

Analogous Composed from a range of tones adjacent in the colour circle, keyed to the same primary colour, e.g. yellow, yellow orange, orange, pale yellow.

Contrasting Sharply contrasting colour schemes can be effective, e.g. red and yellow, but may be most acceptable where quieter colours are used on large areas, e.g. walls, floors and ceilings, and bolder colours are used for accent colours, e.g. pale yellow walls, and red cushions, lamps, etc. Large areas of intense contrasting colour are rarely successful in hotel or institutional settings where the aim is to attract as many people as possible.

Shadows

Shadows contribute a great deal to the definition of an interior design and can be deliberately used or avoided. Lights can be used to create interesting shapes and shadows. The texture and colour of the background will affect the shape and clarity of the shadows and will also alter their quality.

Shape and form

A knowledge of the importance of shape and form, especially when related to the human scale, is of value when selecting and siting furnishings and lighting. The circle is considered the most dominent shape, the square solid and heavy, and the pyramid the most economical. The repetition of any one shape in a design is rarely as successful as one composed predominantly of one shape but dominated by one other, e.g. a series of circles dominated by one square.

Planning design

When planning a design the following points must be considered:

The proportions of the area These must be determined to assess the relationship with adjacent rooms and areas and to achieve the correct scale of furnishings, patterns and textures.

Ease of maintenance The design should minimize cleaning and maintenance.

Reduction of human effort Unecessary repetition of movement both in general use and in maintenance must be eliminated. This may limit the range of designs which can practically be used.

The layout Possible alteration to the existing layout should be considered. For example, where a large open space is required, can partition walls be removed, or can privacy be achieved in an open-plan design?

The users of the area Consideration must be

given to the expectations of those who will use the area, e.g. hotel guests, hall of residence staff and students, and a design devised which will suit the lifestyle and requirements of the majority.

Services   Note should be made of the availability and type of flooring, lighting, ventilation and water services.

The resulting design for any area should be one that has carefully planned the materials, furnishings, lighting and accessories for that area so that the interior design will be appropriate for all users of that area. For example:

1   A restaurant scheme should provide atmosphere and mood, stimulate the appetite and complement the style of food and its service.
2   A hospital ward scheme should be one that has safe, non-slip and easy-to-clean surfaces and which is comfortable for both staff, patients and visitors.
3   A study bedroom should provide durable sleeping, storage and studying facilities, requiring minimal maintenance and using restful colour patterns and textures.

Pattern

Pattern can contribute to the overall design by adding interest and by apparently altering the shape of an area. Stripes, in general, when horizontal make the area appear lower and wider, whilst vertical stripes make an area appear taller and narrower.

Some patterns have a three-dimensional effect which make an area appear to have greater depth.

Pattern should be proportional in size to the room or area in which it is used, e.g. a large pattern will dominate a small area. A large number of patterned surfaces in an area may be overpowering and disturbing to the eye. More

than one pattern may be used in any one design but all patterns used in any design should be complementary. For example:

1   Two wallpapers, the first a green trellis on a white background and the second, the same green trellis and white background but with the trellis entwined with flowers, together with a fabric of smaller scale flowers but the same as those on the second paper.
2   Two wallpapers of small pink and blue flowers on a white background, curtains, a second design of small pink and blue flowers on a white background and cushion covers a third design of small pink and blue flowers on a white background.

Dirt is not as obvious on patterned surfaces as on plain ones. This factor is particularly important when considering the selection of carpets, e.g. plain carpets would be too labour-intensive for a busy reception area of a hotel.

Quantity and quality of light

The minimum amount of light required in a room is governed by the type of activities to be carried out in it (see page 91). However, when planning an interior design, light can be used to good effect in a number of ways. These include:

- The general level of lighting.
- The colours of light used.
- The use of direct, indirect and diffuse lighting.
- The amount of glare and the formation of shadows.
- The positioning of light fittings.

British Standards

BS 4800: 1981, *Specification for Paint Colours for Building Purposes.*
BS 5252: 1976, *Framework for Colour Co-ordination for Building Purposes.*

3 Hygiene

The maintenance of an environment that is safe in all respects and which is pleasant for both accommodation and cleaning services staff and for the users of a building is of paramount importance. In the following chapter are described the various factors which will influence the environment created in a building and those requirements necessary to maintain that environment and hence the health and comfort of all users of a building, its furnishings and equipment.

In Volume 2 are described the requirements and procedures necessary to maintain the general safety of the users of a building.

Soil

Soil may be defined as any substance that is out of place, thereby reducing the standard of appearance and hygiene required.

Composition of soil

Soil in a room or building may arise from four sources. It may be:

1 Carried into a room by the air.
2 Carried in on feet and people's clothes.
3 Carried in on equipment.
4 Caused by activities or operations carried out in a building or by persons within it.

Of the soil brought into a building, 80% will be carried in by footwear. Soil will consist of one or more of nine different types of material and it may be light, heavy, loose, impacted, ingrained, wet or dry. The actual composition, amount and nature will depend upon the building and its environment, together with the activities carried out within it, and upon dust and soil control methods. The types of soiling materials are:

Fumes and odours caused by gases or particles less than 0.5 μ in diameter. They may enter a building through doors and windows or may arise within the building. Typical examples are fine soot and corrosive acid gases, e.g. sulphur dioxide, carbon dioxide and sulphides arising as a result of fuel combustion or chemical processes and odours caused by the presence or activities of people.

Dust is fine particulate material, 0.5 to 20 μ in diameter. It will enter a building via doors, windows, on clothes and on footwear. It will arise within a building as a result of one or more of the following: manufacturing operations; deterioration of fabric, e.g. floors, wall coverings; people, e.g. skin scale, hairs, sputum; vermin, e.g. skin scale, hairs, sputum, excreta; furnishings, e.g. fibres from carpets or upholstery; smoking; faulty air conditioning; fuel combustion; inefficient or incorrect methods of cleaning; food preparation and consumption. It broadly consists of:

Sand, quartz, felspar, silica, limestone	50%
Animal fibres, hairs, sputum	12%
Cellulose (from paper, cotton)	12%
Resins, gums, starches	10%
Fats, oils, rubber, tar	6%
Gypsum	5%
Moisture	3%
Protein, bacteria, spores	2%

The exact composition will depend upon its situation. However, dust is one of the most important agencies for the transfer of bacteria. It may also include hazardous substances, e.g. asbestos, fine quartz.

Grit Large particles (above 20 μ). It will enter a building on footwear or clothing and arises within a building as a result of manufacturing operations and deterioration of the fabric of the building. It will consist of metallic or mineral materials, the cutting edges of which are particularly destructive to many surfaces.

Fats, oil, greases Light or heavy organic materials. They may be brought into a building on footwear or equipment and may arise as a result of eating or food preparation, use of lubricating oils in manufacturing processes, spillages, commodities in food processing, degreasing of soiled equipment, the build-up or trafficking of solvent-based polishes. This type includes animal and vegetable fats and oils, lubricating oils, tars, rubber and other similar materials.

Proteins, starches and water-soluble resins may be brought into a building on footwear, equipment or as a particular commodity. It will arise in a building as a result of eating or food preparation, food processing, spillages build up and deterioration of polishes.

Industrial waste or effluent includes any by-product of a manufacturing process. In particular it will include such materials as swarf, turnings and shavings.

Litter includes any large debris, e.g. cartons, paper and cigarette ends, which may be brought into or arise within a building.

Stains and chemical soilage arise as a result of spillages, accidents or vandalism, including localized staining of floors, upholstery and carpets, graffiti, urine and excreta.

Tarnishing Silver will react with sulphides in the air to produce a dark discoloration of silver sulphide. Copper reacts in moist atmospheres with oxygen to produce a green discoloration, or patina (often not removed).

The composition of soil affecting various buildings, rooms and their surfaces, furnishings, fixtures and fittings is shown in Table 10.

Dust and soil control

Effective dust and soil control is essential for the following reasons:

● Cleaning is a labour-intensive and,

Table 10   *Soil arising in different parts of a building*

Premises or room	Possible composition of soil
Offices, public rooms, foyers, reception areas, hotel rooms, wards, theatres, computer rooms	Fumes, dust, litter, grit; *also* stains and soilage arising from eating, spillages, accidents, vandalism or transferred by footwear
Toilets, washrooms, sanitary annexes	Fumes and odours, dust, litter, grit, soilage from urine and excrement, graffiti and soil washed from human body
Food processing, preparation and consumption	Fats, oils, proteins, starches; *also* dust, litter, grit
Workshops	Fumes, odours and dusts (all of which may be hazardous); oils, grease, dust, grit, swarf, turnings, litter
Warehouses and storage areas	Fumes, odours, dust, grit, oils from handling equipment. Other soil may arise depending on commodity or equipment stored

consequently, expensive process. Reduction in the amount of dust and soil entering a building will reduce cleaning costs.

- Soil, in particular grit, will damage the fabric of a building.
- Dust is a primary agent for the transfer of bacteria.
- Computer rooms, manufacturing processes in the electronics and pharmaceutical industries and clinical areas in hospitals require a dust-free atmosphere.
- Fumes, gases and dust produced by some manufacturing processes are hazardous.
- Dust, grease and oils represent slip hazards.

Control may be exercised either at the point of entry or within a room or building. Point-of-entry control involves prevention of soil entering a building at traffic entrances and air conditioning.

Traffic entrances Of the soil entering a building, 80% will be via footwear. Effective control procedures will remove up to 95% of this soil. In addition, air showers will remove some of the dust adhering to people entering the building if this is required. The effective removal of soil from footwear can be achieved by one of three methods, all of which involve an initial barrier mat to scrape soil from footwear followed by an absorbent mat which removes light soil and water. The methods are:

1 Approach cleaning in which both barriers are situated before the entrance beneath a canopy.
2 Approach and post-entry cleaning in which the scraping barrier is situated before and possibly after the entrance and the absorbent mat is situated within the entrance. The use of a ramp covered with a textile which in wet weather compresses to squeeze water over the undersurface of footwear to leave only clean water to be removed by the absorbent mat is particularly effective when used in this method.
3 Post-entry cleaning in which both barriers are situated within the entrance.

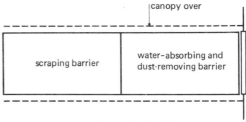

Approach cleaning

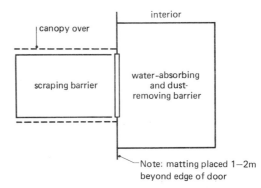

Note: matting placed 1—2m beyond edge of door

Approach and post-entry cleaning

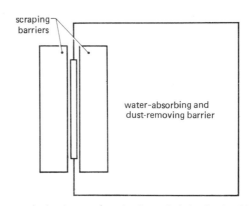

In the absence of two barriers a single barrier should have the best scraping, water-absorbing and dust-removing characteristics that can be obtained

Post-entry cleaning

Figure 37 *Barrier matting at traffic entrances*

Of the three methods the last is the least preferable in that it may not be possible to accomodate a sufficiently large area of matting. The essential requirements of a barrier are that it must retain an acceptable appearance, scrape effectively, remove light soil and dust efficiently,

Table 11   *Types of barrier matting**

Type	Character-istics	Appearance retention	Scrapability	Water removal	Dust/grit removal	Method of cleaning
Coir (made to BS 3959)	Heavy fibre; expensive; becomes waterlogged; should not be used	Fair	Good	Fair	Fair	Difficult to clean by any method
Link	Pieces of rubber linked together	Good	Good	Poor to fair	Poor to fair	Scrub
Open strip	Alternating strips of rubber and aluminium	Good	Good	Poor to fair	Poor to fair	Scrub if required
Metal grid	Metal strips linked together	Good	Good	Poor	Poor	Scrub if required
Natural fibre	Pile fixed to non-slip impervious backing	Poor to fair	Poor to fair	Good	Fair	Suction clean, wash
Synthetic fibre	Pile fixed to non-slip impervious backing	Fair to good	Fair	Fair	Good	Suction clean, wash, extraction
Natural and synthetic fibre †	Pile fixed to non-slip impervious backing	Fair to good	Fair	Fair to good	Fair to good	Suction clean, wash, extraction
Looped pile	Pile forms part of synthetic backing	Good	Fair	Fair; water lodges under loops of pile	Fair to good	Suction clean, wash, extraction

*The properties for each type of matting are broad generalizations since there is wide variation between different mats within the same catagory.
† Matting may be hired which will periodically be returned for cleaning and re-impregnation if required.

remove and hold water efficiently and be easy to clean.

The principle types of barrier mat are shown in Table 11 together with their respective properties. As will be seen, no one type of mat tends to have all the desired characteristics. Open strip or cavity mats situated in a well generally meet the requirements for scraping, whilst mats composed of natural fibres meet the requirements for absorbency and dust removal. Mats consisting of looped synthetic pile meet most of the requirements where scraping followed by an absorbent barrier is not possible, but tend to wear poorly when subjected to heavy traffic. The amount of matting required will depend on the amount of traffic, the degree of wetting and soilage, the preferred traffic lanes and the type of matting selected, but in general the greater the traffic and soilage or wetting, the greater the amount required.

It is always preferable that the matting extend to about 1 metre either side of the entrance to ensure that traffic both feet and wheels, passes over the barrier.

Air conditioning will remove dust and fumes entering a building or room. The standard of filtration required will depend on the activities carried out. BS 5295: 1976 specifies the standard of filtration required for various classes of clean room or area. A clean room or area is one in which the activities carried out require that the particle contamination, humidity and temperature be carefully controlled and meet certain specified requirements.

Required standards of filtration range from an efficiency of 99.995% to 70%. Surgical units in hospitals will require the upper value, while computer rooms require an efficiency of 80%. To ensure the efficiency of air conditioning plant filter screens must must be cleaned and checked regularly, blocked screens must be replaced and all air-conditioning ducts must be inspected to ensure that no accummulations of dust occur which may eventually blow through into a room.

Control within a room or building can be achieved in a number of ways.

Isolation of dust and soil-creating operations can involve barrier matting at entry points leading to other parts of a building; entry points only from outside; vacuuming to remove hazardous dusts; the restriction/isolation of dirt-making processes, e.g. to dining room.

Litter bins and ashtrays must be provided wherever the general public have access. The number provided must be related to usage.

Prevention of smoking will eliminate one source of dust and fumes. To be effective, ashtrays must be provided at entry points to no smoking zones and adjacent to 'No Smoking' signs.

Cleaning equipment will involve the use of static or impregnated sweepers or dusters; suction unit and skirt fitted to scrubber polishers when buffing, burnishing or carrying out high-speed spray maintenance. Vacuum cleaners that cause no, or a prescribed minimum of, air disturbance at surface level and which filter the exhaust air to required standards should be used (see Table 12).

Protective clothing is required to prevent the carriage of soil into clean areas. The type of clothing will depend on the standard of hygiene required, ranging from a simple overall to caps, overalls, overgowns and overshoes. The complete

Table 12

Use of suction cleaner	Filtration requirement
Hospitals (clinical areas)	60% of particles 0.2 to 2 μ: no more than seven bacteria-carrying particles per cubic metre of exhaust air
Mainframe computer rooms	80% of particles greater than 0.5 μ
Pharmaceuticals, electronics, hazardous dusts	Up to 99.995% of particles 0.2 to 2 μ

removal of all normal outer clothing may be required.

Cleaning methods will be governed by the type of soil and the standards of cleanliness required:

a   Dust removal at all levels may be carried out using static or impregnated mops or dusters or suction cleaners suitably filtered. Care has to be taken not to stir up dust during cleaning.
b   Light soil adhering to a surface may be removed by mopping, washing or light scrubbing. Rinsing may increase the efficiency of soil removal. After cleaning, surfaces should be left dry, suction drying being easier and more effective than mopping or wiping dry. Care must be taken to ensure that surfaces other than the ones being cleaned are not splashed.
c   Heavily impacted soil may be removed by heavy scrubbing, scouring or scarifying.
d   High pressure water jets can be used effectively at temperatures up to 60°C to remove proteins and starches and at higher temperatures to remove grease and oils.

Deodorizers should only be used where air conditioning, ventilation and effective regular cleaning cannot contain an offensive odour.

Barrier matting may be used to prevent the transfer of soil from one area to another.

Prevention of surface dusting   Concrete and older thermoplastic or PVC asbestos floors will be subject to dusting and may, therefore, require sealing. PVC sheet, seamless resin and terrazzo floors are most suitable where high levels of dust control are required.

Antisoiling and antistatic finishes   Antistatic finishes applied to plastic surfaces will prevent dust alighting, thereby maintaining the standard of appearance longer. Antisoiling compounds applied to carpets and upholstery prevent soil penetrating the constituent fibres, arresting deterioration in the appearance and making cleaning easier. Finishes applied to walls can prevent penetration of stains and graffiti, thus making their removal easier.

Clean zones and rooms require the highest standards of control. Depending on the standard required it will involve the use of: dust control matting; air showers at entry points to remove dust from clothes; positive air pressure difference between clean zone and outer areas preventing entry of air; appropriate protective clothing; appropriate air filter screens; appropriate cleaning equipment; dirty personnel or equipment prohibited from clear zone.

British Standards

BS 5295: 1976, *Environmental Cleanliness in Enclosed Spaces. Part 1: Specification for controlled environment clean rooms, work stations and clean air devices. Part 2: Guide to the construction and installation of clean rooms, work stations and clean air devices. Part 3: Guide to operational procedures and disciplines applicable to clean rooms, work stations and clean air devices.*
BS 5958: 1980, *Code of practice for the Control of Undesirable Static Electricity. Part 1: General considerations.*
BS 3959: 1965, *Coir Matting.*

Hygiene

Introduction

'Hygiene' can be defined as the practices and procedures essential to the maintenance of health and the quality of life. It has two branches:

1   *Personal hygiene,* including personal habits and practices related to an individual's health and wellbeing.
2   *Environmental hygiene,* including surroundings, situation and circumstances which will effect a person's health and wellbeing.

Personal factors relevant to accommodation and cleaning services that will contribute to the improvement or reduction of health and well-being are habits and practices which lead to or control the spread of infection and disease, and working practices which lead to or prevent accidents.

Environmental factors which are relevant are pathogenic organisms in the environment, pollution, structural defects in a building, e.g. damp proofing, ventilation, lighting, heating, sanitation, general cleanliness and tidiness.

Employers and employees will have a responsibility to maintain high standards of both personal and environmental hygiene. High standards of personal hygiene involve the control of those personal habits and practices that affect the health and wellbeing of themselves and others. High standards of environmental hygiene involve the control of those factors harmful to and the encouragement of factors that promote health, quality of life and working conditions in a person's surroundings, circumstances or situation.

Bacteria and infection

Many of the adverse factors affecting personal and environmental hygiene have in common that they promote the growth of bacteria. Most bacteria are harmless but many are responsible for disease and infections in both man and animals. Harmful bacteria are known as pathogens.

Characteristics of bacteria

Bacteria are usually 0.5 to 2 μ in diameter. Many are capable of forming resting states called spores which resist normal cleaning and disinfection procedures and require sterilization for their destruction.

Disinfection will kill most harmful bacteria. It will *not* kill all bacteria and frequently not spores. Following disinfection, if spores are allowed to germinate, bacteria will multiply and infections may result. Following sterilization, if bacteria are allowed to recontaminate surfaces and are given

Table 13 *Conditions affecting the growth of pathogenic bacteria*

Heat	20⁰ to 45⁰C	Rapid growth
	37⁰C	Optimum growth
	0⁰ to 10⁰C	Controls bacteria
	0⁰ to −18⁰C	Deep freezing
	63⁰ to 115⁰C	Kills them, reducing numbers to acceptable levels
	115⁰C and above	Destroys all living things
Moisture	High humidity encourages bacteria	
Time	Necessary for the multiplication of bacteria	
Food	Certain foods are particularly susceptible to contamination, e.g. stocks, sauces, gravies, soups, meat and meat products, milk and milk products, eggs and egg products, food that is handled, food that is reheated. Those foods less likely to be contaminated are those having a high concentration of vinegar, sugar or salt, or with low protein contents	
Acids	Generally kill most bacteria.	
Disinfectants	Kill bacteria but different disinfectants have different degrees of effectiveness.	

the necessary conditions for growth, infections may result. Many bacteria will multiply by dividing once every 20 min if given the correct conditions for growth (see Table 13).

Freezing, chilling, refrigerating, pasteurizing, disinfecting, sterilizing, dehydrating or denying bacteria the time to multiply will all help to control or kill bacteria.

Reservoirs of infection and the spread of bacteria

The sources of bacteria which may cause infection

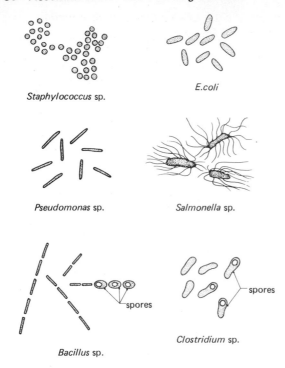

Staphylococcus sp.

E.coli

Pseudomonas sp.

Salmonella sp.

spores

spores

Clostridium sp.

Bacillus sp.

Figure 38 *Appearance of different types of bacteria*

and disease include humans, animals, soil, air, water and refuse.

Humans All humans carry both pathogenic and harmless bacteria. Poor standards of personal and environmental hygiene encourage the growth of the harmful bacteria, which in turn will lead to disease in the individual and the transfer of bacteria and hence disease to others either directly or via an intermediary e.g. food, surfaces, clothing, vermin.

Animals Like humans animals carry harmful bacteria. They also act as vectors, i.e. transmitters of disease, particularly pests, e.g. rats, cockroaches, flies and pets, e.g. cats and dogs.

Soil Ground soil may have up to three million bacteria per gramme of soil. Soil is brought into the building on shoes, etc., and hence dirty floors

must be considered a potential source of harmful bacteria.

Air Air will include harmful bacteria. The number will increase if the temperature and humidity rise or if ventilation is inadequate. Adequate ventilation, and when required, effective filtration, are essential.

Water Untreated water may be contaminated by harmful bacteria, e.g. typhoid. There is a particular risk if untreated or standing water is used in hospitals or clinics. If water used for cleaning is not changed frequently or it is allowed to stand it may become heavily contaminated with harmful bacteria, e.g. *Pseudomas* species.

Refuse This is an excellent growth medium for bacteria. It must be stored in sealed areas. Vermin will be the principle vectors of bacteria from refuse to food, surfaces and equipment.

Disease-causing bacteria

Table 14 lists a number of important disease- and infection-causing bacteria, their sources, method of transmission and their effects.

Prevention and control of bacteria and disease

The prevention of bacteria and disease is essential to the maintenance of health and quality of life. Failure to achieve such control may be due to: lack of knowledge, particularly rules of hygiene, carelessness, negligence, accident, poor facilities and provision of equipment, and/or, lack of supervision. Control can be achieved in a number of ways:

Air conditioning and ventilation will control temperature and humidity and reduce the number of bacteria in the air. Filter screens removing dust particles down to 0.5 μ will remove 99.99% of bacteria and remove all particles of 10 μ and above, below which size particles are incapable of supporting bacterial colonies.

Table 14 *Disease-causing bacteria*

Organism and effects	Source	Transmission
Staphylococcus aureus food poisoning; infections of nose and throat; infects cuts and wounds	1 Mucous membranes of nose, skin of man and animals. 30-50% of non-institutional people carry *S. aureus* in nose. Nasal carriage in hospital staff and patients is 60-80%	1 Touch: nose and mouth; handkerchiefs; sometimes from hair and skin 2 Skin infections: puss from staphyloccocal skin infections, e.g. boils and carbuncles 3 Wounds: even apparently clean, healthy wounds may harbour large numbers of *S. aureus* 4 Passed from raw to cooked foods via hands, containers, surfaces, equipment
E. coli food poisoning; diarrhoea; bladder infections; gastro-enteritis	1 Normal inhabitant of intestines of man and animals, but there are many strains which cause infections and disease 2 Foul water	1 Direct spread in maternity units 2 Contaminated infant feeds 3 Passed from raw to cooked foods via hands, containers, surfaces, equipment 4 Cleaning water not changed frequently or allowed to stand and then used 5 Pests and flies carry bacteria from excreta
Shigella sonnei dysentry	1 Human intestine	1 Failure to wash hands after visiting WC 2 Pests, e.g. flies and vermin, may carry bacteria from infected excreta to food 3 Contamination of toilet fittings
Salmonella group food poisoning; typhoid; paratyphoid	1 Human or animal intestine 2 Foul water 3 Poultry, shell-fish, meats, creams	1 Brought into building on raw foods of animal origin, e.g. meat, poultry, sausages, dried egg. 2 By insects, vermin, birds, domestic pets 3 Failure to wash hands after using WC 4 Water polluted by sewage 5 Passed from raw to cooked foods via hands, containers, surfaces equipment
Pseudomonas aeruginosa wound infections	1 Soil 2 Foul water	1 Cleaning water allowed to stand and then used. 2 Passed from dirty water to surfaces and equipment
Clostridium perfringens food poisoning; infects wounds	1 Human and animal intestines 2 Soil 3 Flies and blue-bottles are usually heavily infected 4 Most protein food	1 Brought into kitchen on raw meat 2 Brought into building in soil, e.g. vegetables, packing cases 3 Failure to wash hands after visiting WC 4 Passed from raw to cooked foods via hands, surfaces, equipment

Cleaning methods if selected and carried out correctly will remove or reduce to acceptable levels the majority of harmful bacteria on a surface. Wet cleaning methods are most effective. Methods likely to transfer bacteria from one place to another e.g. dry dusting which creates dust showers, should not be used. After cleaning, a surface should be left as dry as possible. Most pathogens die in the absence of water.

Cleaning equipment must be selected and used correctly. Dusting should be carried out with dust control mops and suction cleaning with suitably filtered suction cleaners.

To help prevent the transfer of bacteria colour coding will distinguish equipment used to clean different surfaces or areas e.g. different coloured cloths should be used to clean w.c. pans and the rest of a toilet area.

Cloths and mops must not be allowed to stand in cleaning or disinfecting solution but should be washed out and left to dry. They should be disinfected routinely.

Cleaning agents must be used correctly. Generally there will be no advantage in using a bactericidal detergent in preference to a neutral one. Cleaning solutions must never be topped up. They must be changed frequently, thrown away when finished with and always freshly prepared.

Cleaning frequency   The higher the standard of control required the more frequently must cleaning be carried out.

Clean areas and isolation units are required when there is a risk of infection to healthy individuals or to the ill. The operation of such areas can involve the use of protective clothing, barrier matting, air showers at entrances, an air pressure difference between clean and dirty areas and ventilated lobbies between clean and dirty areas.

Disinfection and sterilization is required when it is necessary to ensure that surfaces are, respectively, free from harmful bacteria or free from all bacteria including their spores. Either process should be preceded by effective soil removal.

Disinfection may be carried out by heat or chemically, depending on the circumstances. Sterilization will involve the use of dry heat at very high temperatures or moist heat at lower temperatures. If chemical disinfectants are required they must be used correctly, e.g. no topping up and freshly made.

Building design   Buildings and equipment should be designed to permit easy cleaning and not harbour soil and bacteria. Surfaces should be hard, smooth non-porous and easily assembled. For a description of requirements in kitchens and sanitary accommodation, see pages 49–55.

Barrier matting impregnated with bactericides can be used to prevent the trafficking of bacteria from one room or area to another.

Protective clothing will be required, ranging from an overall to gown, mask, cap, gloves and boots, depending on the situation.

Waste disposal   Waste, in particular wet and clinical wastes, are important potential sources of disease and infection. Procedures for their handling and disposal must be followed.

Personal hygiene   Personal practices and habits will greatly influence the spread and control of infection. The more important aspects are described in the following section.

Important aspects of personal hygiene

Clean Body

1   Daily bathing.
2   Change of underwear.
3   High standard of oral hygiene: clean teeth; visit dentist regularly.
4   Hair must be washed regularly, well groomed and covered for both safety and hygiene reasons.
5   Paper handkerchiefs are preferred to help reduce the transfer of streptococcal infections.

They must be disposed of carefully.

6 Cuts, boils, wounds, etc., should be covered to prevent transfer of staphylococcal infections. Food handlers must cover such wounds with a waterproof dressing.
7 Persons suffering from diarrhoea or similar must not handle food or work in areas where others may be at risk.

Hand care

1 Must be clean, wash frequently, especially after using WC. Essential to prevent transfer of bacteria to food, surfaces, etc.
2 Nails should be short and clean, well manicured.
3 Regular application of hand cream will help prevent roughening. Roughness acts as a bacteria trap.
4 The use of barrier cream, before starting work, will help to protect hands. This is of great importance when there is any risk of a cleaning agent causing dermatitis.
5 The wearing of gloves, rubber or PVC for wet work and cotton for dry work will help protect hands. When operatives suffer allergic reactions to rubber gloves, PVC gloves will normally be tolerated.
6 Jewellery should not be worn, particularly by food handlers, for both hygiene and safety reasons.

Feet

1 Feet must be clean; wash at least daily.
2 Feet must be comfortable.
3 Socks, stockings or tights must be changed daily.
4 Shoes should fit well, providing both support and protection.
5 Shoes worn at work should cover as much of the foot as possible to provide protection against spillages and accidents.
6 Rubber soles are helpful, if there is a risk of slippery floors.
7 Shoes should be kept in a good state of repair.
8 Nails should be kept short and clean.

Clothing

1 Pride in appearance should be encouraged.
2 Clothes should be neat and tidy.
3 Clothes must be clean and laundered frequently.
4 In a work situation overalls are preferred to prevent dirt and bacteria being carried into the work area on outdoor clothes.
5 Overalls must be clean and laundered frequently.
6 There is a danger of transferring bacteria from clothing to people, surfaces, fittings, etc.
7 Outdoor clothes must not be permitted in areas where there is a risk of infection or food is handled.

Personal habits

1 Avoid touching mouth, nose, throat, cuts and wounds, ears.
2 Smoking, spitting, snuff-taking should be prohibited.
3 Bacteria may be transferred from mouth, lips, etc., onto hands and so, onto surfaces, food, etc.
4 Hair must never be combed in the kitchen or where there is an infection risk. Possible transfer of *Staphylococci* from scalp (also dandruff) to food and surfaces.
5 Staff must not dip fingers into food to taste it, nor lick a spoon and return it to food without washing it. Bacteria will be transferred from mouth onto hands or spoon, and so onto food.
6 Fingers should not be licked when separating wrapping paper.
7 Avoid coughing and sneezing over food. Large numbers of *Staphylococci* will be expelled in droplets of moisture and will reach food and surfaces and equipment.
8 Pick up items such as cutlery, glasses by handles and stems, plates by their edges.

Food handling

1 Cooked and raw foods should not be handled together. This involves the use of equipment, surfaces, storage areas, e.g. refrigerators. The transfer of bacteria from raw meat to cooked

food is a frequent cause of food poisoning, i.e. cross-contamination. Hands also need to be washed after handling raw meat, poultry or vegetables.

2 After handling refuse or stale and con-taminated foods, hands must be washed. A great many bacteria will be present in refuse and waste food.

3 Clean utensils and clean cloths should be used in food preparation areas.

4 Chopping boards and work surfaces used for raw meat preparation must be kept exclusively for that purpose. Helps to prevent cross-contamination.

5 All work surfaces and equipment must be washed with detergent after each use, and disinfected at least daily.

6 Damaged utensils and chipped crockery must be discarded. Bacteria will be harboured in the cracks, even with efficient cleaning pro-cedures.

7 Correct storage of food. Frozen foods – freezer (–18°C). Fresh foods – dry store, cool with slatted shelves at least 50 cm from ground, having a hard, impervious floor, and excluding all pests. Perishable foods – refrigerator –4°C. Cooked protein foods – store either below 10°C or above 62°C. Displayed food – must be covered.

8 All frozen meat and poultry should be thoroughly thawed before cooking. Helps to eliminate risk of salmonella food poisoning. Warm food provides ideal temperature for multiplication of bacteria.

9 Food must be kept very hot or very cold before service, never left in a warm temperature for a any length of time.

10 Avoid reheating foods wherever possible. Never reheat meat products more than once. Hazard that food may contain *Clostridium perfringens* spores.

11 Deep frozen foods should not be refrozen once thawed. Pathogenic bacteria may have multiplied during thawing. Also texture suffers.

12 Observe correct cooking times and tempera-tures. Food is a poor conductor of heat. Time

and temperature control is essential to ensure complete cooking.

13 Use all food stocks in rotation.

Lighting

Adequate lighting of the most appropriate types will be required for the following reasons.

Safety Poorly lit areas, e.g. staircases, may result in falls.

Prevention of eyestrain Activities that involve continuous use of the eyes will require higher levels of illumination than other activities.

Contribution to decor The type, level and colour of lights used will significantly affect the appearance and feel of a room. This will also be true of the fixtures and fittings used.

Use of room or building The intended use will affect the level of illumination required.

Cleanliness A well lit room can be more effectively cleaned than one with dark corners where soil can be missed.

General comfort of a room can be reduced by too much glare or too high a level of illumination.

A room or surface can be lit by four types of lighting:

1 *Direct* All the light will come directly from the light source.

2 *Semi-direct* Most of the light will come directly from the light source, but some will have come by reflection via other surfaces.

3 *Semi-indirect* A little of the light will come directly from the light source. The majority will come by reflection from other surfaces.

4 *Indirect* All the light will have come from the light source via other surfaces.

The type of light produced will be governed by the type of light source used, e.g. tungsten filament bulb or fluorescent tube, and whether or not

Table 15 *Lighting levels for different rooms and activities*

Activity	Lux	
Rough or routine work; large detail; medium to light material of good contrast	300	From CP 3: Part 2: 1973, Chapter 1
Ordinary work usually involving workers' inspection; medium detail and contrast	500	
Fairly critical work; fairly small detail or poor contrast	750	
Fine or critical work; very small detail; very poor contrast or very dark material	1000	
Very fine, exacting work	2000	
Minute work	3000	

Area	Lux	Area	Lux
General		**Hospitals**	
Corridors, passageways	100	Corridors	150
Lifts	150	Wards (general)	300
Lift lobbies	150	Bed heads	30-50
Stairs, escalators	150	Reading rooms	150
Entrance halls	150	Laboratories	300
Kitchens (general)	500	Operating theatres (general)	400-500
Kitchens (food preparation)	500	Operating area	Special lighting
Food stores	150	Anaesthetic room	300
		Recovery rooms	300
Medical		Consulting rooms	300
Consulting rooms and first-aid cubicles	500	**Hotels**	
Rest rooms	150	Entrance halls	150
Treatment rooms	500	Reception	300
Medical stores	100	Cloakrooms	150
		Dining rooms	100
Staff restaurants		Lounges	100
Canteens, cafeteria	200	Bedrooms (general)	50
Dining rooms (general)	200	Bedhead	150
Counters	300	Kitchens	500
Staff rooms		**Offices**	
Changing and locker rooms	150	General	500
Cloakrooms and lavatories	150	Print room	300
Rest rooms	150	Drawing	750
		Records	300
Schools			
General	300	**Shops**	
Examination rooms	300	Circulation areas	500
Classrooms	300	Counters	500
Lecture theatres	300	Cash desks	500
Art rooms	500		
Laboratories	500	Computer rooms	500
Needlework rooms	500	Laundries (general)	300

Source: From Lighting Industry Federation Handbook, *Interior Lighting Design.* (5th edition)

diffusers or reflectors are used. Direct light tends to result in glare, uneven illumination and shadows. Indirect light results in reduced glare, more even illumination and fewer shadows. The minimum recommended levels of illumination for different rooms and activities are shown in Table 15. The quantity of light is measured in lumens and a lux is the number of lumens falling on 1 m² of a surface.

Ventilation

Good ventilation is essential to remove: odours and smells; carbon dioxide; water vapour; dust, fumes and grease droplets; excess heat. This can be achieved naturally, e.g. windows, mechanically with extractor fans, or by air conditioning.

Air conditioning can be defined as a system that automatically controls the temperature, humidity, movement and cleanliness of air. BS 5720 specifies the air change requirements for various rooms and buildings. Examples are shown in Table 16.

The relative humidity of a room should be 30–65% and not greater than 70%.

Poor ventilation will have a number of effects:

1   Increase in number of bacteria resulting in increased incidence of infection.
2   Draughts, resulting in discomfort.
3   Excess temperature, humidity and carbon dioxide levels resulting in drowsiness, headaches and increased respiration. These in turn can result in more accidents, lower productivity and general discomfort.
4   Accumulation of dust and grease droplets in the atmosphere will have two results: an increase in the incidence of respiratory complaints and an increase in the soilage of surfaces. Water vapour and grease droplets falling onto a surface tend to hold dust.
5   Excessive condensation will lead to deterioration of the fabric of a building and its furnishings.

Table 16   *Air changes required in various rooms*

Room/buildings	Air changes
Hospital ward	3 per hour
Dormitory	3 per hour
Dining room	3 per hour
Corridor	2 per hour
Internal lavatory/ bathroom	3 per hour
Kitchen	20-40 per hour
Laundry	10-20 per hour
Places of entertainment	28 m³ per hour per person*

Local Authority regulations*

Table 17   *Temperature requirements in various rooms*

Room	Temperature, °C
Bedroom	13-16
Kitchen	18
Office	19-20
Classroom	17
Workshop	13-18
Lavatory	13-18
Hospital ward	19
Public room	20-21
Corridor/stairs	13-18

Temperature

The temperature required in different rooms will depend on the individual person, the amount of clothing they wear, humidity levels, the type of activities carried out and a number of other factors. Accordingly it is less easy to define precisely temperature levels. The temperatures given in Table 17 are those generally recommended.

British standards

BS 5266: 1975, *Emergency Lighting. Part 1: Code of practice for the emergency lighting of premises*

House mouse

German cockroach

Common house fly

Woodworm larva in tunnel

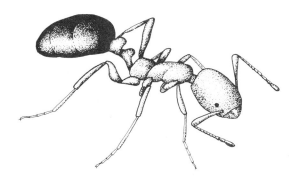
Pharoah's ant
Various pests

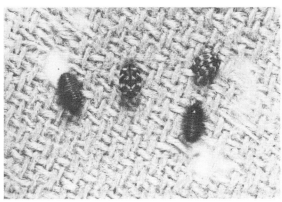
Adults and larvae of carpet beetle

Table 18 *Pests*

Type, class habits and life style	Factors influencing infestation and methods of control
Cockroach (insect):	**Infestation:**
1 Three types: German, American, Common.	1 Poor standard of cleanliness. Not ensuring that all waste food is removed.
2 Sizes range from 1.0-3.5 cm.	2 Food stored incorrectly.
3 Flattened bodies, long antennae, long exposed wings.	3 Poor standard of cleanliness in food stores.
4 Live and breed in very warm moist dark places. Often found in kitchens, dining areas and food stores, e.g. behind ovens, warm pipes.	4 Structure of food store permits entry of pests.
	5 Waste food stored incorrectly.
	6 Poor standard of cleanliness in waste storage area.
5 Prefer sweet and sticky foods but will attack most foods, also paper and clothing.	7 Structure of waste storage area permits entry of pests.
6 Health hazard. Carriers of *salmonella sp.*	**Control:**
	1 Regular, thorough cleaning. Ensure that all waste food is removed.
	2 Store food in closed containers.
	3 Clean food stores correctly.
	4 Food stores should be built to exclude pests.
	5 Waste food should be stored in closed containers.
	6 Clean the waste storage area correctly.
	7 Waste stores should be built to exclude pests.
	8 If infestation occurs, treat with insecticidal dusts and lacquers. Typical insecticides used include deildrin, chlordene, fenctrothian, diazinon or dioxacarb.
	9 When severe infestation occurs, seek specialist help.

Flies (insects):

1   There are a large number of different types, the most common are the housefly and blowfly (green and bluebottles).

2   Feed on dead and decaying vegetable and animal matter, excrement, etc., by secreting digestive juices onto food and then sucking up the partly digested food.

3   Eggs are laid by female in warm moist places, e.g. waste food, rotting meat and refuse.

4   The life cycle is: Adult - Eggs - Larvae (maggot) - Pupae - Adult.

5   Occur throughout the establishment.

Infestation:

1   As for cockroach.

Control:

1   As for cockroach.

2   Insecticidal sprays, but not in food areas. Many sprays contain pyrethrins or pyrethroids.

3   Numbers can be reduced by covering windows and ventilators with gauze.

4   Ultra-violet electric insect killers, e.g. 'Insectocutors'.

5   Infestation as such is not usually a problem. The number of flies in urban environments has decreased recently due to improved refuse and sewage disposal.

Silverfish (insect):

1   A wingless insect, silver grey, 1 cm long.

2   Feeds on cellulose and starchy material, e.g. wallpapers, paste, books, cotton or rayon clothing, debris and remains of starchy food.

3   Nocturnal.

4   Occur in drawers, cupboards and around drains and sinks.

Infestation:

1   Irregular cleaning of cupboards and drawers.

Control:

1   Clean cupboards and drawers regularly.

2   Infestation is rarely a problem but can be dealt with by the use of an insecticidal spray or powder.

(continued)

Table 18 *continued*

Type, class habits and life style	*Factors influencing infestation and methods of control*
Moths (insect):	*Infestation:*
1 The female lays up to 200 eggs which hatch to produce grubs which attack wool, fur skin, feather.	1 Linen and curtains not cleaned before storage.
2 The life cycle is: Adult - Egg - Larvae (grub) - Pupae - Adult.	2 Insufficient inspection of stored linen and curtains.
3 Moths prefer shade, a temperature of about 20o-30oC and soiled areas of fabric.	3 Failure to use a repellent if not already treated.
4 Moths will attack blankets, bedding, quilts, carpets, underfelt, upholstery, curtains, stuffed animals and birds.	4 Insufficient cleaning and inspection of carpets and upholstery, particularly carpet edges.
	Control:
	1 Cleaning of linen and curtains before storage.
	2 Regular inspection of stored linen and curtains.
	3 Use a repellent, e.g. paradichlorobenzene crystals.
	4 Regular vacuuming of carpets and upholstery.
	5 Occasional special cleaning of carpets and upholstery.
	6 If attack occurs, thorough cleaning is required. This involves cleaning both sides of carpets and upholstery. Then subject to heat treatment or a general insecticide.
Carpet beetle (insect):	*Infestation:*
1 Two types: black and the varied carpet beetle.	1 Failure to inspect and clean carpets on a regular basis, particularly carpet edges.
2 Grubs known as 'woolly bears' are responsible for damage.	

3 Attack woollen carpets.

Control:

1 Vacuum regularly.
2 Special clean occasionally.
3 If an attack occurs, treat as for moths.

Woodworm (insect):

Infestation:

1 Unpolished or cracked woodwork.
2 Sapwood, used in many modern buildings, is susceptible to attack.

1 The term woodworm refers to the larvae of several species of wood-boring insect, e.g. *Anobium punctatum.*

2 The adult lays eggs on the rough surface of unpolished wood and in cracks of woodwork.

3 The grubs which hatch out bore into the timber. There is no sign of entry, the grubs tunnel inside the wood.

4 When ready to pupate (usually after 1-3 years), larvae make a pupal chamber just below the surface of the wood.

5 The adult beetle bites its way out, leaving characteristic flight holes.

6 Piles of wood dust on horizontal surfaces indicate grub activity.

7 Close examination will reveal flight holes.

Control:

1 Regular polishing of all wooden surfaces.
2 Checking and making good cracks in woodwork.
3 Careful selection of building timber.
4 A mild infestation can be dealt with by using a specialist preparation, e.g. Cuprinol. It is necessary to thoroughly treat not only the area where woodworm holes are visible, but also the adjacent timbers.
5 Specialist advice is essential for major infestations.

Ant (insect):

Infestation:

1 Two types of ant occur in buildings: garden ants and Pharoah's ants.

2 Garden ants nest outdoors but seek food indoors. They are not known to be a health hazard but are a nuisance in food areas.

1 Poor standard of cleanliness.
2 Careless removal of waste food.
3 Cracks, crevices and defects in walls and floors provide nesting sites.

(continued)

Table 18   *continued*

Type, class habits and life style	*Factors influencing infestation and methods of control*
Ants - continued	**Control:**
3 Pharoah's ants nest in warm buildings and can carry organisms which cause disease. They are a health hazard in hospitals, moving from soiled dressings to contaminate sterile equipment, dressings or food. They are known to carry *Pseudomonas sp., E. coli, C. perfringens.*	1 Maintain high standards of cleanliness.
	2 Remove every item of waste food including crumbs.
	3 Check and maintain structure of building regularly.
	4 If infestation occurs, treat nests of garden ants with boiling water, malathion, paraffin or lindane.
	5 When infestation of Pharoah's ants occurs, there will be many nests which need to be treated systematically. Treatment should start beyond the infested area. Bands of insecticide should be applied at the junction of the wall and floor, around pipe exits, sinks, air vents, cracks, sills and on the underside of cupboard shelves.
	6 Lacquers containing dieldrin or sprays containing chlordane, are suitable. An alternative control method is by using poison bait, e.g. chlordecone mixed with an attractive base such as liver.
Lice (insect-parasite):	**Infestation:**
1 Head lice are most common.	1 Poor personal and environmental hygiene.
2 Head lice bite and suck blood.	2 Can be introduced into situations of high hygiene standards.

Control:

1 Infestation dealt with by the use of special shampoos.

Fleas (insect-parasite):

1 Able to jump considerable distances.
2 Prefer warmth and darkness.
3 Bite and suck blood, causing severe irritation.

Infestation:

1 Introduced into a building in a variety of ways.

Control:

1 Infestation may be dealt with by cleaning, followed by fumigation with formaldehyde and/or heat treatment.
2 Specialist advice should be sought.

Bed bugs (insect-parasite):

1 May be up to 0.5 cm long.
2 Bite and suck blood, causing severe irritation.

Infestation:

1 Introduced via second-hand furniture, clothing, bedding, etc.

Control:

1 Infestation may be dealt with as for fleas.

Rats (rodent):

1 Gregarious, will quickly infest.
2 Live and breed in warm, dark corners, with plentiful and easily accessible food and little disturbance.

Infestation:

1 As for cockroach.

(continued)

Table 18   *continued*

Type, class habits and life style	*Factors influencing infestation and methods of control*
Rats - *continued*	*Control:*
3 Will cut through walls, floors and burrow and eat their way through sacks, bins, packets of food.	1 As for cockroach.
4 Contaminate food with droppings, containing harmful bacteria.	2 Infestation may be dealt with by trapping, gassing or poisoning. This is usually most effective if carried out methodically. Warfarin in suitable bait, e.g. oatmeal, is an anticoagulant which causes death within a period of 8-10 days of repeated doses. Ensure that no other creatures may eat bait.
5 Rats also carry harmful bacteria on their fur and feet and so transfer them to any surfaces they travel across.	
6 Rats carry organisms responsible for food poisoning, dysentry and plague.	3 In the case of infestation by Warfarin-resistant strains of rats, defenacoum or coumafuryl may be used.
7 They are usually creatures of habit and use familiar runs.	
8 Signs of infestation are gnawing marks, droppings, feet marks in dust or grain.	
9 Rats breed prolifically.	
Mice (rodent):	*Infestation:*
1 As for rats, infestation is usually on a lesser scale, but mice are less predictable in their habits. Individual traps may be useful but large scale poisoning can be difficult.	1 As for cockroach.
	Control:
	1 As for cockroach.

Dry rot (fungus):

Infestation:

1 Over one dozen fungi known to cause deterioration of timber. True dry rot is caused by one species, *Merulius lacrymans*

2 Occurs in dark, damp, poorly ventilated areas of wood work.

3 Cannot develop in wood containing less than 25% moisture. Optimum moisture content for growth is 30-40%.

4 Recognised by its smell, filaments, red powdery spores.

5 Will reduce wood to a powdery crumbling state.

6 May also penetrate soft brickwork and mortar.

Infestation:

1 Faulty building design or construction.

2 Neglect of maintenance of building.

3 Faulty plumbing.

4 Continuous damp under floor covering and poor ventilation.

5 No, or faulty, damp course.

Control:

1 High standards of building design and construction.

2 Regular checking and maintenance of building.

3 Correct plumbing methods.

4 Prevention of damp under floor covering and adequate ventilation.

5 Intact damp course.

6 When dry rot occurs, all rotten wood must be cut away and burned. Affected plasterwork or rendering must be removed. Remaining wood and brickwork must be thoroughly cleaned and sterilized. Surrounding plaster should be sprayed with a fungicide before installation. Brickwork and masonry must dry out before redecoration.

Wet rot (fungus):

Infestation:

1 Wet rot is often known as cellar fungus (*Coniphora cerebella*).

2 Outbreaks are twice as frequent as dry rot, but less difficult to treat.

Infestation:

1 Similar to dry rot, but with moister conditions.

(continued)

Table 18   *continued*

Type, class habits and life style	*Factors influencing infestation and methods of control*
Wet rot — *continued*	*Control:*
3 Only occurs in very damp conditions. Optimum water content for growth is 50-60%	1 Similar to dry rot but activity ceases when source of moisture is removed.
4 Sensitive to drying and so activity ceases when source of moisture is removed.	2 If wet rot occurs, treat by removing cause of dampness and allow timber to dry out. Only replace timber if wet rot is severe. Cut out and burn any timber which has suffered surface or sub-surface breakdown. Treat new timber with fungicide before installation.
5 Recognised by fungal strands of dark fern-like shape on surface of wood or damp plaster.	3 Specialist advice is available for outbreak of both dry and wet rot.
6 Wet rot does not penetrate brickwork.	
Birds:	*Infestation:*
The excreta of birds presents a hazard as a result of:	1 Public opinion.
1 The dust produced as it dries is blown into buildings	*Control:*
2 Droppings may contaminate food with organisms of the *Salmonella* group and other pathogens.	1 Screens, e.g. netting on windows, helps to exclude birds.
3 Unsightly. Birds may also be carriers of pests which spoil stored products	2 Stupefying agents. Birds are rendered insensible and can be killed or released as required.
	3 Tactile repellants applied or fixed to roosting sites. These include pliable substances which give birds a sense of unsure footing.

other than cinemas and certain other specified premises used for entertainment.

BS 5720: 1979, *Code of Practice for Mechanical Ventilation and Air Conditioning in Buildings.*

BS 5925: 1980, *Code of Practice for Design of Buildings: Ventilation Principles and Designing for Natural Ventilation.*

CP 3, *Code of Basic Data for the Design of Buildings. Chapter 1: Part 1: 1964, Daylighting. Chapter 1: Part 2: 1973, Artificial lighting.*

Pest control

Pest control is required under the *Prevention of Damage by Pests Act 1949,* which places an obligation on the owner of premises to keep buildings, etc., free from rodents, and also, where applicable under the *Food Hygiene (General) Regulations, 1970.*

Pests require food, water, shelter and time to breed and multiply. Therefore it is necessary to deprive pests of these items to prevent infestation. Table 18 outlines the main types of pest, their life style, factors influencing infestation and methods of control.

British Standards

CP3, *Code of Basic Data for the Design of Buildings. Chapter 10: 1950, Precautions against vermin and dirt.*

Table 18 *continued*

Notes

1 When selecting insecticides for the control of pests, great care must be taken to ensure that:

   a The insecticide will not be a danger to humans or other animals.

   b The insecticide is suitable for the area in which it is to be used. Many are unsuitable in food areas.

   c They are applied strictly in accordance with the manufacturer's instructions.

2 In general, where infestation is severe, specialist help is recommended.

4 Cleaning equipment

Equipment used in the cleaning of a building, its furniture and fittings will include both manual and mechanical equipment. Cleaning and maintenance will also involve the use of access equipment.

There will often be several ways of carrying out any particular cleaning task and a number of different types of equipment that can be employed. It is essential to select the most appropriate piece of equipment in any situation.

In this chapter are described the different types of cleaning and access equipment available, correct and safe methods of using and storing each, selection criteria and the stages involved in the selection of equipment.

Brushes

Brushes are designed to remove dry or wet soil. They consist of a stock of wood, metal or plastic into which bristles of horsehair, nylon or polypropylene are inserted. The stock and handle may be constructed in one piece or alternatively the stock may be attached to a wooden or metal handle. The bristles have a chisel like action which dislodges the soil.

There are three principal types: hard, soft and scrubbing. Hard brushes have bristles that are fairly stiff and well spaced. Soft brushes have bristles that are fairly flexible and set close together. Scrubbing brushes have short, hard and well spaced bristles.

Selection of hard and soft brushes

Since hard and soft brushes should not be used where dust control is essential, this limits their use to exterior areas and to interior areas where dust control is unimportant.

Soft brushes may be used to remove loose soil and litter. Hard brushes are most suitable for the removal of litter. Both are effective on uneven surfaces. The largest possible should be used consistant with ease of manoeuverability around any obstructions and the size of area to be swept. In more congested areas, brushes 30 to 50cm wide are preferable, whilst in large, open spaces brushes up to 1 metre are preferred.

Brushing is a relatively slow process with a high fatigue factor. Typical work performances per hour are shown in Table 19.

Small hand brushes can be used to remove localized soiling or accumulations of soil after sweeping.

Selection of scrubbing brushes

Scrubbing brushes should only be used to remove heavy soiling from small areas or where access by a suitable scrubbing machine is not possible. Manual scrubbing is extremely slow with a very high fatigue factor. The highest work performance factor that can be achieved is 50 m^2/hr.

Methods of use

Brushing requires a steady deliberate action whilst walking forwards. The number of passes made over each area as it is swept will depend on the degree of soiling and impaction.

Hand scrubbing involves scrubbing each section of a surface with cleaning solution using a circular action. The section is then rinsed with clean water and a floor cloth used to mop up and leave the surface as dry as possible. Each section cleaned should overlap adjacent sections which have been cleaned.

Deck scrubbing involves scrubbing each section

of a floor using a backwards and forwards action. The section is rinsed and left as dry as possible using a mop, bucket and press. The cleaning of each section should overlap adjacent sections.

Care

Brushes should never be stored standing on their bristles. If necessary they should be washed in cold water or, if partcularly dirty, in a lukewarm solution of neutral detergent. Tangles can be removed by using a suitable comb. A final cold salt water rinse will help to keep natural bristles firm.

Dust control mops and dusters

Dust control mops and dusters are designed to remove soil and debris from a surface without raising dust which may then settle back onto the surface. They generally consist of a handle to which a metal frame is attached. The mop head or duster is either inserted into the frame or stretched over it, according to type.

Types of dust control mop and duster

There are four principal types:

Impregnated fringe mops consist of dense cotton fringes, 15 cm in length, inserted into a metal frame, 15 to 120 cm in length. The mops are usually pre-impregnated when a hire service is used or will require impregnating by soaking in or spraying with mineral oil or a synthetic

impregnating fluid. In contact with a surface the fringe spreads out, thus increasing the mop's effective surface area. Dust is held on the mop by the oil. They are generally less expensive than other forms of dust control mop. They can also be used for the application of protective finishes. However, only part of the fringe is in contact with a surface. They require regular washing and re-impregnation.

Impregnated mops consist of cotton strands fixed to a flat backing and stretched over a metal frame, 15 to 120 cm in length. A sweeper consists of a single frame or two hinged frames forming a vee sweeper. Mops can be pre-impregnated or require impregnation. In use the fringes splay out to give a large surface area in contact with a surface. They require regular washing and re-impregnation. Following impregnation, sufficient time must be allowed for the mineral oil to cure. Improperly cured mops will leave a film of oil on a surface. They are more effective in terms of dust control than static mops.

Static mops and dusters consist of acrylic, nylon, or polyester strands fixed to a backing which is stretched over a metal frame. In use the fringes splay out to form a large surface area holding dust by means of a static charge which builds up on the fringe. They are more easily maintained than impregnated mops.

Disposable mops consist of cheap cotton or other fibrous material. They are replaced as necessary. They are particularly suitable where infection control is required.

Selection

Dust control mops and dusters are generally the preferred method of removing light soil and debris and can be used on any smooth dry surface. The size and shape of the mop or duster used will depend on the type of surface, area to be cleaned, density of furniture and ease of access.

Mops and frames designed for the dusting of furniture and the high dusting of walls, ledges,

Table 19 *Brush work performances*

Brush width, cm	Unobstructed area, m^2	Obstructed area, m^2	Soiling factor
30	400	200-400	Light soil x 1
50	700	300-700	Moderate soil x 0.75
100	1,200	N/A	Heavy soil x 0.5

Dust-control mops

fixtures and fittings are available. Telescopic poles will frequently make the use of access equipment unnecessary. The largest possible mop should be used for the sweeping of floors consistent with ease of manoeuvrability around and under obstructions. Mops 45 to 60 cm in length are suitable for small to moderately sized areas allowing obstructions to be easily negotiated. Larger mops, in particular vee sweepers, should be used on larger, open areas, e.g. gymnasia, and corridors. Typical work performances are shown in Table 20.

The handle of a mop to be used on floors or walls should swivel through 360° when the mop head is placed on a flat surface and feature a rigid position for straight sweeping.

Method of use

Sweeping or dusting requires a straight, steady action with overlapping passes. When sweeping floors, an S-type action can be employed. Whichever action is used, the sweeper should not be removed from the floor when a change of direction is required. With practice the mop can be manoeuvered around and under obstacles without removing the mop from the floor or altering the basic action.

Accumulations of dust or debris are removed from the surface of the mop using a vacuum cleaner either when the job is completed or during the job if accumulation becomes excessive.

Table 20 *Dust control mop work performances*

Size of mop		Obstructed to unobstructed, m^2/hr
Cm	Inches	
30	12	400 - 800
45	18	600 - 1,200
60	24	600 - 1,600
90	36	3,400
150	60	5,000 - 10,000
	(vee sweeper)	

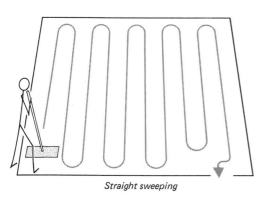

Straight sweeping

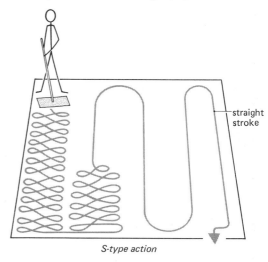

straight
stroke

S-type action

Figure 39 *Sweeping with a dust-control mop*

Care

At the end of a work period, mops and dusters must be vacuumed and stored such that the fringes are not in contact with the floor or any other surface. Mops should be washed periodically in warm detergent solution. Inserting the mop into a net bag will prevent tangling. When dry, impregnated mops require re-impregnation by soaking or spraying. The normal application is 25g of oil per 30 cm length of mop.

If mops are hired, the frequency of exchange of soiled mops for clean is usually specified in the hire contract.

Damp and wet mopping equipment

Mops and buckets are used for the removal of soil adhering to a surface. There are three principal types of mop: do-all, Kentucky and foss.

Do-all mops consist of strands of twisted cotton fixed to a circular metal plate, which in turn is fitted to a stock.

Kentucky mops consist of cotton strands fixed to a length of cotton fabric which is inserted into a flat metal stock. They are available in weights ranging from 330 to 670 g.

Strands may be stitched together or unstitched.

The former are less likely to tangle, can be laundered more easily and are likely to last longer than unstitched mops.

Foss mops consist of a dense cotton fringe inserted into a weighted metal stock. They are available in a range of weights.

Buckets of various types are available including plastic or metal pails, plastic or galvanized do-all buckets incorporating a fixed or detachable straining cone, and single-, double- and treble-galvanized buckets mounted on castors or a trolley and which are used in conjunction with a press (a device to mechanically squeeze water from a mop).

Selection

Mops up to 450 g are suitable for general use. Where large areas are to be wet-mopped, heavier mops can be used. Large mops are very heavy when wet, which can result in a high fatigue factor.

Kentucky and foss mops are designed to be used in conjunction with a press. The size of the press required will be governed by the size of the mop to be used.

Small pails are suitable for the cleaning of surfaces other than floors. Do-all buckets are easily portable and are most suitable for the removal of light soilage or spillages. Larger

Types of mops and buckets

Table 21   *Systems of mopping*

System	Use	Equipment and rate	
Damp mopping	Very light soilage	1	Requires single bucket, part filled with cleaning solution, wringer or strainer and mop
		2	200-400 m²/hr
Single-solution wet mopping	Light to moderate soilage	1	Requires two buckets, one part filled with cleaning solution, one empty, wringer and mop
		2	150-300 m²/hr
Two-solution wet mopping	Moderate to heavy soilage	1	Requires three buckets, one part filled with cleaning solution, one part filled with clean rinsing water and one empty, wringer and two mops
		2	100-200 m²/hr

A do-all or Kentucky mop when used for applying or removing water from a floor is used with a side-to-side figure-of-eight action, taking care to avoid the splashing of furniture or skirting boards. Each stroke should overlap the previous one turning the mop two or three times. A foss mop is used with a backwards and forwards zig-zag action. To avoid splashing of walls or skirting boards the section of floor adjacent to the walls should be mopped with a straight stroke prior to mopping the rest of the floor.

An abrasive pad fitted to the stock will facilitate the removal of stubborn marks.

To prevent strain and reduce fatigue overstretching should be avoided.

Bucket cloths must be placed under buckets during use to prevent marking of a surface.

Cleaning and rinsing solutions should be changed frequently to avoid returning soil to the surface.

Systems of damp and wet mopping

The three major systems and the work performance of each is shown in Table 21. The system selected will depend on the degree of soilage.

Care

After use mop heads should be washed, rinsed, squeezed dry and stored in a dry, well ventilated store with the strands hanging down. Periodically, or as required, they can be boiled or laundered. During work periods, mops not in use should be squeezed dry and not allowed to stand in cleaning solution.

Buckets after use should be washed out, rinsed and wiped dry.

Squeegees

Squeegees are designed to remove water from a surface and, if used correctly, will leave an even surface dry. They consist of a rubber strip fixed to a metal holder and used in conjunction with a stock and handle.

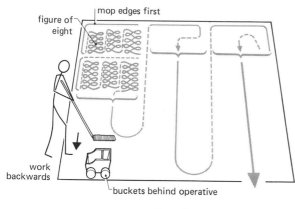
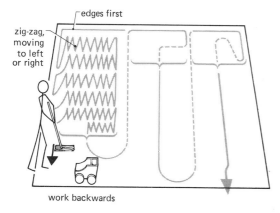

Figure 40 *Damp mopping*

buckets, whether used singly or in double or treble combination, are most suitable for larger areas but are not easily portable when full.

Methods of use

When using a mop it is important to appreciate that it is the weight of the mop which plays a major part in the dislodging and removal of soil from a floor. The mop should be allowed to do the work and, except occasionally, it is therefore unnecessary to apply any undue pressure to the mop.

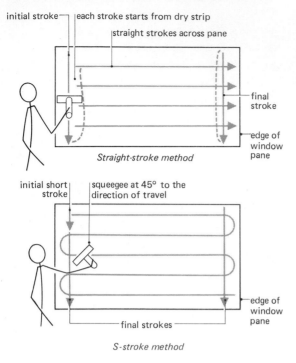

Straight-stroke method

S-stroke method

Selection

Blades of different lengths, telescopic poles and various special fittings enable squeegees to be used to remove water from floors, windows and walls.

Methods

To simply remove large quantities of water from a floor a straight deliberate stroke is used in the direction of a drain, gulley or collection point.

To leave a surface dry the edge of the blade must be firmly in contact with the surface, each stroke commencing from a dry section of surface. There are two principal methods of use both requiring an initial stroke to be made to leave a dry surface from which subsequent strokes can commence. Before commencing a stroke the blades should be wiped dry and each stroke should overlap the previous one. Straight strokes are usually more appropriate for larger areas.

Care

After use squeegee blades must be washed, rinsed and wiped dry.

Cloths

A variety of cloths are available. They must all be kept and used clean.

Wipes and swabs These are cloths used for the wet cleaning of surfaces above floor level. They can take a number of forms. They can be reusable or be disposable. Reusable wipes include loosely woven or knitted cotton cloths and synthetic sponge and non-woven cloths. They must be washed and opened out to dry after use. Disposable wipes must only be used once and then discarded. They can be impregnated with a bactericide during manufacture. During work periods wipes should not be left standing in cleaning or disinfecting solutions between one time of use and the next.

Floor cloths These generally consist of a loosely woven or knitted coarse cotton. They are only to be used for the removal of spillages from a floor.

Chamois leather Natural chamois leathers are either the skin of the chamois goat or split sheep skins (skivetts). They can be used wet for cleaning windows and mirrors or dry for polishing silver and are ideally suited for wiping squeegee blades. After use they should be washed out, rinsed and kept moist by placing in an airtight container. If used irregularly they can be allowed to dry naturally and then rubbed gently to keep them soft.

Cheaper synthetic chamois leathers have to some extent replaced the use of natural ones.

Scrim A loosely woven linen cloth which is absorbent and does not leave linters. They are suitable for the cleaning of glazed areas.

Rags Disposable cloths, usually obtained from the linen room and used for general cleaning. They are discarded when soiled.

Dusters Soft and absorbent checked cotton material or yellow flannelette up to 50 cm square. They are used for buffing or dusting. When used for dusting they must be sprayed with a fine mist of water. In either case they must be folded several times into a hand-sized pad to provide a number of clean surfaces.

Dust sheets Thin cotton sheets used to cover furniture during cleaning or in storage; often discarded items from the linen room.

Bucket cloths Thick fabric placed under buckets to prevent marking of a surface.

Druggets Linen, canvas or plastic sheeting used to protect floor coverings from heavy soilage or during cleaning or redecoration.

Polish applicators

The sets of equipment used for polish application are:

1 Natural or synthetic lambswool applicator and tray with flat area sloping towards reservoir.
2 Natural or synthetic lambswool applicator with built-in polish reservoir.
3 Cotton fringe mop, bucket and strainer.
4 Cotton mop and do-all bucket.
5 Solid wax pressurized applicators.

When a bucket or tray is used the applicator is dipped into the tray or bucket of polish and then squeezed or strained so that polish is retained in the heel of the mop or applicator. Polish is applied in straight flat strokes or, if using cotton do-all mops, in overlapping figure-of-eight strokes.

Applicators or mops used for polish application should only be used for this purpose. After use they must be thoroughly cleaned, wrung or squeezed and stored with the head uppermost.

Box sweepers

These are manually operated mechanical sweepers designed for the removal of spillages or light cleaning of small carpeted areas. A friction roller drives a brush as the machine is pushed over the floor, dislodging soil and carrying it into the soil pan of the machine.

Spray bottles

These are lightweight containers that deliver a fine mist of water or cleaning solution through a fine nozzle. Particularly when used for spray cleaning, it is essential that the nozzle is properly adjusted and free from partial blockage. The nozzle must be cleaned after use by spraying water through it.

Cable drums

Drums are used for efficient storage and transportation of extension cables. It is essential that they are frequently checked. In use all cables must be wound off the drums. Failure to do this

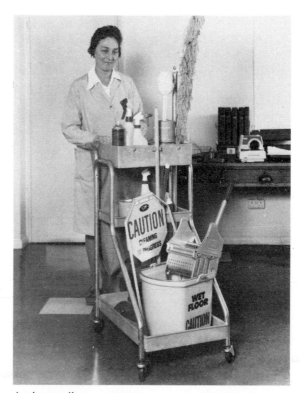

Laden trolley

will result in the cable heating up and eventually fusing.

Abrasive pads

Non-woven nylon pads suitable for the removal of localized heavily impacted soil by abrasion. Pads with different abrasive properties are produced.

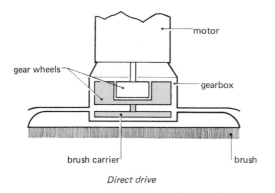

Direct drive

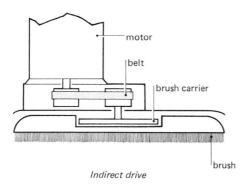

Indirect drive

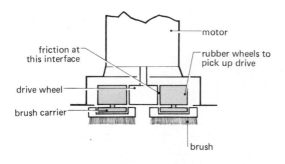

Friction drive

Figure 42　*Scrubber polishers, methods of power transmission*

Wire wool and soap-filled scouring pads should never be used. Particles of iron remaining on a surface will result in rust, making it then necessary to remove rust stains. Soap-filled pads produce a highly polished finish consisting of soap, soil and fine metal particles.

To clean the edges of a floor, pads are available to fit a piece of equipment called an edging tool.

Trolleys

Trolleys are ideal for the efficient removal and carriage of cleaning equipment and materials, linen and replacements and the collection of rubbish. They will eliminate time wasted in assembling equipment at a work location or moving from one place to another.

Scrubber polishers

These are machines designed for scarifying, scouring, scrubbing, buffing, burnishing and spray maintenance.

Principles

The machines consist of one, two or three rotating heads to which a variety of brushes, pads and scouring and scarifying assemblies may be fitted. The heads are driven usually by electric motors, but petrol, propane and air are used. Power is generally transmitted from the motor to the heads by one of three methods:

Direct drive　The motor is situated over the head, power being transmitted via a gear box.

Indirect drive　The motor is situated off-centre or to the rear of the head, power being transmitted via a belt.

Friction drive　The motor drives a wheel or spindle which transmits drive to the brushes.

Depending on the machine specification and the type of brush, pad or assembly fitted, a number of jobs may be carried out:

- *Buffing* The action of the bristle tips of a brush or the surface of a pad on a surface creates a gloss finish. In the case of a surface to which a polish has been applied it will involve the generation of local heat to harden waxes and resins.
- *Scrubbing* The bristle tips of a brush or the surface of a pad abrade and cut the soil to remove it.
- *Burnishing* Tips of a brush or the surface of a pad abrade and cut a surface to create a smooth surface with a gloss finish. In the case of a surface to which a polish has been applied it will involve the removal of a surface layer (or layers) of polish.
- *Spray cleaning* Bristle tips of a brush or the surface of a pad abrade and cut the soil from a surface. It differs from scrubbing in that only a fine mist of cleaning solution is applied to the floor and a thin film with a gloss finish is formed on the surface. It can be used to maintain an unpolished floor or a floor protected by a hard polish, i.e. a metallized or a non-metallized dri-bright polish.
- *Scarifying* Bristle tips or the edge of a cutting tool cut into impacted soil removing it by means of a chisel-like action.
- *Spray burnishing* Essentially similar to spray cleaning but the term is applied to the maintenance of floors where a buffable or semi-buffable polish has been applied and the bristle tips of a brush or the surface of a pad remove both soil and a surface layer of polish to leave a smooth glossy surface. Resins and waxes in the maintenance product form part of the restored finish.

Types of machine

Single brush machines have a single rotating head driven by an electric, petrol or propane motor or by compressed air. Transmission of power to the head may be direct or indirect. Machines are available to drive brushes, pads or assemblies, from 28 to 60 cm, at speeds which fall broadly into four categories:

Slow	120 – 175 rpm
Standard	175 – 300 rpm
High	300 – 500 rpm
Super	1000 rpm

Two-speed machines are also available. Machines intended for heavy-duty scrubbing and scarifying or for high-speed buffing or spray maintenance require more powerful motors than standard speed machines of corresponding size. Backward or forward movement of the machines is affected by the direction of travel of the operative, whilst a sideways movement can generally be affected by moving a fixed handle or fork up or down to transfer the weight of the machine onto the front or back of the brush or pad thus causing the machine to be pulled to the left or right depending on the direction of rotation of the brush. A sideways movement cannot be effected if, when in use, the weight is divided between the brush and a set of wheels.

Single-brush machines are generally subject to some degree of pull on the handle, particularly in the case of faster machines and especially when starting. This pull may be partially eliminated by an offset motor, or the use of dampening devices to counteract the effect of brush torque.

Two-brush machines have two counter-rotating brushes fitted side by side. They are usually designed for polishing or for carpet shampooing, and are only suitable for relatively small areas. The dead space between the brushes is usually considered a disadvantage.

This type of machine should not be confused with scrubber driers many of which have a two-brush arrangement.

Three-brush machines have three rotating heads driven by an electric, propane or petrol motor or by compressed air. The motor is centrally mounted, power being transmitted to the head via a belt. The heads are mounted on a turntable independent of the motor mounting. When starting, or when the brushes experience resistance, the turntable counter rotates, thus eliminating pull on the handle.

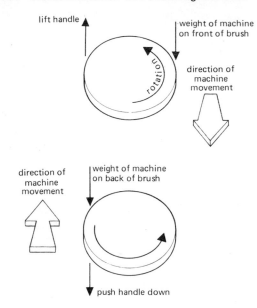

Figure 43   *Sideways movement with a scrubber polisher*

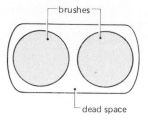

Figure 44   *Dead space of a two-brush machine*

and it may tend to bind with the floor and therefore overload the motor. Pads of an open construction are less durable but more absorbent, thereby reducing the frequency of pad changing, the likelihood of soil being thrown off and the possibility of overloading the motor.

Machines are available with speeds of up to 900 rpm and a working diameter of up to 76 cm.

Three brushes enable the angle of attack between the bristles and a surface to be altered as the machine passes over a particular point, thus increasing the effectiveness of the machine.

Equipment

Brushes, pads, sanding discs and scarifying assemblies are used for a variety of purposes, but the actual tasks that can be performed by a machine will be related to the speed and power of the motor. Table 22 shows the major tasks and the brushes, pads and assemblies that can be used with reference to speed.

Pads are designed to be suitable for particular tasks and to be used at particular speeds. They differ in their abrasive properties and density of construction. Spray maintenance pads in particular must be absorbent as well as abrasive. Densely constructed pads are durable but less absorbent. Once the surface of a pad is filled with soil it will not clean the floor. It will throw off soil

Three-brush scrubber polisher

Table 22   *Pads, brushes and assemblies used in conjunction with scrubber polishers*

Task	Slow	Standard	High
General-purpose cleaning or scrubbing	*Brushes* Nylon Polypropylene *Pads* Green	*Brushes* Nylon Polypropylene *Pads* Green	
Carpet shampooing	*Brushes* Soft nylon		
Heavy-duty scrubbing	*Brushes* Polypropylene Nylon *Pads* Black	*Brushes* Polypropylene Nylon *Pads* Black	
Scarifying	*Brushes* Crimped steel Bronze (non-sparking) Twisted steel *Assembly* Steel cutting tools mounted in groups on a wooden platform		
Carpet skimming Bonnet buffing	White pad Bonnet	White pad Bonnet	
Buffing	*Brushes* Gumati *Pads* Tan White (high sheen)	*Brushes* Gumati *Pads* Tan White (high sheen)	*Brushes* Gumati *Pads* Tan White (high sheen)

(continued)

Table 22 — *continued*

Task	Slow	Standard	High
Spray cleaning Spray burnishing	*Brushes* Spray clean brush	*Brushes* Spray clean brush	*Brushes* Spray clean brush
	Pads Purple	*Pads* Purple	*Pads* Gold (light duty) Red (medium duty) Blue (heavy duty)
Spray stripping	*Pads* Brown	*Pads* Brown	*Pads* Brown
Sanding	Abrasive discs (various grades of nylon mesh coated with silicon carbide)		
Burnishing	*Brush* Crimped steel	*Brush* Crimped steel	
	Pad Steel wool Green	*Pad* Steel wool Green	*Pad* Red Blue

The table is not intended to include all the possible varieties of pads, brushes and assemblies available. It includes those pads, etc., most commonly encountered and provides a comprehensible framework on which the selection of pads, etc., can be based.

Superspeed machines generally utilise a white pad for buffing and a red pad for burnishing.

In general, the heavier the soiling, the more abrasive the pad required to carry out cleaning. However, for broadly similar tasks, the pads used in conjunction with high-speed machines will generally be less abrasive than those used with slower machines.

When selecting pads for the spray burnishing of floors it must be appreciated that the more abrasive the pad and the faster the machine, the greater the amount of polish removed during cleaning. In order to reduce the frequency with which further coats of polish need be applied, the correct choice of cleaning agent and method of use is essential.

Pads are fitted to the machine via a drive disc, the lower surface of which comprises one of a number of different substances, e.g. Velcro strips, studded rubber, creped synthetic rubber, or numerous short nylon bristles. Pads are generally more expensive to use than brushes, but cleaning tasks are quicker. Brushes should, however, be used on uneven floors.

Suction assembly   When buffing, burnishing or using spray maintenance procedures, machines to which a skirt and suction unit can be fitted are preferred since they remove dust as it is produced.

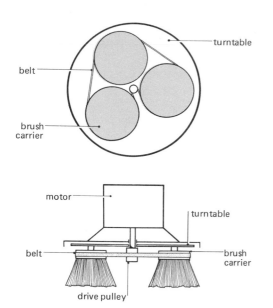

Figure 45 *Head of a three-brush scrubber polisher*

Antisplash guard Will prevent splashing when scrubbing.

Solution tanks Can be fitted to machines used for scrubbing.

Spray unit A spray unit fitted to a machine and operated at the handle will increase the rate of cleaning and reduce the danger of overwetting the floor when spray cleaning.

Selection

The characteristics of single-brush machines that will influence their use in particular situations include the following:

Weight The suitability of a machine for a particular task depends on the weight acting on the unit area of brush or pad. For the same brush diameter, the heavier the machine the greater the weight acting on the unit area of brush and the greater the diameter of the brush the greater the preferred working weight. The preferred working weights on a brush or pad for various tasks are

given in Table 24. In general the weight should be sufficient to ensure contact between the surface being cleaned and the bristle tips, pad or edge of cutting tool. The working weight of some machines can be reduced when required by dividing the weight of the machine between its wheels and the brush.

Motor The power of the motor will influence the type and amount of work which can be carried out in unit time. For heavy-duty cleaning or high brush speeds and for general cleaning, motors of 600–1500 W and 500–700 W respectively are suitable. The larger the brush the faster the brush speed, and the more heavy-duty the cleaning the more powerful the motor must be. However, machines designed for high speed cleaning despite their larger motors are not generally suitable for heavy-duty cleaning.

Brush speed The faster the brush speed the greater the work performance of a machine but this is subject to the power of the motor and the type of cleaning to be undertaken. Table 24 gives the preferred brush speeds for various tasks.

Size of head The larger the head, the higher the work performance of the machine. By doubling the diameter of the head, the floor area that can be covered in unit-time will be quadrupled.

Work performance The maximum possible work performance of a machine will depend on the weight, brush speed and size of brush. For a rotary machine they are approximately related by the following equation:

$$\text{Work rate} = 0.005 \, D^2 \sqrt{R} \, \sqrt[3]{W} \, \text{m}^2/\text{hr}$$

where D is the diameter of the brush in centimetres, R the brush performance in revolutions per minute and W the working weight in kilogrammes.

If the type of cleaning tasks undertaken and the degree of congestion of an area are also considered, some indication of the work performance of a machine in different situations can be determined. Table 23 indicates the

Table 23 *Work performance of single-brush scrubber polishers*

Brush diameter		Weight, kg	Maximum brush speed, rpm	Maximum work performance, m²/hr (approx)	Factor*	
Cm	Inches				Task	Congestion
60	24	66	400	1,500	Buff x 1	Light x 1
48	19	48	400	850	Spray clean/ burnish x 0.75	Moderate x 0.75 Heavy x 0.5
38	15	39	400	550	Spray strip x 0.3	
38	15	28	300	450	Light scrub x 0.5	
38	15	25	160	300	Deep scrub x 0.4	
38	15	30	400	500	Scarify x 0.4	

*Multiplication factors are guides only. In practice, they depend very much on the situation.

maximum work performance of some machines together with factors that they may be multiplied by to indicate performance under various conditions.

Safety A dead man's handle ensures that machines will only be operable when actually held by an operative with the handle in the working position.

Overload protection An automatic cut-out which operates when there is a current overload of the motor.

Portability Although all machines are fitted with wheels, only the lightest can be easily moved from one level to another in a building via a staircase.

Manoeuvrability In congested areas smaller machines can be negotiated around obstructions more easily than large machines and in such areas the work performance may be higher using a smaller machine. An offset motor may make it possible to gain access to floors beneath furniture or fittings.

Power source Petrol- or gas-driven machines are not generally suitable for indoor use. Low-voltage machines are used where an electrical hazard may arise. Air-driven machines are used where a safety hazard may arise or where electrical interference may be a problem.

Method of use

The method of use will be dictated by the type of machine, i.e. the tasks to be performed. In all situations safety and general precautions must be observed.

Most single-brush machines are made to move from side to side by gently raising or lowering the handle to transfer the weight of the machine on to the front or back of the brush while walking slowly backwards or forwards. For three-brush machines and divided-weight single-brush machines the side-to-side action is omitted.

Cleaning is carried out backwards or forwards. The former is often preferred to prevent walking on a wet or cleaned floor. The speed at which an operator can walk and the number of passes to be made over the same area of floor are governed by the performance characteristics of the machine, the task, the degree and nature of the soil and the standard required. With buffing and spray

Table 24 *General characteristics of single-brush machines suitable for particular tasks**

Task	Working weight, kg	Power of motor	Brush speed	Effect of using incorrect machine
Scarify	55 to 65+	High	Slow	Too light: cleaning is ineffective or slow
Heavy-duty scrubbing	45+	High	Slow	Low power: cleaning is ineffective or slow and motor may overload
Light scrubbing	30 to 40+	Moderate	Slow or standard if splashguard fitted	Too fast: splashes when scrubbing
Carpet shampooing	30 to 40+	Moderate	Slow	Too light: bounces over surface Too heavy: overloads and may damage carpet Low power: overloads Too fast: bounces over surface
Spray maintenance Burnishing Buffing	30 to 40+	High or moderate	High/super or standard	Too light: cleaning is slow Too heavy: removes too much polish if spray burnishing Low power: overloads Too slow: too labour-intensive, when buffing takes time to generate heat to harden waxes and resins and create gloss
Carpet skimming	30 to 40	Moderate	Standard	Too light: bounces over surface Too heavy: overloads Low power: overloads Too fast: bounces over surface

*When it is not practical to have machines to suit all jobs, for most purposes, other than heavy duty scrubbing or scarifying, a standard speed machine with a reasonably powerful motor at 30-40 Kg in weight will carry out most tasks reasonably well.

maintenance tasks the faster the machine, the fewer the number of passes required and the faster the operator can walk. When using high speed machines there is a danger that, if a pad is allowed to remain in contact with the same area of floor too long, friction burns will result.

Care must be taken not to knock or splash furniture and skirting boards. The former largely depends on experience and using a machine related to the prevailing circumstances. The latter can be prevented by using splash guards.

Overwetting of a floor should be avoided when scrubbing or carrying out spray maintenance tasks.

To prevent wobble, pads fitted to drive discs must be centralized.

To prevent soil being thrown off, ineffective cleaning and possible overloading of the motor, brushes must be cleaned and pads changed or turned over when no longer absorbent.

Suction units fitted to a machine when buffing or carrying out spray maintenance will eliminate need for subsequent sweeping and control the production of dust.

In addition to all safety precautions, the following points must be observed:

1 Never fit pads or dusters under brushes.
2 When carrying out wet cleaning methods, ensure that either the area is closed or cordoned off or a dry passage is left and indicated by warning notices.

Care of equipment

Care of equipment includes:

- Not using underpowered machines for heavy-duty cleaning.
- Removal of brushes and drive discs from machine after use.
- Not leaving machine resting on brush.
- Emptying and washing out tanks and feed lines.
- Washing out pads and brushes (using a detergent if necessary).
- Placing brushes upside down or hanging when in storage.
- Wiping of all parts of machine, including cables.
- Coiling of cables around machine after use.
- Checking cables, flexes and rest of machine and reporting any defects.

British Standards

BS 5415: 1976, *Specifications for Safety of Electrical Motor Operated Industrial Cleaning Appliances. Part 1: General requirements. Part 2: Section 2.1: Floor polishing, scrubbing and/or carpet cleaning machines.*

Suction cleaners, driers and sweepers

In this section consideration is given to equipment that will remove debris, soil and/or water from a surface by suction. The main types are cylinders, canisters, upright sweepers and back-vacs.

Principles

The principles may be understood with reference to Figures 46–8, which show three of the main types of suction cleaner. In all types a motor drives an impeller which sucks air from an inlet creating a difference in pressure between the air within and outside the machine. Air drawn from the inlet passes through and out of the machine, whilst at the inlet air from the surrounding atmosphere is sucked in together with soil, debris or water picked up from a surface by the air.

Machines differ principally in the way in which they collect soil. There are two categories: those employing the sac principle in which the air flow through the machine passes the motor, soil being trapped by a paper sac or cloth bag situated in front or behind the motor, and those employing the container principle in which the air flow by-passes the motor, soil or water being deposited in a container.

Types of machine

Cylinders generally employ the sac principle and are suitable for most tasks involving light-duty suction cleaning. Soil and debris are trapped in a paper sac enclosed by a cloth bag situated between the machine inlet and the motor. The walls of the sac and bag filter the air to remove fine particles of soil. The air flows past the motor housing leaving the machine at an outlet behind the motor. The fast flow of air from the outlet will be noisy and may blow dust and bacteria from surfaces behind the machine into the surrounding environment. A filter/diffuser fitted to the outlet will remove very

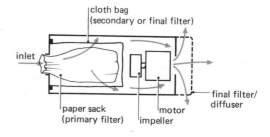

Figure 46 *Section through a cylinder suction cleaner*

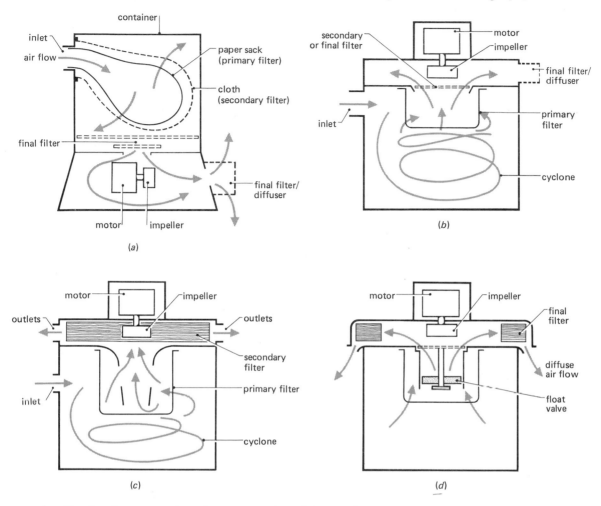

Figure 47   *Sections through various types of canister suction cleaner*

fine particles of soil and bacteria by filtration and reduce air disturbance and noise by breaking up the flow of air from the outlet.

Canisters or tubs employ either the sac or container principle. Tubs employing the sac principle are suitable for most tasks involving light-duty dry suction cleaning. They are illustrated in Figure 47a and are similar to cylinder machines, but rotated through 90°. Generally a cloth filter is situated between the sac and motor housing and will be either a bag enclosing the sac or be stretched across the base of the container. A

fine filter may be positioned at a point between the container and motor housing or a filter/diffuser may be fitted at the outlet port.

Tubs employing the container principle are suitable for most cleaning tasks. The suitability of a machine for light- or heavy-duty suction cleaning, and the removal of wet or dry soil will depend on the actual model. They are illustrated in Figure 47b–d.

The motor is situated so that the air flow through the machine does not pass the motor, the exhaust outlets being positioned between the container and motor. These machines are designed to pick up either water or dry soil. Air entering the machine circles around the wall of the container, before passing through a primary filter. This circling of air is known as a cyclone and will be enhanced where the primary filter projects into the container, the filter tending to force the air around the wall. The cyclone will increase the distance travelled by the air before it passes through the filter, promoting the settlement of dry soil and the collection of water at the bottom of the container. Unlike the cylinder, the primary filter is not the principal means of removing soil from the air flow.

Although paper sacs can be fitted into this type of tub for dry work, they interfere with the efficiency of the machine. However, they can make the emptying and disposal of soil easier. From the container the air flow is via a primary filter constructed of cotton, Dralon or moleskin situated at the top of the container, by-passing the motor on its way to the outlet. Different filters will be required for wet and dry work.

Before the air leaves the machine it passes through a secondary filter and sometimes a tertiary filter. These filters may be situated between the primary filter and impeller (Figure 47b), between the impeller and the exhaust outlets (Figure 47c) or at the exhaust port (Figure 47d).

Air flow is broken up by either the air leaving the machine through several outlets (Figure 47c), the filter acting as a diffuser (Figure 47b) or the air passing out through a fine vent running around the underside of the impeller housing (Figure 47d). Machines to be used for wet work incorporate a float valve (Figure 47d) situated between the container and the impeller and motor housing. When the container is full the water forces the float upwards, thus shutting off the hole through which air is drawn and preventing more water from being picked up. Also available are suction units which may be fitted to any suitable container. These are particularly useful for the removal of debris and waste in workshops.

Uprights are generally designed for carpet cleaning. In order to dislodge soil from the carpet pile, a beater bar (or more usually a rotating brush) is included in the head of the machine. The brush or bar loosens the soil, thus increasing the amount of soil removed by the air drawn through the carpet pile. Machines may employ either the sac or container principle.

Figure 48 illustrates two machines employing the sac principle. That in Figure 48a consists of a cylinder machine linked to an independently powered brush; that in Figure 48b consists of a motor which drives both the suction unit and the brush or bar loosens the soil, thus increasing the sac may fill from the top or bottom.

Machines suitable for the vacuuming of large areas usually consist of an independently powered sweeper linked to a suction unit of the cylinder or canister type.

Back-vacs are particularly suitable for cleaning inaccessible areas or high walls, fixtures and fittings. They are similar to machines of the cylinder type, but are carried on the operative's back.

Equipment

Tools and other accessories are required, the range and type depending on the machine and its use. Cylinders and tubs intended for commercial

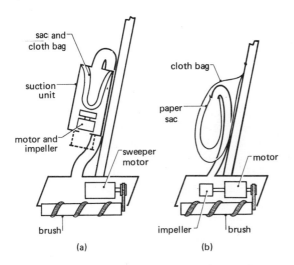

Figure 48 *Sections through upright suction cleaners*

Canister suction cleaner and power brush/wet pick-up and tools

or institutional use require:

1 Floor, wall, crevice, dusting, upholstery, carpet, radiator and venetian blind tools.
2 A lightweight hose incorporating a nylon or steel spiral. The hose should have a smooth internal wall, should not stretch since this tends to increase wear and should, preferably, incorporate an anti-twist device.
3 Extension tubes and angle bends to improve accessibility.

The following points should also be borne in mind:

- A power sweeper consisting of a rotating brush driven by its own motor should be used in preference to a carpet tool since this increases the effectiveness of soil removal and helps raise the pile.
- Suction cleaners intended for medium or heavy duty use require a similar range of equipment to that given above, together with brushes incorporating brass or steel, and a heavy-duty hose.
- The cleaning of electrical equipment or computer accessories will require the use of insulated and tapered nozzles.
- Tools incorporating a squeegee are used for the removal of water from hard surfaces.
- Upright machines intended for carpet cleaning may require a similar range of equipment to cylinders and tubs, but only if intended for multi-purpose use.

Selection

Cleaners have a number of characteristics that affect their suitability for use in particular situations.

Suction power is an indication of the potential work performance of a machine. It depends on vacuum and air flow and is usually measured in watts. The relationship is:

$$S = PA$$

where S is the suction power (in watts), P the suction pressure, or vacuum (in millimetres of water lift) and A the air flow (in litres per second). Suction pressure is the difference in air pressure between the surrounding air and the nozzle inlet as a result of air being sucked from the inlet towards the impeller. It is usually expressed in millimetres of water lift, i.e. the height of the column of water that the difference in pressure would support. The suction pressure of a machine depends on the motor and the cross-sectional area of the nozzle. The greater the cross-sectional area of the nozzle the lower will be the corresponding suction pressure. The more powerful the motor the greater the possible suction pressure which can be generated. It will be at a maximum when the nozzle is closed.

Air flow is the volume of air which will pass through the machine in unit time. It is expressed in litres per second and depends on the cross-sectional area of the nozzle, hose or machine inlet. The greater the minimum cross-sectional area the greater will be the possible air flow. It will be a maximum when the nozzle aperture is equal to or greater than the minimum cross-sectional area of the hose or inlet.

Suction power, and therefore work performance, is improved by increasing the minimum cross-sectional area of the inlet, hose or nozzle, to increase the possible air flow, and utilizing a more powerful motor to increase or maintain the suction pressure.

Suction power will determine the rate of cleaning and the type of soil that can be collected. Greater suction power permits the use of large nozzles, thereby increasing the rate of cleaning, or enables heavy soil or waste to be collected. The suction power of a machine is not always quoted. However, data for the type of motor, air flow (open) and suction pressure (closed) can be used as a reasonably effective guide to the work

performance of a machine. Table 25 includes the motor, air flow and suction pressure (vacuum) characteristics of machines suitable for specific uses. For machines to be used in hospitals, BS 5415 requires that domestic and commercial type machines have suction powers of 54 and 81 W, respectively, when the suction pressure is half that when the inlet to the machine is closed.

Suction power is also influenced by the method of soil collection, hose characteristics and degree of filtration. The extent to which the method of soil collection affects the suction power depends on whether the sac or container principle is employed. With the sac principle, fine particles of dust will block the pores of the sac and bag, thus inhibiting air flow and therefore reducing suction power. Suction power can be reduced by as much as 85% depending on the type of soil and will make it necessary to change the sac when it is less than half full to maintain adequate suction power. Where the container principle is employed, the cyclonic air flow ensures that the rate at which filter pores are blocked by fine soil particles is much reduced, allowing suction power to be maintained. The inclusion of a paper sac in a machine designed to produce a cyclonic air flow will significantly reduce the suction power.

The influence of hose characteristics on machine performance will depend on the length and nature of the inside wall and the occurance of air leaks at joints between the machine and nozzle. Long hoses, internal ridges or air leaks will reduce suction power, long hoses and ridges increasing resistance to air flow.

The degree of filtration will influence air flow and therefore suction power. Filters inhibit the flow of air through the machine. Where a greater degree of filtration is required, a more powerful motor will be required to generate a vacuum and air flow equivalent to that produced by machines which include less filtration.

Air velocity is the speed at which air is sucked over a surface into a nozzle. A low velocity (10–20 m/sec) may be sufficient to dislodge loose soil. A high velocity (70–80 m/sec) will be required to dislodge embedded soil. The velocity depends on

Table 25 *Characteristics of suction cleaners to be used in particular situations*

Use	Type	Motor power, W	Noise, dB(A)	Weight, kg	Capacity, litres	Vacuum, mmH$_2$O	Air flow, litres/sec	Brush/squeegee width, cm	Filteration stages
Domestic Institution Commercial	Cylinder	700	50	8	6	1,600	35	30	2 or 3
Domestic Institution Commercial Light industry	Container (dry suction)	750	60	10	15	2,000	40	30	2, 3 or 4
	Container (wet or dry suction)	1,500	65	25	30	2,000	55	30 (brush) 50 (squeegee)	2 or 3
Institution Commercial Industry	Back-vac	900	70	6	10	2,000	35	—	2 or 3
Light industry	Container (wet or dry)	2,500	70	60	60	2,500	130	—	2 or 3
Institution Commercial	Small carpet sweeper	500	65	10	6	600	35	30	2
	Large carpet sweeper	1,500	65	50	40	2,000	40	70	2 or 3

Note: the figures give a broad indication of the required characteristics of machines at the upper end of the range of each type.

the size of the nozzle and the suction power of the machine. The smaller the nozzle or the greater the maximum suction power of a machine, the greater will be the air velocity.

Filtration will remove from the air passing through a machine fine soil particles or bacteria that are not trapped by a paper sac or deposited in a container. The degree of filtration required depends on the intended use of a machine. In hospitals an efficiency of 60% (BS 5415) with respect to particles in the size range 0.2 to 2 μ is required. In computer rooms, industries handling hazardous materials, e.g. asbestos, and in other situations where a clean environment is required, still higher standards of filtration are necessary.

Filters that remove particles of 1 μ or greater with 100% efficiency, and all particles with an efficiency of 99.995%, meet the highest standards required, but the use of machines whose filtration efficiency exceeds the actual standards required will involve unnecessary expense.

Filtration can be in two, three or four stages. Two-stage filtration consists of a paper sac enclosed by a cloth bag. Machines using this method are suitable for general use. Three-stage filtration includes a paper sac, a filter of cotton, Dralon or moleskin and a third filter of foam, glass fibre or other material. Many machines using this system will meet the highest standards of hygiene required. Four-stage filtration consisting of a paper sac, cloth, impact and HEPA (High Efficiency Particle Air) filters meets the highest standards of hygiene.

However many stages of filtration are used, the largest possible surface area of filter is required in order that maximum suction power is maintained for as long as possible.

Air disturbance To prevent disturbances of dust on a surface the air flow from a machine must be of low velocity and above ground level. The outlet or final filter should be designed to diffuse the air flow. Where air disturbance may be a particular problem, machines to which special diffusers can be fitted are available.

Sweepers Soil in carpets is generally embedded so that suction alone will not be enough to remove it. Upright machines specially designed for carpet sweeping incorporate a brush rotating at up to 5,000 rpm to physically dislodge the soil. In the case of larger machines the rotating brush will help to propel the machine.

Noise A noise level of 70 dB(A) or less is preferred and is a requirement for hospitals. Where lower levels of noise are required, machines are available to which sound suppressors may be fitted to reduce the sound to 60 dB(A), a level equivalent to normal speech.

Suppression Machines should meet the requirements of BS 800 (1977). Machines that interfere with computer, monitoring and similar equipment must not be used in those situations where they occur.

Container or sac capacity The size of the container or sac is usually related to the suction power and hence intended use of a machine. The larger the machine, the larger the container required. A large container will require less frequent emptying, but may present problems unless the equipment includes a mechanical aid to emptying.

Portability Machines weighing less than 10 kg are regarded as being truly portable.

Work performance depends upon the width of the nozzle or head in contact with a surface, the speed at which it is drawn over the surface and the number of passes required to achieve the desired standard of soil removal. For a particular machine the speed and number of passes will depend on the type of surface, degree of soiling and the density of furnishings on that surface, but the greater the maximum possible suction power the larger the head which can be used, the greater the speed and lower the number of passes. Once the desired standard of cleaning has been established for a particular situation the work performance in square metres per hour of

Table 26 *Simple comparison of relative labour costs of carpet vacuum cleaning*

Brush width, cm	30	70
Vacuum (closed), mm of water lift	500	2,000
Air flow (open), litres/sec	40	40
Number of passes	3	1
Speed, m/hr	2,400	2,400
Area/hour, m^2/hr	240	1,680
Area of carpet (open uncongested), m^2	1,680	1,680
Time, hr	7	1
Frequency, per day	1	1
Total time per year (250 days), hr	1,750	250
Labour cost, £/hr	2.00	2.00
Labour cost per annum, £	3,500	500

different machines can be compared. The comparison is particularly relevant when considering the most appropriate machine for the vacuum cleaning of relatively large areas of carpet. The relative cost of using a small and large vacuum sweeper are very simply compared in Table 26.

Manoeuvrability In congested areas a small machine may negotiate obstacles more easily than a larger machine.

Power source Low voltage machines should be used where there is a possibility of an electrical hazard arising.

Type of tool The efficient removal of soil or water from a surface is dependent on air flowing over that surface and the soil or water being lifted into the air stream. To remove dry soil from a hard surface a tool fitted with bristles will ensure that a flow of air over that surface is maintained (see Figure 49a). On a soft porous surface, e.g. woven carpet or upholstery fabric, through which air can be drawn, the use of a tool fitted with bristles will result in air being drawn over the surface of the carpet pile or upholstery rather than through it. A tool with a hard flat surface is required to ensure that air is drawn through the pile or fabric, removing soil from within the pile or fabric and not just from the surface (see Figure 49b). A rotating brush will improve the efficiency of soil removal from a carpet by dislodging from the pile soil that might not otherwise be removed by the air stream (see Figure 49c). In the case of a stuck down carpet or one with an impervious backing, air cannot flow through the carpet and a rotating brush is essential to dislodge the soil from the pile and enable air to flow through the pile rather than just over the surface. When a carpet in this category has a particularly dense, short pile, e.g. flock or no-pile, it is virtually impossible to achieve a satisfactory flow of air through the pile using conventional suction cleaning equipment and tools. Consequently, suction cleaning is not particularly effective, other than to remove surface soiling, and other methods of cleaning are preferred (see Figure 49d).

To remove water from a hard surface a tool with a squeegee is required. For soft surfaces a tool with firm edges is required.

Method of use

This will be influenced by:

1 Type and position of surface to be cleaned.
2 Whether the soil is loose, embedded, wet or dry.
3 The type of machine.

Whatever the situation safety and general precautions must be observed (see page 150). In

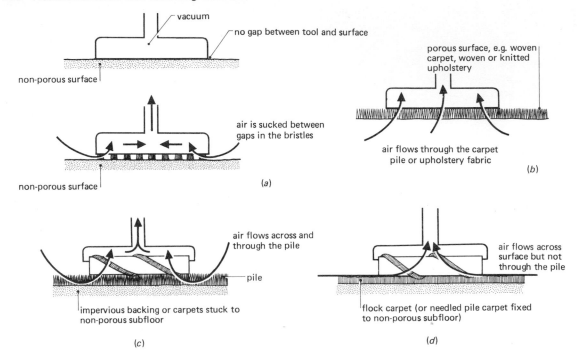

Figure 49   *Maintenance of air flow over a surface using different types of suction cleaner tool*

particular, the float valve on wet suction cleaners and the overload protection device must be checked whenever the machine is used.

To remove dry soil from floors a hard floor tool, carpet tool, power head or the machine as appropriate are moved over each section of floor, the number of passes depending on the degree of soiling and the machine. The height of the tool or machine above the floor should be adjusted to suit the type of floor. To daily clean a carpet up to three passes over each section of floor may be required, moving the tool or machine backwards and forwards and finishing with a pass in the same direction. Cleaning may be carried out moving forwards or backwards. The latter is used where it is preferred not to walk on the cleaned surface and the former where the surface can be cleaned satisfactorily in a single pass. It is usual to start at a point furthest from and finish at the exit.

To remove dry soil from a vertical surface or surface above floor level the tool appropriate to the situation is moved deliberately over the surface in strokes as long as possible, overlapping adjacent strokes and taking care not to scatter dust into the atmosphere.

To remove water from a hard surface it is essential that the squeegee blade is just in contact with the surface. The removal of water from a hard floor is carried out by moving the tool forwards over the surface at a speed which will remove all the water from a particular section in a single pass. When drying upholstery the tool is moved backwards and forwards over each section to leave it as dry as possible. To remove water from a carpet the tool is drawn backwards:

Care of equipment

Care of the equipment will include:

- Not using the machine if bag or container is full since this will overload the motor (indicated by a change in the sound of the motor).
- Removing all tools and accessories from the machine after use.

- Emptying of bags and containers.
- Cleaning and drying of the tank of wet suction cleaners.
- Cleaning of all tools and accessories.
- Wiping the outside of the machine and cable.
- Not running over hoses and hanging up after use.
- Not pulling machine by hose.
- Not using the same hose for wet and dry suction cleaning.
- Coiling cable around machine after use.
- Changing of filters regularly.

British Standards

BS 3028: 1958, *Electric Vacuum Cleaners for Use in Hospitals.*
BS 5415: 1976, *Specification for Safety of Electrical Motor Operated Industrial Cleaning Appliances. Part 1: General requirements. Part 2: Section 2.2: Vacuum cleaners wet and/or dry.*

Spray extraction machines

Spray extraction machines are used to restore the surface appearance of carpets, upholstery and curtains, to remove the more deeply embedded soil not removed by suction cleaning alone and for the application of some soil-retardent finishes. They include hot water extraction machines which are principally used for the cleaning of carpets and to a lesser extent for upholstery and curtains, and solvent extraction machines which are used principally for the cleaning of upholstery and curtains and to a lesser extent for carpets.

This section deals principally with hot water extraction machines. Solvent extraction machines are similar in most respects and reference is made to them where appropriate.

Principles

Spray extraction involves subjecting the surface to be cleaned to a high-pressure stream or mist of cleaning solution delivered from either static or rotating jets. Soil can be removed in upto four

ways:

1. The cleaning solution has a detergent or solvent action.
2. The jet of solution causes a mutual scrubbing of the fibres.
3. The force with which the jets of solution strike the fibres dislodges soil adhering to them.
4. A revolving brush fitted to the cleaning tool scrubs the fibres.

The soil and cleaning solution is subsequently carried from the surface by suction. Cleaning is carried out by drawing a cleaning tool incorporating both jets and suction inlet over the surface. The tool is linked to equipment which generates the high-pressure stream of water and suction.

Machinery and tools

Spray extraction machines consist of four essential parts:

1. A solution tank (which may be heated) to hold the cleaning solution.
2. A recovery tank to collect the soiled solution.
3. A pump to generate the high-pressure stream of solution.
4. A suction unit to remove soiled solution from the surface.

The unit is usually fitted with wheels or is lorry mounted. The machine is linked via a hose to a cleaning tool of which there are several types.

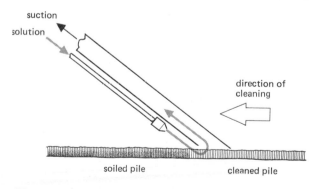

Figure 50 *Injection of solution and removal of soil by spray extraction machine*

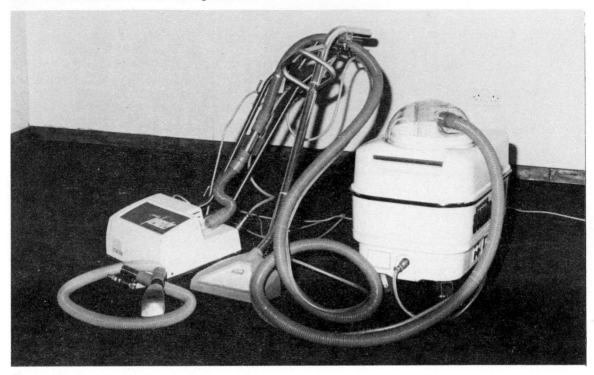

Hot water extraction machine and tools

Hand tools, used for cleaning upholstery, curtains, stairs and inaccessible areas, have a working width of approximately 5 to 20 cm and are fitted with one or two jets. Some upholstery tools are designed to ensure low cleaning solution pressures on the upholstery.

Wands, used for carpet cleaning have a working width of up to 50 cm and are fitted with a number of static jets (usually four to eight). They are weighted to improve contact with the carpet, thereby increasing the effectiveness of cleaning and removal of the solution. Heavy wands usually include rollers which assist in drawing them over the carpet and improve the evenness of the clean. Lighter wands also require the operative to apply pressure to maintain close contact with the carpet.

Floor tools with power-operated brushes, used for carpet cleaning, have a working width of up to 50 cm and are fitted with up to eight static jets. They are heavily weighted to ensure contact between the brush and carpet pile and the suction inlet and the pile.

Floor tools with power-operated rotating jets, used for carpet cleaning, have a working width of up to 50 cm and are fitted with four jets mounted at right angles to each other (see Figure 51).

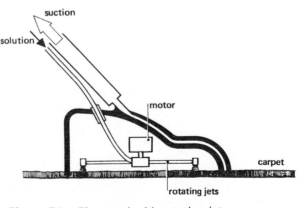

Figure 51 *Floor tool with rotating jets*

Rotation of the jets enables streams of solution to be directed at an area of pile from numerous angles, thereby increasing the effectiveness of the cleaning process.

Hand sprays are used for the application of soil-retardent finishes and are similar to the lances used for high-pressure washing.

Wet and dry suction tools enable spray extraction machines to be used, if required, in a similar way to wet or dry suction cleaners.

Selection

A number of machine characteristics will influence their suitability for use in various situations.

Cleaning solution pressure will effect the degree of penetration, the amount of soil removed and the work performance.

The solution pressure will depend on the volume of water pumped in unit time through the jets and on their shape and size. In general the greater the volume of water and the smaller the jet orifice the greater the pressure. However, it must be appreciated that it is the pressure at the surface being cleaned that is important and that for a given flow rate the pressure at the surface can be varied using different sizes and shapes of jet.

The higher the pressure the greater the penetration of a surface and the greater the amount of soil that can be removed from the constituent fibres. Higher pressure can involve fewer passes of a tool and the drawing of the tool more quickly over a surface, resulting in higher work performances. High pressures are preferred for carpet cleaning, although the use of very high pressures must be related to the type of carpet. A solution pressure of 40 psi is generally considered to be the minimum necessary to achieve satisfactory results.

For upholstery cleaning, subjecting the surface to high pressures can cause excessive penetration, wetting of the stuffing and result in prolonged drying times and possible browning (surface discoloration). Accordingly the combination of tool and machine used should be such that the solution pressure on the upholstery surface is relatively low. Pressures of around 30 to 50 psi will give satisfactory results.

Type of tool used will affect the amount of soil removed, the evenness of cleaning, the extraction of soiled solution, operative fatigue and work performance.

Wands with fixed jets can remove about 40% of the soil in a typical woven or tufted carpet, the jet of water only attacking the fibres at a limited number of angles. Heavy wands are often more effective and give a more even clean, better extraction of soiled solution and less operative fatigue.

Tools with rotating jets rotating brushes can remove up to 60% of the soil in a woven or tufted carpet. When very high pressures are used the type of jets used should be related to the type of carpet. The height of the tool in relation to the carpet pile should be adjustable to achieve the required depth of cleaning and maximum extraction of solution. Tools with rotating jets or power-operated brushes will often achieve a satisfactory standard of cleaning, with a single pass and drawing the tool relatively quickly over the carpet, resulting in higher work performances and less operative fatigue than wands.

Suction power will affect the percentage of solution recovered from a surface and the drying time.

The recovery of solution is normally expressed as a percentage of the total amount of solution applied. The greater the suction power the greater the percentage recovery. It must be emphasized that if a carpet or upholstery has been overwetted such that the backing or stuffing is saturated, no amount of suction will be effective and the drying times will be lengthy.

Machines generating a vacuum (closed) of approximately 2,000 mm of water at air flows of 40 to 50 litre/sec will give recovery rates of over 80% and possible drying times of 4 to 8 hr. Machines generating a vacuum of up to 5,000 mm of water at air flows up to 150 litre/sec will give recovery rates of over 90% and possible drying times of 2 to 4 hr.

The volume of cleaning solution will affect both drying time and cleaning efficiency. The amount of solution delivered per unit area of surface will depend upon the volume of water delivered through the jets in unit time, the number of passes and the speed of drawing the tool over the area. Depending on the combination of machine and tool used the flow rate will range from about one to 10 litre/min. The fewer the number of passes and the faster the tool is drawn over the surface, the lower the volume of solution applied. But the volume of solution delivered must be sufficient to suspend the soil.

For carpets, high pressure in combination with a powered brush or rotating head can reduce the amount of water applied, cleaning being achieved by fewer passes and drawing the tool more quickly over the carpet.

Work performance of a machine and tool will depend on the working width of the tool, speed at which it can be drawn over a surface, the number of passes required and the degree of soiling.

The wider the working width of a tool the greater the work performance, a greater area being covered in a single pass. The fewer the number of passes and the faster the tool can be drawn over a surface, the higher will be the work performance. These will be governed by the cleaning solution pressure, the type of tool and the degree of soiling. For heavily soiled carpets, a number of passes will generally be required.

Work performances of between 50 and 400 m²/hr are possible, depending on the type of machine, tool and degree of soiling.

Cost   When purchasing machines and tools their work performance must be related to their frequency of use and the area of carpet and units of upholstery or curtains to be cleaned. The additional cost of machines with very high work performances can be significantly greater than savings in labour costs alone.

Machines with very high work performances are normally purchased by contractors or by organizations with large areas of carpet to be cleaned. In other situations, a performance of 100 m²/hr is normally suitable.

Consideration should also be given to buying several smaller machines rather than one large or medium-sized machine and issuing each department with its own machine in much the same way as suction cleaners or scrubber polishers are issued.

Portability   Other than the smallest, spray extraction machines cannot be regarded as being portable. They are either designed to run on wheels or are lorry-mounted. Machines intended to be lifted and carried for short distances will usually weigh up to 100 kg. Lorry-mounted machines will be connected to cleaning tools by long extension hoses.

Solution and recovery tanks   The total capacity of the solution and recovery tanks will be similar and should be related to the volume of solution delivered per minute.

The recovery tank will be either filled directly or the soiled solution collected in buckets inserted into it. The latter has the advantage of enabling the machines to be more compact.

Solution tanks and recovery tanks filled directly should be fitted with a tap for emptying into a drain. An estimate of the frequency of filling and emptying can be obtained by dividing the quoted capacity of the tanks by the volume of solution delivered per minute. Used continuously, the frequency is normally once every 10 to 20 min. The lower the frequency the less time spent emptying and refilling.

Cleaning temperature and agents   The ability to heat and maintain cleaning solutions at high temperatures is not normally required for carpet cleaning. Accordingly, hot water extraction machines are frequently not fitted with a heater.

Low-foam neutral detergents are generally used for hot water extraction.

Solvent extraction machines utilize non-chlorinated organic solvents which are heated to high temperatures. The combination of high temperature and organic solvent enables rapid drying times to be achieved and eliminates many of the problems encountered in the cleaning of upholstery or curtains with water and detergents.

Ease of use Machines of up to about 100 kg can be moved fairly easily. Relatively short hoses can therefore be used to connect them to floor or hand tools. Large machines are most conveniently used if they are connected to the tools by long hoses. On large floor areas the complete machine can then be moved less frequently.

The heavier a floor tool the more effort required to pull it, even when fitted with a roller, but unless weighted tools are used, maintaining good contact between the carpet and the tool will result in operative fatigue.

Floor tools are normally designed to be pulled backwards. This makes it unnecessary to walk on a clean carpet and operative fatigue is less. Hand tools in some cases are designed to enable cleaning to be carried out whether they are pushed or pulled.

Carpet, upholstery and curtain cleaning requirements

In this section are summarized the essential requirements of machines and tools to be used for the cleaning of carpets, upholstery and curtains.

Carpets:

1 Cleaning solution pressures in excess of 30 to 50 psi are generally required. The use of very high pressures must be related to type of carpet.
2 The efficiency of soil removal and rate of cleaning, particularly of a heavily soiled carpet, will be increased by using high pressure and floor tools with either rotating jets or power-operated brushes.
3 On heavily soiled carpets the use of low pressures and wands may result in overwetting caused by passing the tool too slowly and too often over the carpet.

4 Suction power must be adequate to recover 80 to 90% of the cleaning solution. A vacuum of about 2,000 mm of water and an air flow of 40 to 50 litre/sec is required.
5 A heavy tool capable of height adjustment in relation to the pile will give a more even clean and better extraction.
6 Tepid cleaning solution will generally be required.

Upholstery:

1 To prevent shrinkage and browning it is essential that fabric and stuffing are not overwetted and that drying is rapid.
2 A low volume of cleaning solution should preferably be delivered per unit area of fabric.
3 The cleaning solution should be delivered at pressures which ought not to exceed 30 to 50 psi at the surface of the fabric to prevent excessive penetration.
4 Solvent extraction machines enable rapid drying times to be achieved and reduce the possibilities of shrinkage, browning and colour bleeding.
5 Suction power similar to that for carpets is required.

Curtains:

1 To prevent shrinkage and colour interchange between curtain and lining as a result of wetting it is essential that drying times be extremely rapid.
2 Solvent extraction machines are particularly suitable for the on-site cleaning of curtains. The possibility of shrinkage or colour problems is significantly reduced.
3 Hot water extraction using conventional detergents is generally limited in its applications.
4 A hand tool with a small notch (pleat tool) makes cleaning easier.

Use and care

The type of tool used in the extraction of carpets,

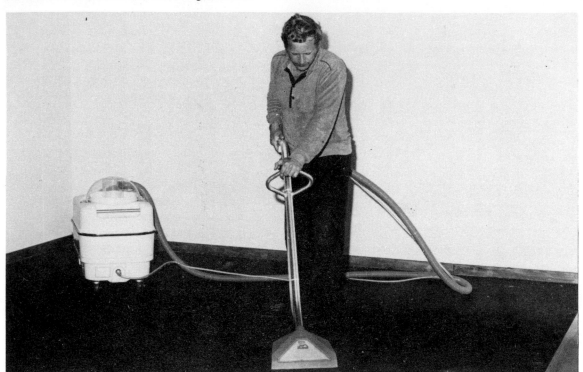

Hot water extraction of a carpet using a wand

upholstery or curtains influences the way in which cleaning is carried out.

To reduce the possibility of overwetting a carpet or upholstery, a 'pre-spotting' cleaning agent can be applied to the more heavily soiled areas with a hand spray before commencing extraction. This should eliminate the need for repeatedly passing the tool over the same area in order to achieve a satisfactory standard of appearance. Also the cleaning agent has time to act on the heavier soil before extraction is actually carried out.

It is essential that buckets or containers are not allowed to overflow when they are full or suction motors allowed to continue operating when the float valve is closed.

Carpets Wands are moved backwards and forwards over successive 1–1.5 m lengths of carpet. The more heavily soiled the area of carpet, the greater the number of passes required over each length. Solution is applied to the carpet and

pressure applied to the wand on the backward stroke. Even pressure is essential for an even clean.

Weighted wands, power-operated brushes and tools with rotating jets are normally drawn backwards over successive long lengths of carpet. The actual rate depends on the degree of soilage, the tool and the machine.

Just before completing a pass over a length of carpet, application of solution should be stopped in order that the suction inlet can be drawn over that last area of carpet to which solution has been applied. Failure to do so can result in excessive wetting of the carpet and the appearance of 'tide' marks.

The cleaning of each length of carpet should just overlap adjacent lengths. It is essential not to overwet the carpet by successively drawing the tool over the same area of carpet.

To reduce drying times and ensure that as much soil as possible has been removed from the carpet, the tool can be drawn over each length of carpet after the application of solution using suction only.

When a carpet has previously been shampooed a defoaming agent will be required in the recovery tank.

Upholstery The hand tool should be moved systematically over the surface of the fabric using long or short strokes (see Figure 52). If the short-stroke method is used, pressure can be applied as the tool is moved backwards and forwards or only when it is drawn backwards, depending on the type of tool used. Each area cleaned should be finished with a suction-only stroke.

Curtains The tool should be drawn systematically down successive lengths of curtain.

Drying times Assuming that cleaning has been carried out correctly, then the rate at which the surface will dry depends on environmental conditions. A warm, dry atmosphere and good ventilation are necessary if drying is to be as rapid as possible.

Care of equipment

This involves removal of all tools and accessories from the machine after use, emptying, cleaning and flushing with clean water of the solution and recovery tanks, cleaning and flushing of tools and the wiping of all exterior parts.

Centralized vacuuming

In centralized systems suction is generated at one point in a building. Soil is removed by suitable nozzles linked by detachable flexible hoses to vacuum points. It is then conveyed by a network of pipes to a central container. The system is expensive to install and is generally done at the construction stage. It does, however, offer a number of advantages:

1 It is extremely hygienic in that all the dust is carried away from the point of cleaning.
2 Maintenance costs are usually lower.

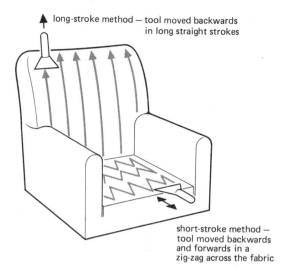

Figure 52 *Systematic use of a hand tool for upholstery cleaning*

3 It is instantly available.
4 Recovery of valuable waste can be more easily achieved.
5 Operative fatigue should be lower.
6 It can be safer in that there is less equipment to be left on floors.
7 Waste collected can be used as part of the fuel used for energy generation.

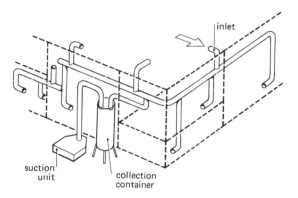

Figure 53 *Centralized vacuuming system*

Scrubber driers

These are machines capable of both scrubbing and drying a floor in the same pass and which may also be used for buffing. The principle is similar to that in individual suction driers or scrubber polishers and whenever relatively large areas are to be maintained they must be considered.

Motors are driven by propane, petrol, battery or electricity via a cable. Self-propulsion is achieved by drive wheels to which power is transmitted through an arrangement of gear wheels or gears and chain. Travelling speeds of up to 15 km/hr are possible, depending on the actual machine, but the actual working speed will be much lower than this and is determined by the degree of soiling, impaction and ease of accessibility.

Cleaning is achieved by one, two or three rotary brushes which may be driven directly via a rack and pinion arrangement or indirectly via a belt or gears and chain. Machines usually have one, two or variable brush speeds in the range 125 to 350 rpm. In some cases the position of the brush or brushes can be altered relative to the machine, as can the pressure of the brushes on a floor.

Some of the largest machines are fitted with cylindrical rather than rotary brushes and these also serve to collect debris.

Cleaning solution is fed to the brushes from a tank, the capacity of which is usually related to the work performance of the machine.

Soiled water is removed from the surface by a squeegee approximately one and a half times wider than the working width of the brushes. The squeegee may float enabling the machine to remove water from uneven floors. Suction pressures of 1,200–1,500 mm of water lift and an air flow of 30–40 litre/sec leave a surface clean and dry. The capacity of the collection tank is related to that of the cleaning solution tank. The tank may be pumped out via a hose or emptied from the bottom, in which case the tank may be removable from the rest of the machine to permit emptying where there are no drains accessible to the whole machine.

Operators may walk behind or ride on the machine depending on its size. Particularly in the

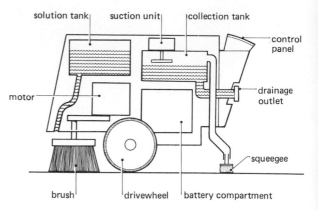

Figure 54 *Section through a scrubber drier*

case of larger machines the turning radius and width of the machine must be considered in relation to the width of access points, gangways, corridors and degree of congestion.

The work performance generally depends on the working width of the brushes and the speed of the machine. Although the degree of soilage will be important, a working speed of about 2 km/hr is a reasonable expectation. The work performance can be estimated from the relationship:

$$\text{Work performance} = \text{Brush width} \times \text{Working speed}$$

Table 27 compares the use of a scrubber drier with a scrubber polisher and suction drier indicating the financial benefits of using a scrubber drier for the maintenance of large areas.

Machines are available with theoretical work performances of up to about 10,000 m²/hr.

Scrubber drier/sweepers

These machines employ the principles described for scrubber driers and sweepers. They are suitable for large areas where both mechanical sweeping and scrubber drying are required.

Power sweepers

These are self- or manually propelled machines designed to remove debris and loose soil from roads, pavements, car parks and large areas of hard floor. There are a number of different types.

Pedestrian-driven sweeper

This consists of a battery- or mains-operated rotating broom which carries soil into a hopper. A side broom, suction unit and filters may be included in the specification. Work performances of 1,000–3,000 m²/hr can be achieved.

Petrol- or gas-driven, pedestrian-driven sweeper

This is a petrol- or gas-powered engine which drives a suction unit and brush. Soil is brushed into the air flow and collected in a large cloth sack situated behind the motor. These are suitable for the sweeping of pavements, car parks and similar areas. Work performances of 1,500–3,000 m²/hr can be achieved.

Self-propelled sweeper

This is a petrol- gas- or battery-powered machine, the power being transmitted to the drive wheels and a rotating broom which carries soil from a surface. The actual specification will depend on the individual machine but typical features will include:

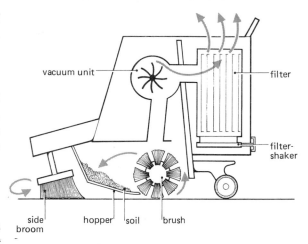

Figure 55 *Section through a self-propelled sweeper*

1 A side broom to carry debris from floor edges into path of main broom.
2 Soil thrown by brush to back of a hopper or on to an elevator which loads the hopper from the top.
3 A water spray or suction at the side broom to prevent the raising of dust clouds.
4 High-volume suction unit which sucks or blows air through a bank of filters as soil is deposited in the hopper.

Table 27 *Simple comparison of using different combinations of machines to scrub a floor*

	Scrubber polisher and suction drier		Scrubber drier, working speed 2 km/hr		
	Working width, cm		Working width, cm		
	38	76	50	100	150
Time to clean 1,000 m², hr	8	2	1	0.5	0.33
Time to clean 5,000 m² 50 times/year, hr	2,000	500	200	100	66
Annual labour cost at £2.00 per hour	£4,000	£1,000	£400	£200	£132

5   Filter shaken or air flow reversed to prevent blockages.

6   Hopper hydraulically lifted for purposes of emptying.

7   Work performance of up to 40,000 m²/hr possible, depending on the machine and type of soil.

Where relatively large areas require regular sweeping power sweepers should be considered. The most suitable machine for a particular situation will depend on:

- The power source.
- The work performance in relation to the size of area to be cleaned.
- The turning radius and width of the machine in relation to the width of access points, gangways, corridors and any congestion.

High-pressure washers

This equipment is designed to remove soil by subjecting a surface to water, steam, air or sand under pressure.

Principles

Water under pressure will physically dislodge soil. The process can be assisted by the use of hot water, steam or sand.

Equipment

There are two principal types:

Mobile washers consist of a header tank to maintain the supply of water, a cleaning agent reservoir, a pump and a heater if hot water or steam are to be generated. The extent to which the pressure, quantity of water and the temperature can be altered depends on the actual machine. The high-pressure stream of water is directed on to a surface via an operator-held lance. In the most widely used types of washer, cleaning agents are injected into the water after the pump and the solution applied under low pressure via the lance. Rinsing off is carried out under high pressure by switching the flow of water through a nozzle of smaller diameter.

Lances with different nozzles and fittings are used to vary the pressure, the angle of the jet, to inject sand and to mix steam and water where appropriate.

In-place washers A high-pressure stream of water is generated centrally and delivered to various points within the building by a system of pipes. The stream of water can be used in a number of ways to clean dirty surfaces or equipment.

A lance can be fitted at outlet points situated at various points through the building to clean floors, walls and exterior surfaces of equipment. Cleaning solution can be introduced into piping, tanks and equipment to clean the interior surfaces without the necessity of dismantling or operatives gaining physical access. The water may be simply circulated through the pipework, tanks, or equipment or be directed on to a surface via a spray head (static or revolving).

Factors influencing the efficiency of cleaning

Temperature Increases in temperature will generally increase the speed of cleaning. However, at temperatures above 60°C proteins will be baked and starch gelatinize, making their removal more difficult.

Hot water and steam will assist in the emulsification, and hence removal, of oils and grease. Hot water and steam can also be used for disinfection.

Steam has the advantage of no recoil, resulting in less operator fatigue but can be dangerous and must not be used on the moving parts of machines, otherwise lubricants may be removed.

Water quantity The greater the quantity of water delivered through a nozzle, the greater will be the pressure at the surface being cleaned. When lances are used, if the quantity of water delivered is less than 400 litre/hr the jet tends to break up before reaching the surface, if above 3,000 litre/hr the recoil is too great resulting in excessive operator fatigue. A range of 750 to 1,200 litre/hr is ideal.

High-pressure washer

Cleaning agents used include neutral and bactericidal detergents, acids, caustic and non-caustic alkalis, organic solvents and sand. Sand is most usually used for exterior cleaning providing no damage occurs as a result of its use. Cleaning agents may be applied before the use of the washer or they are injected into the jet of water.

Pressure An increase in pressure will generally increase the rate of cleaning. The pressure used, however, is governed by the type of surface and the soil to be removed. Lower pressures will be most suitable for lightly bound soil. High pressure may simply scatter the soil. The pressure at the surface will depend on the nozzle pressure, spray angle and distance from the surface. The nozzle pressure is regulated by the amount of water sprayed and the size of the outlet. The smaller the spray angle the greater the pressure, 25°, 25° to 50° and 50° to 80° being used for tightly bound, moderately bound and lightly bound soil, respectively. The ideal working distance is 10 to 30 cm. At closer distances recoil may be too great, and at greater distances the jet may break up.

Operator A skilled operator can increase efficiency by up to 50%.

Uses of high-pressure washers

When used in the situations listed, high-pressure washing can be as or more effective than traditional cleaning methods. It is usually less labour-intensive and therefore less expensive.

The choice of equipment, pressure, temperature and cleaning agents will depend on the nature and type of surfaces and equipment to be cleaned and on the type and degree of soiling.

Typical applications include:

- Cleaning of external walls.
- Routine cleaning and disinfection of hard surfaces and equipment in kitchen and other food premises.
- Periodic and regular deep cleaning of kitchens.
- Initial cleaning of kitchens and sanitary accommodation.
- Vehicle cleaning.
- Swimming pool cleaning and disinfection.

Utensil cleaners

Utensil cleaners are frequently used for the cleaning of small scale equipment and utensils in the kitchen. These consist of a cabinet in which the items to be cleaned are subjected to jets of high-pressure hot or cold water with or without a cleaning agent to physically dislodge soil. The water jets are produced by a rotating head situated at the bottom of the cabinet.

Tank cleaners

Tank cleaners are used in manufacturing industry to degrease plant and equipment by immersing the item in a solution or solvent of alkali, hot or cold, depending on the type of soil. The item to be cleaned is placed in a basket and lowered by an automatic hoist into a tank of cleaning solution, which may or may not be agitated. A second tank of solution linked to the first by a roller may be used for rinsing. When the solution in the first tank is very dirty the second tank is used for washing and the first refilled with cleaning solution and used for rinsing.

Ultrasonic cleaners

Ultrasonic cleaners are used for the cleaning of delicate equipment, for example, printed circuit boards, which will be damaged by other methods. The item to be cleaned is immersed in a solution tank containing organic solvent. Bubbles, generated by high-frequency sound waves, explode exerting a scrubbing action on the soil sticking to the surface.

Scarifying machines

Scarifying is used to remove both light and heavily impacted soil where scrubbing is ineffective. Soil is broken down by the chisel action of a wire brush or by a cutting tool.

Types of machine

One of two types of machine fitted with a scarifying tool can be used:

Heavy-duty scrubber polisher Single or three-brush machines with a brush weight of about 65 kg or more are used in conjunction with a scarifying assembly. Soil has to be removed by a second operation involving sweeping.

Self-propelled scarifier Typical machines consist of a revolving tool, a hopper into which the soil is thrown by the tool and a suction unit and filter to remove finer soil particles.

Assemblies and tools

Assemblies used in conjunction with rotary machines consist of a circular wooden plate into which widely spaced groups of crimped wire or onto which groups of steel cutting tools are fixed. The wide spacing is necessary to prevent clogging when removing wet soil.

The scarifying tool fitted to self-propelled machines is cylindrical and has either numerous crimped wires or a number of steel cutting tools. The crimped wire will be of steel or bronze. Bronze is used where wet cleaning methods or wet soil is

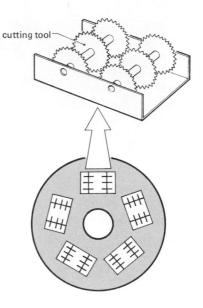

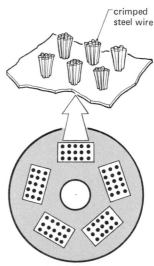

Figure 56 *Scarifying tools*

involved and where there is a danger if sparks are produced.

Crimped wire is used to remove less heavily impacted soil and steel cutting tools to remove very heavily impacted accumulations of soil.

Methods and uses

Where possible scarifying should be undertaken

under dry conditions. Although cleaning agents may be necessary the formation of a sludge can cause problems in its removal.

Self-propelled machines should be considered where larger areas are involved.

The use of crimped wire or steel cutting tools will depend on the type of soil.

Sanding machines

Sanding is used to remove the top layer of material from a surface, most usually a floor, by abrasion.

Types of machine and tools

Three types of machines may be used fitted with a suitable abrasive tool:

Belt sanders consist of an endless belt over which abrasive paper is fitted. Machines arc available in many sizes, the belt being driven by a petrol engine or electric motor. A vacuum unit and sac may be fitted to collect the dust produced. There is usually less risk of damage to the surface being sanded when this type of machine is used.

Orbital sanders consist of an oscillating head to which abrasive paper or a disc is fitted. They are suitable for small tasks, i.e. the fine finishing of a surface.

Rotary sanders are normally slow or standard speed scrubber polishers, under which abrasive paper or discs are used. A vacuum unit and skirt can be fitted to collect the dust produced. In unskilled hands there is a particular risk of damaging the surface by producing swirl marks.

Abrasive tools Three types of tool may be used: nylon mesh discs covered by an abrasive finish, glass paper and carborundum paper. The coarseness of the paper or disc is expressed as the grit number, the higher the number the finer it will be.

Methods of use

Sanders are used to prepare new wood-group floors

Floor-sanding machine

for sealing, to remove seals and to renovate old floors. Sanding should be undertaken by skilled personnel to prevent the risks of scoring or oversanding the surface. If used on a parquet or cork carpet particular care must be exercised.

The process of sanding is a dry one and if possible a machine that will remove and collect dust as it is produced should be used. The degree of abrasion required will depend on the surface but a fine disc or paper will be used after course or medium grades to produce a relatively smooth finish. After sanding, dust is removed by suction cleaning. Before the application of a seal or polish the surface should be damp mopped.

Dishwashers

Dishwashers include a range of machines designed for cleaning crockery, cutlery, glass, food preparation utensils or specifically for glass.

Principles

With the exception of bar-type glass washers, cleaning is achieved by loading the items to be cleaned into a tray or onto a conveyor belt and subjecting them to jets of hot cleaning solution and rinsing water in (or as they pass through) the machine.

Provisions can be made for up to five distinct operations, depending on the type of machine:

1   Pre-rinse with water and detergent at 40° to 50°C to remove all debris.
2   Wash with water and detergent at 50° to 60°C.
3   Power rinse with water at 70° to 80°C.
4   Hot rinse with water at 82° to 100°C.
5   Air drying.

Lower rinse temperatures are required for glass washing. The minimum number of operations required is two: wash and rinse.

Types

The larger the machine the greater the number of operations it will perform and the greater its capacity.

Front-loading   Dishes are loaded on racks which are then inserted into the machine using a front-opening door. The cleaning cycle normally consists of a wash followed by a rinse. Depending on the type of machine, the output of clean pieces will range from 300 to 3,000 per hour.

Hood machine   Dishes are loaded on racks which are individually loaded into the machine from the top, which is closed by a hood. Jets of water produced from beneath the racks are deflected off the hood and on to the dishes. The cleaning cycle includes a wash followed by a rinse. Depending on the size and model of the machine, 1,000 to 3,000 pieces per hour may be cleaned.

Conveyor machines   Dishes are loaded on racks which are inserted at one end of the machine, carried through it by a conveyor belt and removed from it at the other end. The cleaning cycle can

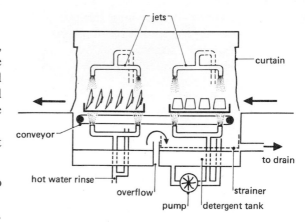

Figure 57   *Section through a conveyor machine*

include up to four operations, cleaning between 3,000 and 10,000 pieces per hour, depending on the size and model of machine.

Flight machines are similar to conveyor machines but dishes are loaded directly on to the conveyor. The cleaning cycle can involve four or five operations, cleaning over 10,000 pieces per hour.

Bar-type glass washers   The most suitable type consists of two small sinks, either free standing or inset into a work surface or drainer. Glasses are inserted individually into the sinks, being washed in the first by spraying or brushing with a hot detergent solution and rinsed in the second by hot water which includes a bactericide.

Use and performance

Correctly operated and maintained dishwashers will be more efficient than hand washing. The size of machine used should be related to the number of pieces per hour to be cleaned. To clean glassware, glass washers are preferred, as they permit the use of lower rinse temperatures. Special low-foam detergents are required; the usual types will produce too much foam. In hard water areas, a water-softening agent, e.g. Calgon, or a water-softening machine, if large machines are in use, will be required. This will reduce the amount of detergent used and eliminate the formation of lime scale in the water jets.

Rinse aids may be used to ensure the removal of all soil and detergent. Bactericides will be required when glass washing.

Continuous effective cleaning will depend on maintaining the detergent action of the cleaning solution. The detergent tanks of conveyor, hood and flight machines will require periodic topping up with detergent.

Straining sieves and detergent and rinse tanks will require emptying and cleaning at the end of each work period.

All dishes should be scraped prior to washing to prevent excessive amounts of debris entering the machine. Sufficient time should be allowed on removal from the machine to allow air drying to take place.

Scaffolds

Types

Independent tied This type consists of two parallel rows of standards (upright poles) tied at intervals to the work surface and erected to standards for light or general-purpose use.

Birdcage A box-like structure with a single working platform used to gain access to ceilings and walls in the interior of large buildings. It is only suitable for light work.

Truss out/cantilever/jib This is used where it is not possible to build up from the ground and the scaffold has to depend on the building for support.

Slung A platform suspended from a ceiling. It is used internally where it is not possible to build up from ground. Secure anchorage preferably from roof girders is required.

Mobile scaffold towers A vertical rectangular tower mounted on wheels. The maximum permitted height is 12.31 m and if above 9.75 m it must be tied to the building, anchored by guy ropes or weighted at the bottom. For internal use the

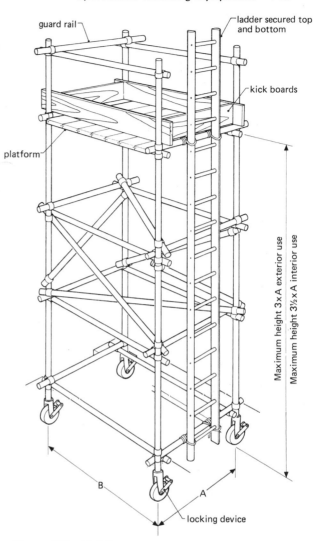

Figure 58 *Mobile tower*

height must not exceed 3½ times the shortest base side and for external use 3 times. A ladder must be fixed, top and bottom and be clear of the wheels. In use the wheels must point outwards and be locked. It must be clear of people and materials when moved.

Interlocking modular scaffold consists of interchangeable standard units which are assembled without the use of separate couplings and have a minimum of individual components. They are used to form temporary load bearing structures which can be assembled quickly.

Safety requirements

Working platform   This will normally be formed from boards of which the minimum dimensions are 40 mm thick, 225 mm wide and commonly 3.9 m in length. Boards of this specification must be supported every 1.52 m.

In all circumstances a minimum of three supports for any board is required. Boards must not overlap each other. They must fit tightly and overhang the end supports by 51–155 mm. The minimum width of the platform must be 640 mm for footing only (three boards), 870 mm for footing and standing of materials (four boards) and 1.07 m to support a trestle. A clear passage of 440 mm is required for personnel and 640 mm for materials. Toe boards and guard rails must be fitted if a fall will exceed 1.98 m. Guard rails must be 920–1,150 mm above the platform. Toe boards must have a minimum width of 150 mm. The gap between the toe board and the bottom of the rail must not exceed 760 mm. A wire mesh can be fitted to prevent materials falling from the platform.

The platform must extend 610 mm beyond the work area.

Access   Where access is by means of a ladder it must be secured so that it meets the general safety requirements for ladders. It must extend 1.05 m above the platform.

An intermediate landing every 9.14 m of vertical height must be provided, fitted with toe boards and guard rails.

Prefabricated frames

These are box-shaped frames which can be placed on top of one another to form a tower which can be mounted on castors. Safety requirements are similar to those for towers, but in particular the total height must not exceed four times the smallest base dimension. The structure must be stiff enough to be stable.

Mobile work platforms

Telescopic work platforms   These are generally

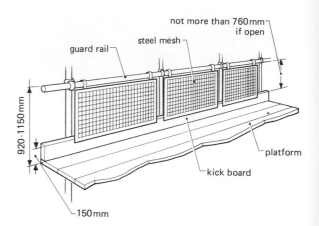

Figure 59   *Scaffold safety requirements*

designed for straight vertical access and for one-man operation. They consist of a vertical light-alloy ladder surmounted with a platform and fixed to a base frame with stabilizers. The tower may be raised or lowered manually or pneumatically depending on the actual type. Such platforms offer considerable advantages over conventional scaffold or mobile towers when access to high parts of a building is required.

Power-operated platforms   These range from small mobile platforms with a self-elevating facility to lorry-mounted hydraulically operated platforms. They must be elevated on firm ground and be operable from the platform. Guard rails and toe boards must be fitted. They must be stable and, unless designed otherwise, the maximum elevation is $3\frac{1}{2}$ times and 3 times the smallest base dimensions, respectively, for interior and exterior use. Where the means of lift is of the scissor type, guard rails must be fitted.

Suspended platforms and cradles

This group includes various types of access equipment suspended by means of wire or fibre ropes from outriggers at the top of a building. The outrigger usually consists of metal joists, poles or framework at the outer end of which is fixed a suspension member. The inboard end may be static

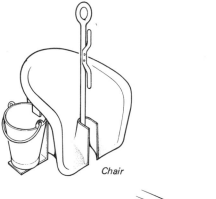

Chair

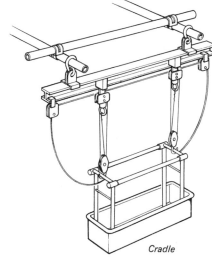

Cradle

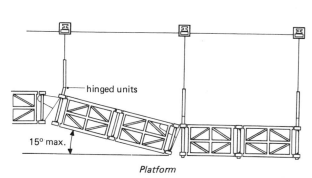

hinged units

15° max.

Platform

Figure 60 *Platform and cradles*

or be fitted to a traversing track. In either case it must be securely fixed and counter-weighted.

Platforms and cradles are raised or lowered by means of a power-operated winch.

Types

Hinged platform A series of platforms hinged together to form a continuous platform. The maximum permitted slope is 15°. They are suspended by wire ropes at each joint or hinge and at each end.

Independent platforms Platforms of various lengths up to 11.95 m, suspended by wire ropes and which can be moved on a traversing track.

Cradles A single platform of up to 3.2 m in length, suspended by wire or fibre ropes which can be fixed or moved on a traversing track.

Chairs A chair suspended by a cable from an outrigger. They should only be used if there is no other reasonable means of access.

General safety requirements

Outriggers and suspension cables Outriggers must be 3 m apart for cradles and no more than 4.57 m apart for platforms. Adjacent outriggers must be tied together.
The resting moment of the counterweight must exceed three times the overturning moment of a platform or cradle and four times that of a chair. For platform sections exceeding 3 m, three outriggers per section are required. Platforms greater than 3.2 m in length must only be suspended by wire ropes. Outriggers and cables must be inspected every week.

Emergency protection should include a secondary wire rope where possible, a fall-arresting device and provision for manual winching in the event of power failure. Control of the platform must be on the platform. Safety harnesses should be worn if necessary.

Working loads and platform dimensions All platforms and cradles must show the maximum safe working load and the number of persons permitted per section.

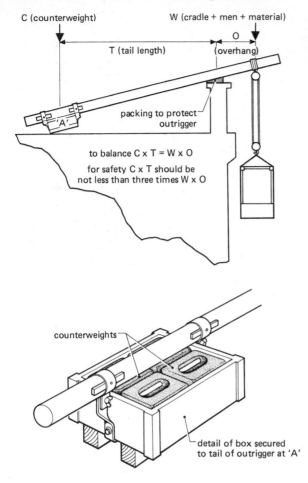

to balance C x T = W x O

for safety C x T should be
not less than three times W x O

counterweight must be fully effective on tail of outrigger

Figure 61 *Support and counterweight for suspended scaffolds*

Guard rails and toe boards The requirements for platforms are similar to those for scaffold. The rail at the working face should be 690 mm above the platform. Chairs must have a continuous back rest and side rails not less than 250 mm in height. The suspension member is fitted such that an operative cannot fall out.

Operating precautions When at work, notices must be displayed at power sources which must be inaccessible to unauthorized personnel. Breakdowns must be immediately reported. No

temporary repairs must be undertaken. When corrosive chemicals are being used, synthetic fibre ropes of approved specification must be used. Platforms and cradles must be rendered inoperative and inaccessible at the end of work periods.

Ladders

These consist, in general, of upright stiles to which cross-members are securely fitted at (normally) 254 mm intervals. They may be constructed of wood or aluminium.

Types

Single-section standing ladder Two rectangular or 'I' beam stiles fitted with turned or 'D' shaped rungs.

Pole ladder Two half-round pole stiles with cleft or sawn, turned or hand-wrought rungs.

Window ladder Two rectangular stiles coming to an apex at the tops with turned rungs. Padding may be fitted to the apex to protect windows.

Step ladder Two flat rectangular stiles fitted with flat treads, a minimum of 76 mm wide, that will be horizontal when the ladder is placed at an angle of 75°.

Extending ladder Two or more standing ladder sections with a provision for coupling when extended. Sections may be raised by a system of ropes and pulleys.

Swingback steps A step ladder with a swing back making them self-supporting. Locking stays are fitted to brace the steps. When open, the treads are horizontal.

Platform steps Similar to swing back steps but the top rung is replaced by a platform. The platform must not be more than 3.85 m above the ground.

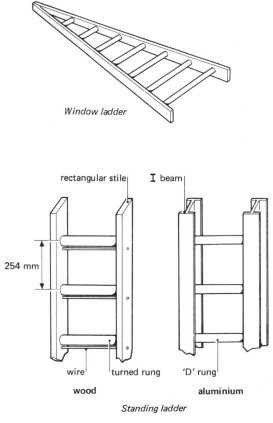

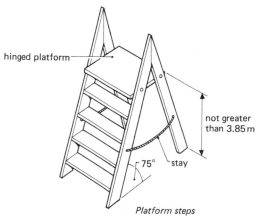

Figure 62   *Types of ladder*

General safety requirements: structural

- Load testing of wooden ladders is not recommended.
- Ladders must not be painted since this will hide defects.
- They must be inspected regularly. This will include checking for splintering, cracking, warping or bruising of stiles; that rungs are all there and not damaged or worn; that there is no splintering of the feet; that the ropes and pulleys are in good order; that there is no play in the stiles in any direction.
- Unsatisfactory ladders must be replaced.
- Aluminium ladders must be fitted with wood or non-metallic non-slip blocks.

General safety requirements: method of use

- Single or extending ladders and steps should be placed at an angle of 75° to the horizontal (1 m per 4 m of vertical height).
- They must be secured by lashing at the top or by fixing by two guy ropes at 45° to the horizontal and staked at the bottom. If neither method is possible then the ladder must be held at the bottom, but this is only suitable for heights up to 6.9 m.
- The ladder must be placed on a flat sound base. On sloping ground safety feet, shoes or spikes must be fitted to the stiles. On stairways an extending foot can be fitted to one of the stiles.
- Aluminium ladders should not be used near electric cables.

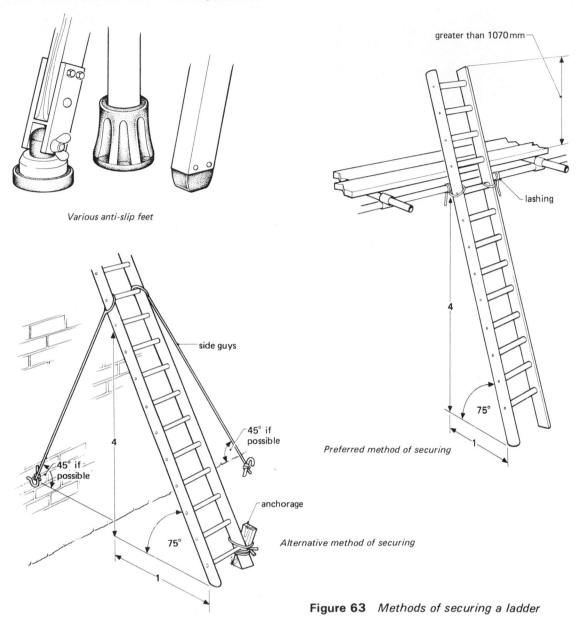

Various anti-slip feet

greater than 1070 mm

lashing

4

75°

1

Preferred method of securing

side guys

4

45° if possible

45° if possible

anchorage

75°

1

Alternative method of securing

Figure 63 *Methods of securing a ladder*

- Reinforcement of rungs and stiles must be on the underside of the ladder.
- Landings must be provided every 9.14 m.
- Extending ladders over 4.92 m when closed must have three rungs overlapping when open and, if over 6.15 m, must have four overlapping rungs.

- Warning notices should be displayed when ladders are in use.

Ladder scaffolds

These are temporary structures consisting of two ladders to which a platform up to 0.92 m wide is fixed by means of cripples. They should only be used if there is no other reasonable alternative.

Staging

Preformed platforms consisting of timber stiles, cross-bearers and decking.

Trestles

Two hinged frames with cross-bearers to support a platform of scaffold boards or staging. They can be of aluminium or wood and are suitable for light work of short duration.

The height of the platform must not exceed 4.570 m. If above 3.6 m the trestle must be tied to a wall. The upper one-third of frame should not be used. The maximum permitted lengths of platform are 1.3 m for 40 mm boards, 2.44 m for 51 mm boards and 3.048 m for staging. The minimum width of platform is 440 mm. Above 1.98 m, a separate ladder must be provided for access.

Folding trestles do not require a guard rail or toe boards. If fixed, and the platform is higher than 1.98 m, requirements are similar to those for scaffolds.

A trestle must be placed on firm level ground.

Safety nets

These are used where it is impracticable to use working platforms with guard rails and toe boards. They may be used in any case. There are two types, personnel nets to catch people and materials or protection nets to prevent objects falling on people. They are normally placed 6.0 m below the working area and will be higher at the outer edges.

Safety belts

These are used where no safe working platform is possible, and only in preference to nets if they are conscientiously worn. They may be either static lines 0.615 or 1.846 m in length, or of the inertia-reel type. BS 5845 specifies requirements for fixed anchorage points for belts. Belt and anchorage points must be inspected each time they are used

and anchorage points must be tested every four years.

Crawling boards

These are used on either pitched roofs (roofs at an angle of greater than 10° to the horizontal) or fragile roofs. They must be 380 mm wide and have cross-bearers at 380 mm intervals. When used on pitched roofs they must be fixed and a catch barrier must be erected at the eaves.

British Standards

BS 1129: 1966, *Timber Ladders, Steps, Trestles and Lightweight Stagings for Industrial Use.*

BS 1139: 1964, *Metal Scaffolding.*

BS 1397: 1979, *Specification for Industrial Safety Belts, Harnesses and Safety Lanyards.*

BS 2037: 1964, *Aluminium Ladders, Steps and Trestles for the Building and Civil Engineering Industries.*

BS 3913: 1973, *Industrial Safety Nets.*

BS 5845: 1980, *Specification for Permanent Anchors for Industrial Safety Belts and Harnesses.*

CP 97: 1967, *Part 1: Metal scaffolding: common scaffolds in steel. Part 2: Suspended scaffolds. Part 3: Special scaffold structures in steel.*

See also Construction Safety, National Federation of Building Trades Employers and BAS Management Services.

Equipment care, safety and storage

A number of general principles apply to the care, safe use and storage of equipment.

Care

The correct care of equipment is essential. Unless equipment is in good working order and reliable, the result will be safety hazards and interruptions in normal cleaning programmes as a result of defective equipment. The essential principles of equipment care are:

1 All staff should know the correct methods of care, cleaning and storage.
2 The correct equipment should be used for each task and used correctly.
3 All equipment should be cleaned after use.
4 Equipment must be inspected before and after use and all defects reported.
5 Manufacturers' instructions for operation and maintenance should be followed.
6 Regular maintenance must be carried out to an agreed programme. For all electrical equipment there should be a card indicating: date of purchase, machine type and serial number, cost, date first used, tools and accessories, maintenance dates and where used.
7 Adequate and correct storage facilities must be provided.
8 Equipment should be stored correctly.

Safety

In addition to regular inspection of equipment by maintenance staff or servicing agents, safety will depend upon:

1 Routine inspection by staff
2 Staff training in the safe use of equipment.

For electrical and access equipment the most important requirements are as follows:

Electrical equipment:

● Check that cables and flexes are not split and are properly clamped into plugs.
● Check that plugs and sockets are not broken.
● Voltage of machine and supply must be the same.
● Plugs must be used correctly.
● Machine and socket must be switched off before plugging in or disconnecting.
● Isolate from mains before carrying out internal adjustments.
● Hands to be dry.
● Machines must not be pulled by the cable or flex.

● Cable should be placed over shoulder when in use.
● Loose cable should lie behind the machine, as close to a wall as possible and pass over door handles if passing a doorway.
● Warning signs should be erected when carrying out wet cleaning methods or where it is not possible to position cable safely.

Access equipment:

● Erect or suspend equipment so that it is firm and secure. Equipment should not exceed the permitted working height. Rails, kickboards and similar equipment must be used where required.
● Never overload platforms.
● Safety lines and nets to be used where required.
● Where equipment is used warning signs must be erected and area cordoned off if necessary.

Storage

Provision should be made for the correct storage of all equipment. The actual size of a store and its facilities will depend on the amount and type of equipment to be stored. It should include, as necessary, the following:

1 Space for each machine.
2 Shelves, cupboards and drawers for all spares, mops, brush heads, squeegees, pads and similar equipment.
3 Hooks for hand mops, sweepers and brushes.
4 Work bench and space to carry out cleaning and maintenance of equipment.
5 Sink with hot and cold water.
6 Lighting.
7 Power points.
8 All the above will be in addition to space and facilities required for storing chemcals and other materials.

Selection of equipment

Equipment selection involves four stages:

1 Analysis of cleaning and maintenance requirements and constraints.
2 Type and characteristics of equipment required.
3 Evaluation of equipment available.
4 Selection and purchasing.

Analysis of cleaning and maintenance requirements and constraints

This involves five elements:

Physical characteristics of building The following must be defined: constraints on the movement of equipment; type and area of each floor; type and degree of soilage; type, quantity and density of furniture and fittings; position, number and type of service points available.

Activities within the building The use to which the building is put will influence the characteristics required of the equipment used, e.g. suction cleaners in hospitals must be filtered and silenced to meet DHSS recommendations.

Requirements for cleaning and maintenance The methods by which the fabric, fixtures, fittings and furniture of the building are to be cleaned and the frequency of cleaning must be defined. This will determine the type of equipment to be employed. The area of horizontal and vertical surfaces and the number of fixtures, fittings and furnishings will indicate the amount and required work performance of the equipment.

Labour The size and skills of the available labour force must be considered. An established unskilled workforce may be reluctant to use new equipment. The labour cost can represent 90% of the total cleaning and maintenance budget. The use of equipment capable of achieving high work performances will frequently reduce labour costs.

Costs The purchase of equipment may be limited by budgetary constraints, in particular capital expenditure. Where there are no constraints, the most cost-effective combination of labour and equipment must be achieved.

A financial analysis should be carried out to compare all the relevant costs of using various combinations of equipment and labour. This will include the financial implications of capital expenditure, the financial implications of revenue expenditure, direct operating expenses and indirect expenditure. In general a combination of high work performance equipment and less labour will be more cost-effective than low work performance equipment and more labour.

The maximum utilization of a piece of equipment is not a good purchasing criterion. Although not necessarily the case, an expensive piece of equipment with high work performance, low associated labour costs and only used for short periods may be the most cost-effective choice.

Type and characteristics of equipment required

Having determined the cleaning and maintenance needs of a building it will be possible to identify the type of equipment required, the amount and the characteristics which will be essential. The characteristics to be considered will include the following:

Safety:

- The use of disposable wipes where high levels of hygiene are required.
- Dust control using impregnated or static sweepers.
- Degree of filtration required by suction cleaners.
- Safety devices, e.g. dead man's handle.
- Insulation of equipment.
- Type of power supply.
- Security of cables and flexes.
- Torque of rotary machines.
- Bumpers to protect furniture and skirting boards.
- Weight of equipment if portability is desired.

Ease of operation:

- Equipment should be designed to be used with a minimum of physical effort. Difficulties experienced in the use of some equipment, e.g. high-speed scrubber polishers are often the result of inadequate training or incorrect method of use.
- Equipment should be easily manoeuverable so that it will negotiate obstacles without difficulty.
- Controls should be simple and easily understood and operated.

Equipment cleaning and maintenance:

- Equipment should be designed so that it can be easily cleaned by operative staff and is sufficiently attractive to give staff an incentive to clean and look after it.
- The cost of a piece of equipment and its durability will influence the type and amount of maintenance required, the costs of which must ultimately be considered.

Size:

- Offset motors will permit equipment to be passed under the furniture.
- The width and turning circle of ride-on machines compared to the width of corridors, access and turning points.
- Furniture density can make it difficult to use and manoeuvre large sweepers, scrubber polishers and other equipment resulting in a work performance well below the maximum possible. The use of large equipment in such situations will not be cost-effective.

Durability:

- Equipment should be of robust construction and capable of withstanding careless use. Durability is best determined by using equipment for a trial period in normal use and by reference to equipment record cards (see Volume 2). Only then are some problems identified.
- The power of the motor should be related to the type of work to be carried out and should be capable of continuous use for several hours. An overload protection device is essential.
- Spare parts must be readily available and repairs not subject to unnecessary delays.

Noise:

- In quiet areas silenced suction cleaners are required.
- Belt-driven machines can be quieter than rack and pinion drives which may become noisy with age.
- Electrically powered machines will be quieter than petrol- or air-driven ones.

Suppression:

- Where interference with other electrical equipment is likely to be a problem, electrically powered cleaning equipment should be suppressed.

Portability:

- If a piece of equipment is likely to be carried, its weight should not exceed 10 kg. Carrying handles should be designed for maximum comfort and undue strain.
- In older buildings or where lifts are not available, the weight of a piece of equipment suitable in all other respects, may prohibit its use.

Power source:

- Petrol-driven machines should only be used outside.
- Air- or electrically-driven machines will be suitable for both interior and exterior use. Air-driven or low voltage equipment will be required where an electrical hazard may arise, e.g. wet areas.
- The voltage of a machine and the power supply must be the same. Alternatively a transformer may be used.
- Suitable power points will be required for electrical equipment.

Type of work and versatility:

• The performance characteristics of equipment must be related to the type of work to be carried out, e.g. a heavy powerful machine for scarifying a floor.

• Frequently versatility is required, achieved for example by the selection of two speed or variable speed scrubber polishers. Accessory tools and special kits can significantly increase the range of tasks a particular piece of equipment will perform. Combination machines can reduce labour costs.

Work performance Subject to other constraints and analysis of the costs involved, equipment capable of achieving high work performance rates with a minimum involvement of labour will be preferred. Analysis of the cleaning requirement will give a broad indication of the work performance equipment will be required to have. In many cases there will be a number of possible combinations of equipment and labour which enable a particular task to be carried out. The equipment actually selected will be that which gives the most cost-effective combination of equipment and labour. For example:

1   Large interior areas and corridors can be swept with vee sweepers. Depending on the size of the area, car parks and court yards can be swept with manually propelled or ride-on sweepers.

2   Combination scrubber driers may be more cost-effective than individual scrubbers and driers.

3   On large areas of uncongested carpet the working width of a suction cleaner and its suction power will affect work rates and hence cost-effectiveness.

4   Work rates achieved when spray cleaning, particularly of uncongested areas, e.g. corridors, can be significantly greater if suction units are used and the application of cleaning solution is controlled from the handle of the scrubber polisher whilst it is in motion.

5   A 38 cm scrubber polisher may be more suitable for spray cleaning a hospital ward, but a 50 cm machine would be more suitable for the corridors.

6   A hot water extraction machine and tools capable of cleaning 40 m^2 of carpet per hour would be suitable where a few hundred square metres of carpet are to be cleaned. Where much larger areas are involved there are two options, both of which may be cost-effective but in different situations. These are the purchase of machines capable of much higher work performances but which are expensive or the purchase of several smaller machines which may be issued to departments in much the same way as suction cleaners or scrubber polishers.

Evaluation of equipment available

Having determined the type of equipment required, all equipment available which appears to meet the requirements for safety, ease of operation, size, durability, noise, suppression, source of power, suitability for work to be carried out, versatility and work performance must be identified and evaluated. The evaluation involves two distinct operations. In addition two other factors should be considered.

Comparison and analysis of costs This will involve two elements:

1   A comparison of the costs of essentially similar machines. This must include the cost of accessory tools, maintenance contracts, etc.

2   A financial analysis to determine the most cost-effective combinations of equipment and labour (see page 137 for a simple analysis).

Demonstration and trial Equipment that broadly meets all requirements, including costs, should be seen and used for a trial period. This is essential because it enables the claims made by manufacturers to be proved and will identify problems that are likely to occur when the equipment is in normal use, e.g. difficulty in handling, unsafe, characteristics of the equipment which interfere with its work performance.

Reputation of companies The reputation and reliability of a company must be carefully considered. Simply put, the machine which appears to be the most cost-effective and which meets all requirements may not in the end turn out to be best.

Servicing and repairs The ease with which spares can be obtained and repairs carried out must be considered. A piece of equipment awaiting spare parts and repairs can result in additional labour costs and costs involved in obtaining a replacement machine.

Selection and purchasing

If the preceding stages are carried out correctly, it should be possible to purchase the most efficient, cost-effective items of equipment for any establishment.

5 Cleaning agents

Cleaning is the removal of soil from any interior or exterior surfaces of a building. The term 'surfaces' includes all fixtures, fittings, finishes and hard and soft furnishings. Soil can be removed by physical or chemical means involving the use of cleaning equipment and cleaning agents. Cleaning equipment will dislodge and remove soil from a surface and bring the cleaning agent into contact with the surface. A cleaning agent is any chemical, including water, that will bring about, or assist either physically or chemically, the removal of soil from a surface. Disinfectants are not cleaning agents and should never be used for cleaning.

Classification of cleaning agents

Cleaning agents are classified according to the principal method by which soil or stains are removed from a surface. This will be determined by their composition. In general they are formulated to suit particular types of soiling and surfaces. The principle classes are:

Water   Acid cleaners
Detergents   Organic solvents
Abrasives   Other cleaning agents
Degreasers

Acidity, alkalinity and pH

To quantify the acidity or alkalinity of a solution the pH scale is used. A knowledge of the pH value is fundamental to understanding the correct use and uses of cleaning agents. The pH of a cleaning agent can be tested using strips of Universal Indicator Paper. The colour of the paper after dipping into the solution is compared with a colour chart and the pH number read off. Figure 64 shows the scale with approximate pH ranges of various cleaning agents. pH meters are also available.

All synthetic detergents and caustic cleaners must be regarded as potentially harmful. The so-called neutral detergents frequently cause dermatitis. Acid cleaning agents are less of a problem but cleaning agents with a pH of 1 to 2 must be handled with extreme caution.

Water

Water is a poor cleaning agent if used alone and has important limitations.

Wetting properties

In order to be effective a cleaning agent must gain

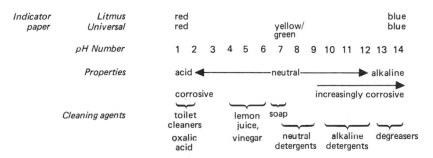

Figure 64 pH scale

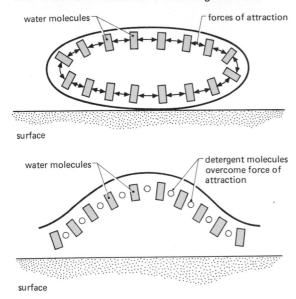

surface

water molecules

detergent molecules overcome force of attraction

surface

Figure 65 *Surface tension of water*

access to the soil adhering to a surface in order to lift or dissolve it. When water is applied to a surface it will tend to form small or large globules which will not penetrate the soil or surface. The globules are formed as a result of high surface tension. Attractive forces between water molecules around the outside of the globule are so great that they tend to form a thin skin preventing the molecules within the globule from penetrating the soil or surface.

Soil suspension

When soil is removed from a surface it must be held in the cleaning water and not allowed to resoil the surface. Water has very limited ability to hold soil in suspension.

Emulsification of grease

Water has little ability to emulsify, i.e. break up, grease or oils.

Hardness

Soft and particularly hard waters contain calcium and magnesium salts which will inhibit cleaning in three ways:

1 In combination with soap the salts form an insoluble scum which reduces the efficiency of the soap and makes rinsing difficult:

Calcium salts + Sodium stearate (soap)
→ Calcium stearate (scum) + Sodium salts

2 Calcium combines with fats in the soil to form a soapy substance, which adheres strongly to the surface.

3 The calcium and magnesium salts tend to cause flocculation, i.e. they tend to cause the soil suspended in the water to be redeposited on the surface being cleaned.

Overcoming the limitations

Despite its disadvantages, water is the most important cleaning agent used, its limitations being overcome in one of two ways:

Cleaning solutions These are formed by combining water with another cleaning agent, the choice of which will depend upon the cleaning task to be carried out.

High-pressure cleaning When soiled surfaces are subjected to water under pressure, the soil is dislodged and carried from the surface. The pressure used, the temperature of the water and the type of cleaning agent used will depend on the type of soil and the surface to be cleaned.

Detergents

Strictly the term detergent can be applied to any cleaning agent. Its usage is now generally restricted to those cleaning agents containing significant quantities of a group of chemicals known as surfactants. A number of other chemicals are frequently included to produce a detergent suitable for a specific use.

Essential properties

A good detergent will possess many or all of the

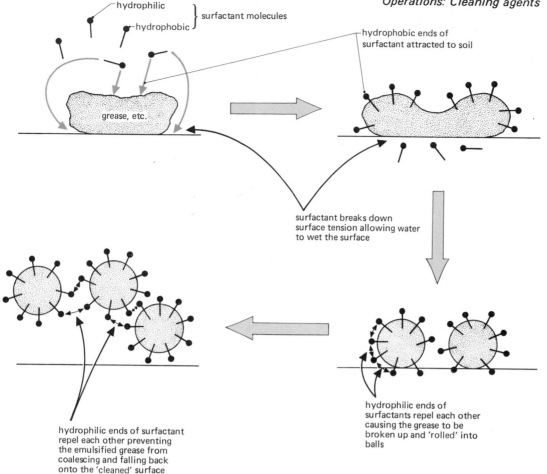

Figure 66 *Surfactant action*

following properties:

1 Reduce the surface tension of water so that the cleaning solution can penetrate the soil and surface.
2 Emulsify soil and lift it from a surface.
3 Suspend soil in the cleaning solution.
4 Be soluble in cold water.
5 Be effective in hard water.
6 Be harmless to user and surface to be cleaned.
7 Rinse easily to leave no streaks or scum.
8 Be economical in use.

Chemical composition

Detergents are formulated from the types of chemicals described in the following:

Surface-active agents (surfactants) are chemicals, the molecules of which when dissolved in water possess a water-seeking (hydrophilic) end and a water-repelling (hydrophobic) end. They may or may not carry a negative or positive electrical charge. The molecules are dispersed through the water so that they reduce the surface tension of the water by overcoming the forces of attraction between the water molecules, thus allowing the water and surfactant molecules to penetrate the soil and surface. The hydrophobic ends of the surfactant molecules are attracted to the soil, surrounding particulate soil particles and lifting them from the surface while breaking and rolling up grease into small particles and lifting them from the surface. The hydrophilic ends of the surfactant molecules point out from the soil

Table 28 *Surface-active chemicals*

Property	Soap (anionic)	Anionic	Non-ionic	Cationic
Chemical nature	☐ Hydrocarbon chain (hydrophobic) COO Carboxylate group (hydrophilic) e.g. sodium stearate Formed by action of caustic soda on vegetable and animal fats	☐ Hydrocarbon chain (hydrophobic) SO_3 Sulphonate group, *or* SO_4 Sulphate group (both hydrophilic) e.g. alkylbenze sulphonate or alkyl sulphates Petroleum by-product	☐ Hydrocarbon chain (hydrophobic) Ether chain (hydrophobic) OH Hydroxyl group (hydrophilic) e.g. alkylphenol ethoxylates Petroleum product	Substituted ammonium compounds, known as 'Quats'
Water solubility	Forms negatively charged ion. Less soluble in cold water	Forms negatively charged ion. Less soluble in cold water	Does not ionize. Less soluble in hot water	Forms positively charged ion. Soluble in hot and cold water
pH	7	7-9 (not neutral)	7	6-7
Surface tension reduction	Good	Good	Fair	Poor
Removal of particulate soil	Good	Good	Good	Fair
Removal of grease	Poor	Fair	Good	Poor
Suspending power	Good	Good	Fair	Poor
Effect of hard water	Scum formed	Less effective	Slight reduction of effectiveness	Inactivated
Foaming	High	High	Low	—
Ease of rinsing	Fair	Fair	Good	—
Safety	Safe	May cause dermatitis or skin allergies	Safe	Safe
Price	Expensive	Cheap	Expensive	Expensive
Antistatic	—	—	—	Good
Bactericidal	Poor	Poor	Poor	Fairly good

particles into the surrounding water. As individual particles approach each other the hydrophilic parts of the surfactant molecules on different particles repel each other keeping the soil in suspension and preventing it from settling back onto the surface.

Table 28 describes the different types of surfactant and their respective properties.

Non-ionics can be combined with anionics or cationics. Anionics and cationics cannot be combined without cancelling out the activity of each because of their opposite electrical charges.

Builders are alkaline chemicals that influence the effectiveness of a cleaning agent in one or both of the following two ways:

1 They sequester (combine with) calcium ions in hard water to form water-soluble salts, thus preventing the adverse effects of calcium.
2 Enhance the emulsifying and dispersing properties of the detergent.

Complex phosphates, e.g. sodium tripoly-phosphate, are included in many detergent powders and act in both of the ways described. Sodium metasilicate and sodium carbonate are included in many liquid detergents and function in the second of the ways described.

Builders in general can have damaging effects on many surfaces, e.g. chrome, aluminium, wool, silk, paints, wood and linoleum.

Water softeners are frequently comprised of complex phosphates e.g. sodium hexameta-phosphate because of their sequestering properties.

Foaming agents increase or stabilize the foam formed by a detergent. Foaming can be used to indicate surfactant activity, the level of foam being dependent on the amount of surfactant active in a cleaning solution. Alkalonamides derived from coconuts oil are frequently used for this purpose.

Other foaming agents can be used to produce stable, relatively thick foams in which the other chemicals are dispersed. The foam will stick to non-horizontal surfaces increasing the contact time between the surface and the cleaning chemicals.

Chelating agents are relatively complex chemicals which are included in many liquid detergents to sequester calcium ions. In simple terms a combination of sodium carbonate or metasilicate and a chelating agent will have a similar effect to tripolyphosphate alone. Tripolyphosphate is not normally included in a liquid detergent because it tends to break down in alkaline solution. Chelating agents are now frequently used as descaling agents, being a more acceptable alternative to strong acids.

Suspending agents, e.g. sodium carboxymethyl cellulose (CMS), increase the amount of soil that can be held in suspension in the cleaning solution.

Bleaches will break down, by oxidation, stains which have not been removed from a surface by surfactants or builders. Sodium perborate, a weak bleach is included in detergents intended for washing textiles.

Bulking agents e.g sodium sulphate, contribute to the volume of detergent powders.

Conditioning agents ensure that the granules in detergent powders are crisp, firm and dry.

Whiteners absorb ultra-violet light and transmit it as visible white light. The whiteness of a surface will normally depend on the amount of natural light reflected from it and received by the eye. Whiteners therefore increase the amount of light received by the eye.

Enzymes are complex proteins that will break down organic substances, e.g. blood stains, adhering to a surface. They are most effective at 30° to 50°C and are inactivated at temperatures above 60°C.

Anticorrosive agents inhibit the formation of water films on a surface. Chemical reactions resulting in corrosion are generally dependent on the presence of water.

Perfumes and dyes are included to increase

consumer acceptability, but increase the risk of allergic reaction.

Types of detergent

Detergents are formulated to be suitable for particular surfaces and types of soil. However, within one particular type of detergent, considerable variation can exist in the actual composition, affecting both cost and effectiveness (see Table 29). It should be noted that the chemical constituents of the various cleaning agents listed in this table are intended to show the range of chemicals that may be included in a particular type of cleaning agent. It does not imply that they include all the chemicals listed.

Abrasives

The cleaning action of abrasives depends on the presence of fine particles which, when rubbed over a soiled hard surface, dislodge the soil and remove tarnishing and surface scratches from metallic surfaces. However, they must be used correctly and on an appropriate surface.

Chemical composition

Abrasive materials used in these cleaning agents may be divided into two categories:

1 Finely powered ash, pumice, felspar or dolomite.
2 Filtered chalk, jeweller's rouge (an oxide of iron).

The former are more abrasive, being relatively larger and coarser. They are combined with a variety of other substances, depending on the intended use of the cleaner. These substances include alkalis to remove grease, an anionic or non-ionic surfactant as a wetting agent, soap as a wetting agent or lubricant to reduce the scouring action of the abrasive material, glycerine as a lubricant, chlorine compounds to remove faecal stains and/or organic solvents to dissolve grease.

Types of abrasive

There are broadly two categories (see Table 29):

1 Hard-surface abrasive cleaners.
2 Metal polishes.

Hard-surface abrasives should only be used on hard surfaces and only if soiling is heavy and localized. Although they are effective cleaning agents, they will eventually damage most surfaces if used regularly. Metal polishes should only be used where heavy soiling, tarnishing or severe scratching occurs. Regular use will tend to remove the surface metal. This is partcularly obvious in the case of silver plate, the metal, e.g. copper, beneath the plate becoming exposed if silver polish is used regularly. Less harmful methods of routine cleaning are available to remove soil and tarnishing.

Degreasing agents

These usually consist of strong alkalis which can dissolve proteins and emulsify and disperse grease and similar substances. They are based on caustic soda (sodium hydroxide) or sodium metasilicate, both of which are available as crystalline powders or form the active ingredient in a number of proprietory products. They are extremely corrosive, damaging most surfaces. Any contact with the human body must be prevented. Although used extensively in manufacturing industry, their routine use elsewhere should be strongly discouraged. Sodium carbonate (washing soda) can be used for the degreasing of blocked drains as it is alkaline in nature, but far less corrosive.

Acids

Cleaning agents with acidic properties react with water-insoluble chemical deposits to produce a water-soluble salt. Either weak (pH 3–6) or strong acids (pH 1–2) are used, depending on the nature of the chemical deposit and the surface to be cleaned. Weak acids include citric acid in lemon juice and acetic acid in vinegar. Strong acids include oxalic acid, phosphoric acid, hydrochloric acid and sulphurous acid released by toilet cleansers. Extreme caution should be exercised when using strong acids and their use should be carefully controlled. Typical chemical processes are:

1 Lime scale (calcium carbonate) *plus* sulphorous, hydrochloric or phosphoric acid *gives* water-soluble, simple or complex, calcium salts.
2 Rust (ferric oxide) *plus* citric acid (in the presence of salt) or oxalic acid *gives* water-soluble citrates or oxalates of iron.

Organic solvents

These are chemicals that will dissolve fats, oils, grease, waxes and similar compounds. Each solvent is capable of dissolving a particular range of substances safely on specific surfaces. Many are used for routine stain removal.

Other cleaning agents

A number of cleaning agents do not easily fall into the categories described above.

Selection and purchasing of cleaning agents

Selection and purchasing will involve a variety of factors:

Type of soil General soiling, chemical deposits, localized stains or soilage, accumulation of grease, and light or impacted soil will generally require different types of cleaning agent.

Type of surface No matter how effective, a cleaning agent must not damage the surface being cleaned. This is particularly important where routine use is being considered.

Method of cleaning It must be established whether cleaning agents other than water are required. The cleaning agent selected must allow the least labour-intensive method to be used, but

not at the expense of ineffective cleaning or damage to surfaces.

Manufacturer's recommended uses Although cleaning agents are frequently recommended for particular types of surface or soiling, it must be recognized that a recommendation does not necessarily make a particular cleaning agent the most appropriate one to use.

Health and safety The least harmful cleaning agent should be used. If a potentially harmful one must be used, then thought must be given to the provision of protective clothing and training.

Cost This should be considered when the most appropriate cleaning agent or types of cleaning agent have been decided. The costs of similar products produced by different manufacturers and the costs of different cleaning agents which are also suitable must be compared. The critical factor will be the amount and type of active ingredients which will determine the amount of cleaning which can be carried out.

Testing Before purchasing a new cleaning product, it must always be tested in the work situation.

Specification Suppliers must be given a specification detailing precisely what is required. It should include the type of cleaning agent, its intended use, health and safety requirements, and particular chemical or physical properties required. Agreed specifications are available for cleaning agents to be used in local government buildings and hospitals (see end of this chapter), but their value is limited.

Methods of use

Once a cleaning agent has been selected for use in a particular situation, effectiveness, efficiency and safety will depend upon the following:

Manufacturers' instructions Generally these

Table 29 *Cleaning agents*

Type and composition	Uses	Factors affecting use
Detergents		
Kitchen and laundry soap: hardsoap builders, dyes, perfumes	1 Bars 2 Handwashing 3 Manual scrubbing of fibres to remove ingrained soil	1 pH 8. Little risk of skin irritation unless large amount of perfumes or dye included 2 Only suitable for removal of soil from those surfaces indicated
Toilet soap: soft soap, dyes, perfume disinfectant	1 Bars or liquid 2 Bathrooms, toilets and wash rooms for personal hygiene 3 Bars used in hotel guestrooms 4 Dispensers of liquid soap used in general toilets and cloakrooms	1 pH 7. Virtually no risk of irritation unless large amounts of perfume or dye included 2 Only suitable for uses indicated 3 Inactivated by hard water 4 Scum formation and excessive foaming can make them difficult to rinse, leaving surface greasy or streaked 5 Limited ability to remove grease, fats and oils 6 Relatively expensive
Soap flakes: soap, perfume	1 Laundering of lightly soiled fabrics, notably wool and silk	
Soap powder: soap, builders, bleach; suspending, whitening, bulking and conditioning agents; perfumes	1 Laundering of textiles 2 Largely replaced by synthetic detergent powders, being relatively expensive and unsuitable for automatic washing machines	1 pH 8-9. Some risk of skin irritation or dermatitis 2 Only suitable for use indicated 3 Excessive foaming can make them difficult to rinse, leaving hard surfaces greasy or streaked 4 Only moderately effective in the removal of heavy soiling
High- and controlled-foam synthetic powders: anionic and non-ionic surfacants, builders: foaming, conditioning, bulking, suspending and whitening agents; enzymes, dyes, perfumes	1 Laundering of textiles 2 High-foam powders are suitable for manual washing or use in non-automatic machines.	1 pH 8-10. Can cause irritation or dermatitis 2 Light-duty and general-duty powders are available 3 May be formulated for hot or cold washes 4 High pH general-duty powders will

Composition	Suitable uses	Points to note
	3 Controlled foam powders are suitable for automatic machines. They contain more non-ionic surfactant and less foaming agent	damage wool and silk fabrics 5 Enzyme action will require soaking of textiles 6 Specifically formulated for textiles making them relatively expensive for other uses. 7 Foam can make them difficult to rinse, leaving hard surfaces greasy or streaked
Low-foam synthetic powders: non-ionic surfactant, builders, conditioning agents	1 Dishwasher powders 2 Hard surface cleaners for use on heavily soiled surfaces only	1 pH 9-12. Will cause dermatitis 2 Low foam essential for automatic dishwashers 3 Hard surface powders will damage many surfaces if contact is prolonged or if used routinely 4 Rinsing is essential
Neutral detergents: anionic surfactant, non-ionic surfactant (light duty and some general duty), builders (none or few in light duty), chelating agents, perfumes, dyes.	1 Liquids or gels 2 Light-duty or general-duty formulations available 3 Light-duty products are variously formulated to be suitable for fabrics, dishes, hard surfaces and hand cleansing 4 General-duty products are suitable for routine cleaning of most hard surfaces	1 Light duty pH 7-9. Risk of irritation or dermatitis with some products 2 General duty pH 8-10. Can cause skin irritation or dermatitis 3 Only some of these cleaning agents can justify the name 'neutral'. This should be remembered when purchasing or using 4 Light- and general-duty products intended for hard-surface cleaning will effectively remove most types of soil and be fairly easily rinsed from the surface 5 General-duty products are usually less expensive than light-duty ones 6 Both types will have little or no damaging effect on most surfaces

(continued)

Table 29 — *continued*

Type and composition	Uses	Factors affecting use
Carpet and upholstery cleaners: anionic or non-ionic surfactant, builders, foaming agents, chelating agents, perfumes, cationic surfactant; *or* surfactant, non-chlorinated organic solvent	1 Are formulated to be suitable for a variety of methods of cleaning: wet shampooing; dry foam shampooing; spray extraction; dry powders; bonnet buffing 2 Surfactant in dry foam shampoo dries to a non-stick powder 3 Cationics (when included in formulation) will reduce static build-up and help reduce soiling	1 Essential that the cleaning agents used for the wet cleaning of carpets dry to a powder which can then be removed by vacuuming. Detergents not drying to a powder may leave a sticky residue which will accelerate resoiling 2 Dry powders are only suitable for light soilage
Alkaline or hard surface liquid detergents: builders, anionic or non-ionic surfactant, chelating agents	1 Cleaning of heavily soiled hard surfaces 2 Stripping of water-based polishes 3 For stripping metallized polishes the detergent must include ammonia or a related compound	1 pH 9-12.5. May cause skin irritation and dermatitis. Avoid all skin and eye contact 2 Will damage wood, lino, PVC, thermoplastic, terrazzo, marble, paint, chrome, aluminium and other surfaces if contact is prolonged or if used routinely 3 Rinsing is essential
Detergents with bactericidical properties: anionic or non-ionic surfactant, builders, chelating agents, chlorine compounds or cationic surfactant	1 General-purpose cleaning of hard surfaces where higher standards of hygiene considered essential 2 Cleaning of plastic surfaces 3 Variety of formulations, some of which have antistatic properties	1 Effective cleaning using a neutral detergent can generally be as effective in removing bacteria 2 Cationic substances will adhere to skin and surfaces; liable to build up of static charges, notably on plastics. This has three useful effects: neutralize any static charge on surface; repel bacteria and dust; a residue of bacteriastatic activity
Buffable detergents: surfactant, waxes, resins, organic solvent	1 Maintenance of hard and semi-hard floors 2 Formulation of products will vary	1 Surfactant or solvent will assist in the removal of soil and may remove part of the surface layer of a coat of polish if one has been applied. Waxes and resins remaining on the floor will form a glossy film or make up part of the surface layer of the polish when buffed

Agent	Uses	Notes
Buffable gel cleaners: non-ionic surfactant, pine oil, organic solvent, fatty acids, cationic surfactant	1 Maintenance of hard and semi hard floors 2 Direct application to many plastic floors may eventually result in breakdown of plasticizer	1 Surfactant or solvent will remove soil. Buffing of the residue of the cleaning agent will form a glossy protective film 2 Remains sticky unless buffed or completely rinsed 3 Periodic stripping of the film may be required

Abrasives

Agent	Uses	Notes
Cream and liquids: surfactant, builder, fine abrasive powder, ammonia	1 Heavily soiled hard surfaces, notably walls and work surfaces 2 Glazed ceramic bathroom, toilet and kitchen fittings if very heavily soiled	1 pH 8-12. Considerable variety in formulation. Effect on skin will depend on pH 2 Must not be used routinely on surfaces likely to be scratched, e.g. paintwork, enamel and plastic
Paste: surfactant, soap, abrasive powder, builders, glycerine	1 Removal of small localized heavy deposits of soil on hard surfaces 2 Graffitti removers	1 pH 8-12. Considerable variety in formulation. Effect on skin will depend on pH and abrasive properties 2 Must never be used routinely on any surface, particularly paintwork, enamel and plastics
Powder: surfactant, builder, abrasive powder, chlorine compounds	1 Scouring powders are available to remove heavy localized accretions of soil on some hard surfaces notably quarry tiles and glazed ceramic surfaces 2 Very mild powders for use in bathroom	1 Extremely abrasive and will damage most surfaces, including glazed ceramic surfaces 2 Avoid use if at all possible and never use routinely on glazed ceramic surfaces
Soft metal polishes: whiteing or jeweller's rouge, solvent, acid or ammonia	1 Available as liquid, impregnated cloth or wadding, plate powder 2 Removal of heavy soiling, scratches or tarnishing from silver and silver plate	1 Plate powder (whiteing or jeweller's rouge) requires mixing with water, meths or ammonia before use 2 Regular use will tend to remove surface metal 3 Some polishes will leave a 'long-term' finish on metal, thus reducing frequency of cleaning needed

(continued)

Table 29 — *continued*

Type and composition	Uses	Factors affecting use
Hard metal polishes: whiteing or very fine abrasive powder, organic solvent, acid or ammonia	1 Liquid suitable for removal of heavy soiling, scratches or tarnishing from brass and chromium 2 Removal of surface scratches from glass fibre bath surfaces	1 Regular use will tend to remove surface metal 2 Use of polishes leaving a 'long-term' finish are preferred 3 The use of soft and hard metal polishes for routine cleaning should be avoided 4 Soft and hard metal polishes must not be used on other metallic surfaces
Degreasers		
Sodium metasilicate or sodium hydrosilicate crystals	1 Degreasing of machinery and equipment 2 Drain cleaning 3 Detergent crystals (include a surfactant) are used for removal of accumulated grease and soil from concrete or asphalt floors 4 No other suitable uses	1 pH 12-14. Extremely corrosive.. Full protective clothing must be worn 2 Equipment or machinery is soaked in hot or cold solutions 3 Drains are flushed with a concentrated solution 4 Detergent crystals are applied in a concentrated solution, followed by scrubbing after allowing 30 min to act 5 Rinsing is essential 6 Seriously damage wood, silk, rayon, cotton, wood, lino, PVC, thermo-plastics, terrazzo, marble, aluminium, chrome
Gels and foams: sodium hydroxide, surfactant, gelling or foaming agent	1 Oven cleansers available in aerosol sprays or gels	1 pH 12-14. Extremely corrosive. Protective clothing must be worn 2 Use an alternative cleaning agent if possible

Agent	Uses	Notes
Sodium carbonate	1 Drain cleaning 2 Used in Polivitt process for cleaning of silver	1 Fairly corrosive. Will cause skin irritation or dermatitis 2 Drains flushed with a hot concentrated solution

Acidic

Agent	Uses	Notes
Phosphoric acid	1 Removal of lime scale and rust	1 pH 1-2. Very corrosive. Protective clothing must be worn
Oxalic acid	1 Used in concentrated solution as a rust remover in the engineering industry 2 Removal of rust marks and lime scale from a variety of surfaces	1 pH 1-2 in concentrated solution. Very corrosive. Protective clothing to be worn if used in concentrated solution 2 When used for removing lime scale or rust marks it is effective in dilute solution. Several applications may be required
Toilet cleaners: sodium bisulphate and chlorine compounds *or* hydrochloric acid *or* phosphoric acid	1 Cleaning of lavatory bowls and urinals 2 Products based on sodium bisulphate available as powders	1 Sulphurous acid, produced by sodium bisulphate when in contact with water, and hydrochloric acid remove lime scale and urine stains 2 Chlorine compounds will oxidise faecal deposits 3 pH 1-2. Extremely corrosive. Protective clothing must be worn 4 Hydrochloric acid is extremely reactive. Toilet cleaners based up on it are not recommended for general use 5 Never mix with bleach. Chlorine gas is produced
Lemon juice and Vinegar	1 Removal of rust marks from a variety of surfaces 2 Removal of tarnish from copper and bronze	1 Useful alternative to a dilute solution of oxalic acid 2 To remove rust marks and tarnish from metals, lemon juice or vinegar are mixed with salt. The mixture is applied as a thin paste, allowed a few minutes to act and then rinsed. Several applications may be required

(continued)

Table 29 – *continued*

Type and composition	Uses	Factors affecting use
Solvents		
Methylated spirits (methanol and ethanol)	1 Spot cleaning to remove resins, ball-point, iodine, vegetable dyes	1 Extremely volatile and highly inflammable 2 Can be used safely on plastic surfaces
Acetone	1 Spot cleaning to remove resins, lipstick, nail varnish and some dyes and paints	1 Extremely volatile and highly inflammable 2 Will dissolve and therefore damage cellulose acetate, and many plastic surfaces. Test surface should be cleaned before using
White spirit and paraffin	1 Spot cleaning to remove tar, rubber, fats, oils and waxes 2 Thinning of many solvent-based seals, polishes and paints	1 Fairly volatile and inflammable 2 Must not be used on PVC, thermoplastics or rubber surfaces 3 Always test surface to be cleaned before using
Carbon tetrachloride and benzene	1 Must never be used	1 Produces carcinogenic fumes
Tetrachloroethylene	1 Spot cleaning to remove fats, oils, wax, tar, pitch, some paints, resins, rubber	1 Moderately volatile but not inflammable 2 Must not be used on PVC, thermoplastics, rubber, asphalt and some other plastic surfaces 3 Always test surface to be cleaned before using
Methylene chloride	1 Paint and solvent-based seal stripper 2 Too effective a solvent for other uses	1 Extremely volatile with a noxious odour 2 Use should be avoided and, if essential, only in well ventilated conditions 3 Full protective clothing together with face mask or respirator to be worn

Other cleaning agents

Agent		
Glass and window cleaners: ethylene glycol, non-ionic surfactant	1 Removal of grease and inorganic soil from glass or windows 2 Replaces older products consisting of ammonia, water and whiteing	1 Removes light soiling 2 Non-abrasive and does not leave streaks 3 Apply in very dilute solution
Solvent-based detergent: white spirit, builders, anionic surfactant	1 Stripping of solvent-based polishes 2 Removal of accumulation of grease from hard surfaces not affected by white spirit 3 Degreasing of manufacturing equipment, etc 4 Oven-cleaning formulations	1 Combination of organic solvent and alkaline builders is a particularly effective combination for removal of waxes 2 Must not be used on PVC, thermo-plastics, rubber and some types of asphalt
Multipurpose cleaners: organic solvents, surfactants, chelating agent	1 General-purpose cleaning of hard surfaces	1 Only to be used for the cleaning of hard surfaces 2 Can be used on PVC, thermoplastics and rubber
Chewing gum removers	1 Aerosol sprays which freeze gum enabling it to be chipped off	1 Freezing caused by carbon dioxide which forms the spray
Polishes	1 Maintenance of polished floors by spray burnishing	1 Polish identical to that used to maintain floor is applied in dilute solution 2 The surface layer of polish and soil is removed and replaced in part by fresh polish
Bleach: sodium hypochlorite	1 Destaining of sinks, lavatory bowls and urinals 2 Removal of stains from textiles 3 Decarbonizing	1 Bleach will oxidize faecal and other organic staining substances to colourless compounds 2 Unless effectively rinsed it will damage wool, cotton and nylon 3 Never mix with acids. Always wear protective gloves

should be followed, particularly with respect to dilution and safety warnings.

Dilution Different types of cleaning agent, or similar cleaning agents differing in the amount of active ingredient, will require diluting to different extents to carry out the same job. But, for any particular cleaning agent, the dilution must be related to the amount of soiling and the method of cleaning used. Typical dilutions and floor areas cleaned by a liquid neutral detergent conforming to PAS 12 are as follows:

> *Quantity:* 5 litres undiluted.
> *Single-solution wet mopping:* diluted 200:1 will clean 4,000 m².
> *Two-solution wet mopping:* diluted 100:1 will clean 2,000 m².
> *Spray cleaning:* diluted 10:1 will clean 10,000 m².

Protective clothing Essential protective clothing must be worn.

Training Staff must be trained in the correct method of use of all the cleaning agents within a building.

Contact time Sufficient time must be allowed for the cleaning agent to act on soil.

Rinsing Adequate rinsing is essential to remove all soil and cleaning agent from a surface. Many cleaning agents will damage a surface if contact is prolonged.

Temperature Most cleaning agents work more effectively at higher temperatures, particularly when removing grease, fats and oils. However at temperatures above 60°C protein hardens and starches gelatinize, making their removal more difficult.

Topping up The removal of soil will generally inactivate the chemicals responsible for its removal. Once a cleaning solution ceases to have effective cleaning properties it must be discarded. Dirty water must not be topped up with new cleaning agent.

Mixing Cleaning agents when mixed may inactivate each other and may be hazardous. This practice should be discouraged.

Storage Containers must be correctly and clearly labelled. When not in use they must be kept in locked stores.

British Standards

PAS 11: 1974, *Floor Polish Stripper.*
PAS 12: 1974, *General-purpose Liquid Detergent.*
PAS 13: 1974, *Laundry Detergent.*

6 Disinfection and sterilization

Disinfection is the destruction of potentially harmful micro-organisms. It does not destroy all micro-organisms or their spores. Sterilization is the destruction of all micro-organisms including their spores.

Methods of disinfection

Disinfection of a surface can be achieved by cleaning, pasteurization or the use of chemicals. Effective cleaning will remove the majority of bacteria, a standard of hygiene acceptable for most surfaces and situations. Pasteurization or chemical disinfection are used where it is considered essential that all potentially harmful organisms are destroyed. A combination of cleaning and pasteurization, rather than cleaning and chemical disinfection, is preferable as it is easier to ensure the efficiency of pasteurization. Chemical disinfection should only be used when high standards of hygiene are considered essential and when the surface to be disinfected cannot, for practical reasons, be pasteurized.

Pasteurization

This process involves hot water or steam treatment of a surface or equipment at a temperature of 60–100°C for 1 to 15 min. The time will depend on the temperature. It must always be preceded by washing.

Medical equipment not requiring sterilization is disinfected by either immersion in hot water at 65–75°C for 10 min in a purpose-built hot-water pasteurizer or by exposure to steam at 73°C for 15 minutes. Combined washer/pasteurizers are available.

Linen requiring disinfection includes bed linen, babies' nappies, handkerchiefs and drying cloths. In hospitals and institutions carrying out their own laundering a distinction is made, as appropriate, between normally soiled, fouled and special-category linen. All will be disinfected by holding at 65°C for 10 min or 71° for 3 min during washing. If contamination by hepatitis virus is suspected, disinfection must be carried out at 95°C for 10 min. Each type is placed in plastic bags protected by a fabric sack. The bags are colour-coded to distinguish between the types that must be washed separately. Water-soluble bags should be used where possible. The bag and linen are placed directly into the machine, thus minimizing the infection risk to staff. Fouled linen is sluiced in cold water prior to hot washing. Staff who deal with dirty linen should not handle clean linen which must be kept separate from dirty items.

Cleaning equipment used in areas requiring high standards of hygiene, e.g. kitchens, hospital wards and operating theatres, requires disinfection. Mop sweepers, dusters and similar equipment may be disinfected by holding at 65°C for 10 min or 71°C for 3 min in a washing machine. Solution tanks, scrubbing brushes and similar equipment may be disinfected by immersion in hot water at 82–65°C for 1–10 min. All equipment must be dried before storage.

Crockery and small-scale food preparation and processing equipment is disinfected by rinsing in hot water at 82°C for 1 min, 77°C for 5 min or 65°C for 10 min. Small-scale equipment may also be exposed to steam at 100°C for 10 min in a purpose-built cabinet. Clean crockery or equipment must be kept separate from and not handled by staff dealing with soiled crockery or equipment.

High-pressure hot water used for cleaning sanitary accommodation

Hard surfaces and large-scale equipment are disinfected by subjecting them for 5 min to steam, either generated centrally or by portable equipment.

Chemical disinfection

Chemical disinfectants will kill or check the growth of micro-organisms on surfaces and equipment. Two related terms are:

1   *Germicide,* a general name for anything that kills bacteria.

2   *Antiseptic,* similar to disinfectant, but used on the human body.

Chemical disinfectants should not be used where a pleasant smell is required as an indication of cleanliness. Deodorizers are available for this purpose. An effective check on the necessity of using a chemical disinfectant is to ask the question: 'Is there any particular reason for using a disinfectant on this surface?'

Selection of a disinfectant will depend on a number of factors:

1　Broad specificity is required. Many disinfectants will control only a limited number of types of bacteria.
2　Bactericidal or bacteristatic disinfectants are available; the former kill bacteria, the latter stop their growth. Bactericides are preferable. The kill rate should exceed 99.999% of all bacteria present on a surface. pH will effect the activity of some disinfectants.
3　Time is required for maximum efficiency. The contact time will depend on the type of disinfectant, its dilution and the cleanliness of the surface.
4　Deterioration of disinfecting solutions will occur. Some disinfectants will deteriorate faster than others and must be discarded after use.
5　Inactivation by a variety of substances takes place. Each type of disinfectant will be inactivated by a different range of substances and to differing extents. Activity in the presence of organic substances is always preferred.
6　Solubility in hot and cold water is required. A disinfecting solution should not separate out on standing.
7　The safety of people using a disinfecting solution and of people subsequently using a disinfected surface and equipment must be considered. Only a few disinfectants can be considered to be completely safe.
8　Kelsey–Sykes test data should be made available by the supplier. The data indicate the dilutions to give a kill rate of 99.999% for specified organisms.
9　The effectiveness of a disinfectant is also quoted in a number of other ways. Data based on BS 3286 indicate for quarternary ammonium compounds the dilutions to give a kill rate of 99.999% for specified organisms. Chick–Martin and Rideal–Walker co-efficients indicate the effectiveness of the disinfectant when compared with standard solutions of phenol.

Types of disinfectant, their composition, uses and factors effecting their use are shown in Table 30.

Using a disinfectant correctly will influence its efficiency:

- Clean surface or equipment thoroughly. Inactivation will be reduced and accessability to bacteria will be improved.
- Clean just before disinfection. Surfaces are quickly recontaminated.
- Containers or 'pots' must be clean, dry and not constructed of plastic materials.
- Dilution must follow manufacturer's instructions. A too dilute solution will significantly reduce effectiveness.
- Do not mix different disinfectants or disinfectants with cleaning agents. The different chemicals may inactivate each other.
- Hot water should be used. Most disinfectants are more active at high temperatures.
- Apply solution generously to ensure sufficient disinfectant activity to control bacteria present.
- Contact time between surface and solution must be adequate.
- Remaining solutions must be discarded. Deterioration followed by growth of bacteria in the solution can result in gross contamination of a surface or equipment if used subsequently.
- Never top up solution.
- Never leave cleaning equipment to stand in a disinfectant solution. Deterioration of the solution will again result in contamination of surfaces being cleaned by the equipment.
- Protective clothing must be worn if required.

British Standards

BS 541: 1934, *Technique for Determining the Rideal–Walker Coefficient for Disinfectants.*
BS 808: 1938, *Modified Technique for Chick–Martin test for Disinfectants.*
BS 2462: 1961, *Black and White Disinfectant Fluids.*
BS 3286: 1960, *Method for Laboratory Evaluation of Disinfectant Activity of Quaternary Ammonium Compounds by Suspension Test Procedure.*

Table 30 *Types of disinfectant*

Types and composition	Uses	Factors affecting use
Chlorine: a green gaseous highly toxic element. It reacts with water to produce 'active' oxygen which controls microbes	1 Swimming-bath water, the concentration being maintained at 5 ppm 2 Water in food-processing plants, the concentration being maintained at 1–2 ppm for general use and 100 ppm for disinfection	1 Bactericidal activity will depend upon the amount of free or available chlorine and is expressed in parts of chlorine per million of water (ppm) 2 Very wide range of specificity 3 Will react with any organic matter 4 Reacts with phenols to produce strong smelling chlorophenols 5 Safety considerations generally limit its use. Storage and chlorine levels in water must be carefully controlled
Sodium hypochlorite: normally sold in solution. In water free chlorine is released which reacts with the water to produce 'active' oxygen	1 Hard surfaces, fixtures, fittings and equipment in kitchens, toilets, sluice rooms, laboratories and food processing areas at a concentration of 100–200 ppm for cleaned surfaces and 1,000 ppm for soiled surfaces 2 Crockery at a concentration of 100 ppm 3 Surfaces, equipment, materials contaminated with blood, particularly if risk of hepatitis, at a concentration of 10,000 ppm	1 Activity of a solution depends upon the amount of free chlorine that it will yield to react with water to produce 'active' oxygen. The concentration of a solution is normally expressed as a percentage or ppm of free or available chlorine 2 Decomposes during storage, thus reducing activity. The higher the concentration of sodium hypochlorite, the faster the rate of breakdown 3 A 10% (100,000 ppm) solution is most suitable when purchasing 4 Very wide range of activity 5 Little odour or taste in dilute solution 6 Relatively inexpensive 7 Inactivated by organic matter, e.g. blood, protein, soap, cationic detergents and some plastics 8 Very reactive, damaging cotton, nylon, some plastics and blackening many metallic surfaces, notably cutlery 9 Protective gloves must be worn

	Uses	Properties
		10 Must never be mixed with acids. Poisonous chlorine gas is produced
		11 A mixture of anionic or non-ionic surfactant and bleach forms a good bactericidal detergent but it deteriorates rapidly
Chloramines and isocyanurates: powder	1 Similar to hypochlorites 2 Component of dishwashing and scouring powders	1 Do not decompose in a solid dry state 2 Release chlorine when combined with water 3 Other factors similar to hypochlorites 4 Chloramines are used as an alternative to hypochlorites, but are more expensive 5 Both are suitable for use in dishwashing and scouring powders
Iodophors: complexes involving non-ionic surfactants which release iodine	1 Equipment and work surfaces in food preparation areas, e.g. milk and ice cream machines	1 Activity depends upon the amount of free iodine released in solution 2 Non-toxic or corrosive 3 Fairly wide range of specificity 4 Inactivated by organic matter, e.g. proteins, and many plastics 5 Rather expensive 6 Use restricted to situations where any possible tainting must be avoided
Quaternary ammonium compounds (QACs): cationic detergents, e.g. Cetrimide	1 Surfaces and equipment in food preparation areas 2 No other uses 3 Use in hospitals can be hazardous	1 Very limited range of specificity 2 Bacteristatic rather than bactericidal 3 Many micro-organisms, notably species of *Psuedomonas*, can grow in it 4 Inactivated by soap, anionic surfactants, organic matter (e.g. protein), many plastics, cellulosics (e.g. cotton), hard water 5 No odour or taste 6 Relatively expensive 7 Will bind with surface giving antistatic and residual bacteristatic activity

(continued)

Table 30   *continued*

Types and composition	Uses	Factors affecting use
Diguanines: cationic, e.g. chlorhexidine	1 Skin 2 No other uses	1 Limited range of specificity 2 Species of *Pseudomonas* are tolerant but activity is improved in a 4% alcohol solution 3 Other factors similar to the QACs
QACs and diguanines	1 Skin 2 No other uses	1 An attempt to overcome limitations of each type but only partially successful
Clear phenols: cresol, or similar, dispersed in soap solution	1 Drains 2 Not recommended for other uses	1 Very corrosive or may cause severe dermatitis 2 Very wide range of specificity 3 Strong smell prevents use in food and other areas 4 Inactivated by cationic surfactants and rubber
White fluid phenols: emulsion of refined phenols *Black fluid phenols:* emulsion of coal-tar phenols	1 Hard surfaces and some fixtures and fittings in toilets, hospital theatres and sluice rooms 2 Drains 3 No other uses recommended	1 Cause severe dermatitis 2 Wide range of specificity 3 Very effective 4 Strong smell prevents use in food and other areas 5 Inactivated by cationic surfactants and rubber 6 Must not be mixed with chlorine-releasing chemicals 7 Health hazards increasingly make their use inappropriate
Chlorinated phenols: chloroxylenol dispersed in soap solution	1 General skin disinfectant 2 No other uses	1 Limited range of specificity particularly with respect to species of *Pseudomonas* 2 Inactivated by cationic surfactants, organic matter, hard water, rubber 3 When dispersed in water forms a cloudy suspension

Substance	Uses	Comments
Complex phenols, e.g. hexachlorophane	1 Skin disinfectant incorporated in toilet soap	1 Fair range of specificity 2 Research in progress has suggested that it may be a health hazard
Pine fluids	1 Use not recommended	1 Very limited range of specificity 2 Limited effectiveness in general
Formaldehyde: colourless gas	1 Fumigation as part of terminal cleaning	1 Highly irritant 2 Fogging with a mixture of steam and gas can be used for terminal cleaning where certain pathogens are involved, e.g. smallpox
Alcohols: ethanol or isopropanol	1 Skin 2 Hard surfaces in theatres and clinical areas, e.g. dressing trolleys	1 Wide range of specificity 2 Very effective 3 Little inactivation 4 Low flash point
Oxidizing agents: potassium chlorate or potassium permanganate	1 Drains	1 Can be used in drains where it may not be possible to ensure completely effective cleaning

BS 5197: 1976, *Specification for Aromatic Disinfectant Fluids.*

BS 5283: 1976, *Glossary of Terms Relating to Disinfectants.*

See also Kelsey, J.C., and Sykes, G., *Pharmaceutical Journal,* Vol. 202, pp 607–9 (1969).

Sterilization

Sterilization is a much abused term. It should only be applied where it is intended to destroy all micro-organisms and their spores. The process has little relevance to accommodation and cleaning services except in specific hospital situations, e.g. sterilization of medical equipment. In this section only the broad principles are described.

Methods of sterilization

Heat sterilization can be achieved by one of two methods:

1 In an autoclave (a refined pressure cooker); equipment is subjected to temperatures of 121° to 134°C for 15 to 3 min in a moist atmosphere.
2 In an oven; equipment is subjected to temperatures of 160° to 190°C for 45 to 15 min in a dry atmosphere.

Of the two methods the former is preferred. The efficiency of the sterilization process is checked by including Browne control tubes within the batch of equipment to be sterilized. A colour change is used as an indication of effective sterilization.

Low-temperature gas sterilization can be used for heat-sensitive materials, but this method can be less satisfactory.

Disposables are increasingly preferred. Equipment or materials are prepackaged and sterilized by radiation or heat.

Handling and disposal

All sterile equipment must be stored in unopened packages in a warm dry atmosphere. Storage on open racks will make general cleaning easier.

Used non-disposable equipment is placed in disinfectant solution and returned for sterilization.

Used disposable syringes and similar equipment are placed in 'sharps' boxes to reduce the risk of accidents. Other used disposables are placed in suitably coded polythene sacs. Both types are incinerated.

7 Protective finishes

Seals and polishes are finishes applied to a surface to protect it *(a)* against the direct effects of abrasion and *(b)* from soil, grease, oils and other chemicals. This they do by forming a thin layer or film over the surface. They will help to maintain and often enhance the appearance of a surface.

The distinction between the two is mainly in the way that they are used. Seals are semi-permanent materials which, when appplied, will remain on the surface for several years being restored as required. Polishes are applied to and removed from a surface at more frequent intervals. Seals are more durable, more resistant to soil, chemicals and stains and more resistant to abrasion than polishes, but are less easily restored to their original finish.

Seals

Functions

Seals are applied to a floor or other surface to perform one or more of the following functions:

- Prevent entry of dirt and soil into a floor.
- Increase life of a floor by eliminating direct wear.
- Protect floor from chemicals.
- Improve appearance.
- Reduce dusting.
- Arrest further deterioration of a badly worn or porous floor.
- Increase ease and reduce costs of routine maintenance.
- When applied to a floor the seal will penetrate the floor to a greater or lesser extent but will leave a hard impervious film on the surface.

Requirements

The seal selected for a particular floor or surface must meet a number of requirements although their relative importance will depend upon the particular situation. The principal requirements are:

- Prevent entry of dirt and soil into the floor.
- Protect floor from water and chemicals.
- Good adhesion and resistance to flaking, chipping or cracking.
- Easy to apply.
- Easy to repair, re-coat and remove.
- Durable.
- Good appearance.
- Resists scuffs.
- Does not alter colour of floor or yellow with age.
- Quick drying.
- Mild solvent odour.
- Realistic cost.
- High flash point.

A seal must be compatible with the surface to which it is applied, i.e. it must not damage the surface. It must be capable of complete removal without damaging the surface because, although durable, it will be subject to wear and may eventually be unsuitable for repair or recoating.

Types of seal

Seals can be classified according to their principal chemical components and the process whereby they form a protective film. There are two major classes of seal:

Solvent-based seals consist principally of various types of resin dissolved in an organic solvent. They can be pigmented or clear and may contain oils.

Water-based seals consist of acrylic or other materials dispersed or dissolved in water.

Table 31   *Types of seal, their composition and sealing process*

Class	Type	Composition	Sealing process
Solvent-based	Oleoresinous	Oils, phenolic resins, driers, solvents	Penetrates floor and leaves surface film. Hardening involves evaporation of solvent and oxidation of oils accelerated by driers
	One-pot polyurethane (oil-modified)	Polyurethane, oils, solvents, additives	As oleoresinous
	One-pot polyurethane (moisture-cured)	Polyurethane, solvents, additives	Penetrates floor and leaves surface film. Hardening involves chemical reaction with water drawn from atmosphere
	Two-pot polyurethane	Two components: a polyester resin base and a hardener (accelerator) such as isocyanate in solvent	Base and hardener mixed together just before application. Some penetration of floor and surface film formed. Chemical reaction between base and hardener
	Pigmented, two-pot polyurethane	Similar to clear, two-pot polyurethane but base contains pigments and additives resistant to alkali	As for two-pot polyurethane
	Epoxy resin (two-pot)	Two components: base and initiator	Base and initiator mixed just before application. Penetration of floor and surface film formed. Chemical reaction between base and initiator
Water-based	Water-based emulsion	Acrylic polymers: large molecules, plasticizer, water	Polymer molecules fill pores and form a plastic skin over surface. (Molecules are larger than similar chemicals in polishes)
	Silicate dressing	Sodium silicate, water	Sodium silicate reacts with the lime in concrete to form insoluble calcium silicate which helps form seal. Water evaporates leaving deposit of silicate glass

The chemical composition and type of solvent will determine the way in which a seal forms a protective film. Table 31 lists the major types of seal and the method whereby they form a protective film. (See also 'Surface coatings' for a further explanation.) The composition will also determine the properties of a seal and accordingly its uses. Table 32 shows the more important properties of seals.

Selection

The sealing of a floor is an expensive operation, but when taken as part of an overall method of maintenance it will reduce the costs of routine and periodic cleaning and maintenance. Conversely, it must be remembered that the use of the wrong seal can increase costs. It is essential that the most appropriate seal is selected for any particular situation.

When selecting a seal a number of factors must be considered. These will include:

1 Prevention of water and soil entering the floor.
2 Reduction of deterioration caused by traffic.
3 **Prevention of deterioration caused by** chemicals.
4 Improvement of appearance.
5 Reduction of dusting.
6 Prevention of further deterioration of a badly worn or porous floor.
7 Improvement in efficiency and reduction of cost of routine maintenance methods.

Sealing of a wood-block floor with light traffic with **oleoresinous seal would be adequate if** reasons (1), (2) and (7) were the principal objectives. However, increased usage would make the use of a more durable seal, e.g. a two-pot polyurethane, desirable. To reduce dusting of a concrete floor, a silicate dressing would be adequate. However, if good resistance to chemicals and appearance were also important, then an epoxy resin could be applied. Normally, thermoplastic and PVC asbestos floors will not need sealing, but should the floor become worn and excessively porous, a water-based seal will help reduce further deterioration.

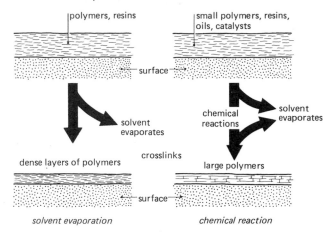

Figure 67 *Films formed by seals drying by solvent evaporation and/or chemical reaction*

Types of floor The type of floor will have a major influence on the type of seal that can be used. The points to be considered are:

● Will the seal adhere to the floor?
● Will the seal have a detrimental effect on the floor?
● Can the seal be removed relatively easily without damaging the floor?

Solvent-based seals adhere well to wood, wood composition and cork floors. They have no detrimental effects and can be renewed without damaging the floor. Conversely, they adhere poorly to terrazzo and marble floors. They have a detrimental effect on flexible PVC, PVC asbestos, thermoplastic and rubber floors; the solvent causes PVC to swell and pigments to bleed in PVC and thermoplastic floors and cannot be removed without damaging the floors. Water-based seals cannot be used on porous floors, i.e. wood, wood composition and cork, but adhere well to, have no detrimental effects and can be removed easily from **terrazzo,** marble, flexible PVC, PVC asbestos, thermoplastic, linoleum and rubber floors. Solvent-based are generally not suitable for asphalt floors but, subject to testing, two-pot polyurethane can be used sometimes. The alkaline nature of concrete makes the use of seals not resistant to alkali unsatisfactory. Table 33 shows the major types of floor.

Table 32   *The properties of the major types of seal*

Types	Oleoresinous	One-pot polyurethane	Two-pot polyurethane	Epoxy resin	Pigmented rubber	Pigmented two-pot polyurethane	Water-based emulsion	Silicate dressing
Colour	Dark, yellows with age	Oil-modified*, dark; moisture cured, very pale	Pale	Clear or pigmented	Coloured, e.g. red, grey	Coloured, e.g. red, grey, black, green	Very pale	Varies
Chemical resistance	Limited resistance to organic solvents, acids and alkalis	Oil-modified, moderate resistance to acids, alkalis, solvents, oils, grease; moisture-cured, good resistance to acids, and fair to alkalis, solvents, oils and grease	Excellent resistance to acids, and fair to alkalis, solvents, oils and grease	Excellent resistance to alkalis. Good resistance to oils and grease and fair to acids and solvents	Good resistance to acids, alkalis, grease, oil. Softened by white spirit and other solvents	Very good resistance to acids, alkalis, oil, water, grease. Poor resistance to solvents	Poor resistance to acids, solvents and strong alkalis. Fair resistance to oil, grease and weak alkalis	Good resistance to oil, grease solvents. Poor resistance to acids and alkalis
Adhesion	Good for most floors, but poor on stone group	Poor to fair depending on state and type of floor	Moderate to good on most floors, but poor on stone group. Depends largely on state of floor	Good on most floors including stone group if there is a reasonable key	Moderate to good on most floors depending on state of floor	Moderate to good on most floors, but can be poor on stone groups	Good on all floors	Only suitable on concrete

Chemical properties	Damages flexible PVC, PVC asbestos, thermoplastics, rubber	Damages flexible PVC, PVC asbestos, thermoplastics, rubber and asphalt	Damages flexible PVC, PVC asbestos, thermoplastics, rubber	Damages flexible PVC, PVC asbestos, thermoplastics, rubber	Damages flexible PVC, PVC asbestos, thermoplastics, rubber	Damages flexible PVC, PVC asbestos, thermoplastics, rubber	Water in seal can affect wood floors	Only suitable on concrete
Ease of removal	Use sanding machine or nylon mesh discs under scrubber/polisher. Chemical strippers can be used, but more difficult	Use a sanding machine or nylon mesh disc. Chemical strippers can be used on oil-modified, but not moisture-cured	Use a sanding machine. Nylon mesh discs are partially effective. Chemical strippers have little effect	Use sanding machine. Nylon mesh discs not very effective. Chemical strippers have little effect	If floor flat, use a sanding machine or nylon mesh disc. If floor ribbed, use chemical stripper	Use a sanding machine. Nylon mesh discs are partially effective. Chemical strippers have no effect	Use a strong alkaline detergent and course pad under scrubbing machine	Very difficult
Ease of re-coating	Apply to clean dry floor	Difficult to ensure good inter-coat adhesion. Requires roughening of surface and mopping with solvent to produce good key	Difficult to ensure inter-coat adhesion. Requires roughening of surface and mopping with solvent to produce a key	Good inter-coat adhesion if surface roughened to give a good key	Apply to clean dry floor	Difficult to ensure inter-coat adhesion. Requires roughening and mopping with solvent to produce a key	Apply to clean, grease-free floor	Apply to clean floor
Odour	Mild	Mild	Strong	Moderate	Mild	Moderate	None	None
Durability (years)	1 to 2	0.5 to 5, moisture-cured better than oil modified	2 to 6	2 to 10	1 to 2	1.5 to 5	1 to 3 if suitably maintained	0.5 to 5

Table 33 *Seals for major types of floor*

Floor and need for sealing	Suitable seals	Unsuitable seals
Wood, gran-wood, cork (must be ideally)	Oleoresinous: one-pot and two-pot polyurethane; epoxy resin	Pigmented rubber; pigmented two-pot polyurethane; water-based seals and dressings
Magnesite (can be)	Most types of solvent-based seal depending upon reason for sealing	Water-based seals and dressing
Flexible PVC, PVC asbestos, thermoplastics, rubber (if old and porous)	Water-based	All others
Linoleum (if old and porous)	Water-based (two-pot polyurethane possible, but not recommended)	All others
Asphalt (can be)	Water-based; two-pot polyurethane (test first); pigmented rubber (test first); pigmented two-pot polyurethane (test first)	Oleoresinous; one-pot polyurethane; silicate dressing
Terrazzo, marble, quarry tile (not normally)	Water-based	All others
Stone (not normally)	Water-based; pigmented rubber; pigmented two-pot polyurethane; epoxy resin	Oleoresinous; one-pot polyurethane; silicate dressing
Concrete (can be)	Silicate; pigmented rubber; pigmented two-pot polyurethane; two pot polyurethane; water-based (depends on formulation); epoxy resin	Oleoresinous; one-pot polyurethane

Existing state of floor If no seal has been used previously, but the floor has been maintained correctly, then the choice of seal will be limited by other factors. If little or no maintenance has been carried out then in some circumstances it may be impossible to seal the floor, e.g. where a wooden floor has become thoroughly permeated with oil and grease. Where the floor has been sealed previously and it is not possible to remove completely or be sure of completely removing the previous seal, the choice will be limited by the compatibility of the new seal with the old. The more important incompatible combinations are:

1 Oleoresinous applied to one-pot or two-pot polyurethanes.

2 One-pot moisture-cured and two-pot polyurethanes applied to oleoresinous or pigmented rubber.

3 Silicate dressing applied to any other seal and *vice versa.*

Durability The most durable seal suitable should be used consistant with the amount of wear experienced by a floor, and whether or not a polish will be used. Floors experiencing heavy usage, e.g. foyers, reception areas and gymnasia, will require very durable seals. A polish will increase the life of a seal.

Drying time This will become important where the floor is only available for sealing for a short period. A two-pot polyurethane seal may be the only possibility.

Odour May occasionally be important. Typical situations where a seal with a mild odour must be used include opthalmic wards, burns units and units dealing with respiratory tract infections and areas where food is handled or stored.

Colour Pigmented seals in addition to their protective role will improve the appearance of concrete and of worn magnesite, asphalt and stone floors, but are unsuitable for floors where the inherant colour or design is required. The non-pigmented seals are suitable in most situations. The darker colour of oleoresinous seals tends to yellow with age.

Slip resistance In general, a seal applied correctly will increase the slip resistance of a floor. All seals have a coefficient of friction, seal to leather, of greater than 0.5. Although there is no correlation between gloss and slip resistance, where there is a possibility of this correlation being made then a seal drying to a matt or subdued gloss should be used, e.g. oleoresinous, water-based. Specialised non-slip finishes can be applied to a floor.

Flexibility Most seals are regarded as being flexible, i.e. when subjected to identation they distort rather then puncture. If the seal is broken, water can enter eventually causing the seal to lift. The one-pot polyurethanes are least suitable in this respect.

Ease of recoating When it is expected that a seal will require regular recoating or repair and where experienced labour is unavailable, a seal which can be easily repaired or recoated should be selected, e.g. oleoresinous and water-based.

Ease of removal Can influence the type of seal selected. Oleoresinous and polyurethane seals can be removed with varying degrees of ease from wood, granwood and cork floors by sanding and without damage to the floor. Their removal from fleixible PVC, PVC asbestos and thermoplastic floors will generally damage the floor. Conversely, a water-based seal can be removed from these floors without damage.

Initial dressing The use of an intial dressing or priming coat is desirable where the floor is uneven, porous or where there is a possibility of poor adhesion because of previous treatments.

Cost The cost of sealing must include the need for subsequent resealing, repair and recoating. The most durable possible seal will reduce these costs.

Preparation, application and maintenance

Preparation of a floor is intended to provide a clean, dry, oil- and wax-free surface to which the seal will adhere. If the floor is damp, oily, greasy or waxy, adhesion will be poor. If the floor is dusty the appearance will be poor and will accelerate deterioration. Adhesion of the seal to the floor will depend upon the formation of a good key between the seal and the floor.

When preparing a floor for sealing, training and safety must be emphasized. Many of the tasks involved require well trained staff who know the methods of carrying out each task and who are aware of the relevant safety precautions. The use of sanding machines in the hands of untrained

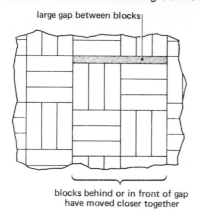

Figure 68   *Rafting*

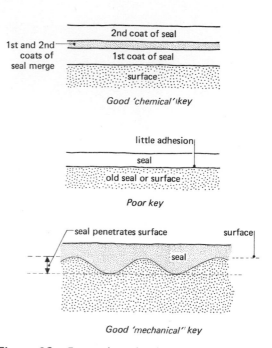

Figure 69   *Formation of a 'key'*

operatives can result in major damage to floors, e.g. cork tiles and carpet. Stripping compounds, in particular methylene chloride, are particularly dangerous and should be used in well ventilated areas and by operatives wearing appropriate protective clothing, in particular face masks. The drinking of milk during such operations is considered to be very efficacious.

Application of a seal can be carried out using brushes, mops, bonnets or rollers, the actual method chosen depending on the type of seal and floor. In general, application will be successful if the following points are remembered:

- Water will cause lifting, bubbling and blistering of solvent based seal.
- Floors on which water-based (unless formulated for concrete), oleoresinous and one-pot polyurethane seals are to be used must be neutral. Alkalis will cause the seals to break down.
- Waxes remaining on a floor will cause seals to adhere badly. If all wax cannot be removed, then either do not attempt to seal or an initial dressing can be tried.
- Large paint brushes can be used to apply most seals.
- Cotton mops can be used for spreading oleoresinous and water-based seals.
- Lambswool bonnets can be used for rapid application of thin coats. They are not, however, suitable for two-pot seals.

- Rollers can be used for rapid application of all seals but, unless great care is taken, there is a danger of applying coats too thickly.
- Apply seal from bucket or tray.
- Allow seals to dry before applying next coat, but do not allow seal to over-harden.
- Always mix two-pot seals just before application.
- Main traffic lanes and entrances will require extra coats if the use of a polish does not form part of the subsequent method of maintenance.
- Always clean equipment in the appropriate solvents.

Repairing or recoating depend on a *mechanical* key in the case of water-based seals and on both a *mechanical* and a *chemical* key when solvent-based seals are applied. The presence of water, wax, oil or grease interfere with the successful formation of the key.

A solvent-based seal applied to a suitable floor penetrates the floor to a greater or lesser extent forming a *mechanical* key between the floor and the seal. Subsequent coats soften the earlier coat

Table 34 *General methods of preparing floors for sealing*

Floor	Preparation
New	Sanding, etching, scrubbing to remove surface dressing or washing as appropriate to type of floor
Old floor - no protective finish	As for new floors, but may require additional treatment to remove build up of oil, grease, dirt
Old floor - protected by solvent or water-based polish but not seal	Removal of polish using method appropriate to type of polish and floor. Essential to test that old wax has been removed by applying new seal to 2 or 3 m^2 of floor and checking that it dries in the correct time and to the correct degree of hardness
Old floor - protected by solvent or water-based seal but not polished	If seal badly deteriorated or incompatible with new seal then it should be removed by method appropriate to seal and floor. Compatibility of seal can be checked by applying new seal to 3 or 4 m^2 of floor in a main traffic lane and checking adhesion and durability after a period of 3 to 4 weeks. If seal is in good condition and compatible with new seal, floor is prepared for re-coating or repair using method appropriate to type of seal in use
Old floor - protected by both polish and seal	Remove polish and then proceed as for sealed floors

allowing the formation of a *chemical* key between the old and new coats. When a water-based seal is applied, the polymer particles penetrate the pores of the floor forming a *mechanical* key. The type of penetration will depend upon: the type of floor, whether the floor is old or new, the previous method of maintenance, and whether it is better to seal, repair, recoat or reseal. The general methods of preparation are shown in Table 34.

Always apply coats thinly. Thick coats can bubble or, in the case of two-pot polyurethane, appear white. Thinning of the first coat applied can improve adhesion between floor and subsequent coats. It also makes feathering in of seal (see Figure 70) during repair easier. Marking lines should always be applied between first and second coats.

Maintenance Seals can be maintained by sweeping, vacuuming, mopping, scrubbing, and spray cleaning. The durability of the seal can be enhanced by the use of an appropriate polish.

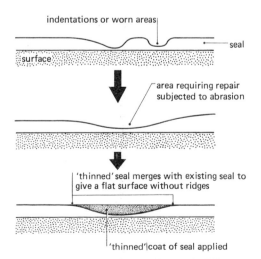

Figure 70 *Feathering*

Polishes

Functions of a polish

Polishes are substances that when applied to a surface form a relatively impervious barrier intended to serve one or more of the following functions:

- Protect the surface by preventing the entry of dirt, soil, grease, oil and water and resisting chemicals and stains.
- Increase the durability of a surface or seal by reducing the effects of wear and tear.
- Improve the appearance of a surface by filling minor imperfections and giving it an attractive sheen or gloss.
- Adjust the slip resistance of a floor.
- Improve the efficiency, effectiveness and reduce the costs of cleaning and maintenance.
  Polishes are made for use on a wide range of fixtures, fittings, furnishings and surfaces.

Requirements of a polish

A polish must meet a number of specific requirements depending on the type of polish and its intended use. These are:

- Prevent dirt and soil entering a surface.
- Resistant to water and chemicals.
- Durable.
- Good gloss and sheen.
- Will not yellow with age or alter colour of surface.
- Resistant to scuffing.
- Resistant to carbon heel marks (floor polishes only).
- Buffable after wear.
- Good antislip properties (floor polishes only).
- Easy to apply.
- Good levelling and flow characteristics.
- Good adhesion.
- Easily recoated.
- Easily removed when required.
- Quick drying.
- Indefinite shelf life.
- Mild odour.
- Realistic cost.

Types of polish

These are tabulated in Table 35 and fall into the following categories:

Table 35   *Types of polish*

Solvent-based		Water-based emulsion		
Type	*Uses*	*Type*		*Use*
Paste wax	Furniture, floors	Non-metallized	Fully buffable	Floors
Cream wax	Furniture		Semi-buffable	
Liquid wax	Furniture, floors		Dri-bright	
Spray wax	Furniture			
		Metallized	Semi-buffable	Floors
			Dri-bright	
		Wash and wax		Floors
		Acid-sensitive		Floors

Solvent-based waxes consist of a blend of waxes in an organic solvent, usually turpentine or white spirit. The term 'wax' is a nebulous one and has come to mean chemicals which resemble beeswax, either physically or chemically. Dyes, masking agents and silicones are also added, depending on the particular use intended for the polish. Evaporation of the solvent leaves a relatively impervious layer of wax on the surface to which the polish is applied.

Their use is restricted to surfaces unaffected by the solvent, e.g. wood group of floors.

Water-based emulsions consist of a suspension of emulsified wax, alkalis, soluble resins, polymers and various additives in water. During manufacture water and wax are emulsified by heating them together with emulsifying agents and then adding the emulsified waxes to hot water. The wax solidifies as fine particles (water in wax solid emulsion) dispersed in the water. To this mixture the other ingredients are added. Evaporation of the water leaves a relatively impervious layer of wax, resin and polymers on the surface to which the polish is applied.

The major types of water-based polish are shown in Table 35. The essential characteristics of each can be defined as follows:

- *Fully buffable:* requires buffing to produce a high gloss.
- *Semi-buffable:* dries to a subdued gloss and requires buffing to produce a high gloss.
- *Dri-bright:* dries to a high gloss without buffing.
- *Metallized:* contains zinc or zirconium metals which link the polymer molecules together, thus increasing resistance to detergents.
- *Wash 'n' wax:* has the gloss characteristics of a dri-bright polish, and is a formulation of detergent and polish which both cleans and applies a layer of polish to the floor. It is not to be confused with buffable detergents.
- *Acid-sensitive:* special formulation which can only be removed by special acid strippers.

Metallized and non-metallized polishes are formulated to have a solids content ranging from

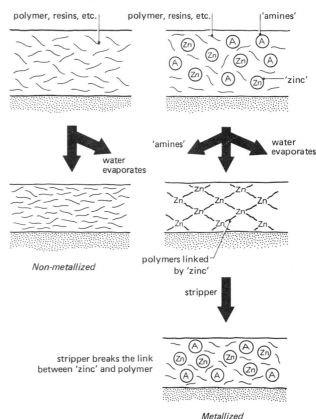

Figure 71 *Film formation by metallized and non-metallized polishes*

12—15% (normal) to 25–30% (high solids). A high solids polish will enable a thicker coat of polish to be applied.

The difference between buffable, semi-buffable and dri-bright is related to the relative amounts of wax and polymer each contains. The greater the content of wax the more buffing required to establish a gloss. The greater the amount of polymer the more able it is to dry to a gloss finish without buffing. A buffable emulsion contains relatively more wax than polymer, while a dri-bright contains more polymer than wax.

Water-based polishes can be used on a wide range of floors, including the wood group, providing they are sealed.

Table 36 shows the general characteristics of each of the main chemicals used in the manufacture of polishes.

Table 36   *Chemicals used in manufacture of polishes*

Class and characteristics	Examples	Specific characteristics
Solvents		
1 Organic solvents in solvent-based polish 2 Water in water-based polishes 3 Evaporation of solvent leaves a deposit of wax, resins, polymers, depending on type of polish	White spirit	1 Flash point 41°C, flammable 2 Drying takes about 30 min. If a flash evaporating solvent is included, drying takes about 10 min
	Water	1 Non-flammable 2 Drying takes 30 min
Waxes		
1 Contribute to gloss, durability and flexibility of polish 2 Require buffing to produce gloss 3 Require buffing to increase hardness and hence durability 4 Generally limited scuff resistance, but removed by buffing 5 Generally good resistance to carbon heel marks 6 Good chemical resistance other than to solvents 7 Moderate slip resistance, but exceptions	Beeswax	1 Mainly obsolete - but still used in fine furniture polish
	Carnuba	1 Obtained from leaves of carnuba plant 2 Good gloss and durability 3 Used in small amounts in solvent base
	Montan	1 Extracted from brown coal 2 Good gloss and durability 3 Very slippery
	Paraffin	1 Synthetic, cheap 2 Good gloss, and durability if combined with natural waxes
	Polyethylene	1 Synthetic, cheap 2 Excellent antislip properties 3 Powdering caused if more than 25% of solids in wax 4 Excellent gloss and durability 5 Used extensively in water-based polishes
	Microcrystalline	1 Good gloss and durability if combined with natural wax
Polymers		
1 Complex high-molecular-weight compounds	Polystyrene	1 Yellows with age

Table 36 — *continued*

Class and characteristics	Examples	Specific characteristics
2 Very durable, buffing unnecessary to increase hardness 3 Gloss develops on drying; no buffing necessary 4 Generally good resistance to scuffing; buffing will not remove scuffs easily 5 Generally poor resistance to carbon heel marks 6 Good chemical resistance other than to alkalis, but exceptions 7 Good slip resistance	Polyacrylate	1 Less resistance to scuffing and more resistant to carbon heel marks than polystyrene 2 Resistant to water spotting
	Copolymer of styrene and acrylate	1 Polymers are held together with zinc or zirconium 2 Excellent durability and resistance to scuffing, carbon heel marks, heat. 3 Resistant to alkalis below pH 11.5 4 Further complexing of polymer molecules can take place making them very difficult to remove
Alkali-soluble resins 1 Alkali-soluble polymers, related to natural products 2 Contribute to gloss 3 Make wax easier to remove 4 Contribute to levelling, flow and adhesion 5 Too much makes film brittle 6 Can crack with age	Terpene phenolics	1 As for general characteristics
Additives 1 Substances added in small amounts to improve specific performance characteristics	Plasticizer	1 Improves initial gloss and buffability 2 Reduces soil and scuff resistance
	Wetting agent	1 Improves flow of polish
	Silicones	1 Modified derivatives of silica 2 Difficult to remove 3 Improves resistance to chemicals, soils, water 4 Used in furniture polishes and protective finishes for carpets
	Coalescing agents	1 Improves film formed

Table 37 Types, composition and properties of polishes

Type	Composition	Gloss	Durability	Resistance to water, dirt, chemicals	Effects	Scuff resistance	Carbon heel mark resistance	Slip resistance	Removeability
Solvent based									
Paste wax	Wax 25-30% solvent, silicones if furniture polish	High gloss when buffed	Good; requires buffing to harden	Good, except solvents, oil and grease	Flammable; unsuitable for surfaces affected by solvents	Good, but scuffs can be removed by buffing	Very good	Good	Use solvent-based detergent. Difficult if silicone is present
Cream wax	Wax 20%, solvent, silicones	As paste wax	As paste wax	As paste wax	As paste wax; solvent gives wax cleaning properties	As paste wax	Not applicable	Not applicable	As paste wax
Liquid wax	Wax 8-12%, solvent, silicones if furniture polish	As paste wax	As paste wax	As paste wax	As paste wax	As paste wax	Not applicable	Not applicable	As paste wax
Spray wax	Wax 8%, solvent, silicones	As paste wax	As paste wax	As paste wax	As paste wax	Good	Not applicable	Not applicable	As paste wax
Water based									
Fully buffable	Polymer 20-40%, wax 45-60%, resin 5-15%	High gloss when buffed	Good, requires buffing to harden wax	Good except alkalis, oil and grease	Water and alkali cause wood to swell and discolour	Fair, but scuffs removed by buffing	Good	Good	Use mild alkaline detergent
Semi-buffable	Polymer 45-60% wax 25-40% resin 5-15%	Subdued gloss when dry, high gloss when buffed	Very good, buffing will harden wax	Good except alkalis, oil and grease	As for fully buffable	Good and scuffs removed by buffing	Moderately good	Very good	As buffable
Dri-bright	Polymer 50-70%, wax 5-15%, resin 5-15%	Dries to high gloss	Very good	Good except alkalis, oil and grease	As for fully buffable	Very good, but less easily removed	Poor	Excellent	As buffable
Metallized emulsion	Polymers cross-linked with zinc or zirconium	As for dri-bright or semi-buffable	Very good to excellent	Good to very good except oil or grease, resistant to	As for fully buffable	As for dri-bright	As for dri-bright	Excellent	Strong alkaline detergent or ammonia stripper

Type								
Wash and wax	Good gloss when buffed	Combination of wax and detergent permits washing and waxing in one step	Moderate	Good resistance to dirt and chemicals but not oil and grease. Some early products were poor	Application softens surface of previous coat, removing it, together with dirt, and replacing it with a fresh layer of wax	Moderate, but scuffs removed by buffing	Very good	Moderately good	Use alkaline detergent
Acid-sensitive	Good gloss	Special polymers resistant to alkalis and detergent	Excellent, very expensive and limited application	Highly resistant to many chemicals, particularly alkalis and detergents, but not oil and grease. Affected by acids, e.g. fruit	Only affects wood or cork materials but acid stripper used for removal may affect surfaces	Very good	Poor	Very good	Use acid stripper but has disadvantage of increasing range of maintenance products required

The properties of each of the two major classes of polish and of specific types in each class reflect the properties of the substances used in their composition. The properties of each type of polish are shown in Table 37. Of these properties, scuff resistance and resistance to carbon heel marks require more explanation. Scuff resistance includes resistance to the creation of scuff marks and their ease of removal. The softer polishes containing higher proportions of wax than polymer are less resistant to the creation of scuff marks than the harder polishes containing more polymer than wax, but scuffs can be more easily removed.

Resistance to heel marks is not the same as scuff resistance. The softer polishes are more resistant to the creation of marks and marks can be more easily removed.

Selection for furniture

A number of polishes are formulated for use on wooden furniture and should only be used for this purpose. They include paste wax, cream wax, liquid waxes, liquid no-rub waxes and spray polishes. The inclusion of silicone makes them difficult to remove but increases the resistance of the polish to heat, soil, chemicals and water.

Selection for floors

Before selecting a polish it must be decided whether a polish is required at all. Frequently a method of cleaning not involving the use of a polish will provide a satisfactory standard of cleanliness, appearance, protection and slip resistance.

The decision to use a polish will generally be based on the following criteria.

- Protection required to prevent entry of soil and water into floor. For example, it may be preferable to use a polish on unsealed, semi-porous floors subject to moderate to heavy soilage and regular wetting.
- Protection required to prevent deterioration of a seal or of unsealed surface experiencing moderate to heavy traffic.

- Protection required to prevent damage to floor caused by chemical spillage.
- Adjustment of antislip characteristics of a floor. A polish can be used to improve the non-slip properties of a surface.

If it is decided that a polish is necessary then the actual selection will depend on the following factors:

Method of cleaning and maintenance employed in the building   As far as possible the use of a large number of different polishes within a building is undesirable. Two or three polishes will generally be sufficient to deal with most types of surface requiring cleaning and maintenance. The use of many different types can be both expensive and present problems with respect to standardization of procedures and their control. If a floor is taken in isolation from the rest of the building one polish may give better results than another but in relation to the whole building the advantages may not be significant.

Method and frequency of cleaning and maintaining the polish   A dri-bright should be used where the system of maintenance involves spray cleaning or when it is not intended to buff the polish. Buffable and semi-buffable polishes are used where the system involves spray burnishing. When mop and buff systems are employed buffable, semi-buffable or dri-bright may be used although a case can be made for the more widespread use of dri-brights. Metallized polishes can be used as an alternative to a non-metallized dri-bright polish. They should be used where the system of maintenance involves routine light scrubbing and as a base coat where the system employed requires the periodic stripping of polish. The base coat is resistant to detergent and so remains intact, making it only necessary to apply the top coats of polish.

A requirement to apply further coats of polish at regular intervals should be minimized and the frequency of application, if further coats are required, should be reduced if the type of polish to be used is selected correctly and the appropriate methods of cleaning used.

Resistance to soil and water   Polishes in general have good resistance to water and soil, but where the floor is likely to become greasy and oily their use is not recommended, the surface tending to become slippery.

Durability   When traffic and therefore wear is heavy a high solids polish should be used to increase the thickness of film applied. This will reduce the necessity to apply and the frequency of applying further coats of polish at regular intervals.

Resistance to chemicals   When floors are likely to be subject to chemical spillage, protection will generally be a function of a seal rather than a polish. For unsealed surfaces, polishes will provide reasonable protection in the event of occasional spillages. Solvent-based polishes should never be used where there is any possibility of spillage of organic solvents.

Appearance   The appearance that a polish gives to a floor will depend on the following characteristics of the polish: gloss, scuff resistance and ease with which scuffs can be removed; resistance to carbon heel marks; colour and yellowing with age. Solvent- and water-based emulsion polishes will all give a high gloss which can be maintained using the appropriate method of cleaning. In most instances a good gloss is required. However, if there is a possibility of psychological links being formed between slipperiness and gloss, then a semi-buffable polish can be used. Resistance to and ease of removal of scuff and heel marks should be considered. As a general principle it is easier to remove scuff and heel marks from a buffable polish.

All solvent-based polishes will yellow to some extent with age making them unsuitable, irrespective of other factors, for use on any floors where 'true' colour is important, e.g. linoleum. On wooden surfaces this may not matter. The water based polishes are, ideally, colourless when dry, making them suitable for all floors.

Type of floor The selection of a polish for a particular floor must take into account the previous history of the floor, the adhesion of polish to the floor and the effect of polish on the floor. If the floor has been sealed, then the type of polish that can be used will be determined by the seal. All types of floor polishes can be used on top of solvent-based seals. Conversely, water-based polishes can only be used on top of water-based seals. A solvent-based polish will not adhere to a water-based seal; it softens the seal and creates slippery conditions. If the floor has not been sealed, but polishes have previously been used, the polish to be used must be compatible with the polish previously used unless they can be removed completely. Adhesion and the effect of the polish on the floor will be important. Water-based polishes will adhere well to terrazzo, marble, PVC asbestos, flexible PVC, thermoplastic and linoleum and will not damage them, but on unsealed wood, granwood and cork floors they may cause swelling of the surface. More importantly, stripping of the polish from the floor may involve the regular use of water and alkali both of which will result in damage to the floor. They may be used quite satisfactorily on well maintained sealed wood, granwood and cork floors.

Polishes should not be used on the stone group of floors except under exceptional circumstances and solvent-based polishes should never be used. (See Table 41, page 220, for polishes to be used on various types of floor.)

Location of floors In general it is preferable to use either water-based or solvent-based polishes in the same building, but not both. If both are used then they must not be used in adjacent rooms where the solvent polish can be carried onto the water-based polish, thus creating slippery conditions. This transfer of polish from one floor to another is known as 'walk off'. A similar situation can occur when solvent-based polishes are carried onto a terrazzo floor.

Slip resistance Generally all the polishes used have acceptable slip resistance:

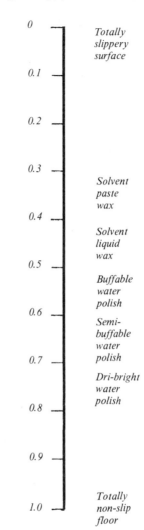

Coefficient of friction

0	Totally slippery surface
0.1	
0.2	
0.3	Solvent paste wax
0.4	Solvent liquid wax
0.5	Buffable water polish
0.6	Semi-buffable water polish
0.7	Dri-bright water polish
0.8	
0.9	
1.0	Totally non-slip floor

Although there is no correlation between gloss and slip, where this question might be raised, a semi-buffable water-based polish should be used. It must be remembered that the antislip properties of a polish are only as good as the prevailing system of maintenance. Dirt, soil, water, grease, trafficking of solvent-based polishes, breakdown of a polish because of failure to correctly neutralize a floor after stripping will all reduce the antislip properties of a surface.

Odour   Most polishes are mild but that of the stripping agent may not be. Where odour is important, e.g. opthalmic areas, stripping agents with a mild odour should be selected.

Cost   The major element of cost (80–90%) of a floor maintenance programme is labour. Accordingly, the materials, equipment and methods used will be selected to reduce labour costs to a minimum. This can be achieved by selecting a polish that can be most easily restored to an acceptable standard in the context of the methods of cleaning and maintenance used in the building and by selecting a polish with the greatest possible durability, thereby reducing the frequency of periodic maintenance.

Preparation, application and maintenance

The achievement of the best results from a polish, assuming that it has been selected correctly, will depend on the following:

Preparation is intended to provide a clean, dry, grease and oil free surface to which the polish will adhere. When water-based emulsions are applied the surface must be neutral and free from any wax or solvent, if a solvent-based wax has previously been used. The method of preparation will depend on the type of surface, whether the surface is sealed or not, whether the surface has previously been polished and whether the surface must be stripped of polish.

When preparing a floor for the application of a polish the following points should be observed.

- If a floor has not previously been polished or a further coat of polish is to be applied all dirt, grease and oil must be removed by mopping or scrubbing with a neutral or alkaline detergent depending on the amount of the soil.
- If previous coats of polish are not to be completely removed then as far as possible a compatible polish must be used.
- A polish can be removed by scrubbing or spray stripping. Solvent- and water-based polishes will, respectively, require a solvent-based detergent and an alkaline detergent when scrubbing.

- Removal of a metallized polish will involve the use of a strong alkaline detergent or one containing ammonia or related compounds. If a metallized base coat has been applied to the floor its removal should not be required every time stripping is carried out.
- When an alkaline detergent has been used, it is most important to remove all the alkali and to neutralize the surface by rinsing the floor with a dilute acid ($\frac{1}{2}$ pint vinegar in 1 gallon of water). Rinsing must be continued until indicator paper records a pH of 7.
- When a solvent-based detergent has been used it is most important to remove all solvent and wax by thorough rinsing.
- Before application is commenced the floor must be dry and dust free. It is advisable to damp mop or suction clean immediately before application.

See Table 41, pages 220, for methods of preparing various types of floor. With respect to furniture the surface should be clean and dry, using routines described on pages 231–233.

Application   The method of application will depend to some extent on the type of polish used. The methods applicable to floors and furniture are outlined on pages 215 and 234 respectively. Pastes can be applied to floors as a hot spray using appropriate equipment. Care must be taken that polish is only applied to the floor.

Application will be successful if the following points are remembered:

- Apply polish thinly. If too thick it will dry slowly, wrinkle and be soft.
- Apply evenly, ensuring that there are no puddles of polish.
- Allow polish to dry between coats.
- If appropriate, and when polish is dry, buff between coats using a pad or brush.
- The first coat of polish should be applied within 25 cm of the skirting boards. Only the

top coat should be applied upto the skirting board. This will reduce the possibility of build up of polish on areas not generally walked on.

- The number of coats applied will depend to some extent upon the type of polish used and durability required. Normally two or three coats will be applied, greater film thickness being achieved not by applying more coats but by using a polish having a higher solids content. If greater durability is required, a further coat can be applied, e.g. on main traffic lanes.
- Wash all equipment.

- Preferably, polish should not be walked on for 12 hrs. This is the ideal. It will be possible to walk on the polish once it is dry.

Maintenance will involve mopping and buffing, spray burnishing or spray cleaning depending on the system employed.

British Standards

PAS 8: 1974, *Light Wax Floor Polish.*
PAS 9: 1974, *Metallized Polymer Floor Polish.*
PAS 10: 1974, *Acrylic Emulsion Floor Polish.*

8 Accommodation services

In addition to cleaning and maintenance, accommodation services will involve, depending on the establishment, the provision of linen, food and beverage and laundry services. Each of these services is described in this chapter. It is generally true that the largest part of the accommodation services or housekeeping department's budget will be spent on the provision of cleaning services. In order to be cost-effective and to provide an appropriate standard of service, an understanding of methods and principles involved in the cleaning of various parts of a building, its fabric and furniture and of the procedures and routines employed is required.

Cleaning services

Reasons for cleaning

Cleaning will be required for five reasons:

Prevention of the spread of infection and disease   When maintaining a clean environment prevention of the spread of disease-causing bacteria and their removal can be of paramount importance. Cleaning is the most important method of achieving this. Effective cleaning will remove the majority of bacteria present on a surface.

The highest standards of hygiene will be required in high risk areas and operating theatres of hospitals. High standards will also be required in patient and treatment areas of hospitals and clinics, kitchens and sanitary accommodation.

Dust Control   In some situations dust control is of paramount importance. In industries

manufacturing hazardous materials or when hazardous dust and fumes are a by-product of the processes involved, levels of dust within the atmosphere must meet specified levels. In other industries, e.g. pharmaceuticals and electronics, dust may interfere with the manufacturing process.

Preservation of the fabric, fixtures, fittings and furnishings   Accumulation of dust, grease and other types of soil will lead to a progressive deterioration of a building and its furnishings. When cleaning is neglected, this process of deterioration will accelerate and when eventually carried out may require drastic methods which will cause further damage.

Provision of a socially acceptable environment   A clean and attractive environment is essential to live and work in. Guests are unlikely to return to a poorly maintained and cleaned hotel. People using a building are more likely to respect one that is clean and well maintained. Employees are likely to be happier and more productive.

Safety   Standards of cleaning and maintenance must be at least sufficient to meet the requirements of the *Health and Safety at Work etc. Act 1974.*

Standards of cleaning

The standard of cleaning to be achieved will be governed by the user's or customer's requirements and will depend largely on the type of establishment and the activities carried out within it. The standard set for a particular area will define the appearance and level of hygiene required. Table 38 indicates the five major standards used and their application. The standard set will be

Table 38 *Cleaning standards*

Standard	Characteristics	Uses
Clean to BS 5295 standards	Highest standards of appearance, dust and infection control	Hospital operating theatres and isolation units, industrial applications
Hygienically clean	High standard of cleanliness and appearance	Kitchens, toilets, hospital wards
Prestige	High standard of cleanliness and appearance	Public rooms, foyers, reception areas, hotel guest rooms, board rooms, senior management offices
General/domestic	Good standard of appearance and absence of soil	Bedrooms of residential establishments, general offices
Basic	Absence of disorder and visible soil	Basements, workshops

achieved by:

1 Correctly selecting the method of cleaning, and the equipment and materials to be used for each of the surfaces involved.
2 Carrying out cleaning tasks at suitable intervals.
3 Effective quality control.

Methods, equipment and materials

Cleaning will only be cost effective if the combination of equipment, materials, labour and method selected is correct and is selected in relation to the standard required. Methods employed, materials and equipment will depend on the following:

User or customer requirements Consultation with the user or other relevant persons will enable the standard and any other requirements for an area to be established.

Building usage Activities carried out within the building will determine what is required, e.g. in hospitals only wet methods should be used in the cleaning of operating theatres.

Fabric, fittings, fixtures and furnishing The types of surface, the materials from which they are made and their physical and chemical properties will determine the methods of cleaning employed and the equipment and materials used.

Nature and degree of soiling The type and amount of soil brought into or arising within a building will influence methods, materials and equipment employed.

Traffic The amount of traffic entering a building will affect the amount of soil brought in and the amount of wear and tear experienced by surfaces in particular floors. It will effect the system of floor maintenance used.

Density of furnishing This may affect the size of cleaning equipment that can be used. It will certainly influence the ease and speed with which cleaning can be carried out.

Safety The safety of cleaning staff and users of a building must be considered when selecting methods, equipment and materials, e.g. air-driven equipment can be required in wet areas.

Design and nature of building Access and lifts

Table 39 *Methods of cleaning and general applications*

Group	Method	Surfaces	Equipment
Dry	Dusting	Walls, ceilings, fixtures, fittings, furniture	Damp, static or impregnated duster or mitten
	Sweeping	Hard floors	Mop sweepers, brooms or powered sweeper
		Carpets	Mechanical sweeper
	Suction cleaning	Carpets, upholstery, curtains, hard floors, walls, ceilings	Suction cleaner and accessories as necessary
	Buffing	Floors	Scrubber/polisher and pad or brush
		Fixtures, fittings, furniture	Soft cloth
	Burnishing	Hard floors, polished	Scrubber/polisher and pad or brush
	Spray cleaning	Hard floors	Scrubber/polisher and pad
	Spray burnishing	Hard floors, polished	Scrubber/polisher and pad
	Spray stripping	Hard floors	Scrubber/polisher and pad
Dry/Wet	Scarifying	Stone group floors	Scarifying machine or scrubber/polisher and scarifying head

may be limited in older buildings. The fabric and furnishings may be badly deteriorated, create dust and make cleaning more difficult.

The methods of cleaning employed can be broadly divided into two groups: dry and wet. Table 39 summarizes the main methods of cleaning. These are described more fully in the following sections.

Frequency of cleaning

In all buildings there will be a progressive decline in the standards of appearance and cleanliness. The frequency with which the various surfaces are cleaned will depend on the standard required and the degree of soiling. In general the higher the standard required and the greater the amount of soiling the greater will be the frequency with which cleaning is carried out:

Frequency of cleaning increasing ↑

Infection/dust control
Hygienically clean/prestige
General/domestic
Basic

Cleaning tasks can be carried out at one of the following frequencies:

Table 39 — *continued*

Group	Method	Surfaces	Equipment
Wet	Damp mopping	Hard floors	Mops, buckets, gear press
	Wet mopping	Hard floors, usually non-porous	Mops, buckets, gear press
	Scrubbing	Hard floors, usually non-porous	Scrubber/polisher and brush or deck scrubber
		Hard, non-porous surfaces	Scrubbing brush or nylon pad
	Washing	Walls, ceilings, doors	Hand spray, wall-washing machine or high-pressure washer
		Furniture in general	Hand spray or high-pressure washer as appropriate
		Windows	Squeegee, chamois, scrim
	Damp wiping	Walls, ceilings, doors, furniture in general	Cloths
	Skimming	Carpets	Scrubber/polisher and pad or bonnet
	Shampoo	Carpets	Scrubber/polisher and brush or dry-foam machine
		Upholstery	Dry-foam machine
	Spray extraction	Carpets, upholstery	Spray extraction machine

Daily Any task carried out at least once per day. Where high standards of hygiene are required some tasks will be carried out routinely several times per day.

Check clean Task carried out several times per day but only as necessary, e.g. mop sweeping of floors to control dust.

Weekly Tasks carried out at least once per week. It may include tasks carried out 2 or 3 times per week.

Special Tasks only carried out as necessary, e.g.

removel of spillages, terminal cleaning of wards.

Periodic Tasks carried out less than weekly. The frequency may range from once every two weeks to once a year. Spring cleaning is a special type of periodic cleaning.

The higher the standard required the greater the number of tasks carried out daily and the more frequent will be periodic tasks. The DHSS lays down minimum frequencies for the various tasks to be carried out in hospitals (see *Hospital Management Advice Notes: No. 1 Cleaning Frequencies in Acute and General Hospitals,* 1972).

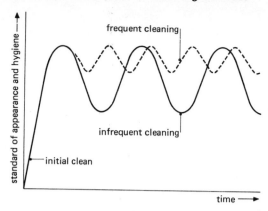

Figure 72   *Effect of cleaning frequency on standards*

Quality control

Effective systems of checking are essential to ensure that all work is carried out and that standards are being adhered to.

Order of Cleaning

The order in which cleaning tasks are carried out depends to some extent on the situation, but there are some broad principles:

1   Clean areas should be cleaned first and the dirtiest last to avoid transferring soil from dirty to clean areas.
2   Cleaning should be carried out working from the top to the bottom. This avoids the necessity of having to reclean or remove splashes. Wall washing is an exception.
3   Walking on cleaned surfaces during the cleaning of others should be avoided.
4   All work should be planned in accordance with work study principles, avoiding any unnecessary walking or movement.

A typical order of work conforming to these principles is:

Ventilate rooms
Remove all litter and debris
Remove all items requiring off-site cleaning
Clean high surfaces

Clean sanitary fittings
Spot clean walls and fittings
Clean furniture
Clean floors

Factors influencing when work is carried out

The time when cleaning can be carried out will be influenced by the following:

Traffic   Cleaning when traffic is lightest will have a number of benefits:

1   Dust will settle and can be removed more effectively.
2   There will be fewer interruptions. The cleaning can therefore be completed more quickly.
3   It will be more methodical allowing operatives to progress directly from one area to the next.

Occupancy   It is preferable to clean an empty building. Work should be carried out when the building has been vacated, between one period of use and another, or as parts of the building are vacated.

Other services   Where operatives are required to provide other services at set times, e.g. meals and beverage services, cleaning must be scheduled around those times.

Exterior fabric

Other than the maintenance of forecourts, most exterior cleaning tasks are usually undertaken by contractors.

Forecourts

To maintain a satisfactory standard, regular sweeping will be required, the frequency being governed by the amount of litter and usage. For small areas a stiff brush will be adequate, but for larger areas a power sweeper should be used with a work performance related to the size of the area to be cleaned. Litter bins, strategically placed and frequently emptied, will reduce maintenance costs and improve the overall standard of appearance.

Walls

The cleaning of all exterior surfaces of a building will seldom be required. However, the removal of soil at or just above ground level and the removal of graffiti may be required more regularly. The methods employed are governed by the degree and type of soiling, the hardness of the surface and the

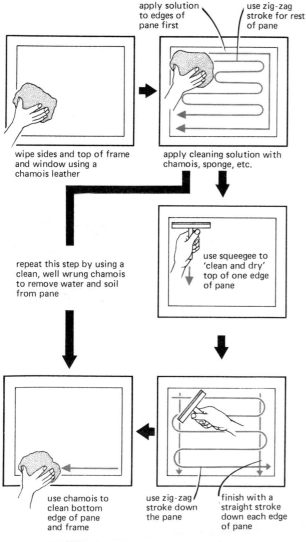

Figure 73 *Window cleaning procedure*

need to retain a surface with as little porosity as possible.

Small areas and soil not heavily ingrained The soiled area is treated with a sulphate free detergent (sulphates will attack the mortar) and left to work for several minutes. Soil and detergent are then removed by brushing and rinsing with a stiff brush attached to a water hose.

Large areas, ingrained soil or graffiti Methods employed usually involve the use of high-pressure water with or without the use of cleaning agents and sand. Cleaning agents used include neutral detergents, alkalis, methylene chloride and strong acids. The pressure used, the type of cleaning agent and the amount of sand depend on the type of soil, the hardness and porosity of the wall and, to some extent, on the skill of the operator. In general, the pressure and the amount of sand should be kept to a minimum.

Protective clothing is required, the extent of the protection being governed by the type of cleaning agent used.

In principle, the method employed involves spraying the surface with a mist of water and cleaning agent if required, allowing the solution to stand for several minutes and then rinsing using a brush and stream of water or by spraying with high-pressure water. If this is unsuitable or where the surface will withstand sand blasting, the surface is sprayed with a mixture of sand and water under pressure.

Roofs

On fragile and pitched roofs crawling boards must be used. On pitched roofs a catch barrier at the eaves will also be required.

The methods employed may involve the application of a cleaning agent such as a gel or foam followed by scrubbing and rinsing, or the use of high-pressure water and cleaning agents followed by rinsing.

Windows

The method, equipment and cleaning agents

employed depend on the height of the windows above the operative, the size of windows and the degree of soiling. Unless windows are particularly dirty, water to which a cleaning agent (dilute 1:100) has been added will produce satisfactory results. If very dirty a neutral detergent will be required. Traditional products based on whiting are too labour-intensive to use. Cleaning agents containing abrasives or ammonia must not be used. Ammonia may soften the putty while abrasives may scratch the panes and in the case of anodised aluminium frames will ruin the protective film, resulting in the appearance of whitespots.

Cleaning solution can be applied with a sponge or cloth, although for larger windows a purpose-designed applicator with a long wool bonnet is preferred. To remove the solution and soil a squeegee is most suitable although for small panes a chamois leather or scrim may be the most practicable means. When the tops of the panes are no more than 8 m above the ground extension poles to which the applicator and squeegees are fitted may be used.

The typical procedure for cleaning is as follows (although for larger panes it may be easier to work section by section):

1 Apply cleaning solution to window frames, edge of pane and then systematically to the rest of the pane.
2 If using a chamois or scrim:
   a wipe vertical and top edges of pane and parts of frame;
   b use a zig zag stroke down the pane;
   c wipe bottom edge of pane and part of frame.
3 If using a squeegee:
   a wipe vertical and top edges of frame with scrim or chamois;
   b make a vertical stroke down side of upper part of the pane with squeegee;
   c commencing from the dried part, use a zig-zag stroke down the pane always keeping the blade at an angle of 45° to the direction of travel and never lifting the blade off the surface.

   d if required, make a vertical stroke down the length of each side of the pane;
   e wipe bottom part of frame with chamois or scrim.
4 If the windows are very dirty and a detergent has been used it will be necessary to repeat the procedure using clean water.

The initial cleaning of windows will involve a modified procedure:

1 Protect frames with masking tape.
2 Apply alkaline cleaning solution to the pane and allow to stand for a few minutes.
3 Remove stubborn marks with a scraper.
4 Rinse the pane thoroughly with clean water.
5 Remove masking tape and clean panes and frames using the normal procedure.

Interior fabric

Equipment, materials and methods

Cleaning and maintenance involve routine and periodic tasks including low and high level dusting, damp wiping, suction cleaning, wall ceiling and window washing, stain removal, restoration and high-pressure washing.

Wall, window and high pressure washing are frequently undertaken by contractors.

Access equipment if required must be erected and used safely and all equipment must be cleaned after use.

Dusting Low and high level dusting is undertaken routinely or periodically to remove loose soil from walls, doors and ceilings. It is most suitable for smooth surfaces.

To dust doors and the lower part of walls methods and equipment are used similar to those for furniture (see page 232). To clean ceilings and the upper parts of walls or complete walls it is preferable to use a wall dusting tool. A typical routine for wall dusting is:

1 Assemble equipment required including wall dusting tool, access equipment if appropriate, and suction cleaner and hose.

High-level suction cleaning

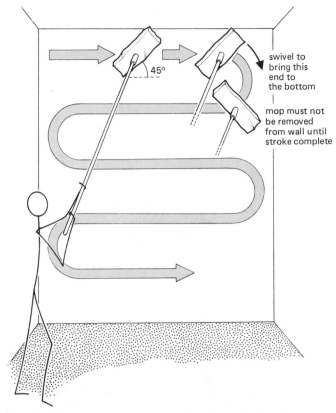

45°

swivel to
bring this
end to
the bottom

mop must not
be removed
from wall until
stroke complete

Figure 74   *High-level dusting using a wall dusting tool*

2   Divide the surface into suitably sized sections and clean each section by drawing the mop over wall or ceiling using an S-type stroke, ensuring that all the dust is carried in front of the mop. When cleaning walls work from top to bottom.

Suction cleaning is used routinely or periodically to clean loose soil from walls or ceilings with textured finishes and from wall hangings. It will require the use of a brush, hard-surface tool, upholstery tool and curtain tool as appropriate to the surface. A typical routine will be similar to that described for furniture (see page 232), but will include:

1   Divide surface into suitably sized sections and clean section by section.
2   To clean hard or semi-hard surfaces draw tool back and forth horizontally, overlapping adjacent strokes, working from top to bottom of a wall.
3   To clean hangings, draw suction tool down the length of the hanging, overlapping adjacent strokes.

Damp wiping is used routinely to remove light soil and localized stains adhering to walls and doors. It can be used periodically to clean surface finishes that cannot be washed. A typical routine is similar to that described for furniture, but if large areas are to be cleaned divide surface into suitable sections and clean each section in turn, overlapping adjacent sections.

Wall washing is used periodically to remove accumulations of soil not removed by other

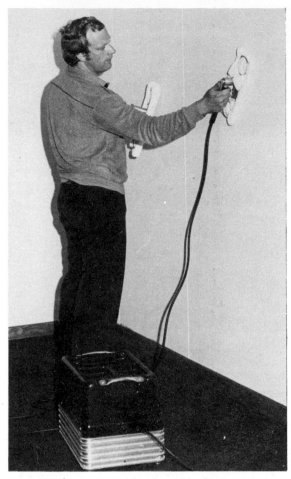

Wall washing machine at work

cleaning methods. It is also used routinely where particularly high levels of hygiene are required, e.g. operating theatres. Surfaces to be washed will generally be painted. The task can be undertaken manually or by using wall washing machines. Washing must be preceded by suction cleaning or dusting and the surface should be left on completion as dry as possible.

For manual washing one of two methods can be used:

1 This is generally suitable where the walls to be washed are in areas that can be taken out of use during cleaning. Walls are divided into vertical strips about 1 m wide and each strip is washed in turn by applying cleaning solution to the wall, commencing at the bottom and finishing at the top, and then rinsing with clean water from top to bottom. The method has the advantage of being relatively quick but operative fatigue can be high and splashes and spillages can occur which will require subsequent removal.

2 This method is generally suitable where the walls to be cleaned are in areas that cannot be taken out of use. A typical routine for this method is outlined below. In principal it differs from the first method in that the cleaning solution is applied with a hand spray rather than with a cloth. It has the advantages that splashing and streaking are virtually eliminated and contact time for the cleaning solution is uniform. It has the disadvantage that it is more time-consuming than the first method.

A typical routine for wall washing:

1 Assemble equipment, which should include a bucket half filled with cleaning solution, hand spray filled with cleaning solution, bucket half filled with clean water, empty bucket, bucket cloth, cloth for rinsing, nylon abrasive pads, cloths or paper towels for drying and dust covers.

2 Remove or protect furniture and carpets with dust covers.

3 Divide wall into vertical strips about 1 to 2 m wide and clean each strip, section by section, working from bottom to top. Working downwards can result in streaks down the wall, creating runs which are subsequently very difficult to remove. Where access equipment other than step ladders is required, clean the lower part of the wall before erecting equipment.

4 To clean wall, apply solution with hand spray to a 1 or 2 m^2 section of wall, taking care not to overwet, and wipe systematically using a side-to-side action. More stubborn marks can be removed using a nylon pad or brush. Remove as much of the soiled water from the wall as possible into the empty bucket. Rinse wipe

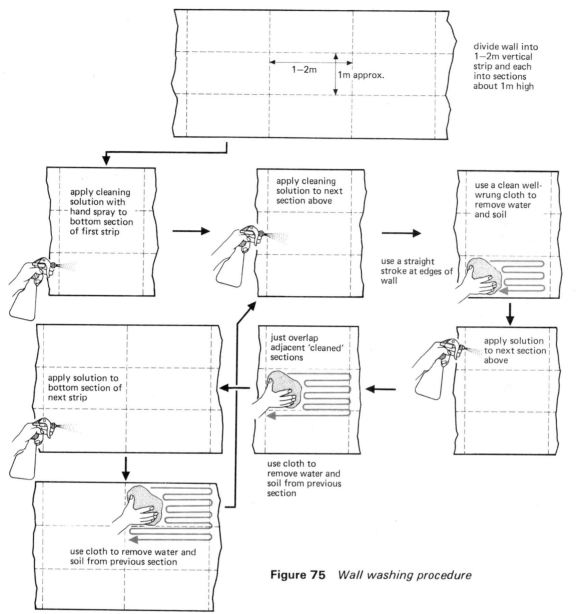

divide wall into 1–2m vertical strip and each into sections about 1m high

apply cleaning solution with hand spray to bottom section of first strip

apply cleaning solution to next section above

use a clean well-wrung cloth to remove water and soil

use a straight stroke at edges of wall

apply solution to next section above

apply solution to bottom section of next strip

just overlap adjacent 'cleaned' sections

use cloth to remove water and soil from previous section

use cloth to remove water and soil from previous section

Figure 75 *Wall washing procedure*

with clean water to leave surface as dry as possible.

5 Proceed to the next section above or to the bottom of the next strip of wall as appropriate. When cleaning each section, overlap adjacent sections.

6 Remove any splashes or runs on cleaned sections of wall as they occur using a clean, dry cloth.

7 If a particularly high standard of finish is required, when all parts of a wall have been washed, working from top to bottom, wipe each strip with a well wrung cloth and dry and buff using a dry soft cloth. If access equipment has been erected, complete the upper part of the wall before completing the lower part.

A wall washing machine will significantly increase the rate at which washing can be accomplished. The procedure is essentially similar to that outlined for the second manual method but differs in that the cleaning solution is applied to each section of a strip of wall with a glider and is immediately removed with a second glider before proceeding to the next section of a strip of wall.

Window cleaning   The procedure is similar to that described for exterior windows. It will be undertaken periodically. It is normally desirable to minimize the amount of water used and to avoid splashing. Accordingly, chamois and scrim are generally used both for the application and the removal of cleaning solution.

Stain removal and restoration   The removal of stains and graffiti can be attempted using abrasive pads, solvents or proprietary cleaners if damp wiping or washing is ineffective or inappropriate to the type of surface finish. The method employed must be tested on a non-visible part of the surface. It may be better not to attempt removal, the result being worse than the stain.

Painted surfaces can be repainted and wallpapers may be restored by resticking or cutting out and replacing torn or stained pieces. Success depends on the position of the affected area. The restoration of other types of finish will be similar to those described for furniture.

High-pressure washing can be undertaken to clean heavily soiled walls and ceilings in kitchens, toilets, workshops and similar areas.

Selection of methods and frequencies

The methods of cleaning and maintenance employed will depend on the type of surface (wall, ceiling, windows, or door), the nature of the surface (smooth, textured, porous, non-porous, or abrasion-resistant) and on the type of soil. The frequency with which the various methods employed are used will depend on the standard of cleanliness required, governed largely by the location of the surface, and on the degree of soiling. Methods that make the use of access equipment unnecessary are preferred, being quicker and safer. Where routine washing of ceiling and walls is required or where large areas are to be washed, the use of a wall washing machine is preferred.

Neutral detergents should be used although alkaline cleaning agents can be used on surfaces less affected by alkalis, but not routinely. Abrasive pads should be used to remove stubborn stains from hard surfaces, rather than abrasive powders which will damage the surface finish or steel wool which will leave fine particles to rust and stain a surface. The use of other cleaning agents or protective finishes will depend on the type of surface finish.

A number of general rules can be applied with regard to the suitability of methods to be used:

- Loose soil is removed from flat surfaces by high or low dusting.
- Loose soil is removed from textured surfaces by suction cleaning.
- Soil adhering to non-porous surfaces is removed by damp wiping or washing.
- Soil adhering to porous surfaces is removed by damp wiping only.

Walls will usually require routine spot cleaning, e.g. by damp wiping, and stain removal or restoration as necessary. Washable surfaces will require routine or periodic washing depending on the standard of hygiene and appearance required and the degree of soiling.

The range of methods that can be employed to achieve a particular standard or to remove soil will be limited by the nature of the surface.

- *Smooth paint:* dust, damp wipe or wash.
- *Textured paint:* suction clean or wash.
- *Non-washable paper:* dust, suction clean or damp wipe avoiding an excess of water or abrasion.
- *Washable papers:* dust, suction clean or wash using a minimum of water.
- *PVC:* dust, suction clean, damp wipe or wash.
- *Laminates:* dust, suction clean, damp wipe or wash.

- *Wood panelling:* dust, suction clean, damp wipe or wash using a minimum of water. A waxed or french polished finish will require a periodic application of polish.
- *Cork:* dust, suction clean, or damp wipe. It can be washed if sealed.
- *Hangings:* suction clean. Other cleaning methods will depend on whether the hanging is a curtain, tapestry, silk or carpet (see page 243).
- *Leather:* dust or suction clean. As required, damp wipe or wash using method described for furniture (see page 238). Alkalis and solvents must not be used for removing stains.
- *Glass:* damp wipe or wash using a minimum of cleaning solution. Use either a 1% solution of glass cleaning agent or neutral detergent. Finish with a scrim or lintless cloth.
- *Metallic:* dust, suction clean, damp wipe or wash. An appropriate metal polish may be used on very badly tarnished surfaces, but must be followed by washing.
- *Ceramic tiles:* dust, damp wipe or wash. Regrout when necessary.
- *Brick and stone:* suction clean. If heavily soiled scrub with detergent solution and rinse.
- *Marble and terrazzo:* dust, damp wipe or wash. Do not use acids, alkalis or abrasives which will, respectively, etch, cause surface flaking or roughen the surface.

Ceilings In new buildings or following the washing of a ceiling, routine high-level dusting can be introduced if required to remove soil of a non-greasy nature. It should not be introduced in older buildings without washing first. The result will usually be unsightly. If the soil is of a greasy nature cleaning is better restricted to periodic washing.

Where high levels of hygiene are required ceiling washing must be carried out regularly.

Windows are normally washed periodically, for example at three-monthly intervals.

British Standards

CP 153: 1969, *Windows and Roof Lights. Part 1: Cleaning and safety.*

Hard and semi-hard floors

Methods of cleaning

Cleaning usually involves daily, weekly and periodic tasks. Routine tasks include sweeping, dry suction cleaning, damp mopping, wet mopping, buffing, spray cleaning, spray burnishing, and light or heavy scrubbing. Periodic tasks include burnishing, light or heavy scrubbing, spray stripping, polish application and scarifying. Less frequently some floors will require sealing, resealing, recoating or repair of the seal. These tasks are discussed more fully on pages 185–187.

General procedures and safety precautions

1. Assemble all equipment and materials required before commencing job.
2. Prepare cleaning solutions to recommended dilutions.
3. Add detergent to hot water rather than water to detergent to prevent excess foaming.
4. Erect warning signs and cordon or close off areas when using wet cleaning methods or applying polish since loose cable may result in accidents.
5. Do not walk on wet or newly polished floors.
6. Work backwards when using wet cleaning methods or applying polish to avoid walking on wet or polished floor.
7. Work from the point furthest from the exit to the exit point to avoid being marooned.
8. Do not flood floors affected by water.
9. Remove furniture if necessary to make cleaning and maintenance easier.
10. When moving furniture make a note of its position and always return it to that place.
11. To prevent rust marks appearing when wet cleaning methods have been used, card or foil should be placed under the feet of returned furniture.
12. Protect the legs and bases of furniture which cannot be moved, particularly if carrying out wet cleaning methods.
13. Avoid the splashing of skirting boards and furniture and remove splashes that do occur.

14 Do not knock skirting boards and furniture with cleaning machines. Report any damage.
15 Observe all safety precautions relevant to the use of electrical equipment (see page 150).
16 If working backwards, plug machine in at socket furthest ahead of work route. If working forward, plug in a socket nearest starting point.
17 When task is completed, clean equipment and return to store.

Sweeping will remove loose soil such as litter, grit and dust. It can form the principal means of cleaning or may precede other cleaning tasks. It involves the use of dust control mops, brushes or powered sweepers. A typical routine using dust control mops is as follows:

1 Assemble equipment: mop, vacuum cleaner and hose.
2 Determine most appropriate work route, preferably starting at point furthest from and ending at the door.
3 If necessary, remove any obstructions, noting the position of any furniture moved.
4 Sweep with straight or S-type strokes, pushing soil in front of mop. Overlap each stroke. Do not remove mop from floor when changing direction of sweeping.
5 Remove accumulations of soil with vacuum cleaner. A long handled dust pan and brush can be used if a vacuum cleaner is not readily available.
6 Return furniture to its correct position.
7 Clean mop head with a suction cleaner.

Suction cleaning will remove loose soil. It can be more suitable than sweeping where large amounts of loose soil are to be removed or very high standards of dust control are essential. A typical routine is as follows:

1 Assemble equipment: suction machine, hoses, hard floor tool, crevice tool.
2 Check flex, plugs and sockets.
3 Check that bag or container are empty.
4 Plan work route.
5 Remove furniture as necessary.

6 Plug in machine to work backwards or forwards as required.
7 Switch on and commence cleaning, passing machine or tool backwards and/or forwards over each section of floor in turn until removal of soil from each section is satisfactory. Overlap the cleaning of adjacent areas. Use a crevice tool to clean corners or inaccessible areas. Clean under furniture.
8 Observe safety and general precautions with respect to cable and use of machine.
9 Return furniture to correct position.
10 Empty container or bag, clean machine and retun to store.

Damp mopping can be used for the removal of light soil. A typical routine is:

1 Assemble equipment: mop, bucket, wringer and sweeping equipment.
2 Sweep floor.
3 Half fill bucket with hot water and add detergent. A dilution of 1:200 is usual.
4 Plan work route.
5 Remove furniture or protect legs and bases as necessary.
6 Erect warning signs and cordon or close off area if required.
7 Mop floor using a very well wrung mop. Mop edges of floor with a straight stroke. Mop rest of floor in 1–2 m² sections working backwards. Use a figure-of-eight stroke, turning mop frequently. Wet mop and wring thoroughly before moving from one section to the next. Avoid splashing other surfaces and remove any splashes that do occur.
8 When floor has dried, return furniture to its correct position.
9 Wash out bucket and mop and return to store and leave to dry.

Wet mopping involves a single-solution method for light to moderately soiled floors and two solutions for heavily soiled conditions. A typical routine for single-solution wet mopping is similar to damp mopping, with the following modifications:

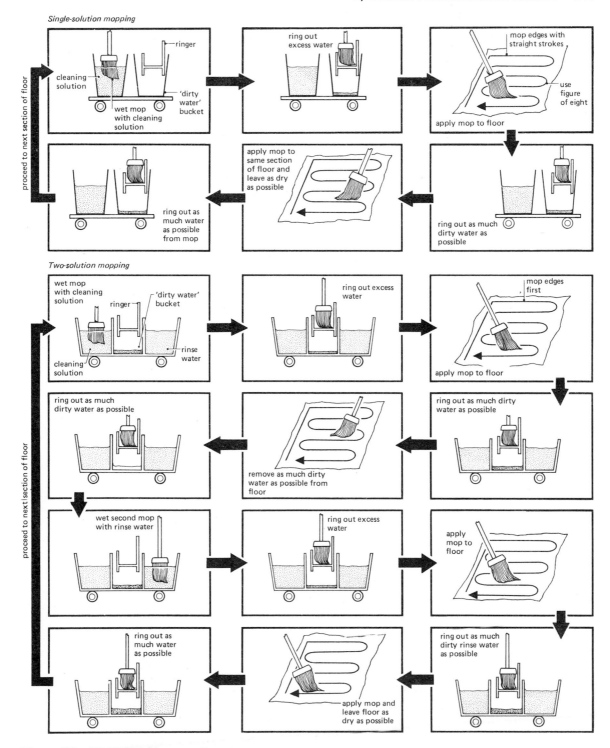

Figure 76　*Wet mopping procedure*

1 Equipment required: two buckets, mop and wringer.
2 Half fill one bucket with water and detergent diluted 1:100 to 1:200. Second bucket left empty and used to collect dirty water.
3 To mop edges and 1–2 m² sections of floor, wet mop with cleaning solution and wring out excess water; mop edges or sections of floor; remove as much dirty water as possible into empty bucket wringing mop thoroughly; proceed to next section. Always wring mop into dirty water bucket.
4 Leave floor as dry as possible.

A typical routine for two-solution wet mopping is also similar to damp mopping, with the following modifications:

1 Equipment required: three buckets, two mops and wringer.
2 Half fill one bucket with water and detergent, diluted 1:50 to 1:100. Half fill second bucket with clean water. Leave third bucket empty to collect dirty water.
3 To mop edges and 1–2 m² sections of floor, wet mop with cleaning solution and wring out excess water; mop edges or sections of floor; remove as much dirty water as possible into empty bucket, wringing mop thoroughly; wet second mop with clean water and wring out excess water; mop rinse edge or section of floor; remove as much dirty water from floor as possible into empty bucket, wringing mop thoroughly; proceed to next section. Always wring mop into the dirty water bucket.
4 Leave floor as dry as possible.

Buffing removes scuffs and restores the shine of a polished floor or creates a shine after application of polish. Except after polish application it should be preceded by sweeping and if required by damp or wet mopping. It must be followed by sweeping unless a suction unit is fitted to the polishing machine. A typical routine is as follows:

1 Assemble equipment: polishing machine, polishing brush or buffing pad and drive disc, sweeping equipment or suction unit and skirt, and mopping equipment if required.
2 Sweep or suction clean and mop if required.
3 Check flex and plug of polisher.
4 Erect warning signs and cordon or close off area if necessary.
5 Plan work route.
6 Remove furniture if necessary.
7 Plug in machine to work backwards or forwards as required.
8 Switch on machine and buff floor. Work systematically, moving the machine forwards or backwards and from side to side as determined by the type of machine. Overlap the buffing of adjacent areas. Negotiate carefully furniture and skirting boards along the work route. Reverse direction of brush or pad from time to time if possible.
9 Observe safety and general precautions with respect to cable and use of machine. Do not use pads under brushes or dusters under pads or brushes.
10 Replace furniture.
11 Clean machines pads and brushes.
12 Do not leave machines standing on brushes.

Spray cleaning and burnishing   Spray cleaning is used for the routine cleaning of light or moderately soiled floors. A fine mist of water, dilute neutral detergent, gel cleaner or buffable detergent is applied to the floor and a spray cleaning brush or pad under a scrubber/polisher machine is passed over it. The process of spray cleaning is significantly more efficient when a high-speed machine is used.

The water or cleaning solution assists in the removal of soil and acts largely as a lubricant preventing damage to the floor. abrasion between the bristle tips or pad and the floor dislodges the soil which is then held in the pad or brush.

Spray burnishing is essentially similar to spray cleaning but differs to the following extent. Spray burnishing is carried out on a floor to which a non-metallized buffable or semi-buffable polish, has been applied and a buffable detergent or polish is generally used as the cleaning and lubricating agent. Abrasion between the brush or pad and the polish removes both the surface soil and a surface layer of polish ingrained with soil. The restored surface will include resins and waxes contributed by the cleaning agent. The lubricating properties of the cleaning agent are essential to minimize the amount of polish removed by abrasion during burnishing.

The term spray buffing is frequently applied to either technique.

The routine is essentially similar for both methods and with the following exceptions almost identical to buffing:

1 Assemble equipment: scrubber polisher, spray cleaning or burnishing brush or pad (determined by task and speed of the machine), suction unit and skirt, and cleaning agent and spray bottle (hand or fitted to the machine) or aerosol cleaning agent.
2 Unless an aerosol is used, dilute cleaning agent (usually 1 to 10) and fill spray bottle.
3 Plug in machine to work forwards.
4 To clean floor spray a fine mist of cleaning agent over that section of the floor immediately adjacent to the machine and buff until dry. Repeat the procedure for each subsequent section of floor until all the floor has been cleaned. If a hand spray is used apply a fine mist of the solution over 2–3 m² of floor in advance of the machine and then buff.
5 Do not overwet floor. Overwetting will have two effects. More buffing will be required to leave the floor dry and on a polished floor softening of the polish film may occur resulting in excessive removal of polish and the rapid clogging of pads.
6 Do not allow the machine to linger at one point. Particularly on an unpolished floor and when using a high speed machine, excessive abrasion may result in burning of the floor.
7 Replace pads or brushes when clogged. Soil-saturated pads will throw off rather than hold soil, fail to clean effectively and cause overloading of the motor.

Scrubbing and stripping will remove impacted soil or surface layers of polish by a combination of abrasion by the tips of a scrubbing brush or

Spray cleaning

abrasive pad and the action of a cleaning agent.

Light scrubbing will remove lightly impacted soil or a surface layer of polish. Deep scrubbing will remove heavily impacted soil. Stripping is essentially the same as deep scrubbing but usually refers to the complete removal of polish from a floor.

The procedures are essentially similar for each of the three tasks, the principle differences arise in the type of cleaning agent, the type of brushes or pads, whether the soil is to be removed by means of mop and bucket, wet suction cleaner or scrubber drier, and whether polish is to be applied to the floor after light scrubbing or stripping. A typical routine is:

1 Assemble equipment as appropriate from:
   Scrubbing machine, solution tank, mop, bucket and wringer, wet suction cleaner, scrubber drier.
   Scrubbing brush, green pad for light scrubbing, black pad for deep scrubbing, drive disc.

Neutral or alkaline detergent for light scrubbing, alkaline detergent for deep scrubbing and stripping non-metallized emulsion polishes, (ammonia) stripper for metallized polishes, solvent based detergent for solvent based polishes.

Vinegar if intending to apply water based polish after the use of an alkaline detergent.

2   Check all electrical equipment.

3   Dilute cleaning agent. A dilution of 1:50 is used, although a 1:5 dilution of alkaline detergent can be used to replace an ammonia stripper if required. Fill tank.

4   Erect warning signs and cordon or close off area.

5   Plan work route.

6   Remove or protect furniture.

7   During cleaning observe all safety and general precautions.

8   Apply cleaning agent to floor and scrub. Do not overwet floor. Speed of scrubbing depends upon the amount of soil and whether light scrubbing, deep scrubbing or stripping is being carried out. Unless a scrubber drier is being used it is preferable to work backwards and to allow cleaning agent to remain on the floor for a few minutes before its removal.

9   Remove soiled water from floor using mop and bucket or wet suction cleaner. Work forwards from a dry area.

10   If a single person is to carry out all tasks, only 4–5 m² should be scrubbed at a time and the soiled water then removed. Do not allow floor to dry out.

11   If using a scrubber drier omit 9 and 10.

12   Check floor and rescrub if necessary.

13   If the task does not involve the removal of polish and/or a wet suction cleaner or a scrubber drier is used it will frequently be unnecessary to scrub rinse the floor. This step and steps 14 and 15 can then be omitted. Suction drying removes virtually all the cleaning solution and the soil suspended in it from the floor. If rinsing is required, empty the solution tank and refill with clean water.

14   Scrub floor (usually twice) using similar procedures to scrubbing with cleaning solution and removal of soiled water.

15   If water-based polish is to be applied, check the pH of the floor using Universal Indicator Paper. If still alkaline, scrub rinse with a solution of water and vinegar (1 cup per gallon of water).

16   Floor must be left clean, dry and neutral.

17   Unless polish is to be applied, return all furniture.

18   Clean and return all equipment.

Burnishing is the removal from a surface of a layer of polish or other material by abrasion using a steel wool pad, burnishing brush or abrasive pad to restore appearance and gloss. The routine is similar to that for buffing, but a suction unit should be fitted to the scrubber polisher.

Spray stripping involves the stripping of a polish from a floor by spraying it with a fine mist of detergent and passing a spray stripping pad under a high-speed scrubber polisher over the floor. It should be carried out with a machine to which a suction unit and skirt have been fitted.

An extremely fine mist of cleaning solution, which will act for the greatest part as a lubricant, must be applied to each section of floor. The polish is removed largely by abrasion and is either absorbed into the pad or removed from the floor as a powder by the suction unit. The slightest excess of cleaning solution will result in very rapid clogging of the pad and the almost constant need for changing it.

Care must be taken not to damage the floor as the final part of the polish film is removed.

A typical routine is similar to that for spray cleaning or burnishing.

Scarifying removes heavily impacted soil and involves the use of a scarifying machine or suitable scrubber polisher. Soil is chipped away by the bristles of a steel brush or edges of a cutting tool. The operation can be carried out under wet or dry conditions depending on the actual situation. The loosened soil is removed using a mop and bucket, high-pressure hose or sweeper.

Scrubbing and drying of a floor

Polish application normally follows scrubbing or wet mopping. Before commencing application, the floor must be clean and dry. A typical routine is as follows:

1   Safety and general precautions are similar to those for wet mopping or scrubbing.
2   Assemble equipment: mop or applicator, tray or bucket and strainer, polishing machine and brush or pad.
3   Ensure that warning notices are erected and area cordoned off or closed.
4   If any delay between wet cleaning and application, sweep or damp mop floor.
5   Plan work route carefully.
6   Partly fill tray or bucket.
7   Apply a thin coat of polish to floor. After dipping an applicator into polish, remove all excess polish so that reservoir of polish is held only in the heel of applicator or mop. Use figure-of-eight strokes if using mop and straight strokes if using applicator. Overlap adjacent strokes. Only apply final coat up to skirting board. Remove all splashes.
8   Allow to dry.
9   Buff.
10 Sweep.
11 If required, apply second and third coats. Use same procedure for further coats. After application of each coat, allow to dry, buff and sweep. Apply each coat at right-angles to the preceding coat.
12 Return furniture.
13 Empty tray or bucket, clean all equipment and return to store.

For larger areas spray application may be preferable.

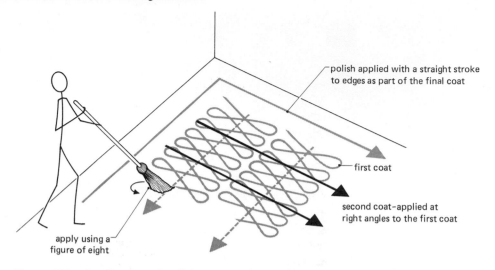

polish applied with a straight stroke
to edges as part of the final coat

first coat

second coat–applied at
right angles to the first coat

apply using a
figure of eight

Figure 77   *Application of polish: mop action and coats at right-angles*

Use of cleaning agents and protective finishes

The use of particular cleaning agents and protective finishes is determined by the floor's porosity, resistance to various chemicals (including water) and the requirement to maintain the floor's anti-static properties. A number of rules can be applied.

Protective finishes:

- Porous floors, e.g. wood group, must be sealed or protected.
- Semi-porous floors, e.g. linoleum, rubber, PVC, PVC asbestos and thermoplastic tiles, do not normally require sealing unless they have become porous through age or poor maintenance.
- Concrete floors should be sealed to prevent dusting.
- Non-porous floors, e.g. stone group, asphalt and rubber and PVC sheet, do not require sealing unless they have become porous.
- Solvent-based seals must not be used on stone or resilient floors with the exception of linoleum.
- Some types of solvent-based seal may be used on asphalt.
- Solvent-based seals are most suitable for the wood group floors.

- Polishes are not required on stone group floors.
- Polishes are applied to resilient floors when the degree of soiling, traffic or possible exposure to chemicals will result in rapid deterioration of the floor. Where these conditions do not prevail this is unnecessary, methods of maintenance involving the use of polishes being more expensive.
- Polishes are generally considered necessary to enhance the life of the wood or sealed wood group floors.
- Solvent-based polishes must not be used on PVC, thermoplastic, asphalt, rubber and stone group floors.
- Water-based polishes can be used on top of a solvent-based seal.

Cleaning agents:

- Excessive wetting of unsealed porous and semi-porous floors must be avoided.
- **Strong alkalis must not be used routinely. In** particular, they will alter the colour of linoleum and damage the surface of most floors rendering them porous.
- Acid cleaners must not be used.
- There are occasional instances where acid cleaners may be used to deal with particular

staining problems, but only after seeking specialist advice.

- Gel cleaners should not be used directly on any of the resilient floors.
- Anti-static flooring should only be maintained with neutral or mildly alkaline detergents which are non-film forming.
- Conventional polishes and seals should not be used on anti-static floors.

Floor maintenance and cleaning systems

The use of protective finishes, cleaning agents and methods of cleaning and maintenance can be combined to form cleaning and maintenance systems. Table 40 outlines a number of systems and their applications. With some exceptions the systems outlined cover the most commonly occuring combinations of circumstances and requirements.

Spray cleaning is generally less labour intensive than spray burnishing but neither system is necessarily less labour intensive than equivalent damp mop and buff systems. The various systems are rarely completely effective at removing all the soil on a floor. The film formed by spray cleaning and the restored surface of a spray burnished floor will both include soil. Particularly in the case of spray burnishing there is a tendency for the surface appearance to deteriorate progressively making it necessary to strip and reapply polish to the floor.

Spray stripping has a number of advantages over scrubbing and drying. It is less labour-intensive. There is less chance of overwetting or leaving alkalis on the floor. Neutralization should not be required.

Scrubbing followed by the use of wet suction cleaners is generally most effective in the removal of soil and bacteria present on a surface.

Systems involving the use of polishes are more labour-intensive than comparable systems not using them. But they must be used where protection of the floor or seal is a primary consideration. As far as possible the system selected for a floor must be the least expensive consistent with the standard of cleanliness,

appearance and protection of the floor that is required.

The frequency of carrying out periodic maintenance and routine cleaning tasks depends on the standard of cleanliness and appearance required and the degree of soiling and traffic. For example, a system involving mopping, buffing and the use of a water-based polish under conditions of light soiling and traffic may require daily sweeping, damp mopping and buffing twice weekly and the polish stripping twice a year. With moderate traffic and soiling, mopping and buffing may be increased to daily and polish stripping may be required four times a year. In all cases, however, a build up of polish must be avoided and the film should be removed from time to time.

For any individual floor the use of protective finishes and systems of cleaning and maintenance will depend on the floor type, the prevailing conditions of soilage and traffic and the standard of hygiene and appearance required. Table 41 shows the seals, polishes and systems of maintenance applicable to each of the different types of floor.

Before changing from one system to another which involves different cleaning agents and finishes all traces of the previously used materials

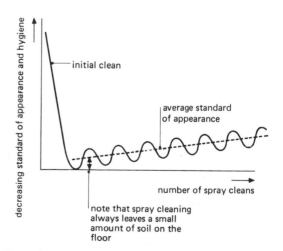

Figure 78 *Deterioration of surface appearance/ cleanliness of a floor maintained by spray cleaning*

Table 40 *Systems of floor maintenance*

No.	Routine	Special	Periodic	Application
1	Sweep			Loose soiling. Light to heavy traffic
2	Sweep. Damp mop or wet mop using single-solution method	Wet mop using two-solution method or light scrub with neutral detergent		Light to moderate soiling. Light to heavy traffic. Floor requires no additional protection
3	*a* Sweep. Spray clean with neutral detergent, buffable detergent or gel cleaner. (Sweep) *b* Sweep. Damp or wet mop using single-solution method with buffable detergent or gel. Buff. (Sweep)	Wet mop using two-solution method with neutral detergent	Light scrub with neutral detergent to remove film of resin, detergent, oil, fats and soil	Light to moderate soiling. Light to heavy traffic. Floor requires no additional protection. Gloss required
4	*a* Sweep. Spray clean with buffable detergent or gel. (Sweep) *b* Damp or wet mop using single-solution method with neutral detergent, buffable detergent or gel cleaner. Buff. (Sweep)	Wet mop with neutral detergent using two-solution method or light scrub Scrub and apply polish to worn areas	Spray strip or scrub with alkaline detergent. Apply 1/3 coats of dri-bright polish depending on amount of wear expected. Use a metallized polish if scrubbing of the floor is to occur with any regularity and strip with an ammonia stripper.	Light to moderate soiling. Light to heavy traffic. Protection of floor required. Gloss required

5 *a*	Sweep. Spray burnish with buffable detergent or gel. (Sweep) *b* Sweep. Damp or wet mop using single-solution method with neutral detergent, buffable detergent or gel cleaner. Buff (Sweep)	Wet mop using two-solution method with a neutral detergent. Light scrub with neutral detergent and apply coat of polish to worn areas	Spray strip or scrub with alkaline detergent. Apply 2/3 coats of non-metallized buffable or semi-buffable polish. A base coat of metallized rather than non-metallized polish may be used which need not be removed every time stripping is carried out	Light to moderate soiling. Moderate to heavy traffic. Floor requires protection. Gloss required
6 *a*	Sweep. Spray burnish with liquid solvent-based polish. (Sweep) *b* Sweep. Damp mop or wet mop using single-solution method with neutral detergent. Buff. (Sweep)	Wet mop using two-solution method with neutral detergent. Burnish. Light scrub and apply coat of polish to worn areas	Scrub with solvent-based detergent. Apply 2/3 coats of solvent based polish	Wood floors; no seal used
7	Sweep. Wet mop using two-solution method or light scrub with neutral detergent	Scrub with neutral detergent		Heavy soiling. Light to heavy traffic. Floor requires no additional protection. No gloss required. Not floors affected by excessive wetting
8	Sweep. Wet mop using two-solution method or light scrub with neutral detergent. Buff if required. (Sweep)	Light scrub with neutral detergent and apply a coat of polish to worn areas	Spray strip or scrub with (ammonia) stripper. Apply 2/3 coats of metallized polish	Heavy soiling. Moderate to heavy traffic. Floor requires protection. Gloss required. Frequent scrubbing necessary
9	Sweep. Light scrub using scrubber drier. Buff if required. (Sweep)	Apply coat of polish to worn areas if polish used	Apply up to three coats of metallized polish if floor requires protection or a gloss is required	Large areas of floor. Light to heavy soiling. Not floors affected by regular wetting

Table 41 Methods of floor maintenance

Floor	Seals	Polish	Maintenance	Precautions
Concrete	1 Use silicate dressings, two-pot pigment/non-pigmented epoxy resins, rubber or polyurethane 2 New floors allowed to harden for up to six months before application 3 Scrub with alkaline detergent, detergent crystals or solvent-based detergent as appropriate to remove grease, oils and waxes 4 Etching with strong acid will improve adhesion	1 Not normally required 2 A water-based polish may be used on a sealed floor 3 Scrub with neutral or alkaline detergent, rinse, neutralize and dry	1 Unsealed: use systems 2 and 7. Heavy impactions of soil removed by scarifying 2 Sealed: use system, 2 and 8 although other systems involving spray cleaning and the use of polishes may be used if there is an established requirement 3 Solvent-based seals can be removed by sanding or use a chemical stripper	1 Sealing is preferred to prevent dusting 2 Regular use of strong alkaline cleaners will damage floors if unsealed
Granolithic, terrazzo,	1 Only sealed if badly deteriorated 2 Use water-based acrylic seals 3 Do not use solvent-based seals 4 Scrub with neutral or alkaline detergent, rinse, neutralize and dry before application	1 Not normally required 2 Water-based polish may be used 3 Never use solvent-based polish 4 Scrub with neutral or alkaline detergent, rinse, neutralize and dry	1 Use systems 2, 3, and 7 as appropriate 2 Systems involving use of water-based polishes will be very rarely required 3 Old seals may be removed by scrubbing with alkaline strippers	1 Detergents leaving a film, e.g. soap, must not be used 2 Regular use of alkaline detergents will damage surface 3 Oil/grease stains may be removed using a poultice of of white spirit and whiting
Quarry	1 Only sealed if badly deteriorated 2 Water-based acrylic seals used 3 Do not use solvent-based seals 4 Scrub with neutral or alkaline detergent, rinse, neutralize and dry before application	1 Only used if tiles are principally intended to be decorative 2 Not used in kitchens or toilets 3 Scrub with neutral or alkaline detergent, rinse, neutralize and dry	1 Use systems 2 and 7 2 Spray cleaning may be used if soilage light 3 Systems involving buffing and the use of polishes only used if tiles are intended to be decorative or a high standard of appearance is required without creating a safety hazard 4 Periodic scrubbing with alkaline detergent using a brush rather than nylon pad to remove grease	1 Detergents leaving a film must not be used 2 Regular use of alkaline detergents will damage surface

	Sealing	Polishing	Maintenance and renovation	Notes
Stone	1 Only sealed if badly deteriorated 2 Water-based acrylic seals are preferred if required 3 Pigmented/non-pigmented two-pot epoxy resins, rubber and polyurethanes may be used 4 Scrub with neutral or alkaline detergent, rinse, neutralize and dry before application	1 Seldom used 2 If required a water-based polish should be used 3 Solvent-based polishes not used 4 Scrub with neutral or alkaline detergent, rinse, neutralize and dry	1 Use systems 2 and 3 (using a brush) and 7 2 Systems involving buffing and polishes may be used on sealed floors if requirement established 3 Floors may be renovated by abraiding with a sander or abrasive disc 4 Acrylic seals can be removed by scrubbing with an alkaline stripper 5 Solvent-based seals may be removed by abrasion	1 Rough surface will destroy pads 2 Minimum of water must be used to prevent alkali being drawn to surface of tile
Brick	1 Only sealed if badly deteriorated 2 Water-based acrylic seals are preferred if required 3 Solvent-based seals are difficult to remove or renovate and should not be used 4 Scrub with neutral or alkaline detergent, rinse, neutralize and dry before application	1 Not normally required 2 If required, a water-based polish should be used 3 Solvent-based polishes not used 4 Scrub with neutral or alkaline detergent, rinse, neutralize and dry	1 Use systems 2 and 3 with scrubbing or polishing brush as appropriate 2 Systems involving the use of polishes used if there is an established requirement 3 Water-based seals may be removed by scrubbing with alkaline stripper	
Asphalt	1 Only sealed if badly deteriorated 2 Water-based seals are preferred if required 3 Pigmented/non-pigmented two-pot epoxy resin, rubber or polyurethanes may be used, but it is essential to test compatibility of seal with floor by first applying to 3-4 m² and checking adhesion after 4 weeks 4 Surface dressing of new floors must be removed if sealing to prevent crawling of seal 5 Scrub with mildly alkaline detergent, rinse, neutralize and dry	1 Used if there is a particular requirement to protect floor 2 Water-based polish if required, used on unsealed or sealed floors 3 A solvent-based polish can be used on floors sealed with solvent-based seal 4 Scrub with mildly alkaline detergent, rinse, neutralize and dry	1 Use systems 2, 3 and 7 2 Systems involving the use of polishes determined by prevailing conditions and requirements 3 Old floors may be renovated and solvent-based seals removed by sanding or abraiding with nylon web discs 4 Water-based seals can be removed by scrubbing with alkaline stripper	1 Regular use of strong alkalis on unsealed floors must be avoided 2 Use of pine-oil-based buffable gels may cause long-term deterioration

(continued)

Table 41 - *continued*

Floor	Seals	Polish	Maintenance	Precautions
Thermo-plastic, PVC, PVC asbestos, rubber	1 Only sealed if badly deteriorated 2 Use water-based acrylic seals 3 Do not use solvent-based seals. They will damage floor and are difficult to remove 4 Allow 28 days for adhesive to dry if floors new 5 Surface dressing of new floors removed by scrubbing 6 Scrub with neutral or mildly alkaline detergent, rinse and dry	1 Used if there is a particular requirement to protect floor 2 Use water-based polishes if required 3 Scrub with neutral or alkaline detergent, rinse, neutralize and dry	1 Use systems 2 and 3 on sheet and tiles 2 System 7 may be used on welded sheets 3 Systems 2 and 7 would preferably not be used on rubber floors 4 Systems involving the use of polishes determined by prevailing conditions and requirements 5 Thermoplastic and PVC floors renovated by deep scrubbing 6 Rubber may be renovated by abraiding with a fine abrasive disc (120) and finishing with a fine abrasive pad 7 Water-based seals removed by scrubbing with alkaline stripper 8 If solvent-based seals have been used it is preferable to recoat and repair rather than attempt to remove by abrasion	1 Do not use water on tiles until 28 days after laying 2 Avoid regular use of strong alkali 3 Do not use any product that includes organic solvents 4 The use of pine-oil-based buffable gels can cause long-term deterioration 5 Rubber is prone to surface oxidation and requires a method of maintenance which leaves a protective film
Linoleum	1 Only sealed if badly deteriorated 2 Use a water-based acrylic seal 3 A two-pot polyurethane, epoxy resin or urea formaldehyde seal can be used, but is difficult to remove 4 Surface dressing of new floor must be removed to prevent scrawling 5 Scrub with neutral or mildly alkaline detergent, rinse and dry	1 Used if there is a particular requirement to protect floor 2 Use water-based polish if required 3 Surface dressing must be removed from new floor 4 Solvent-based polishes will keep lino supple 5 Scrub with neutral or a mildly alkaline detergent, rinse, neutralize and dry	1 Use systems 2 and 3 2 Systems involving use of polishes determined by prevailing conditions and requirements 3 Floor may be renovated by deep scrubbing with neutral or mildly alkaline detergent 4 Water-based seal removed by scrubbing with alkaline stripper 5 Solvent-based seals are better repaired or recoated	1 Regular use of alkalis will cause colour changes in pigments

granwood, cork, soft-woods	1 cork are normally sealed by oleoresinous or two-pot epoxy resin, urea formaldehyde or poly-urethane 2 A solvent-based wax will also form an effective seal 3 New floors should be sanded with a medium and then fine grade paper, vacuumed, damp mopped and dried 4 Old floors will require sanding with grade paper necessary to remove all soil and wax 5 Cork requires great care when sanding 6 Apply thinned steel before sealing to penetrate between blocks to prevent rafting 7 Soft wood floors are not normally sealed	woods, a solvent-based wax should be used 2 On sealed floors solvent- or water-based polish may be used 3 If a highly slip-resistant finish is required or there is no particular reason for the use of a polish, a sealed floor does not require a polish 4 Floors sealed by wax prepared as for sealing 5 Sealed floors prepared by mopping or scrubbing with neutral, alkaline or solvent based detergent, rinsing, neutralizing and drying as appropriate	depending on situation and particular requirements 2 Floors reconditioned after removal of polishes if appropriate by sanding 3 Softwood floors not sealed may be recon-ditioned by light scrub-bing using neutral detergent and a minimum of water 4 End grain paving recon-ditioned by scarifying	be used in all maintenance of wood floors 2 Systems of cleaning and maintenance selected for a particular situation must not encourage the build-up of polishes or result in regular special applications of further coats of polish
Magnesite	1 As for wood group but water-based acrylic seal may also be used 2 New floors require scrubbing to remove surface dressing	1 As for wood group, but only use water-based polishes on water-based seals	1 As for wood group	1 Any excess of water can result eventually in cracking of floor
Antistatic	1 No seal used	1 No polish used	1 Sweep and damp mop frequently with minimum of water and neutral detergent 2 A mild alkaline detergent may be used periodically	1 Avoid use of any cleaning agent that will leave a film
Seamless resin	1 Screed or self-levelling floors only sealed if very badly deteriorated 2 Decorative floors will require coat of solvent-based seal. Clean and lightly abraid before application	1 Screed and self-levelling floors do not normally require a polish 2 Decorative floors can be protected with water-based emulsion polish 3 Scrub with neutral or alkaline detergent, rinse, neutralize and dry	1 For screed and self-levelling floors use systems 2, 3 and 7. Heavy impactions of soil removed by scarifying 2 For decorative floors use systems 2, 3 and 7. Use of systems involving polish will be determined by prevailing conditions and requirements 3 To renovate unsealed floors scrub with alkaline detergent	1 Detergents leaving a film should not be used 2 Epoxy resin softened by boiling water or steam 3 Epoxy resins attacked by organic acids, e.g. acetic and citric, and chlorinated solvents. 4 Abrasive pads may damage decorative floors

should be removed to avoid possible problems caused by incompatability of products.

British Standards

CP 209: 1963, *Care and Maintenance of Floor Surfaces. Part 1: Wooden floors.*
BS 6263: 1982, *Care and Maintenance of Floor Surfaces. Part 2: Sheet and tile floors.*

Carpets

Methods of cleaning

Cleaning can involve both *in situ* and off-site cleaning. *In situ* cleaning involves routine sweeping or suction cleaning and periodic skimming or bonnet buffing, dry foam shampooing, hot water extraction, wet shampooing and the application of soil-retardent finishes.

General procedures and safety are similar to those for hard and semi-hard floors. They also include the following:

1   Areas being cleaned by wet methods should be cordoned or closed off until the carpet is perfectly dry.
2   Working backwards when using wet methods to avoid walking on a wet carpet is preferred.
3   Wet cleaning methods must be preceded and followed by vacuuming when dry. Failure to vacuum before wet cleaning can result in the build up of a hard compacted layer of soil at the base of the pile, particularly when rotary machines are used. Vacuuming after cleaning will raise the pile uniformly.
4   Cleaning agents used should be tested on a non-visible part of the carpet. Discoloration can arise as a result of reaction between carpet dyes, moisture and cleaning agent. For example, the dyes of woollen carpets are often sensitive to alkalinity and it can be necessary to acidify the cleaning solution. Conversely the dyes of carpets made from synthetic fibres

are less likely to bleed if the solution is slightly alkaline.

5   Shampoos leaving a resinous residue on the carpet should be avoided. The sticky nature of the residue will accelerate deterioration of the surface appearance of the carpet.
6   To reduce the possibility of shrinkage and minimize drying times, overwetting of the carpet must be avoided, particularly if the pile and/or the backing are made from natural fibres. Natural fibres are more absorbent than synthetic fibres and carpets with backing made from natural fibres are more likely to shrink than those made from synthetic fibres. Overwetting, particularly of the backing, is more likely in carpets having short and/or low density piles.
7   Tepid water rather than hot should generally be used to reduce the possibility of shrinkage and to avoid the possibility that the dyes used are not fast at higher temperatures.
8   The application of a prespotting agent to the more heavily soiled parts of a carpet before actually commencing wet cleaning can help reduce the possibility of overwetting in an attempt to restore those badly soiled or stained areas. The prespotting agent has time to act on the soil before cleaning is actually carried out.
9   Carpets must be permitted to dry completely and as quickly as possible. Where the atmosphere within a building is affected by external humidity a dry day is preferred.
10 Overwetting and prolonged drying times may result in surface staining, particularly if the carpet is generally of a light colour.
11 The possibility that damage may occur to the pile if excessive abrasion or agitation is used should be considered.

Sweeping   A manual box sweeper can be used to remove light, loose soil from the surface of a carpet. A typical routine is:

1   Collect sweeper and ensure that it is empty
2   Plan work route
3   Clean all sections of carpet moving backwards

passing the sweeper over each part of carpet as many times as necessary to restore surface appearance to an acceptable standard. Always finish each part with a stroke in the same direction.

4   Empty sweeper and return to store.

Suction cleaning will remove loose particles of soil from the surface and upper layers of the carpet pile but is less effective in removing it from the base of the pile, or from a woven backing (see page 127 for a discussion of the principles involved in the removal of soil from different types of surfaces by a suction cleaner). The typical routine is similar to that for hard floors and, in particular, involves:

1   A machine which includes a sweeper should be used. Where a cylinder or tub is used, a power head incorporating a sweeper will be more effective than a carpet tool.
2   If adjustable, the height of the head should be set to suit the length of the carpet pile.
3   Up to three passes over each section of floor is generally considered to give an acceptable standard of soil removal, always finishing in the same direction to ensure that pile runs the same way throughout. The number of passes and the direction of working will be governed by the characteristics of the suction cleaner used.

Stain removal and application of prespotting chemical   Stain removal is described on page 243. It should be carried out before commencing any of the periodic methods of carpet cleaning.

The application of a prespotting cleaning agent to the more heavily soiled or stained areas of a carpet may make it unecessary to attempt to remove specific stains and can increase the effectiveness of the overall cleaning process. After application, usually with a hand spray, the chemical can be worked into the pile if necessary and it should be given several minutes to react with the soil.

Carpet skimming and bonnet buffing are similar to spray cleaning of hard and semi-hard floors.

Carpet skimming is carried out with a white abrasive pad. Bonnet buffing employs a thick bonnet composed either of a dense cotton fringe or a mixture of polypropylene, polyester or cotton.

Ingrained soil is removed from the surface and upper 2 or 3 mm of the pile by light abrasive action and the action of a non-resinous shampoo, the soil being absorbed and held by the pad or bonnet.

When carpet skimming, the cleaning solution (diluted as per manufacturer's instructions) is applied by means of a spray. When bonnet buffing, the cleaning solution can be applied by spray, from a tank, if soiling is particularly heavy, or the bonnet may be dipped into the cleaning solution and well rung prior to fitting to the machine.

Suction cleaning, stain removal and/or the application of a prespotting agent should be carried out before commencing skimming or buffing.

A typical routine is as follows:

1   Assemble equipment: scrubber polisher, drive disc, white pad or bonnets, cleaning agent, and spray, tank or bucket as required.
2   Observe all general and safety precautions.
3   Erect warning signs and close or cordon off area.
4   Remove furniture if required.
5   Plug in machine to work backwards.
6   If applying cleaning solution by means of a spray, spray a fine mist over 5–10 m² of carpet and pass bonnet or pad over the area. If using a tank, pass bonnet over carpet as for scrubbing a hard floor, releasing small amounts of solution onto the carpet. If using a pre-wetted bonnet, pass over carpet as for buffing hard floors, rinsing out the bonnet periodically in the cleaning solution.
7   Turn pads or bonnet as they become heavily soiled.
8   When bonnet buffing, rebuff whole carpet using a clean dry bonnet. This will further remove soil and reduce the drying time.
9   Replace any furniture. If furniture legs are of metal or have metal studs stand the legs on

Dry foam shampooing of a carpet

pieces of cardboard or foil to prevent the formation of rust marks.

10 Wash out pads or bonnets and leave to dry.

11 When completely dry, vacuum carpet to raise pile.

Dry foam shampooing will remove ingrained soil, largely from the surface and upper 2–3 mm of carpet pile, by a combination of detergent action, abrasion and suction cleaning. It must be preceded by suction cleaning, stain removal and/or application of prespotting agent. A typical routine is:

1 Assemble equipment: dry foam shampoo machine, non-resinous shampoo, bucket and scrubbing brush.

2 Cordon off area to be cleaned and erect warning signs.

3 Dilute cleaning solution, usually 1:30, and fill tank and bucket.

4 Check effect of cleaning solution on carpet.

5 Plan work route.

6 Remove furniture if required and protect legs and bases.

7 Use brush to clean edges and corners.

8 Observe safety and general precautions.

9 Plug in and work backwards.

10 Clean, section by section, moving the machine backwards and forwards systematically over each section. Push the machine slowly over each successive length of carpet on the forward pass, feeding foam onto the carpet carefully to avoid overwetting and just overlap adjacent lengths of carpet.

11 Unless a machine incorporating a wet pick up is used, a separate wet pick up should be used

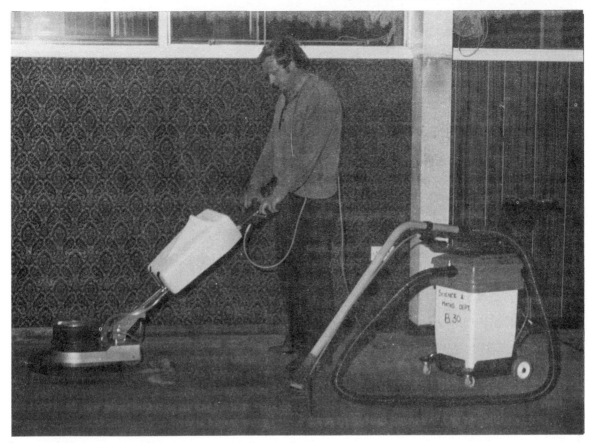

Wet shampooing of a carpet

to remove as much of the foam and soil as possible.

12 Allow carpet to dry completely.
13 Vacuum to remove residue of shampoo and soil and to raise the pile.
14 Replace furniture.
15 Clean and return all equipment to store.

Wet shampooing will remove ingrained soil from a surface and upper 2–3 mm of pile, but also to some extent from pile more than 2–3 mm beneath the surface by a combination of detergent action, abrasion and suction cleaning. When used in combination with a shampoo that includes a soil-retardent finish, it can be used usefully to build up a resistance to soil. It must be preceded by suction cleaning, stain removal and the application of a prespotting chemical.

Ideally two operatives will be required. If only one is available then the carpet should be shampooed and rinsed section by section.

A typical routine is:

1 Assemble equipment: scrubber polisher machine, tank, non-resinous shampoo preferably incorporating a soil-retardent finish, carpet shampoo brush, bucket and hand brush and wet suction cleaner to be used in conjunction with a hot water extraction wand.
2 Initial preparations are similar to those described for dry foam shampooing.
3 To clean carpet, pass shampoo brush over the carpet, releasing a minimum of cleaning solution into the carpet. Do not overwet.
4 When 4–5 m² of carpet have been shampooed,

commence removal of soiled water using wet pick up. It is essential to ensure that water is not allowed to soak into the backing if shrinkage or prolonged drying is likely.

5 When shampooing has been completed, empty solution tank, wash out and refill with clean water.

6 Rinse carpet using similar procedure to that for shampooing and removal of soiled water.

7 Clean and return all equipment.

8 Allow to dry completely.

9 Vacuum.

10 Replace all furniture.

Hot water extraction will remove loose and ingrained soil from the surface and from other parts of the pile including the base. The efficiency depends on the machine and the type of tool used. Soil is removed by a combination of physical and chemical processes. It must be preceded by suction cleaning, stain removal and the application of a prespotting chemical to the more heavily soiled areas. The methods of using the various types of tools are described on page 133–134.

A typical routine is:

1 Assemble equipment: hot water extraction machine, carpet and upholstery tool, cleaning agent and defoamer.

2 Initial preparations are similar to those described for other wet cleaning methods.

3 Fill extraction tank with cleaning solution (usual dilution 1:30). The water should only be tepid.

4 If carpet has been shampooed before, place defoaming agent in the collection tank.

5 Observe all safety and general precautions.

6 Plug in machine to work backwards.

7 Use hand tool to clean edges and corners.

8 As dictated by the type of tool used, clean the carpet either section by section, drawing the tool over successive short lengths of carpet and releasing cleaning solution and applying pressure to the backward stroke, or by drawing the tool over successive long lengths of carpet. Application of solution should be stopped just before completing a pass. Do not overwet the carpet by drawing the tool too slowly over the carpet or by repeatedly drawing it over the same section of carpet. As cleaning proceeds, re-extract each length of carpet using suction only.

9 Allow carpet to dry completely.

10 Wash out all equipment thoroughly including tanks, hoses and wands and return to store.

11 **Vacuum.**

12 **Replace the furniture.**

An alternative technique is to prespray the carpet with cleaning solution from a hand spray and use the hot water extraction machine to rinse the carpet with clean water.

Application of soil-retardant finishes will reduce the rate at which a carpet deteriorates to a point at which it is no longer possible to restore its appearance to an acceptable standard. It should be applied after wet shampooing or hot water extraction of old carpets of after the vacuuming of new ones.

It is essential to check the effect of a soil-retardant finish on a carpet before application. Some finishes can cause colour changes, dulling or stiffening of the pile. The finish must be applied in straight even strokes just overlapping adjacent strokes. The coverage must be that recommended by the manufacturers. The appliance must be one that will give the required output.

Application of anti-static finishes will reduce a build up of static charge on a carpet. Application will be similar to that for soil-retardant finishes.

Selection of cleaning methods and frequencies

Cleaning methods and frequencies depend on the standard of surface appearance and soil removal required, the types of soilage, the degree of soilage, the advantages and disadvantages of the different methods of carpet cleaning, and the type of carpet including construction, type of fibre and dye fastness. When these have been evaluated a suitable programme can be prepared. Table 42 indicates some possible programmes. However,

Table 42 *Possible carpet cleaning programmes*

Carpet type and soilage	Possible programmes
Low profile, heavy soilage	Suction clean daily. Bonnet buff weekly. Hot water extract every six months
Low profile, light soilage	Sweep daily. Suction clean weekly. Hot water extraction yearly
Deep pile, moderate soilage	Suction clean daily. Hot water extraction every six months

the actual programme prepared and methods used will depend greatly on prevailing circumstances.

Standard of surface appearance and soil removal This will be governed by the principal objectives of carpet cleaning:

1 To restoɩe surface appearance.
2 To remove as much soil of all types and from all levels but particularly dust and grit from the base of the pile and in the backing.
3 To prolong the life expectancy of a carpet by removing grit and arresting the long-term rate at which the surface deteriorates to a point where it is no longer possible to restore it to an acceptable standard.

Unless the correct combination of methods and frequencies are employed, failure to achieve the first and second objective will result in failure to achieve the third. For example, regular suction cleaning of a heavily trafficked area of carpet coupled with regular periodic hot water extraction may not be as efficient in arresting the long term rate of deterioration of surface appearance as a similar programme which also includes bonnet buffing. Conversely, insufficient suction cleaning will rcsult in an accumulation of soil at the base of the pile which may form a hard pad following wet cleaning methods.

Types of soilage affecting carpets can be conveniently divided into three groups.

1 Dust and grit detract from the surface appearance and contribute to a reduction in the life expectancy when lodged at the base of the pile. Dust and grit at or within 2–3 mm of the surface can be relatively easily removed by sweeping or suction cleaning, but at a greater depth or in the backing, although not actually adhering to the pile, sweeping will remove little, and suction cleaning using a suitable machine only part, of the dust and grit present. See also page 127 and the following pages.
2 Ingrained soil of grease, oil, starch, protein and similar materials detracts significantly from the surface appearance and if allowed to accumulate the appearance may quickly deteriorate to a point where it is no longer possible to restore it. Because this type of soil adheres strongly to the pile, sweeping and suction cleaning are relatively ineffective, wet cleaning methods being required.
3 Localized stains have a similar effect to the second group of soils, particularly if several parts of a carpet are affected. They must be removed as they occur and, depending on the type of stain and the extent to which they are fixed in the carpet, specialist techniques may be required.

Degree of soilage The greater the soilage and the more frequently it occurs, the more frequent will be the various methods of cleaning required. Under conditions of light soilage a combination of sweeping, suction cleaning and very occasionally hot water extraction are adequate. When soilage is heavy and frequent daily suction cleaning, less frequent bonnet buffing and periodic hot water extraction may be appropriate.

Methods of cleaning The use and advantages and disadvantages of the various methods are as follows:

Sweepers:
● Will remove surface dust and grit.

- Have little effect on ingrained soil.
- May be preferred to suction cleaners for daily removal of soil to restore surface appearance, but cannot replace them.

Suction cleaning:
- Will remove dust and grit from surface and to a depth of 2–3 mm reasonably effectively, but is less effective in removing it from the base of the pile or backing. Effectiveness is further limited when it is used on carpets which are stuck to the floor, which have a non porous backing or have a particularly dense pile. Only 20 to 25% of the soil in a carpet may be removed.
- Will not remove ingrained soil.
- Can be used several times per day, daily or weekly, depending on the degree of soiling, to restore surface appearance.
- Will prolong the life expectancy of a carpet by removing some of the dust and grit from the base of the pile.

Stain removal:
- Must be carried out as stains occur.
- Will help restore surface appearance.
- Will reduce the long-term rate of surface deterioration.

Carpet skimming or bonnet buffing:
- Will remove soil adhering to the surface and to a depth of 2–3 mm.
- When used in conjunction with suction cleaning before and after, will remove about 30% of the soil present in a typical woven or tufted carpet.
- Can be used weekly or less frequently depending on the degree of soilage, to maintain surface appearance.
- Will prolong the life expectancy of a carpet by preventing build up of ingrained soil adhering to it and which subsequent hot water extraction or wet shampooing may be unable to remove.
- May decrease the frequency with which hot water extraction or wet shampooing is required.
- Will, unlike other methods, leave the carpet virtually dry enough to walk on immediately.
- Skimming pads lose their absorbancy relatively quickly and require frequent changing.

Wet shampooing:
- Will remove soil effectively from the surface of the pile and to a depth of 2–3 mm and remove it to some extent at greater depths.
- Used in conjunction with suction cleaning before and after, it can remove about 50% of the total soil present in a typical woven carpet.
- Can be used (principally as a periodic routine) to restore the surface appearance by removing ingrained soiling and to remove some of the dust and grit not removed by suction cleaning.
- Is generally more effective than other methods in the removal of heavy accumulations of ingrained soiling affecting surface appearance.
- Can prolong the life of a carpet by removing grit and accumulations of ingrained soil not removed by other methods.
- May damage the pile of some carpets.
- May result in shrinkage as a result of overwetting.
- May accelerate resoiling if conventional shampoos are used.
- Is extremely labour-intensive.
- Will involve prolonged drying times.
- Can be used in conjunction with a soil-retardent shampoo to build up a resistance to soiling and therefore reduce the rate at which long-term deterioration of surface appearance occurs.

Dry foam shampooing:
- Will remove soil adhering to the surface of the pile and to a depth of 2–3 mm.
- Used in conjunction with suction cleaning before and after, it will remove about 30% of the soil present in a typical woven carpet.
- Can be used periodically to restore the surface appearance by removing ingrained soiling.
- Will prolong the life expectancy by preventing accumulation of ingrained soiling.
- Is less effective in removing heavy

accumulations of ingrained soiling than wet shampooing.
- Is less likely to involve overwetting.
- Is less labour-intensive than wet shampooing and in some circumstances may be less labour-intensive than hot water extraction.
- Will involve shorter drying times than wet shampooing or hot water extraction.
- Will involve specialized machine.

Hot water extraction:
- Will remove ingrained soil from the surface and from other parts of the pile, including the base.
- Used in conjunction with suction cleaning before and after, it can, depending on the machine used, remove up to 60% of the total soil in a typical woven or tufted carpet.
- Can be used as a periodic routine to restore the surface appearance by removing ingrained soil and to remove dust and grit not removed by other methods of cleaning. The frequency will depend on the degree of soilage and whether any form of interim maintenance, i.e. skimming or dry foam shampooing, is carried out.
- Will prolong the life expectancy of a carpet by removing grit not removed by suction cleaning and by preventing the accumulation of ingrained soil to a point where surface restoration is no longer possible.
- Is less likely to involve overwetting than wet shampooing.
- Is less labour-intensive than wet shampooing.
- Will involve shorter drying times than wet shampooing.
- Will require specialist machines.

Wet shampooing and hot water extraction:
- Can be used together to attempt the restoration of very heavily soiled carpets.

Soil-retardent finishes:
- Will help prolong the life of a carpet by reducing the long-term rate of surface appearance deterioration by preventing soil penetrating carpet fibres.
- Will improve the effectiveness of cleaning methods.

Type of carpet The types of fibre, methods of construction, dye fastness and the method of laying will affect the method of cleaning chosen and the way in which it is carried out.

Carpets generally require routine suction cleaning, although the effectiveness of the process depends on the porosity of the carpet backing, whether the carpet is stuck down, the length of the pile and whether the tool used is of the appropriate type (see page 127).

Difficulties can sometimes be experienced with the suction cleaning of flock carpets. Carpets with a very dense pile tend to be less easy to overwet than those with a more open pile. Conversely cleaning can be more difficult.

Carpets made from natural fibres are more absorbent than those with synthetic fibres and are therefore more likely to be overwetted during cleaning.

The types of dye and its fastness can affect the choice of cleaning agent and the cleaning temperature. The dyes may not be fast at high temperatures and they may change colour or bleed if the cleaning agent is too alkaline or acid (see page 224). Acid rinses are sometimes used to restore the colour to a carpet.

Carpets with short dense pile are particularly suited to bonnet buffing. Generally this technique should not be attempted on carpets with long open pile. It can also cause friction burns on polypropylene carpets.

Flock carpets can be wet scrubbed although hot water extraction is the most effective method of deep cleaning. Chlorine bleaches should not be used to rinse flock carpets.

Oriental carpets require specialist cleaning. Wet cleaning of Chinese carpets will remove the sheen.

Hair carpets must be sprayed routinely with water, usually at fortnightly intervals.

Furniture

Methods, equipment and materials

Furniture cleaning and maintenance involves both routine and periodic tasks. The former include dusting, damp wiping, suction cleaning, stain removal and washing and the latter, washing or scrubbing, polish application, restoration, dry foam shampooing and spray extraction.

Dusting is used to remove dust not adhering to a hard or semi-hard surface. Dry dusting with an ordinary duster must not be permitted. It will not hold the dust; rather it will disturb it and disperse it into the air to settle again later.

One of two methods can be used: damp dusting or dry dusting with an impregnated or static mitten. A routine for damp dusting is as follows:

1   Assemble equipment: duster and hand spray filled with clean water.
2   Lightly spray duster with a fine mist of water, taking care not to overwet, and then fold.
3   Lightly draw duster over the surface, taking care not to disturb the dust. Turn to a clean part of duster as necessary. Work in straight strokes, overlapping adjacent strokes.
4   When finished, wash out dusters and leave to dry.

Routine for dry dusting:

1   Assemble equipment: mitten, extension poles and frame if high dusting, suction cleaner and hose.
2   Clean surface as for damp dusting.
3   Suction clean mitten as necessary and when cleaning is finished. Do not shake.

If required, surfaces can be buffed after dusting using a dry duster, or a scrim or lintless cloth if cleaning a glass surface.

Damp wiping is used to remove light soil and a variety of marks and stains which adhere to a surface. A cleaning agent will generally be required, the type being governed by the type of soil or surface. It may also be used as an alternative to dusting where higher standards of hygiene are required. General-purpose cleaning will require neutral detergent usually diluted 1 to 100 or 1 to 200.

Mirrors and glass can be cleaned using a 1% solution of glass cleaning agent and water. The solution will dissolve grease and leave no surface smears. However, if it is intended to buff when dry with a scrim or lintless cloth, a neutral detergent will be suitable. Alternatively, if the mirror is more heavily soiled, e.g. by hair lacquer, a solution containing both methylated spirits and neutral detergent or a general-purpose solvent-based detergent can be used.

Heat marks or grease on waxed or french polished surfaces can be cleaned using a solution of vinegar and water (1 cup per gallon). If this is unsuccessful, a 1% solution of methylated spirits can be used, but it will remove the polish if used directly on french polish.

Damp wiping should be preceded by dusting or suction cleaning. After cleaning, the surface should be left dry. A damp surface will hold dust and therefore accelerate resoiling.

The routine is as follows:

1   Assemble equipment: cloths, scrim or lintless cloth and a bucket half filled with warm water and cleaning agents. If cleaning glass surfaces, paper towels and bucket cloth.
2   Clear surface to be cleaned.
3   Wet cloth with cleaning solution and wring out well. Systematically wipe all surfaces.
4   Wipe with a cloth, scrim, lintless cloth or paper towels as required to leave the surface dry. In some cases this step is omitted.
5   Buff with a soft cloth, scrim or lintless cloth to enhance standard of appearance, if this is required.

Suction cleaning can be used to remove loose soil from all surfaces but, in particular, is used for upholstery or surfaces difficult to dust. It is generally more time-consuming than dusting when used for flat surfaces.

The routine is as follows:

1   Assemble equipment: suction cleaner and tools.
2   Observe precautions and procedures relating to the use of suction cleaners.
3   Plug in machine at point nearest furniture.
4   To clean hard surfaces systematically, move tool backwards and forwards over the surface in straight strokes, overlapping adjacent strokes.

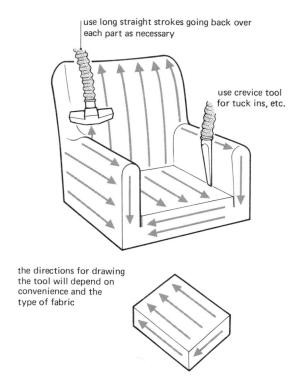

use long straight strokes going back over each part as necessary

use crevice tool for tuck ins, etc.

the directions for drawing the tool will depend on convenience and the type of fabric

Figure 79 *Suction cleaning of upholstered furniture*

5 To clean upholstery systematically, clean all parts, including back and front of cushions using an upholstery tool or crevice tool for tuck ins. Use straight strokes and finish in same direction if the upholstery covering is a pile fabric.

Satin removal for upholstery fabrics is described on pages 243–248.

Washing is used to remove heavy soiling generally from hard or semi-hard surfaces. It is not suitable for upholstery.

A cleaning agent will be required, usually a neutral detergent diluted 1 to 50 or 1 to 100. Alkaline cleaning agents can be used on more heavily soiled surfaces relatively unaffected by alkali. In particular circumstances salt or saddle soap are used..

When cleaning fixtures, fitted furnishings or large items, the cleaning solution can be applied either with a hand spray or a cloth. A spray has the advantage that cleaning is quicker and overwetting is less likely. However, it is unsuitable where overspray is likely to affect other surfaces.

Cleaning should be preceded by dusting or suction cleaning. After cleaning a surface must be left as dry as possible.

The routine is:

1 Assemble equipment: bucket half filled with cleaning solution and hand spray filled with cleaning solution, bucket half filled with clean water, empty bucket, bucket cloth, cloths, hand scrubbing pads or brushes, paper towels, dust covers and, if cleaning glass, a scrim or lintless cloth.
2 Clear surfaces to be cleaned.
3 If possible remove furniture requiring washing to a suitable work area. If washing is to be carried out *in situ,* protect carpet or other furniture with dust covers.
4 Apply cleaning solution systematically to all surfaces using either the spray or cloth. Care should be taken not to overwet surface, particularly if wood. If possible leave solution in contact with surface for a few minutes.
5 Scrub or wipe as appropriate and remove as much water as possible from surface into an empty bucket.
6 Rinse all surfaces with clean water and remove as much water as possible into the 'empty' bucket.
7 Wipe dry with a clean dry cloth or paper towels.
8 When dry, and if a higher standard of appearance is required, buff with a soft cloth, scrim or lintless cloth.
9 Return furniture or remove dust covers as appropriate.
10 Wash out all equipment and return to store.

Application of wax polishes enhances the appearance and protects a wood surface. Wax polish should not be applied to any other type of surface finish and is generally not required on wood surfaces finished with a catalysed lacquer. In general their use should be reserved for high-

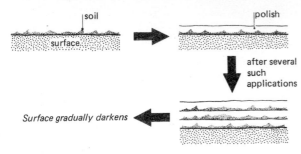

Figure 80 *Effect of applying polish to an uncleaned surface*

quality wood furniture finished with a wax or french polish. On wood finished with a lacquer they should only be used if they are particularly required.

In general it is preferable not to use polishes containing silicones and they should not be used on surfaces finished with a wax or french polish. Over-application of polishes containing silicones will lead to a build up that is difficult to remove and will ultimately affect the appearance of the wood.

Aerosol sprays are convenient when applying polish to lacquered surfaces but over-application, indiscriminate use and spraying surfaces other than that requiring polish application can be a drawback.

Application when required should be made sparingly and generally only once or twice per year. It may be required after the removal of grease or heat marks and the treatment of scratches.
The routine is:

1 Apply only after damp wiping or washing to ensure that the surface is perfectly clean. Failure to do so will eventually affect the appearance.
2 Apply polish on a cloth and rub in well to give a high gloss.
3 If using sprays, it is preferable to spray onto a duster and not onto the surface directly, thus avoiding the possibilities of over-application or spraying onto other surfaces.

Restoration involves tasks necessary to restore the appearance of furniture, but which normal cleaning methods will not achieve. Methods used will depend on the type of damage or deterioration and the materials and finishings used in making the furniture. The many methods of restoration include some of the examples below.

- Metal surfaces when badly tarnished or scratched can be restored using metal polishes. The polish is applied on a soft cloth in long straight strokes. Circular strokes may result in the appearance of swirl marks. They must not be used as a routine method of cleaning, particularly on plated surfaces. A surface must be washed, rinsed and dried both before and after application. Polish remaining on a surface will accelerate tarnishing.
- Cigarette burns on wood surfaces can be partially removed by rubbing with metal polish. After washing, rinsing and drying, teak or linseed oil, depending on the colour of the wood, should be rubbed in and a wax polish applied if appropriate.
- Scratches on a wood surface can be hidden by rubbing in teak oil, linseed oil or iodine, followed by the application of a wax polish if appropriate.
- Blooming, caused by the over-application of wax, can be removed by wiping with white spirit or vinegar solution.
- Scratches in plastic surfaces may be removed by polishing with a metal polish followed by washing, rinsing and drying.

Dry foam or residue shampooing is used to restore the surface appearance of upholstery fabrics. The routine is:

1 **Assemble equipment as required:** bucket containing dry residue shampoo usually diluted 1 to 30, dry foam machine if available, soft scrubbing brush, bucket, cloth, suction cleaner, hose, upholstery and crevice tools.
2 Suction clean all surfaces.
3 Remove stains as appropriate.
4 Check the affect of the cleaning agent on a non-visible part of the fabric.
5 Systematically clean each part applying a

minimum of cleaning solution and using either a hand scrubbing brush or a tool consisting of two rotating brushes linked to a dry foam upholstery cleaning machine. Care should be taken not to overwet the fabric or to damage it by excessive abrasion.

When using a hand brush on a loop pile or plain fabric roughly divide the surface into 30 cm squares and clean each in turn using circular strokes working from the outside in and overlapping adjacent squares. On a cut pile fabric use straight strokes in the direction of the pile, overlapping adjacent strokes.

6 After cleaning each part, use a suction cleaner and upholstery tool to remove as much of the cleaning solution as possible.
7 When upholstery is dry, suction clean all parts.

Spray extraction is used to restore the appearance of upholstery fabrics. Hot water extraction using water and a detergent shampoo may be used but in many situations the use of solvent extraction machines enabling hot non-chlorinated organic solvents to be used is preferable. The routine is:

1 Systematically suction clean all parts.
2 Check the effect of the cleaning solution on a non-visible part of the fabric.
3 Solution temperature should be related to the type of fabric and the fastness of the dyes, but it should be as hot as possible.
4 Systematically extract all parts, taking care not to overwet, particularly if trying to clean heavily soiled areas of the fabric. Depending on the type of tool used (see page 135) use either long straight strokes, preferably in the direction of the pile, applying pressure as the tool is drawn backwards over the fabric and just overlapping adjacent strokes, or use short strokes moving the tool backwards and forwards in a zig-zag across each section of fabric, applying pressure in both directions.
5 Pass the hand tool over each part a second time using suction only.
6 When fabric is dry, suction clean all parts.

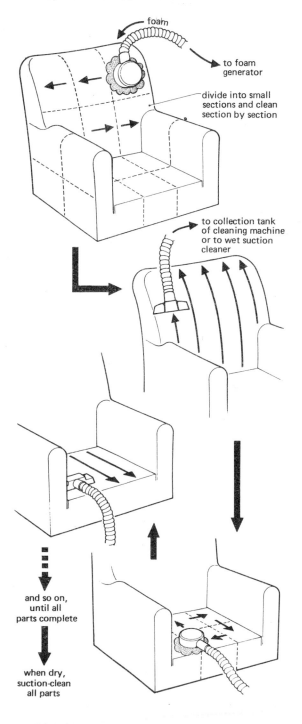

Figure 81 *Dry-residue shampooing of upholstery*

Selection of methods, cleaning agents and frequencies

The methods of cleaning and the cleaning agents and materials that can be used for a particular item of furniture will depend on its type, construction materials and finish. The following pages indicate in alphabetical order the methods of cleaning and maintenance that can be applied to different types of construction materials, finish and major types of furniture.

The actual method of routine cleaning and maintenance and its frequency will be governed by the type of soil, but in general all items of furniture will require daily or regular dusting, damp wiping or suction cleaning.

The frequency of periodic cleaning and other maintenance tasks will be governed by the degree of soiling, the standard required and the usage of the particular item of furniture.

The types of cleaning agent and protective finish used will be influenced by the type of surface, but the following points should be remembered:

- In general, neutral detergents are preferred although alkaline cleaning agents may be used periodically on surfaces little affected by alkalis.
- Alkaline cleaning agents should not be used routinely on any surface.
- Strong abrasives will scratch. Acids will attack most surfaces and should not be used.
- Steel wool tends to leave fine particles which will rust and stain a surface.
- Metal polishes must only be used to remove heavy tarnishing. They should not be used for routine cleaning.
- Wax and polishes should only be used on wood furniture with surface finishes that specifically require its use.

Alabaster ornaments should not be placed over open fires since smoke can cause discoloration. To clean, dust, damp wipe or wash with warm water and neutral detergent. Strong acids will etch surface and strong alkalis cause surface flaking. Abrasives score surface. Steelwool leaves rust marks.

Aluminium   Dust, damp wipe or wash with warm water and neutral detergent. Strong alkalis will react chemically. Abrasives remove the surface coating from anodized aluminium resulting in white spotting.

Ash trays   Empty into a fire-proof container. Either damp wipe or wash in warm water and neutral detergent. Polish glass ash trays with a scrim or lintless cloth.

Bamboo   Dust, suction clean or light scrub with a 1% salt solution. After scrubbing, rub with linseed oil and after 2 hours buff vigourously with a soft cloth.

Beds   Dust framework and headboards. Periodic work will include: turning of interior spring mattress, washing frames, vacuuming springs, repairing and removing stains from upholstery, vacuuming mattresses and upholstered bases. Plastic and rubber sheeting will protect mattresses.

Blinds   Venetian and vertical blinds require regular suction cleaning or dusting of slats and cords. The procedure is:

1   Lower blind and clean the upper parts.
2   Tilt slats to one side and clean each slat by drawing duster or suction tool across slats.
3   Reverse slats and clean other side.
4   Clean tapes and cords.
5   Adjust blind.

Periodically blinds require washing. If *in situ,* the procedure is:

1   Similar to dusting or suction cleaning.
2   Each slat washed with neutral detergent.
3   Wax polish can be applied to wooden slats when dry.

Roller blinds should be suction cleaned as required. Periodically they will require washing. The procedure is:

1   Remove blind and lay it on a flat surface.
2   Dust or suction clean.
3   If washable, wash or light scrub with neutral

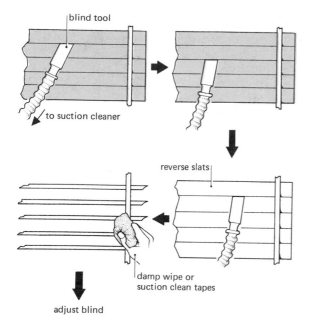

2   Apply metal polish on a soft cloth and rub gently using straight strokes.
3   Wash, rinse, dry and buff.

Metal polish left on a surface will accelerate tarnishing.

If surface is lacquered metal polishes must not be used. To remove lacquer:

1   Wash, rinse and dry.
2   Wipe with acetone to remove original lacquer.
3   When dry, brush or spray apply lacquer (cellulose butyrate) to give a smooth thin coat.

Bronze as for brass. Antique bronze requiring other than routine cleaning will require expert advice.

Cabinets, cupboards   Dust or damp wipe tops, sides and legs. Suction clean and damp wipe drawers as required and always when room is vacated. Washing and other maintenance will depend on soilage and nature of finish.

Catalysed lacquers   Dust or damp wipe. Polish is generally unnecessary. To remove heavy soiling wash using a minimum of water and neutral detergent.

Ceramic tiles   Dust or wash with warm water and neutral detergent. Do not use abrasive powders. Strong alkalis will attack grouting.

Chairs   Dust or damp wipe seats, backs, legs and stretchers. Wash or carry out other maintenance as dictated by degree of soiling, construction materials and type of finish. Polish should only be applied appropriately and sparingly.

Chromium   Dust, damp wipe or wash in warm water and neutral detergent. White pitting may be removed by using a chrome polish. The procedure is similar to that used to remove tarnish from brass. Do not use abrasive powders or routinely use chrome polish. Strong alkalis will eventually blacken surface.

Figure 82   *Blind cleaning*

detergent using circular strokes, overlapping each stroke.
4   If not washable, damp wipe.
5   Turn over and clean other side.
6   When dry replace and correct tension springs.

It is essential that blinds are always properly dried.

Books can be cleaned individually using a soft brush working outwards from the spine. Specialist advice is required before attempting periodic maintenance of leather bindings and antique books.

Brass   Dust, damp wipe or wash with warm water and neutral detergent. Do not use strong acids or abrasives. Tarnish can be removed by one of two methods:

Procedure 1:
1   Wash and rinse.
2   Rub gently with a mixture of salt and vinegar.
3   Wash, rinse, dry and buff.

Procedure 2:
1   Wash, rinse and dry.

Clocks   Dust case and buff glass face. Glass can be damp wiped when necessary. Heavier soiling can be removed from case by damp wiping or washing. Restorative procedures will depend on type of finish. Care must be taken to ensure that no water enters the back of the clock.

Copper   As for brass. A mixture of equal parts of salt, flour and vinegar can be used to remove heavier soiling.

Cork   Dust or vacuum. Only wash if sealed.

Desks   Dust or damp wipe tops, sides and legs. Do not disturb paper and files left on desks. Interior surfaces including drawers require suction cleaning, damp wiping or washing when desks are vacated. Other forms of maintenance are dictated largely by construction materials and type of surface.

Leather coverings require periodic application of conditioner. Polish should only be applied occasionally and sparingly to appropriate wood finishes.

Dressing tables   Similar to desks and cabinets, but may also include mirrors.

Door frames   Dust, damp wipe or wash with warm water and neutral detergent.

Door furniture   Damp wipe and buff metallic surfaces. Heavier soiling can be removed by washing with warm water and neutral detergent. Restoration measures will depend on the type of finish.

Fire surrounds   Dust, damp wipe or wash.

French polish   Dust and buff with a soft cloth. A wax polish can be applied very occasionally. Heavier soiling can be removed by damp wiping or washing using a minimum of water and neutral detergent.

Gilded objects   Dust only. Before attempting any other cleaning, specialist advice should be sought.

Glass table tops   Dust or damp wipe. Buff with lintless cloth. As required, wash with warm water and neutral detergent.

Glass vases, bowls and ornaments   As for glass tops. Water, if too hot, may crack the glass. Stains can be removed from vases by soaking in water, salt and vinegar.

Horizontal surfaces   Dust, damp wipe, or wash with warm water and neutral detergent.

Ivory   Damp wipe or wash in warm water and neutral deteregent. Do not attempt to remove surface yellowing.

Laminates   Dust, damp wipe or wash with warm water and detergent. Polishes should not be used.

Lacquers and varnishes   As for french polish.

Leather   Dust using impregnated or static duster, or suction clean as appropriate. Periodically, to prevent drying out, apply castor oil, neats foot oil, leather conditioner or Vaseline sparingly on a soft lintless cloth. Rub in well and finish with a clean lintless cloth. Neats foot oil leaves the surface dull. Vaseline is most appropriate on very light leathers. Heavy soiling can be removed by the following method:

1   Wipe with water to which 4 teaspoons of vinegar and 1 teaspoon of ammonia have been added per 2 pints of water, or wash with saddle soap.
2   Rinse and dry.
3   Apply chosen conditioner as described above.

When using saddle soap, care must be taken not to splash adjacent surfaces. Avoid using wax polishes, synthetic detergents and organic solvents.

Lights (ceiling, wall)   Dust as required using high level dusting tool as necessary or suction clean. Report all fused tubes or bulbs. Periodically all parts will require more extensive cleaning as per the following procedure:

1 Assemble equipment.
2 Isolate from mains or switch off and ensure no possibility of being switched on by accident.
3 Erect access equipment if required, observing all safety requirements. Erect warning signs and cordon or close off area.
4 Remove shades, diffusers or reflectors if not possible to clean *in situ*.
5 Damp wipe bulbs or tubes. Do not attempt to clean if warm.
6 Damp wipe or wash fittings according to degree of soiling, using neutral detergent. Use an absolute minimum of water, taking care not to wet sockets.
7 Clean shades, diffusers and reflectors according to type.
8 Replace shades, reflectors and diffusers.
9 Clean and return all equipment to store.

Lights (table, floor) Dust routinely. Report all fused bulbs and defective lights. Periodically all parts may require more extensive cleaning as follows:

1 Assemble equipment.
2 Isolate from mains.
3 Remove shades if necessary.
4 Remove and damp wipe bulbs. Do not attempt to clean if warm.
5 Damp wipe or wash base according to degree of soiling using neutral detergent. Use an absolute minimum of water, taking care not to wet lamp fitting.
6 Clean shades and bulbs.
7 Replace shades and bulbs.
8 Clean and return all equipment to store.

Restorative maintenance of the base may be required.

Shades, diffusers, reflectors Periodic maintenance will depend on type. Glass, metal, glass fibre and plastics can be damp wiped or washed with warm water and neutral detergent. Paper must only be damp wiped. Parchment must be damp wiped and castor oil applied on a soft cloth and gently rubbed in to prevent drying out.

Imitation parchment is treated in a similar way to real parchment but solvent-based wax is used. Fabric shades must be suction cleaned and then damp wiped if glued to frame or washed in warm water and neutral detergent if stitched to frame, using a soft brush to rub fabric. Rinse, and when drip-free, place in a warm, well ventilated situation to dry.

Light switches Damp wipe, wipe dry and buff with a soft cloth.

Marble As alabaster.

Mirrors Dust or damp wipe. Buff with a soft lintless cloth. If necessary, wash using a minimum of cleaning solution. Dust or damp wipe frame. Essential that back of mirror not wetted.

Nickel plate Dust, damp wipe or wash with warm water and neutral detergent. Do not use metal polishes.

Notice boards Dust or suction clean depending on nature of surface. Care must be taken not to disturb notices. Periodically frame may require damp wiping or washing.

Ornaments Dust or damp wipe. Other maintenance dictated by nature of ornament. Specialist advice may be required.

Paint Dust, damp wipe or wash with warm water and neutral detergent. Do not use a polish. The use of abrasives and strong alkaline cleaning agents should be avoided if possible, particularly on emulsion paints.

Paintings and pictures Dust or suction clean frame. If required, damp wipe. Only clean frames of oil paintings. Glass covered pictures may be cleaned by dusting and buffing with a lintless cloth or by damp wiping if necessary. Any over wetting of glass frame may result in wetting of pictures which must be avoided.

Pewter Dust and buff with a soft cloth. When

necessary, wash with warm water and neutral detergent. Metal polishes should not be used on pewter.

Plastics   Dust, damp wipe or wash with warm water and neutral detergent. An anti-static finish can be applied. Do not use wax polishes or abrasives. Avoid routine use of strong alkaline cleaning agents. Organic solvents for stain removal should only be used where it is known that the solvent will not effect the plastic on which it is to be used.

Plastic-coated fabrics   Dust or suction clean as appropriate. As necessary, damp wipe or wash with water and neutral detergent. Wax polishes and strong alkali must not be used.

Pianos   Dust and buff with a cloth, including keyboard. The requirement for polish will depend on the surface finish. If required, apply only occasionally and sparingly. Heavier soiling may be removed by damp wiping. Brass or other fittings may require restorative maintenance according to type. No attempt must be made to restore the colour of ivory keys. After cleaning it is normal to leave the lid down and the keyboard open.

Radiators   Dust, damp wipe and spot clean if required. At weekly intervals or as required, all parts should be suction cleaned using a crevice tool as necessary. This will include front, back, sections, sides, wall behind the floor beneath. As necessary, wash with warm water and neutral detergent.

Room dividers   Dust, damp wipe or suction clean according to type of finish. Spot clean if necessary. Periodically may require washing.

Silver   Dust or damp wipe and buff with a soft cloth. When necessary, wash with warm water and neutral detergent. Tarnish can be removed in a number of ways. Each method should be preceded by washing:

1   Polivitt process involves immersion in a hot solution of sodium carbonate containing pieces of aluminium foil.
2   Silver dip involves immersion in an acid solution of thiourea.
3   Sparing application of metal polish on a soft cloth and rubbing using straight strokes.
4   Burnishing involves ball bearings immersed in water in a rotating drum removing tarnish by abrasion.

Whatever method is used the item must, after treatment, be washed, rinsed, dried and buffed. The use of metal polish and burnishing are least appropriate, particularly if cleaning silver plate.

Slate   Dust, damp wipe or wash with water and neutral detergent.

Stainless steel   Dust, damp wipe or wash with water and neutral detergent. See page 19 for effect of various cleaning agents on stainless steel.

Staircase furniture   Damp wipe hand rail and newel post. Damp wipe and buff stair rods. All parts may require periodic washing. Bronze rods may require removal of tarnish. Depending on type of finish, wooden parts will require occasional sparing application of polish after thorough cleaning.

Tables   Dust or damp wipe tops, legs and sides depending on degree of soiling. As necessary, wash or carry out other maintenance as dictated by degree of soiling, construction materials and type of finish. Polish should only be applied occasionally and sparingly to appropriate wood finishes.

Teak (oiled)   Damp dust or wipe depending on soilage. As necessary, wash with warm water and neutral detergent, rinse and dry. Occasionally, after thorough cleaning, apply linseed oil sparingly on a soft cloth and rub in well.

Television   Before commencing any cleaning always isolate from mains. Dust screen and buff with cloth. If required screen can be damp wiped. Dust or suction clean cabinet including back, paying particular attention to controls and area around screen. If required damp wipe and buff. Depending on type of cabinet finish, polish may be applied occasionally and sparingly.

Telephone Although dusting and buffing will produce an acceptable standard, it is better to damp wipe all parts with a 1% solution of cationic detergent and buff.

Terrazzo As for alabaster.

Upholstery fabrics Suction clean regularly. Remove all stains as they occur. Before attempting stain removal, check the effect of cleaning agent on non-visible part of fabric. Periodically, cleaning will be required to restore surface appearance and remove ingrained soiling. This will involve either spray extraction or dry foam/residue shampooing. Application of a

prespotting chemical to the more heavily soiled areas of upholstery before carrying out hot water extraction can improve the effectiveness of the cleaning process in some instances.

It is essential that the method employed does not result in:

1   Overwetting of the fabric, which can result in shrinkage. Fabrics made from natural fibres are both more susceptible to overwetting and to shrinking.
2   Wetting of the stuffing, which may result in surface staining/browning.
3   Colour change caused by chemicals in the cleaning agents or by the pH of the cleaning solution.
4   Bleeding of the dyes caused by the dyes not being fast at the cleaning solution temperature or at the pH of the cleaning solution.
5   Resinous material being left in the fabric as a

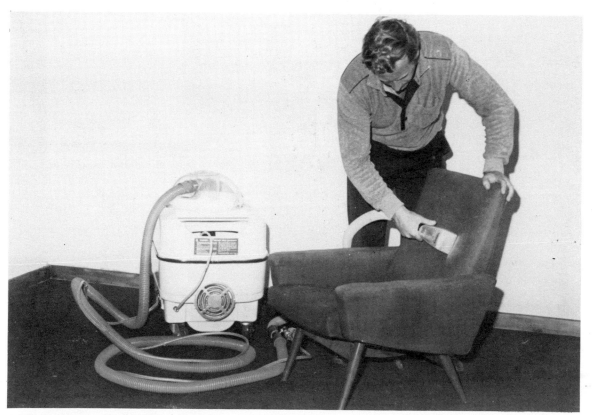

Spray extraction of upholstered furniture

result of using the wrong cleaning agent; this will accelerate subsequent resoiling.

6   Alkaline materials being left in the fabric; this may lead to deterioration.

7   Deterioration caused by organic solvents.

8   Excessive use of labour.

9   Prolonged drying times.

The merits and demerits of the methods of wet cleaning upholstery are outlined below. Wet shampooing:

- Is likely to result in overwetting of the fabric.
- Is likely to result in wetting of the stuffing.
- May leave resinous material in the fabric.
- Will involve an excessive use of labour, in that rinsing will be necessary.
- Will involve prolonged drying times.

Spray extraction:

- Should not result in overwetting of fabric or wetting of stuffing. This may occur when using hot water extraction if tool is passed too many times over fabric or cleaning solution is sprayed at too high a pressure.
- May result in colour changes. This is less likely with non-chlorinated solvents.
- Will not leave a resinous deposit.
- May leave an alkaline residue if detergent shampoo used.
- Is less likely to cause deterioration if non-chlorinated solvents used.
- Is less labour intensive than other methods.
- Will have a shorter drying time than wet shampooing unless overwetting occurs. If hot non-chlorinated solvents are used, drying times will be rapid.
- Is most effective on light to moderately soiled fabrics.
- In the case of some wool and cotton fabrics or where colours are likely to bleed or fade, spray extraction may only be possible if non-chlorinated solvents are used.

Dry foam/residue shampooing:

- Should not result in overwetting or wetting of the stuffing, but they may occur if the cleaning agent is over applied.

- May result in colour changes.
- Should not leave a resinous deposit in the fabric.
- May leave an alkaline residue.
- Will have a similar drying time to hot water extraction unless hot non-chlorinated solvents have been used.
- **May be more** effective on heavily soiled upholstery than spray extraction.

Completely effective restoration of upholstery fabrics can often only be achieved by using a combination of spray extraction and dry foam/residue shampooing. Whichever method of cleaning is selected the primary consideration must always be its effect on the fabric.

Upholstered furniture   Dust or damp wipe and buff all wood and metallic parts. Regularly suction clean all covers using upholstery tool and crevice tool for tuck-ins, including both sides of cushions. Periodic maintenance will be governed by the type of upholstery (leather, plastic-coated or fabric) and the nature of wood or metallic parts. If polishes are to be used occasionally it is essential that they are not allowed to come into contact with the upholstery.

Wardrobes   Dust or suction clean all exterior surfaces. Damp wipe if necessary. Interior surfaces, including shelves and drawers, must be suction cleaned and damp wiped regularly and always when a room is vacated. When necessary wash using a minimum of water or carry out other maintenance as dictated by construction materials, type of surface and degree of soiling.

Wax finishes   Dust and buff or damp wipe and buff. Heavier soiling can be removed by washing with a minimum of water and neutral detergent. Occasionally apply wax polish sparingly on a soft cloth and buff.

White wood   Dust, damp wipe or wash/scrub with water and neutral detergent. Rinse with cold water and dry.

Whicker   Dust or suction clean. Damp wipe if

required. When necessary, wash with water and neutral detergent. Polish can be applied occasionally and sparingly.

Window frames and fittings   Dust, damp wipe or wash. Carry out other forms of maintenance as dictated by soiling and type of finish.

Soft furnishings

Curtains

Curtain cleaning involves both regular tasks carried out *in situ* and periodic tasks which may be carried out either *in situ* or off-site.

Regular cleaning tasks for all curtains other than net ones will involve suction cleaning and stain removal. This will also include pelmets and valances if fitted. Suction cleaning requires the use of a curtain tool which will include a cleft for pleats, a suction cleaner fitted with a hose and access equipment if necessary. Cleaning involves systematically drawing the tool down successive lengths of curtains.

Stain removal should be undertaken as necessary.

Net curtains should be laundered at frequent intervals. Ideally all curtains within a building should be laundered at the same time to maintain a uniform standard of appearance. To prevent problems of matching curtains to windows when refitting they should be marked to indicate their respective rooms.

Periodic cleaning carried out *in situ* involves spray extraction with either hot water and detergent or hot non-chlorinated solvents. Numerous problems can be encountered when using detergents, limiting the usefulness of the method. However, where extraction can be carried out using solvents formulated to suit the different types of fabric, extraction can, with some exceptions, eliminate the need for off-site cleaning. The method employed is similar to that for suction cleaning. It is normally carried out by contractors.

Off-site cleaning involves either washing or dry cleaning according to the type of fabric. Lined curtains should always be dry-cleaned to prevent problems caused by dyes bleeding from one fabric to the other and the two fabrics possible shrinking at different rates.

Loose covers

Regular suction cleaning is required using similar procedures to those for any upholstered furniture. Stain removal should be carried out as required. Periodically covers should be removed and washed or dry cleaned according to the type of fabric.

Stain removal

The removal of stains, particularly from textile surfaces, is dependent upon the strict observation of a number of basic rules.

Rules of stain removal

- Deal with a stain as soon as it occurs. Once a stain has hardened or sunk into a surface it will be much more difficult to remove.
- Soak up as much of the stain as possible before using any other procedure and without rubbing. If a stain is fixed, scrape away build up above the surface.
- Identify stain and surface.
- This can save time spent in trying inappropriate methods and prevent the use of methods that might damage a surface.
- Always test effect of any cleaning agent on part of surface which cannot be seen.
- If the effect of stain removal is likely to be worse than stain do not attempt removal.
- Always use the mildest method first. Hard scrubbing or the use of solvents will frequently be the last resort.
- Always clean from the outside of the stain towards the centre using a soft absorbent cloth. This will prevent spreading of the stain.
- Always rinse with cold water and leave the surface as dry as possible.

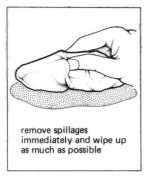

remove spillages immediately and wipe up as much as possible

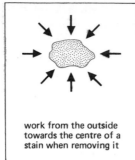

work from the outside towards the centre of a stain when removing it

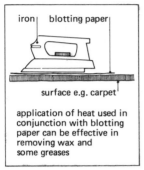

application of heat used in conjunction with blotting paper can be effective in removing wax and some greases

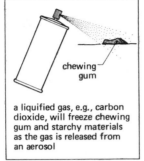

a liquified gas, e.g., carbon dioxide, will freeze chewing gum and starchy materials as the gas is released from an aerosol

Figure 83 *Methods of stain removal*

Methods and chemicals

A variety of methods and chemicals can be used for stain removal. Table 43 indicates the possible use of the various methods described below to remove commonly occuring stains.

Absorbtion (1) To prevent a stain spreading or penetrating a surface an absorbent cloth is placed over the stained area and worked from the outer margins towards the centre. Greasy stains can frequently be removed by working french chalk or Fullers earth into the affected area, leaving for a while and then brushing away.

Poultice (2) Used to remove ingrained or embedded stains. The appropriate cleaning agent is mixed with wallpaper paste and applied to the stained area. After 15 to 20 minutes the paste is removed and the surface rinsed and dried.

Friction (3) Scraping, brushing or rubbing can remove dried-on stains but the amount of friction applied must be related to the surface.

Heat (4) Used to remove materials softened by it. The stain is covered with blotting paper and a warm iron applied.

Freezing (5) Sticky substances, e.g. chewing gum, can be frozen using a carbon dioxide spray and then chipped off.

Cold water (6) Used to remove stains which may be fixed by heat or detergent

Cold water and salt (7) Diluted 1:50 can be used to remove fresh blood.

Warm water and liquid neutral detergent (8) Diluted 1:20 will remove a variety of stains from hard surfaces.

Warm water and shampoo (9) Diluted 1:20 will remove organic and inorganic stains from carpets, upholstery and curtains.

Water and ammonia or sodium bicarbonate (10) Diluted 1:50 is used to neutralize acid stains.

Water and alkaline cleaning agent (11) Diluted 1:50 or stronger if required. will remove many oil-based stains.

Water and white vinegar (12) Diluted 1:1 is used to neutralize alkaline stains, to remove light grease from hard surface and remove stains.

Lemon juice and salt (13) Used to remove rust marks. It can be applied as a poultice.

Oxalic acid (14) Used to remove severe rust marks. It can be diluted with water (1:50) and applied as a poultice if required. Care must be exercised in its use.

Hydrogen peroxide and sodium thiosulphate (15) Stubborn stains can be removed by

Table 43 *Stain removal*

| Stain | Carpets, upholstery, curtains | | Hard and semi-hard surfaces | |
	Method	Notes	Method	Notes
Acid	1, 6, 10, 21	—	1, 10, 21	—
Alcoholic beverages, fresh	1, 8, 9 or 21	—	1, 8, 21	—
Alcoholic beverages, dried	17, 8 or 9, 21	Use meths. 12 can be effective. If severe use 16	3, 8, 21	—
Alkali	1, 6, 12, 21	—	1, 12, 21	—
Blood, fresh	1, 7, 21	—	1, 7, 21	—
Blood, dried	3, 8 or 9, 21	If persistant use 15, but not on dyed fabrics	3, 8, 21	If persistant use 15
Chewing gum, sweets, etc.	5	—	5, 8, 21	—
Cigarette burns	Brush away charred fibres	Use 22 if severe and a replacement piece is available	Permanent on most surfaces. Can involve major restoration	Wood can be polished with metal polish and a suitable oil rubbed in
Coffee/tea	1, 6, 8 or 9, 21	If dried, use 12. 16 can also be used	1, 8, 21	—
Crayon-wax	17, 8 or 9, 21	Use tetrachlorethylene. If persistant use 11, 12 21	3, 17, 8, 21	Use tetrachlorethylene. If persistant, use 11, 21
Dyes	8 or 9, 20	If persistant, use 16 and then 15	8, 21	—
Faeces	1, 3, 6, 8 or 9, 12, 21	—	1, 3, 8, 21	—
Fats and oils	1, 8 or 9 21	If stain persists, use 17 or rub in french chalk	1, 8, 21	If stain persists use 17 with suitable solvent, or 11
Food	1, 3, 8 or 9, 21	Use 17 if stain persistant	1, 3, 8, 21	Protein stain can be removed from wood by scrubbing with 7

(continued)

Table 43 — *continued*

	Carpets, upholstery, curtains		Hard and semi-hard surfaces	
	Method	*Notes*	*Method*	*Notes*
Fruit juice	1, 8 or 9, 21	Use meths if stain persistent	1, 8, 21	—
Glue, water-soluble	1, 3, 8 or 9, 21	—	1, 3, 8, 21	—
Glue, plastic	1, 3, 17, 21	Use acetone	1, 3, 17, 21	Use acetone on surfaces not affected by it. Otherwise omit 17 and use 3 and 8 together
Grass	17, 8 or 9, 21	Use meths	17, 21	Use meths on surfaces unaffected by it. Otherwise omit 17 and use 3 and 8 together
Grease, light	1, 8 or 9, 21	Can use 4 before 8 or 9. If stain persists use 17 or rub in french chalk	1, 8, 21	Can wipe non-porous surface with dilute vinegar. If stain persists, use 17 with suitable solvent or 11
Grease, heavy	1, 17, 8 or 9, 21	If very bad use 11, 12, 21	1, 8, 21	If very bad use 11, 21 or solvent-based detergent depending on effect of solvent or alkali on surface
Ink, biro	17, 8 or 9, 21	Use meths as solvent. Use 15 if stain persists, but not on dyed textiles	17, 21	Use meths as solvent except on french polish. Other alternatives are a combination of 3 and 8 or 13, either in combination with 3 or applied as a poultice
Ink, permanent	1, 17, 8 or 9, 21	As biro ink	1, 17, 21	As biro ink
Ink, washable	1, 8 or 9 21	A poultice of sodium citrate (10% solution) can be applied to leather	1, 8, 21	As biro ink
Ink, oil-based	10 or 11, 12, 21	As washable ink	10 or 11, 21	As biro ink

(continued)

Table 43 – *continued*

| | Carpets, upholstery, curtains | | Hard and semi-hard surfaces | |
	Method	Notes	Method	Notes
Mud	3, 8 or 9, 21	Remove when dry	3, 8, 21	Remove when dry
Nail varnish or make-up	17, 8 or 9, 21	Use acetone. On acetates omit 17 and use 8 or 9 in combination with 3	3, 17, 21	Use acetone
Paint, water	1, 8 or 9, 21	If dry, use 3 in combination with 8 or 9	1, 8, 21	If dry, use 3 in combination with 8
Paint, solvent	1, 17, 8 or 9, 21	Use white spirit or xylol depending on type of paint	1, 17, 8, 21	If solvents affect surface use abrasion only
Polish	1, 17, 8 or 9, 21	Use white spirit	1, 8, 21	Use a solvent only if stain has penetrated surface
Rust	3, 13, 21	If persistent or bad use 14, 10, 21	3, 13, 21	If persistent use 14, 10, 21. 13 or 14 can be used in combination with 2
Tar	3, 17, 8 or 9, 21	Use white spirit	Mix with oil and then 1, 16, 8, 21	Omit using oil and do not use white spirit if surface affected by either. Use either 3, 16, 8, 21 or 3, 8, 21
Urine	1, 6, 8 or 9, 21, 10, 21	Use 11 if set	1, 6, 8, 21	—
Vomit	1, 6, 8 or 9 10, 21	Use 3 if dry	1, 6, 8, 21	—
Wax	3, 4, 17, 8 or 9, 21	—	3, 8, 20	Use a solvent if ingrained

bleaching. Apply 20 vol. hydrogen peroxide diluted to 1:6 to the affected area. After 2 to 3 min, rinse with a solution of sodium thiosulphate diluted 1:50.

Glycerine (16) Diluted 1:1 with water is worked into the stained area and then rinsed out.

Solvents (17) Can be used to remove greasy stains and stains not soluble in water or water and detergent. To be most effective they should be applied to dry surfaces. After application, the solvent is allowed to dry and the residue brushed away. When cleaning curtains, an absorbent cloth can be placed beneath the fabric to assist removal.

The principal solvents used are alcohols, white spirit, tetrachloroethylene and acetone. The type of stains they will remove and surfaces on which they should be used are described on page 168. Carbon tetrachloride and benzene must not be used. The vapours are carcinogenic.

Furniture polish (18) Used to remove stains from the surface of polished furniture.

Solvent-based wax (19) Used to remove surface stains from waxed floors.

Emulsion polish (20) Used to remove surface stains from emulsion-polished floors.

Rinse and dry (21) On completion of any stain removal procedure always rinse with cold water and leave as dry as possible.

Cookie cutter (22) If carpets are badly stained or burned, the affected area can be cut out and replaced with a new piece.

Sanitary accommodation

The cleaning and maintenance of toilets, bathrooms and washrooms requires high standards of hygiene to be maintained. The maintenance of these standards may necessitate the cleaning of these areas several times a day, depending upon the degree of soilage and usage.

Equipment and materials

Equipment to be used in sanitary areas should be colour-coded and used only for cleaning these areas and that used for urinals and WC pans should have a colour code to distinguish it from equipment used elsewhere in toilet areas. Neutral detergents will be most suitable for all normal cleaning tasks. Bactericidical detergents may be used in preference to neutral detergents, although effective cleaning using the latter is likely to be as effective. Alkaline cleaning agents can be used to remove soil of a greasy nature. In this respect they

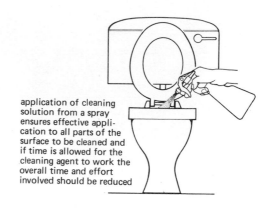

application of cleaning solution from a spray ensures effective application to all parts of the surface to be cleaned and if time is allowed for the cleaning agent to work the overall time and effort involved should be reduced

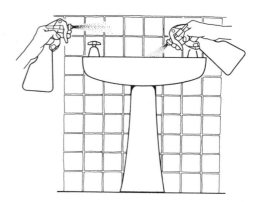

Figure 84 *Application of cleaning solution to sanitary appliances using a hand spray*

are particularly useful in removing tide marks formed largely from body fats.

Abrasive cleaning agents, particularly powders, should not be used.

Acid toilet cleaners must not be used routinely.

They will be required periodically to remove iron marks or accumulations of lime scale on glazed surfaces. On other surfaces vinegar (acetic acid) or lemon juice (citric acid) can be used but, if staining is severe, oxalic acid should be used. Acid cleaners containing chlorine compounds will also remove faecal stains. Sodium hypochlorite is not generally required for routine use but it can be used to remove faecal stains.

Bleach and acid toilet cleaners must never be used together. Chlorine gas will be produced.

Disinfectants must not be used as a substitute for the effective use of cleaning agents. Nor should strong smelling disinfectants be used to cover offensive odours. The source of the odour should be removed.

Channel blocks or deodorizers can be used to provide an attractive smell. They will mask any odours produced as a result of normal usage of the accommodation between one clean and the next.

Polishes must not be used in any sanitary accommodation.

Methods

The cleaning of sanitary accommodation involves methods and routines particular to sanitary appliances together with methods common to other areas, namely sweeping, wet mopping and scrubbing of floors (see pages 210–214), damp wiping and washing of walls, doors, windows, appliances and other furniture (see pages 204–209).

When damp wiping in sanitary accommodation an additional step may be included. After wiping with a cloth to clean a surface it maybe wiped again using a second cloth and clean water to rinse the surface.

Walls Damp wipe or wash using a neutral detergent depending on degree of soilage.

Hand basins The procedure is as follows:

1 Clear sinks of soap, brushes and other items.
2 Remove hair from plugholes.
3 Spray all surfaces with cleaning solution including soap holders, splash backs, taps and

inner and outer surface of basin and allow to stand for a few minutes.
4 Remove tide marks using an abrasive pad or soft scrubbing brush.
5 Run tap and rinse off all surfaces with clean water.
6 Dry and buff all surfaces using disposable towels.

Ledges, handles and similar fittings Depending on degree of soilage, damp wipe or wash. Always rinse, dry and buff with disposable towels.

Mirrors Damp wipe using a cleaning solution containing neutral detergent. Always rinse, dry with disposable towels and buff if required with a scrim or lintless cloth.

Baths As for hand basins.

Showers The procedure is similar to that described for hand basins. It must also include wiping the shower curtain. When task is complete the curtain is normally left hanging in the bath or shower basin.

Bath and safety mats Disposable mats are replaced. Mats requiring laundering are replaced by freshly laundered mats. Cork and rubber mats are washed, rinsed and left to dry.

WCs The procedure is as follows:

1 Flush and then push back all water from the pan with a brush.
2 Spray all surfaces inside the bowl with cleaning solution and allow to stand for several minutes.
3 Damp wipe or wash all other surfaces as necessary including outside of pan, top and bottom of seat, cistern, pipework and handles.
4 Rinse and wipe dry with disposable towels.
5 Scrub inside of bowl with a brush taking care not to miss any part.
6 Flush.
7 Note if an acid cleaner will be required next time.

8   Depending on custom the seat is normally left upright.

Urinals   The procedure is as follows:

1   Flush and remove all debris from channel particularly from drain cover.
2   Spray all inner surfaces including pipework with cleaning solution and allow to stand for several minutes.
3   Damp wipe or wash all other surfaces as for WC.
4   Scrub inner surfaces with brush.
5   Flush.
6   Renew or replace channel blocks.

Floors   The procedure is as follows:

1   Sweep.
2   Wet mop using two-solution method or scrub.
3   Leave floor as dry as possible.

Routine for daily cleaning

The number of items included will depend on the actual appliances and furniture, but in general the order of work is as outlined:

1   Cleaning equipment will include mopping buckets and press, two mops, toilet brush, waste receptacle, rubber gloves, cleaning agent, hand spray, pales, cloths, scrim, paper towels, broom, dust pan and brush. Where appropriate the use of a scrubber polisher, suction drier and associated equipment should be considered.
2   Supplies required will include paper towels, soap, clean linen and toilet paper.
3   Dilute cleaning agent usually 1:50 to 1:100.
4   Ventilate premises if possible.
5   Flush all WC pans.
6   Remove all soiled linen, paper towels, bath mats, incinerator ash.
7   Wash bath and safety mats and leave to dry.
8   Sweep up all loose litter from floor and place in plastic sac.
9   Remove all soap and brushes from sinks and showers.

10   Clear plugholes of hairs and litter.
11   Push back water from WC pans.
12   Clear urinal channel.
13   Spray cleaning solution into WC bowl, urinals, sinks, baths and showers.
14   Clean walls, partitions, door frames, ledges, mirrors, shelves and cupboards.
15   Complete cleaning of sinks, showers and baths.
16   Complete cleaning of WC.
17   Complete cleaning of urinals.
18   Replenish all supplies as necessary.
19   Check that incinerators, hand driers and automatic cisterns are working. Report if defective.
20   Mop or scrub floor leaving it as dry as possible.
21   Check all work.
22   Wash out all equipment thoroughly, emptying dirty water down slop hopper or sluice sink and not down WC pan.

Special tasks

Stained WC pans, urinals and pipework   Accumulation of lime scale, urine salts and iron salts may occur. Removal can be affected using strong acid cleaners. After normal cleaning and in the case of WC pans, after pushing back the water from the pan, apply a liquid acid cleaner with a sponge applicator to all affected areas. Allow to stand for several minutes and then scrub with stiff brush. Apply further cleaner as necessary and continue until all staining is removed. Rinse thoroughly with clean water by flushing several times.

Stained and scratched baths   Heavy deposits of body fats can be removed by spraying with an alkaline cleaning agent, leaving for a few minutes and then rinsing off. Water marks may be removed by successive application of a mild acid, e.g. vinegar, and rubbing vigorously with a cloth or soft brush. Scratched acrylic or GRP baths can be restored by polishing with a metal polish.

Stained floors   In older toilets, floors may have become stained by urine salts. Although acid

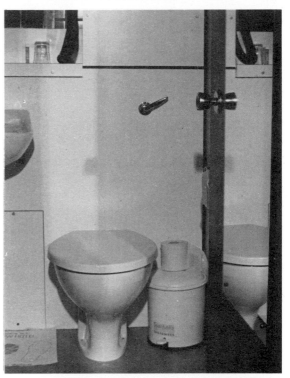

Hotel bathroom showing furniture and required standard of appearance and hygiene

cleaning agents can be used for their removal it must be recognized that restoration will be at the cost of making the floor even more porous than before.

Odours may be caused by ingrained soiling of floor by urine salts, partially blocked drains or dirty overflows from basins and baths. To remove odours caused by urine salts, mopping with a strong phenolic disinfectant which is then allowed to stand before rinsing may be successful. Partially blocked drains can be cleaned by introducing caustic soda into the drain. Overflows can be washed out by using a rubber tube attached to a tap.

Extensively soiled toilets   After treatment to remove scale, stains and odours, high-pressure hot water and detergent is used to clean all surfaces and appliances.

Kitchens

The cleaning and maintenance of kitchens should allow the highest standards of hygiene to be maintained. All surfaces coming into contact with food must be disinfected. This will be achieved largely by effective cleaning and in part by the use of heat or chemical disinfectants.

Cleaning operations in a kitchen can be divided into two categories:

1   Dishes and kitchen ware: crockery, cutlery, glass, food preparation equipment and utensils.
2   Walls, floors and kitchen furniture.

Dishes and kitchen ware

Efficient and effective cleaning and disinfection will depend upon:

1   Correct choice of equipment.
2   Correct choice of cleaning agent.
3   Temperatures employed.
4   Inclusion of a specific disinfecting procedure.
5   Method of cleaning and disinfection.

Equipment   The choice of equipment is governed by the number of individual pieces to be cleaned per hour. A two-sink system is suitable for washing up to 300 individual pieces of crockery, cutlery, glasses or small scale equipment per hour. The equipment consists of two stainless steel sinks with drainers, normally manufactured as a one-piece unit. Preferably each sink should be fitted with a thermostatically controlled heating element. One sink is used for washing, the second for rinsing and disinfection. In the absence of a thermostatically controlled heating element, or if rinsing glassware, a bactericide will be required in the rinsing sink to ensure effective disinfection. Rinsing sinks fitted with heating elements have two principal advantages; they eliminate the need for using bactericides and ensure that the pieces being washed are hot enough to air dry.

Deep sinks are similar to the sinks employed in the two-sink system but are much deeper. They are specifically designed for the washing of large utensils or pieces of equipment.

Dish washing machines can be installed in preference to a two-sink system where the number of pieces to be cleaned exceeds 300 per hour. The machine selected should have a work capacity related to the number of pieces to be cleaned per hour (see page 142). The number of stages depends upon the model of machine, but the minimum requirement will be a wash and rinse stage.

Utensil cleaners can be installed as an alternative to washing food preparation utensils in sinks or washing machines where the number of utensils to be cleaned warrants it (see page 139).

Glass washers, either of the bar or dishwasher type, are installed where the number of pieces of glass used makes hand washing impracticable. Unless specifically designed to be heat resistant, glassware may crack if exposed to high temperatures, making the use of dishwashers other than those specifically designed for glass unsuitable.

Drying cloths are unsuitable for general use. Bacteria from a series of dishes that have been dried will contaminate the cloth and hence contaminate other dishes. If used, they must be discarded as soon as they become wet and be boiled before using again. When it is necessary to hand dry or polish crockery, cutlery or glassware, paper towels should be used.

Handtools to remove soil firmly stuck to a surface will include nylon bristled brushes or abrasive pads. Soap-filled steel wool pads must not be used as they tend to polish rather than remove the soil.

Cleaning agents The choice of cleaning agent is influenced by the use of manual or mechanical means of washing, the degree and nature of the soil and the effect of the cleaning agent on the surface being cleaned. Liquid, neutral detergents are suitable for hand washing and the removal of most types of soil. Dishwashers normally require a low-foam synthetic powder. In hard water areas a water softener, e.g. Calgon, or where larger machines are installed a water softening machine should be used.

Alkaline detergents can be used for the removal of heavy soiling from cooking utensils. They will, however, discolour aluminium. A mixture of equal parts of vinegar, flour and salt may be used to clean copper.

Carbonized materials can be removed by boiling utensils in a mixture of water and sodium hypochlorite (1 oz of bleach to 1 gallon of water).

Abrasive powders should not be used, particularly on crockery. Metal polishes must not be used on silver or copper. Some detergents will effect the head on beer if it is not completely rinsed from glasses.

Temperature Washing should be carried out at about 50°C. If the temperature exceeds 60°C protein hardens and starches gelantinize making their removal more difficult. Higher temperatures will, however, assist in the removal of grease.

Rinsing temperatures should be hot enough to effect disinfection and allow utensils and dishes to air dry.

High temperatures may crack glassware or soften the glue securing the handles of cutlery with plastic, bone or wooden handles.

Disinfection Effective disinfection will in the first

instance depend on the removal of all soil by washing. Effective washing should remove most of the bacteria present. Complete disinfection will normally be achieved by one of two methods:

1 Immersing in water at a minimum temperature of 82°C for a minimum of 1 min.
2 Immersing in water to which a bactericide has been added.

The choice of method and bactericide, if used, will depend on a number of factors. High temperatures will allow dishes and utensils to air dry, thus eliminating the need for drying cloths and reducing the possibility of crockery being stacked whilst still wet.

Bactericides are used when high temperatures will have a detrimental effect on the surfaces and where it is not possible to maintain the temperature at 82°C plus.

Sodium hypochlorite may be used in rinsing sinks at a concentration of 50–100 ppm of active chlorine. However, there are a number of disadvantages. It is toxic and, unless control procedures are good, its use in food premises is generally discouraged. It has a distinctive odour and will darken stainless steel.

Quaternary ammonium compounds and iodophors are non-toxic and odourless but more expensive. Bactericides used as sterilizers for rinsing glasses must not destroy the head on beers.

Methods

Hand washing The usual order of washing is glass, cutlery, crockery, utensils and small equipment. The washing and rinsing water should be changed frequently and never topped up. The procedure is:

1 Scrape or pre-wash, depending upon the degree of soilage.
2 Wash in water and detergent diluted 1:100 to 1:200 at about 50°C using a nylon bristle brush or an abrasive nylon pad, as appropriate, to remove soil.
3 Rinse and disinfect by immersing in water at

82°C for 1 min or in hot water to which a bactericide has been added.

4   Allow to air dry or wipe with disposable paper towels.

Machine washing   The actual washing and rinsing steps will be similar to that for manual methods but will be carried out automatically. There are, however, a number of important points that should be observed.

Flat ware must be loaded into a tray or belt at a slight angle with the upper surface uppermost. Hollow ware is loaded upside down. Cutlery should be stood vertically in purpose-made racks.

The handling of dirty and clean dishes should, if possible, be undertaken by different operatives to eliminate risk of re-contamination.

Efficient washing will depend on the efficient operation of the machine and the detergency of the washing water must be maintained and sieves or strainers emptied periodically.

The air drying of stainless steel cutlery passed through a machine can cause surface staining. It is generally preferable to wipe such cutlery with paper towels as they are removed from the machine.

Crockery with an on-glaze decoration must not be passed through a dishwasher.

Mincers, slicers and mixing machines   The exact procedure will depend on the machine, but it should involve the following steps:

1   Break down machine as far as possible.
2   Pre-rinse all detachable parts.
3   Wash, rinse and disinfect all detachable parts manually or in a dishwasher.
4   Damp wipe or wash remainder of machine with a detergent solution, using a brush to clean less accessible areas. If available, high pressure steam or water can be used.
5   Rinse all surfaces; a bactericide can be included in the rinse water if desired.
6   Dry thoroughly with paper towels.

Ice cream and milk machines   The procedure is similar to that for other machines. When clean and

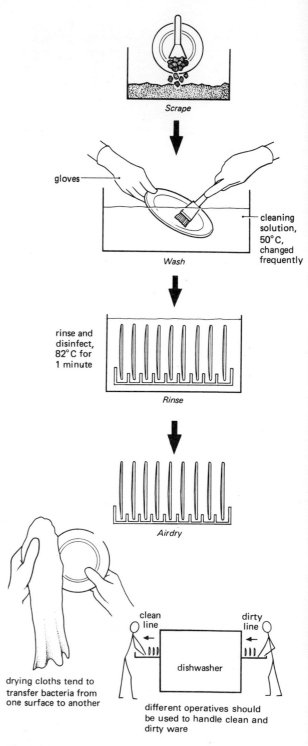

Figure 85   *Major stages and precautions for ware washing*

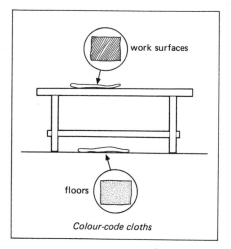

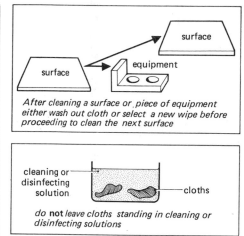

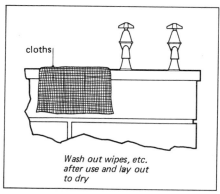

Figure 86 *Hygiene hazards in kitchen cleaning*

dry the machine is re-assembled and filled with water and a non-toxic, odourless bactericide and left overnight. Thorough rinsing with clean water will be required before re-use.

Walls, floors and kitchen furniture

The cleaning of kitchen furniture, appliances and fabric involves two types of cleaning operation: routine cleaning of furniture and fabric undertaken on a daily basis (but may also involve some periodic tasks) and deep cleaning usually undertaken at three- or six-monthly intervals. The operation is usually undertaken by contractors. No matter how effective the daily cleaning, there will be a progressive accumulation of soil, particularly grease, on less accessible surfaces,

notably canopies, ducts, light fittings, floors and walls behind equipment, ceilings and the upper half of walls. Methods employing the use of high pressure water and steam are generally used. Routine cleaning will generally include cleaning agents, machines and methods used elsewhere, but the particular need to maintain high standards of hygiene should be observed.

Equipment and materials Neutral detergents are suitable for most cleaning tasks, although alkalis may be used to remove heavy accumulations of grease while sodium hypochlorite may be required to remove carbonized material. Abrasive powders should not be used on any surface. Soil that adheres strongly to a surface can usually be removed by spraying it with cleaning solution, allowing the solution to stand for a few minutes and then rubbing vigorously with an abrasive pad. Further application of solution may be required if the build up is heavy.

If all cleaning is carried out effectively there should be no requirement for the use of disinfectant. Strong disinfectants must never be used. Floor cloths must be distinguished from cloths used for wiping work surfaces by means of a colour code.

Wet mopping equipment (preferably colour-coded) should be used for the removal of spillages. Wet mopping using the two-solution method can be employed for the cleaning of floors although the use of scrubbing machines and wet pick-ups will give a more satisfactory standard.

Cloths and mops must never be left standing in cleaning solutions or disinfectants. Each time they are used they should be washed out thoroughly and left to dry.

Cleaning solutions must not after use be left for re-use later. A fresh solution should be made up as cleaning is required.

Methods   The cleaning of the kitchen fabric and furniture will include methods common to other areas, namely sweeping, wet mopping or scrubbing of floors (see pages 210–214), damp wiping or washing of walls, doors, windows and furniture (see 204–207). However, the routine used will depend on the actual appliances to be cleaned. It is generally easier to clean cookers, hot cupboards and similar appliances while they are still warm.

Walls   Damp wipe or wash depending on the degree of soilage.

Drains and gulleys   Clean grease traps at least twice per week. Clear and wash out silt traps or strainers of rumblers daily. Gulleys must be cleaned daily with cleaning solution. A typical procedure is:

1   Remove grids and clear channel of debris.
2   Scrub grid and channel with cleaning solution using a stiff brush.
3   Replace grids and flush with hot water.

Blocked drains may be cleaned by the following procedure:

1   Flush with hot water.
2   Sprinkle with washing soda (sodium carbonate) or caustic soda if available. Observe safety procedures.
3   Allow time for soda to act.
4   Flush with cold water.

Cookers, hot plates and cupboards, bain marries   The following procedures, if used on a daily basis, should make the use of stronger cleaning agents unnecessary:

1   Remove all shelves and containers as appropriate and wash. The removal of stubborn soil will be made easier by soaking in hot cleaning solution before scrubbing with a nylon pad. Rinse and dry.
2   Spray all other surfaces both inside and out with a solution of neutral or alkaline detergent depending on degree of soilage and allow to stand for a few minutes. Rinse off all surfaces with clean water and cloth using a nylon pad as necessary.
3   Dry all exterior surfaces with paper towels.
4   Return shelves and containers.

Periodically, if appropriate, burners should be removed and cleaned to ensure jets are clear.

Food service trolleys   The procedure is similar to that for cookers. After use, empty the trolley, spray all surfaces with cleaning solution, rinse thoroughly and dry exterior surfaces.

Refrigerators   Daily cleaning will involve damp wiping, rinsing and drying of exterior surfaces. Periodically the interior must be cleaned:

1   Remove all food to another fridge if possible and defrost. Alternatively, defrost and remove food to a cool place.
2   Remove all shelves and wash, rinse and dry them.
3   Wipe down interior with a solution of bicarbonate of soda.
4   Rinse with clean water and wipe dry.
5   Replace shelves and food.

Fryers The frequency of carrying out the following procedures will depend on usage of the equipment:

1   Drain fat and strain off debris.
2   Wash with neutral detergent or, if badly soiled, fill with a mixture of neutral detergent and sodium hypochlorite and boil.
3   Rinse all surfaces thoroughly with clean water and dry.
4   Ensure that the fryer is completely dry before returning fat.

Work surfaces Damp wipe or wash with neutral detergent, rinse and dry as frequently as necessary during and after use.

Sinks Clear sinks of all debris, dishes and utensils. Spray all surfaces, including taps, with cleaning solution and allow to stand for a few minutes. Run taps, rinse all surfaces and wipe dry drainers and edges with paper towel. After using a sink it is important to always flush with hot water to reduce the possibility of blockages.

Cupboards Daily cleaning will involve damp wiping of exterior surfaces. Periodically cupboards used for food storage must be emptied and all interior surfaces washed, rinsed and dried.

Floors Sweep with a stiff brush. Wet mop using two-solution method or scrub, rinse and dry using scrubbing machine and wet suction cleaner. Leave the floor as dry as possible.

Daily routine When all food preparation and service are completed, all kitchens should be cleaned as per the following routine:

1   Open doors and windows, if appropriate.
2   Complete all washing up.
3   Clean all furniture and equipment, while warm if possible, and as appropriate.
4   Clean all work surfaces.
5   Clean walls and other vertical surfaces.
6   Dispose of all litter and waste
7   Clean floors.
8   Close doors and windows if opened.

Vending machines

The standard of hygiene expected of vending machines is similar to that expected of any equipment coming into contact with food. There are, however, a number of major problems encountered. They are frequently situated away from a source of water and, in order to maintain security, kitchen and cleaning staff do not have keys. They may be installed under contract and maintained by the supplier. Any cleaning agents used must be non-toxic and completely odourless. Cleaning and maintenance will generally involve:

● Damp wipe or washing of the exterior surfaces.
● Removal of spillages from the interior.
● Washing of all interior parts with hot water and neutral detergent followed by rinsing with a bactericide solution. Where possible, surfaces should be wiped dry.
● Detailed procedures depend on the type of machine.

(See *Quality Control in Food Service,* Thomer and Manning, AVI, for a more comprehensive discussion.)

Public and circulation areas

Corridors, reception areas, waiting rooms and lounges require high standards of cleaning and maintenance, the standard achieved reflecting directly on the establishment. Foyers, reception areas and waiting rooms can be subject to considerable soilage. This can be reduced by the use of dust control matting.

Daily routine

1   Empty waste bins and ashtrays and damp wipe or wash as necessary.
2   Ventilate rooms.
3   Dust or damp wipe fixtures, fittings and fitted furniture.
4   Spot clean walls, particularly around doors and switches.
5   Dust or damp wipe moveable furniture.
6   Clean floors according to agreed method.

7 Remove spillages and check clean floors as necessary.

Periodic tasks

1 High dusting.
2 Suction clean upholstery, radiators and curtains.
3 Scrub or strip floors and reapply polish.
4 Wash furniture, fixtures and fittings as necessary.
5 Deep clean upholstery and carpets.
6 Clean or replace curtains.
7 Wash walls, windows, blinds, ceilings and light fittings.
8 Preventive maintenance, e.g. application of polish to furniture.

Offices

The standard required in offices is extremely variable depending upon user requirements, the establishment and the position within the organization of personnel using the office.

The daily routine and periodic tasks will be similar to those for public areas. However, where lower standards are required, this will be reflected in the daily routine where dusting, damp wiping and spot cleaning may only be carried out once or twice per week. Periodic tasks will also be carried out less frequently. It is essential in offices that the confidentiality of papers is respected and that they are not disturbed during cleaning.

Stairs

It is essential that stairways are safe. This will include ensuring that they are not likely to be slippery and nothing is left that will cause falls. When carrying out wet cleaning methods, clean half the width at one time and leave to dry before commencing other half. Care should be taken to ensure that cleaning solutions do not splash over the edges on to the lower surfaces.

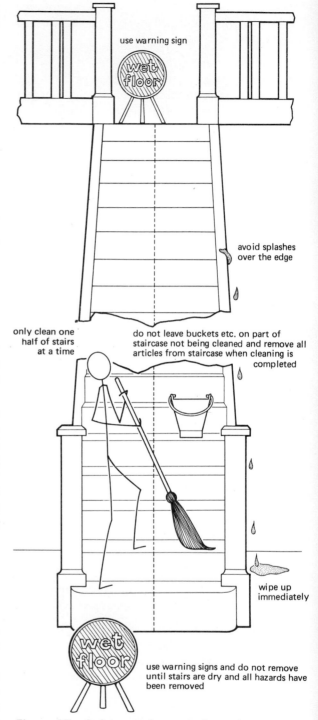

Figure 87 *Safety requirements for staircase cleaning*

Daily routine

1 Remove all litter.
2 Dust or damp wipe bannister rail, newal post and stair rods.
3 Clean string and spindles as necessary.
4 Spot clean walls, particularly around light switches.
5 Sweep or suction clean hard floors and damp mop.
6 Suction clean carpets.
7 Remove spillages as necessary.

Periodic tasks

1 High dusting.
2 Jogging of stair carpet.
3 Deep clean carpet.
4 Wash walls, windows, blinds, ceilings and light fittings.
5 Polish stair rods if fitted and if necessary.

Lifts

Lifts should be cleaned when traffic is lightest and not all at one time.

Typical routine

1 Damp wipe and buff area around signal button.
2 Dust, damp wipe or wash outer door as necessary and buff with a dry cloth.
3 Call lift and switch off.
4 Clean inner surface of door.
5 Clean tracks either by scrubbing with a damp brush or suction cleaning.
6 Dust or damp wipe all interior surfaces as necessary and buff all metal surfaces.
7 Clean floor according to agreed method.

Dining rooms

High standards of hygiene are required reflected in frequent and effective cleaning methods.

Daily routine

Many tasks will be required several times per day and will follow each period of food service. These will include:

1 Emptying and wiping or washing of ashtrays.
2 Damp wiping and washing of tables.
3 Damp wipe chairs.
4 Suction clean and remove stains from upholstered seats.
5 Sweep and damp or wet mop hard floors.
6 Suction clean carpets and remove stains.

Other tasks will include:

7 Dust or damp wipe all other fixtures, fittings and furniture.
8 Spot clean walls and area around light fittings and doors.

Periodic tasks

To maintain high standards of appearance, many tasks will be carried out relatively frequently:

1 Scrub or strip and reapply polish to hard floors.
2 Deep clean carpets and upholstery.
3 Other periodic tasks will be similar to those listed for public areas.

Classrooms

A general standard is normally required. Many periodic cleaning tasks will be carried out together during vacations.

Daily routine

1 Empty waste bins and wash out if necessary.
2 Dust or damp wipe furniture, fixtures and fittings. This may be carried out once or twice per week.
3 Spot clean walls.
4 Clean floor according to type and agreed method. This will involve mop sweeping or suction cleaning, and damp mopping and

buffing or spray maintenance as frequently as necessary.

Periodic tasks

1   High dusting.
2   Wash walls, ceilings, light fittings and blinds.
3   Strip floor and re-apply polish.
4   Deep clean carpets and upholstery.
5   Wash furniture, fixtures and fittings.

Gymnasia

The essential requirement is that floors are maintained to give a non-slippery surface at all times. Floors will usually be wood strip or granwood finished with a suitable seal. A polish is not normally used.

Daily routine

1   Dust or damp wipe fixtures, fittings and furniture.
2   Spot clean walls.
3   Clean floors by mop sweeping and damp mopping using a neutral detergent.

In large gymnasia a scrubber drier will be the most appropriate piece of equipment to use.

Periodic tasks

1   High dust, wash walls, ceilings and light fittings.
2   Wash furniture, fixtures and fittings.
3   Reseal floor.

Swimming pools

High standards of hygiene are required to control bacteria levels. This is reflected in the methods of cleaning and maintenance and their frequency.

Wet areas are constructed of hard impervious materials.

Cubicles, sides of pools, duck boards and other wet areas must be scrubbed frequently through the day with sodium hypochlorite.

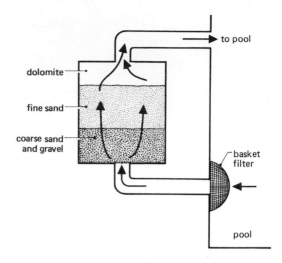

Figure 88   *Swimming pool filtration*

Humidity and temperature will be controlled by air conditioning. Maintenance of the air temperature above that of the pool will help to reduce the humidity of the air.

Water in the pool is continually filtered. The filter has three elements: a basket filter to remove large objects, sand or gravel to remove particulate soil and dolomite or other medium to control pH.

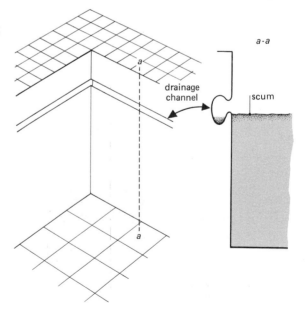

To clean the filters back washing is carried out periodically. This involves reversing the flow of water through the filters.

Skimming of pool to remove surface scum is carried out by displacement into a drainage channel around the side of the pool. Channels must be cleared of debris and cleaned at least daily.

To control the level of bacteria in the water, chlorine is introduced into the water. The level is checked throughout the day; too little has no effect, too much will affect users.

The pH of the water must be maintained at 7.2 to 7.8. If the pH falls or rises outside these limits it can be adjusted by the direct addition of soda ash (sodium carbonate) or dry acid (sodium bisulphate) to the water.

The emptying of interior pools is seldom necessary. Underwater vacuuming and other techniques make it unnecessary.

Increasingly chlorine will cease to be the principal method of disinfecting pools, being replaced by methods requiring the use of ozone, sodium hypochlorite or bromine compounds.

Computer rooms

In computer rooms it is essential that dust levels, humidity and temperature remain within specific limits. Noise, vibration, electrical interference and build-up of static electricity should be avoided. Floors may have conducting properties and be anti-static. There are, therefore, a number of rules which should be followed.

Rules

1 No dry dusting or sweeping. Dust should be removed by suction cleaners and damp, impregnated or static mops and mittens.
2 Dust control equipment must be cleaned elsewhere.
3 Unless specifically agreed with user, floor polishes should not be used. There are polishes specially formulated for conducting floors, but their value is limited. The required con-

ductivity of the floor must not be significantly affected.
4 Aerosol polishes containing silicones must not be used.
5 Wet cleaning should involve a minimum of water.
6 Detergents should leave no resinous deposit on the floor and should be used in minimal quantities.
7 Suction cleaners must be filtered, suppressed and silenced to required standards (see **pages 126–127**).
8 Scrubber polishers must be suppressed and should be fitted with a suction unit.
9 The items of computer equipment to be cleaned must be specifically agreed with user.

Daily routine

1 Remove waste bins and empty elsewhere.
2 Dust all fixtures, fittings and furniture.
3 Clean computer equipment as agreed.
4 Mop sweep or suction clean floor according to type. Damp mop or spray clean hard floors at agreed frequency but usually not less than once per week.

Periodic tasks

1 Change dust control mats.
2 Dust or suction clean walls, ceilings, partitions, light fittings, air conditioning grills and unpolished furniture.
3 Remove heavy soiling by damp wiping with a detergent which includes a cationic surfactant.

The frequency of carrying out these tasks is normally monthly and not less than three-monthly.

Laboratories and technical areas

In such areas cleaning duties are normally restricted to the floor. Any other tasks are only carried out by agreement. Two general rules apply: equipment must not be touched or switched off and chemicals and experimental apparatus must not be touched.

Bedrooms

Cleaning tasks and their frequency will depend on the type of establishment, whether the room is vacated or occupied, and whether the room includes a sink or there is a bathroom en-suite.

Daily routine for cleaning an occupied room

1 Ventilate room.
2 Strip bed and remove soiled linen if it is to be replaced. In hostels bed-making will usually be the responsibility of the occupant.
3 Place soiled linen in laundry bag.
4 Empty ashtrays, waste paper baskets.
5 Remove crockery and all rubbish and litter.
6 Clean washbasins or bathrooms as appropriate (see page 248).
7 Remake bed.
8 Dust or damp wipe all fixtures, fittings and fitted furniture.
9 Spot clean walls, especially areas around light fittings and doors.
10 Dust or damp wipe moveable furniture.
11 Clean floor according to type and by agreed method.
12 Replace soap, towels and toilet paper as necessary.
13 Replace stationary and house notices if appropriate.
14 Adjust windows.
15 Check any defects and report.
16 Check work.

In hostels the cleaning of walls, fixtures, fittings and furniture may only be carried out weekly.

Routine for cleaning a vacated room

In hotels when a room is vacated all possible and relevant tasks identified for daily cleaning of an occupied room will be carried out. In particular it will include changing all linen and checking that no property has been left by previous occupant. In hostels and institutions the possible tasks involved in cleaning a vacated room are frequently incorporated into a routine involving various periodic cleaning tasks.

Periodic cleaning

In addition to the tasks involved in the daily cleaning of a room the following (as required) will be carried out:

1 High dusting.
2 Suction clean upholstery, curtains, underside of bed frame and radiators.

In hotels and hostels it is usually the practice to periodically clean all surfaces, fixtures and fittings in a bedroom, private sitting room and bathroom (if included) together. In hotels this will be carried out during a quiet period and in hostels during vacations. Other maintenance tasks including redecoration and major repairs will be carried out at the same time. Tasks will include wall, ceiling and window washing, furniture washing, relining of draws and cupboards, on- or off-site cleaning of curtains, deep cleaning of carpets and upholstery, special treatments of surfaces, e.g. polish applications, and stripping and repolishing of floors. A typical order of work might be:

1 Ventilate room thoroughly.
2 Strip beds and remove all items of soft furnishing to be cleaned off-site.
3 Remove all mobile furniture if possible and damp wipe or wash all surfaces.
4 Take down curtains if not already removed for off-site cleaning.
5 Cover carpets and remaining furniture with dust covers.
6 Dust and then wash walls.
7 Clean windows unless contractors are involved.
8 Damp wipe or wash all fixtures, fittings and fitted furniture.
9 Rehang curtains if to be cleaned on-site and deep clean.
10 Deep clean upholstery.
11 Deep clean carpets or strip and repolish floors.

12 Replace all furniture when floor is dry on small pieces of card, plastic or aluminium to prevent possibility of rust marks.
13 Reline drawers and shelves.
14 Rehang curtains if cleaned off-site.
15 Remake bed.
16 Suction clean or sweep floor according to type.
17 Check room.

Hospitals

Wards and clinical areas

High standards of hygiene and appearance are required. The frequency with which the various cleaning tasks are carried out should normally meet DHSS recommendations.

Daily routine:

1 Empty waste bins and ashtrays.
2 Remove soiled linen.
3 Damp wipe fixtures and fittings.
4 Spot clean walls particularly areas around switches and doors.
5 Damp wipe bed frames.
6 Damp wipe lockers, trolleys and other items of moveable furniture.
7 Clean wash hand basins.
8 Clean floors according to agreed method. This will include suction cleaning of carpets and damp mopping and buffing or spray cleaning of hard floors.
9 Replenish linen, soap and other supplies.
10 Check clean floor and remove spillages during the day as necessary.

Periodic tasks:
1 High dusting.
2 Suction clean upholstery and radiators.
3 Wash furniture, fixtures and fittings.
4 Curtain cleaning or changing.
5 Wash walls, ceilings, lights and windows. These tasks are frequently carried out by contractors or maintenance staff.
6 Scrub or strip and reapply polish to floors.
7 Deep clean carpets and upholstery.

Terminal cleaning is carried out following the discharge of a patient. The extent of the work depends on whether patient is in a single room or ward and whether isolation is involved. A typical order of work will involve the following:

1 Gown up if necessary.
2 Check bed and lockers to ensure that no items have been left behind. Two persons should be involved for security reasons.
3 All waste and rubbish to be moved.
4 Strip bedclothes by folding corners towards centre to prevent scattering of dust and bacteria and despatch to laundry.
5 Clean all items of furniture and fabric. This can include: high dusting of walls and lights; dusting, damp wiping or washing, as required, of lower half of walls, doors, fixtures and fittings; damp wiping of pillow and mattress covers and changing if badly soiled or damaged; suction cleaning of mattress; damp wiping or washing of bedframes including the underside; damp wiping or washing of lockers and other items of moveable furniture; cleaning of the floor by the agreed method.
6 Prepare bedspace or room for next occupant. This will include replacing of soap and towels and possibly bedmaking.

Isolation and high-risk units

These units are designed and operated to prevent communicable disease organisms from spreading directly and indirectly, to protect other personnel from contracting infections and to isolate patients from secondary infections. The actual tasks carried out by domestic services staff will depend on the unit concerned but in general a number of special methods and precautions are required.

Protective clothing All persons working in those areas must be gowned and masked if required. They will protect the wearer and prevent the transfer of microbes both into and out of the unit. Gowns may be disposable or made of cotton. Once used they may be treated as infected. Cotton gowns will then require specific disinfection.

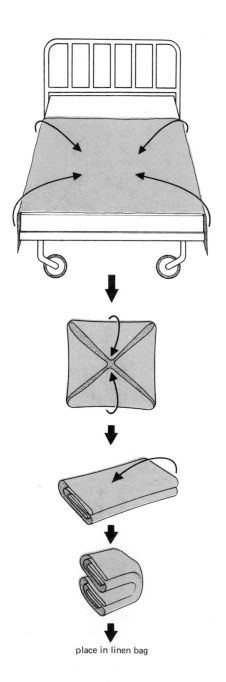

place in linen bag

Figure 90 *Method of stripping and folding bed linen*

Procedures for the putting on and taking off of gowns and masks are specified.

Hands must be washed before entering, before leaving and after leaving a unit. They must be washed after removing gowns, masks or gloves. Hands and gloves should be washed before moving from one room or cubicle to the next and as appropriate between carrying out one task and the next.

Cleaning equipment used in these units will be suitably coded and used exclusively in these areas. All machinery must be clean before commencing work and must be cleaned before moving from one room to the next.

Mop heads must be detachable and auto-claveable.

Disposable cloths and wipes are generally preferred.

Cloths and mop heads must be changed between one room and the next.

Cleaning solutions should be changed frequently and always between one room and the next.

Waste Handling Waste arising in isolation units may be infected. Bins must be lined with plastic sacs of the appropriate colour code. Sacs must not be overfilled to prevent the risk of splitting during disposal. When removing sacs, only the outside of the sac should be handled. They must be sealed and then be placed in a paper sac or the waste receptacle on the domestic assistant's trolley. In order that infected waste arising in these areas can be handled and disposed of safely it must be segregated from domestic and general waste arising in other areas.

Linen handling All linen arising in isolation units may be considered to be infected. Bed linen must be removed by folding towards the centre. Infected linen will be placed in plastic sacs sealed with water-soluble alginate thread. The sealed sacs are placed into a laundry bag of the appropriate colour. It is essential that infected linen arising in isolation units is segregated from linen arising elsewhere.

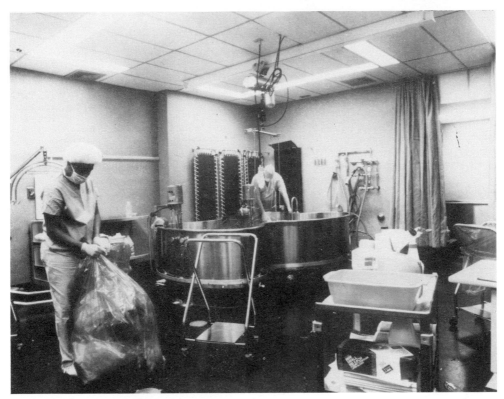

Gowned domestic staff in a burns unit

Procedures will be similar to those used in other hospital areas but all tasks must be carried out to the highest standards. A typical order of work will involve the following:

1 Assemble all equipment and cleaning materials: cleaning solutions, laundry and waste sacs, mops, etc., on a trolley. The trolley will be left outside each room or cubicle.
2 Wash hands and put on gown and, if required, a mask.
3 Enter each room in turn and carry out all tasks, observing all necessary precautions. Always work from the dirtiest to the cleanest areas and finish with the floors.
4 When all cleaning is completed, dispose of cleaning solutions, clean equipment, remove gown and place in a laundry or waste sac and place linen and waste into the laundry and waste chutes, respectively, or leave at the appropriate point for collection.

After the discharge of a patient, terminal cleaning and disinfection will be carried out. This will involve a specific programme of cleaning which is rigorously carried out, using disinfectant sprays and other methods as appropriate.

Theatres

The risk of infection to patients will be high unless the highest standards of hygiene are maintained.

Requirements These will be similar to those for isolation and high-risk units. Within an operating theatre and its associated rooms, e.g. anaesthetic and scrub rooms, there are both clean and dirty zones. Dirty zones include those areas used for the disposal of waste and soiled linen. At no time should personnel or materials move from the dirty to the clean zones.

Caps and overshoes will be required in addition to gowns and masks. Protective clothing must be removed on leaving the theatre areas and replaced on returning.

The following points should be noted:

- Hands must be washed before entry and after leaving.
- Waste and linen must be regarded as infected.
- Cleaning equipment and materials must be colour-coded and only used in theatre areas. All mops and cloths must be autoclaveable.
- Only wet cleaning methods are permitted.
- Floors are anti-static. No build-up of detergent or disinfectant must be allowed.
- Machine scrubbing, rinsing and drying is the most effective method of cleaning.
- Technical equipment will be cleaned by technicians.
- Cleaning tasks and their frequency are defined by the DHSS.

Tasks and order of work

1 *Between sessions* Remove linen and waste and wipe and reline bins; spot clean walls; clean tables; clean floors by agreed method.
2 *Daily* Remove linen and waste; remove furniture and wash; spot clean walls; clean lights; replace furniture; scrub, rinse and dry floors.
3 *Periodic* Wash walls weekly and ceilings monthly.

Waste disposal

Essential requirements

A system of waste disposal must meet five basic requirements:

Security The confidentiality of any written matter must be respected. Confidential material requiring disposal must be either shredded or burnt under supervision. To prevent papers being disposed of by mistake it may be advantageous to retain all waste paper for two days.

Safety All waste must be disposed of in a safe manner. The following points must be remembered:

- Ashtrays should be emptied into metal bins and not into paper sacs.
- Disposable scalpels and syringes used in hospitals must be placed into a 'sharps' box.
- Broken glass should be wrapped before placing in an ordinary bin.
- Hands should not be placed into waste bins. If it is necessary to sift through waste then thick protective gloves must be worn.
- Wax and oil soaked rags must be stored separately from other waste.
- All dry waste must be considered a fire hazard and should be stored accordingly.

Hygiene Wet waste and clinical waste must be considered a potential source of disease. Such waste must be stored in either sealed sacs or covered bins as most appropriate. Waste bins or sacks must be coded either by colour or sign to distinguish between general and hazardous waste. Bins should be thoroughly cleaned inside and out when emptied. Waste stores must be vermin-proof. Hands must never be placed into hazardous waste.

Salvage Waste, e.g. paper, can have a salvage value. Such waste should be collected and stored separately from other waste.

Environment Overflowing dustbins and untidy waste stores demonstrate poor standards of supervision and management.

Types of waste

There are three classes of waste:

Domestic and commercial can arise from a variety of sources. There are four types (see Table 44) which are normally stored and disposed of separately. Further segregation will depend on the type of establishment.

Clinical includes all dressings, disposable scalpels, swabs, etc., arising in a hospital. It must be

Table 44 *Types of commercial and domestic waste*

Type of waste	Example	Methods of disposal
Wet	Food	Sold as swill, incinerated, or removed and tipped by local authority
Dry	Paper, cardboard, rags	Each example may have a salvage value and should be stored separately if necessary. Incinerated, or removed by local authority
Indestructable	Bottles, cans	Cans can be incinerated before removal. Bottles can be broken using a glass breaker if large quantities are involved. Both are removed by local authority
Aerosols		Must not be incinerated. Removed by local authority

regarded as infected and be handled and stored separately from other waste. Syringes and scalpels will be placed in a sharp's box to prevent subsequent handling. Other items must be placed in suitably coded plastic bags. All infected waste must be incinerated. The security of syringes is of paramount importance.

Industrial includes any material arising from an industrial or similar process producing dangerous chemicals and radioactivity. There are strict regulations governing their disposal.

Methods of collection

This will depend on the type of waste and the type of establishment:

Kitchen waste includes wet, dry and indestructible waste. Wet waste can be passed down a waste disposal unit as it is produced or placed in large plastic bins, which must be kept covered at all times. A wall-mounted sac holder fitted with a plastic or waterproof paper sac and a close-fitting lid should be provided for small items of dry waste and for indestructible waste. When no more than three-quarters full it should be sealed and removed to the waste storage area. Cardboard should be transferred to waste storage area as it is produced.

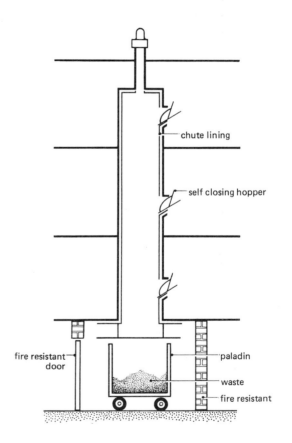

Figure 91 *Waste chutes*

Compactor

Hospital waste   Separate sac holders or bins lined with different coloured polythene sacs are usually provided for clinical and general waste. Holders or bins used for clinical waste require tight fitting lids. Lids are not necessarily required for bins used for general waste. Sharp's boxes are required for scalpels and syringes. Sacs must be changed when no more than three-quarters full. Clinical waste sacs must be sealed and removed to the incinerator separately from general waste.

Sacs containing general waste can be sealed if desired and placed into a larger paper sac or waste receptacle for removal to the incinerator or waste store.

General waste arising in hotels, offices, bedrooms and public areas is usually deposited in a metal bin (which may be lined). This will normally be emptied into a large plastic or paper sac which should be sealed when no more than three-quarters full and despatched to the waste storage area.

Frequency of waste collection

All waste should be removed at least once per day or more frequently if necessary. It is essential that bagged waste, particularly if it contains food, should not be left overnight but must be removed to the waste storage area either immediately or at the end of each work period.

Waste disposal equipment

Bins and sac holders are the most convenient to use. Bins should be lined unless they are likely to be used for cigarettes. Lined bins should be damp wiped when changing sacs. Soiled bins should be washed, rinsed and dried (if small) and hosed with hot water and dried (if large).

Chutes   To overcome the problem of handling waste in larger buildings, chutes may be installed. Refuse, preferably in sacs, is placed in the chute port and collected at the bottom in large containers or fed to an incinerator. To clean the inner surface of a chute sprays are installed. The ports, however, will require daily washing, rinsing and drying.

Disposal units are installed under sinks or as separate units for the disposal of foodstuffs. The food is broken up and reduced to fine particles by an impeller rotating at high speed.

Glass breakers are installed where the number of waste bottles and dead fluorescent tubes produced is sufficient to cause storage problems.

Compactors are used to reduce the volume of stored waste. A ram acting within a confined space compresses the waste already fed in. They are useful where storage space is limited.

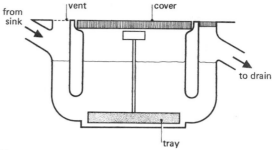
Figure 93 *Grease trap*

Storage of waste

Storage areas must be clean, well ventilated, cool, dry and inaccessible to vermin. Walls must have a 1 hour and doors a ½ hour fire rating. A tap must be provided outside the door and the floor must be drained into an externally trapped gulley.

Traps and similar devices

Before liquid waste is discharged to a sewer or where no main sewer is available there are a number of possible requirements.

Petrol interceptors It is illegal to discharge inflammable materials to the main sewer. In garages and similar situations an interceptor is installed. It allows the petrol to evaporate before other liquids are discharged into the sewer.

Grease traps prevent the discharge of grease into a sewer, e.g. from a kitchen. Grease entering the trap is congealed by the water and settles into a perforated tray. The tray must be removed periodically but not less than once a week to be cleaned using hot water.

Silt traps are similar to grease traps but are used to collect the fine deposits produced by rumblers and similar equipment.

Water traps prevent foul odours entering a room from a drain. They may form an integral part of a kitchen or sanitary applicance. If not, a trap must be fitted to any appliance discharging to drain.

Septic tanks are installed where it is not possible to discharge sewerage to a main drain. It consists of an airtight chamber in which the sewerage is acted upon by bacteria which convert it into a liquid, gasses and sludge. The liquid flows out of the tank whilst the sludge settles to the bottom of the tank which is periodically removed, usually every six months.

British Standards

BS 5906: 1980, *Code of Practice for the Storage and On-site Treatment of Solid Waste from Buildings.*

Bedroom services

The range of services provided in addition to cleaning depends on the type of establishment, e.g. hotel, hostel or institution.

Bedmaking

The actual method will depend on the situation but broadly the following procedure is satisfactory:

1 Place a chair near the bed.
2 Loosen and strip all clothes from the bed. If the sheets and blankets are to be changed, turn the corners towards the centre and roll the sheets and blankets into a bundle. If they are to be returned to the bed they should be individually folded into three and placed over the back of the chair.
3 Clean and turn the mattress if required.

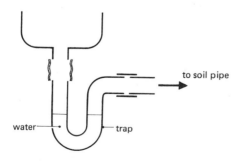
Figure 92 *Water trap*

4 Place on the bottom sheet and either fit to the corners of the mattress or mitre each corner. To mitre a corner, tuck in along bottom and top of the sheet; lift the flap of the sheet about 30 cm from the corner and tuck in the remainder; drop the flap and tuck in.

5 Place on the top sheet, the top to extend just above the top of the mattress.

6 Place on the blankets in turn, the tops to be 30 cm short of the top of the sheet.

7 Mitre one bottom corner and turn over the sheets and blankets at the top and on the same side of the bed to leave a 60 cm space. Repeat this step for the other side of the bed.

8 Fit pillow cases to the pillows and position them at the top of the bed such that the openings face away from the door.

9 Place on the quilt or bedspread as appropriate.

Turning down

This is carried out in luxury hotels. The method used will be determined by house custom. One example would be the following:

1 Remove bedspread, fold and put away.
2 Untuck one side of top of linen and blankets and fold back to form a right angled triangle.
3 Neaten edges and tuck in.
4 Lay night attire on bed, dressing gown on chair and slippers at foot of bed.

In addition to turning down, a number of other tasks are usually carried out:

5 Empty ashtrays and litter bins and generally tidy room.
6 Wipe hand basins, baths and other furniture as necessary.
7 Adjust towels.
8 Check lights.
9 Adjust windows and close curtains.

Food and beverage services

To a limited extent staff involved in accommodation and cleaning services may also be

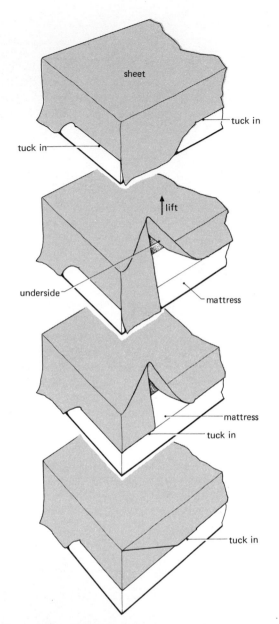

Figure 94   *Mitring of a corner*

involved in the preparation and service of food and beverages.

Hospitals

Food and beverage service in patient areas will be the responsibility of the nursing and dietetic staff.

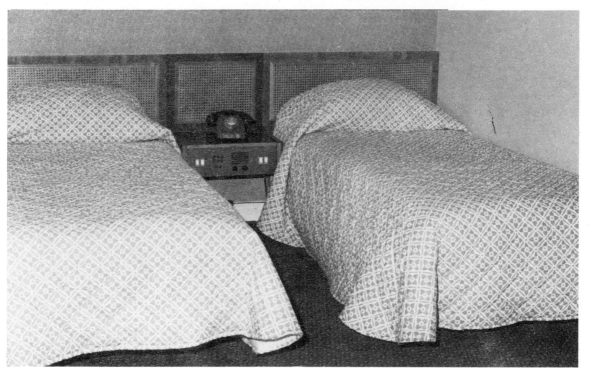

'Ready' hotel bedroom

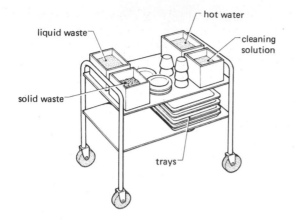

Figure 95   *Collection trolley*

Types of meals service   There are three principle types of service, all of which involve distribution of food to the wards in trolleys:

1   Bulk service in which the food is distributed in containers and plated at ward level. Domestic staff can be involved in both plating and the washing of dishes.
2   Plated service in which the food is plated in a central kitchen. The food is served course by course or the courses are set out on a tray at ward level. All crockery is returned to the kitchen for washing.
3   Trayed service in which the food is plated and all courses set out on a tray in a central kitchen. All crockery is returned to the kitchen for washing.

Food service   Depending on the actual hospital the essential requirements are that:

1   Hot trolleys are plugged in immediately they are received.
2   Hands must be washed before handling or serving food.
3   All food hygiene rules must be observed (see page 54).
4   Trays are laid correctly.
5   Only permitted food must be served to each patient.
6   Food should be attractively presented.

7   Assistance should be given as necessary.

Beverage service   Unless automatic vending machines are installed, domestic staff will be involved in both the preparation and service of beverages. The essential requirements are that:

1   Beverages must only be served as dictated by nursing staff.
2   A range of beverages is available.
3   Beverages are served according to a patient's particular requirements.
4   Drinks are poured individually.
5   Cups are not overfilled or beverages allowed to slop into the saucers.
6   Patients are assisted as necessary.

Collection of crockery   should be made using a correctly prepared trolley which should include two shelves, a bowl half full with hot water, a disposable or launderable cloth, two plastic waste containers and a bowl half filled with cleaning solution. The essential requirements are that all waste is emptied or scraped into a liquid waste or a solid waste container as appropriate, crockery is stacked methodically, cutlery is placed into hot water and trays and bedside tables are wiped clean.

Hotels

In the more luxurious hotels the service of morning tea will be required. Trays may be made up in the kitchen or by the room attendant in the floor service room. The attendant will be provided with a list of guests requiring tea from the night porter or reception.

When trays are made up in the service room a supply of crockery, cutlery, tea and sugar will be kept in the room. Crockery and cutlery will be distinguished from that of the restaurant. Milk will be supplied on a daily basis. Dirty dishes will be washed up by the room maid. Trays for the next day will normally be made towards the end of the previous day's work. They must have a clean surface and, if required, be covered with a paper napkin or tray cloth.

When trays are made up in the kitchen and where room service is required throughout the day, dirty dishes will usually be returned to the kitchen. A typical routine for room service might be:

1 Knock. If no reply knock again and enter.
2 Switch on light and say 'good morning'.
3 Place tray and newspaper within easy reach of guest.
4 Ensure guest awakes.
5 Draw curtains if required.
6 Leave room.

Laundry services

The laundering of linen, soft furnishings and clothing involves three types of cleaning. The types are:

1 Satin removal.
2 Washing, which will include drying and ironing or pressing.
3 Dry cleaning, which will include ironing or pressing.

Stain removal is described on page 243 and will usually be carried out prior to dry cleaning or washing.

Laundering may be carried out on-site using an establishment's own equipment, off-site by a laundry company, off-site in a group laundry or may involve any combination of the three, e.g. all washing may be carried out on-site and dry cleaning off-site.

Types of laundry equipment

From the range of equipment available, laundry facilities can be provided to suit any establishment or situation.

Washer extractors most usually consist of a horizontal drum which, when washing and rinsing, rotates backwards and forwards, agitating the water and articles inside. To extract water from the laundry the drum spins at high speed. The articles to be laundered are loaded and removed via a door in the front of the machine. When it is necessary to separate the clean and dirty linen, e.g. in hospitals, the machine will be fitted with a second door through which the cleaned laundry is removed.

A smaller number of machines are made which consist of a vertical drum, the machine being loaded from the top.

Loading capacities range from about 5 to 250 kg dry weight and give outputs of cleaned laundry of between 10 and 600 kg dry weight per hour.

Machines may be programmed to give a specific number of different wash, rinse and extract cycles or they may be programmed by the user, e.g. using punched cards to give the cycles and conditions selected by the user. Depending on the machine, programmes can be varied to give different wash and rinse temperatures, different degrees of agitation and different wash, rinse and extraction times.

Tunnel washers These are only installed in the largest laundries. They essentially consist of a series of compartments linked together. The laundry is loaded in batches at one end and removed at the other end. Such machines can process approximately 250 to 2,000 kg dry weight per hour, depending on the actual machine installed.

Rotary washing machines These have largely been replaced by the washer extractor. They consist of a horizontal drum which rotates during washing and rinsing to agitate the articles inside.

Hydro-extractors (also known as spin driers) They consist of a perforated vertical cylinder which spins at high speed. Water is removed (extracted) utilizing the centrifugal force principle. Machine capacities range from about 2 to 100 kg dry weight capacity, giving outputs up to about 600 kg per hour.

Tumbler driers consist of a horizontal perforated cylinder through which hot air is blown. The drum

Laundry showing washer extractors

rotates in alternate directions to bring all articles inside into contact with the air stream and to prevent entanglement. Machine capacities range from about 5 to 50 kg dry weight.

Dry cleaning machines are similar in some respects to washer extractors. Solvent is introduced into a horizontal perforated drum which rotates in alternate directions. The machine will spin dry and then air dry the articles inside. The solvent is filtered during the extraction stage and reused.

Ironers (also known as calendars) consist of heated, padded rollers which rotate against each other. They are used for ironing sheets, pillow cases and other flat articles. They are not suitable for blankets or fluffy items.

Presses essentially consist of padded plates which are heated. The items to be pressed are placed on the lower plate and pressed with the upper one. The principle types are rotary and scissor presses. Presses may be designed for the pressing of a variety of articles or for specific types of garment, e.g. shirts, trousers or coats.

Hand irons essentially consist of a hand-held heated plate. Steam irons include a reservoir of water which can be used to generate steam. Older irons include up to five heat settings:

Cool	120°C
Warm	160°C
Medium hot	180°C
Hot	210°C
Very hot	Over 210°C

Ironer

Newer irons usually have three settings corresponding to the International Textile Care Labelling Code:

Cool   110°C
Warm   150°C
Hot   200°C

Folding machines are used when large numbers of sheets and other linen are being laundered. They automatically fold sheets, etc., fed into them. Machines are also available to fold specific items, e.g. shirts.

Criteria for the establishment of on-site or group off-site laundry facilities

The type of laundry facilities and associated equipment established will depend on a number of factors (see Table 45):

Costs involved in purchasing, maintaining and operating laundry facilities and equipment to launder the number of items to be cleaned must be compared with the cost of laundering those items by a laundry company using discounted cash flow analysis. The analysis will include financial implications of capital expenditure, financial implications of revenue expenditure, direct operating costs, and indirect costs.

Excepting other considerations on-site or group laundering is not usually cost-effective where the number of items to be cleaned is less than 20–30,000 per week.

Table 45 *Comparison of on site or group and contract laundering*

On site or group	Contract
1 More cost-effective if number of articles exceeds 20-30,000 per week	More cost effective if number of articles less than 20-30,000 per week
2 Involves capital expenditure which may be used more effectively elsewhere	Revenue expenditure
3 Space required for facilities	No space required
4 Lower linen stock possible	Higher linen stocks required
5 More operative and supervisory staff needed	Less operative and supervisory staff
6 Scope of administrative functions greater	Administrative functions reduced
7 Better control of standards	Limited control of standards
8 Life expectancy of linen stocks greater	Life expectancy of linen stocks will be less
9 Will meet particular requirements of establishment, e.g. fouled and special category linen	May not be able to meet or respond to requirements
10 Rapid service for guests and residents	

Alternative uses for capital must be considered since they may be more effective and profitable.

Space that laundry facilities will require. Alternative uses of that space if available must be considered.

Supervisory and management functions will be increased by on-site or group laundering.

Control of the standard of appearance, finish and cleaning methods can be better exercised in on-site or group laundries. Greater control of cleaning methods may significantly increase the life expectancy of linen and soft furnishings.

Types of soilage Fouled and special category linen will be laundered in an on-site or group laundry. Where linen of this type is involved, e.g.

hospitals and some residential establishments, on-site or group laundry facilities will be essential.

Convenience On-site or group laundries will be better able to respond to changes in requirements and to meet the particular requirements of an establishment. Virtually all establishments require some form of laundry facility to deal with emergencies, e.g. fouled linen, failure of off-site laundry to deliver and strikes.

Linen stocks The turn-round time between despatch of linen to a laundry and receipt of clean linen should be less where laundering is carried out in on-site or group laundries. This will result in smaller stocks being required.

Services offered by establishment Where washing, dry cleaning and pressing of guests' or

Table 46   *Laundry facilities required by various types of establishment*

Establishment	Linen hire	Own linen	
	On-site facilities	Use of off-site laundering by laundry company	On-site or group/district facilities
Small hotel	Small washer extractor, tumbler drier, ironing and pressing equipment	Used for most items	Small washer extractor, tumbler drier, ironing and and pressing equipment
Medium hotel	Small washer extractor, tumbler drier, ironing and pressing equipment	Used for most items	Medium washer extractor, tumbler drier, ironing and pressing equipment
Large hotel	Small to medium washer extractor(s), tumbler drier(s), dry cleaning machine, ironing and pressing equipment	Cost-effectiveness and other considerations will probably favour on-site facilities	Medium to large washer extractor(s), tumbler driers, dry cleaning machine, ironing and pressing equipment, folding machines
Hospital	Only applicable for some items, e.g. roller towels	Only used if there are no on-site or group facilities available	Large washer extractors, tunnel washers and hydroextractors or presses, driers, folding machines, ironing and pressing equipment
Residential establishment	Generally not applicable. If applicable, on-site facilities will be small to medium washer extractor(s), tumbler driers, ironing and pressing equipment	Can vary from very limited use to being used for most items, depending on the actual establishment	Depending on number and relative amounts of linen to be cleaned on- or off-site, requirements will range from those of a medium-size hotel to those of a hospital

residents' clothing is undertaken, the installation of the appropriate equipment can be more convenient and enable a more efficient service to be offered.

Number and type of articles When the requirement for an on-site or group laundry is established, the type of equipment, number and capacity must be determined. Facilities may be installed for both washing and dry cleaning or for washing alone.

The number and capacity of washing machines, Hydro-extractors, tumble driers and ironing equipment will be governed by the number and type of articles to be cleaned per day or week and the turn-round time required. Machines should be selected so that maximum utilization is achieved with a minimum of unnecessary delay. The actual facilities will depend very much on the type of establishment. Table 46 indicates the broad requirements for a range of establishments when hired or own linen is involved.

Table 47 *Textile care labelling code*

WASHING

Symbol	Washing temperature		Agitation	Rinse	Water extraction
	Machine	Hand			
1 / 95°	Very hot 95°C	Hand hot, 50°C, or boil	Maximum	Normal	Normal
2 / 60°	Hot 60°C	Hand hot, 50°C	Maximum	Normal	Normal
3 / 60°	Hot 60°C	Hand hot, 50°C	Medium	Cool	With care
4 / 50°	Hand hot, 50°C	Hand hot, 50°C	Medium	Cool	With care
5 / 40°	Warm 40°C	Warm 40°C	Maximum	Cool	Normal
6 / 40°	Warm 40°C	Warm 40°C	Medium	Cool	With care
7 / 40°	Warm 40°C	Warm 40°C	Minimum, do not rub	Normal	Normal spin, do not hand wring
8 / 30°	Cool 30°C	Cool 30°C	Minimum	Normal	With care
9 / 95°	Very hot 95°C	Hand hot 50°C, boil	Minimum	Normal	Drip dry

Do not machine wash   Do not wash

Explanatory notes 100°C - boiling; 95°C - very hot, nearly boiling; 60°C - hot, too hot for the hands; 50°C - hand hot, as hot as the hand can bear; 40°C - warm; 30°C - cool

DRY CLEANING

(A) Dry clean any solvent

(F) Dry clean in white spirit or solvent 113

(P) Dry clean in tetrachloroethylene

⊗ Do not dry clean

BLEACHING

△/CL Chlorine bleach may be used

⊠ Do not use chlorine bleach

DRYING

▢ Tumble dry   ▢ Dry flat

▢ Drip dry   ▽ Line dry

IRONING

Cool iron 110°C   Hot iron 200°C

Warm iron 150°C   Do not iron

Laundering requirements of different types of linen, soft furnishings and clothing

The methods of laundering will depend on the physical and chemical properties of the constituent fibres, colour fastness and the fastness of any finish applied to a fabric. In particular these will govern washing temperature, amount of agitation, rinsing temperature, method of extracting water, e.g. spinning, wringing or drip drying, type of cleaning agent, use of bleach, method of drying and ironing temperature.

Textile care labelling code This enables some of the problems associated with selecting the correct method of laundering to be overcome. The code consists of a series of symbols (see Table 47) which defines the method of laundering, i.e. washing or dry cleaning, washing conditions or dry cleaning solvent, whether a chlorine bleach can be used, method of drying and ironing temperature. The appropriate symbols are attached or fixed to an article and define exactly the way in which it must be cleaned, dried and ironed. In the case of washing, the symbols usually correspond to many of the preset programmes of the smaller washer extractors.

Laundering categories

Linen, soft furnishings and clothes will normally be sorted into a number of categories before laundering is carried out. Each category will include articles requiring similar washing conditions and dry cleaning solvent and will be washed or dry cleaned separately from other categories. Where the international care code is available, selecting the appropriate category presents few problems. But in other cases knowledge of constituent fibres, colour fastness and the fastness of any finish is desirable and as far as possible this information should be obtained in order that the most appropriate methods and conditions for laundering can be established. If there is any doubt a test item should be selected, if possible, to be laundered using the most likely method and conditions. If the conducting of a test

Table 48 *Laundering categories*

Group	Category	Care code
Machine washable	Cotton and linen	1 / 95°
	Cotton, linen or rayon with dyes fast at 60°C	2 / 60°
	White nylon and polyester/cotton mixtures	3 / 60°
	Polyester, cotton/acrylic mixtures, coloured nylon, coloured cotton/polyester mixtures and cotton or rayon with special finishes	4 / 50°
	Cotton, linen and rayon with colours and finishes fast at 40°C, but not 60°C	5 / 40°
	Acrylics, acetate, triacetate, including mixtures with wool	6 / 40°
	Machine washable wool, and woolen mixtures with cotton or rayon, silk	7 / 40°
	Silk and printed acetate with colours not fast at 40°C	8 / 30°
	Cotton with finishes that can be boiled, but must be drip dried	9 / 95°
Handwash	Non-machine-washable wool, delicate fabrics and fabrics with very poor dye or finish fastness	(handwash symbol)
Dry clean	Articles with poor dimensional stability, dye or finish fastness in water	Ⓐ Ⓟ Ⓕ

Note: Heavily soiled articles must be pre-washed, soaked or dry cleaned separately from less heavily soiled articles in the same category. Fouled or special category linen must be washed separately from other linen in the same category

is not feasible and shrinkage, loss of colour or loss of finish is possible, laundering should be carried out either by dry cleaning or by washing using minimum agitation and cool or warm water.

If dyes are likely to bleed, despite using the most appropriate method and conditions, then articles involving such dyes must be laundered separately from other articles.

Tables 48 and 49 show the major categories together with the corresponding care code. The category into which an article falls is governed by:

Degree of soiling Heavily soiled articles must be cleaned separately from less heavily soiled.

Nature of the soiling Fouled linen should be sluiced in cold water before washing. Fouled and special category linen produced in hospitals will be washed separately from each other and from normally soiled linen. The need to distinguish between the three types has been questioned where effective disinfection is carried out during the wash cycle. The disinfection of linen is described on page 171.

Type of cleaning agent that can be used Fabrics containing wool or silk should not be washed in alkaline cleaning agents or bleached with chlorine bleaches. Linen, rayon and cotton must be rinsed thoroughly after the use of a chlorine bleach. Bleaches should not be used on coloured articles.

Items with poor dimensional stability, dye fastness or fastness of applied finishes when washed should be dry cleaned. Tetrachloroethylene is the most usual solvent, although white spirit is often used. The type of solvent will be identified by the care code label.

Temperature, degree of agitation and method of water extraction The conditions suitable for various fibres, colours and finishes can be determined by comparing Tables 47 and 48.

Ironing and pressing

Pile fabrics or fabrics with fluffy surfaces, e.g. blankets, should not be ironed. The majority of

Table 49 *Ironing temperatures*

Iron temperature	Fibre
Cool, 110°C	Acetate, triacetate, nylon, polyester, acrylic, chlorofibre (with cloth over)
Medium, 150°C	Wool, silk, polyester mixtures
Hot, 200°C	Cotton, linen, rayon, rayon mixtures

other fabrics can be ironed. The safe ironing temperature will be primarily governed by the constituent fibres. Table 49 gives the safe ironing temperatures of the major fibres.

British Standards

BS 1006: 1978, *Methods of Test for Colour Fastness of Textiles and Leather.*
BS 2747: 1980, *Textile Care Labelling Code.*
BS 4961: 1980, *Methods for Determination of Dimensional Stability of Textiles by Dry Cleaning in Tetrachloroethylene. Part 1: Machine method. Part 2: Laboratory method.*
BS 5377, *Specification for Assessment of Laundering Effects by Means of a Cotton Control Cloth. Part 1: 1976: Preparation and use of the cotton control cloth. Part 2: 1980: Method of analysis and test for the unsoiled cotton control cloth.*
BS 5651: 1978, *Cleansing and Wetting Procedures for Use in the Assessment of the Effect of Cleansing and Wetting on the Flammability of Textile Fabrics and Fabric Assemblies.*
BS 5807: 1980, *Method of Test for Determination of Dimensional Change of Textiles in Domestic Washing.*

Linen services

The provision of linen in an establishment will involve a number of distinct operations and functions. The type of services and the operations involved will depend on the type of establishment, whether a linen room is involved, whether laundering is carried out on- or off-site and whether linen is hired. In larger establishments linen services and linen room operations, where they exist, are supervised by a linen keeper responsible to the manager of the accommodation services department.

Operations and functions

Purchase of launderable and disposable linen   The quantity and type of linen to be purchased is determined by the manager of the accommodation services department. Criteria for the purchase of launderable linen are described on page 68. Disposable linen will be used following an analysis of the comparative advantages and disadvantages (see page 69).

Linen hire service will be used following analysis of the comparative advantages and disadvantages (see page 68).

Laundered linen can be received from one of three sources:

1   Linen received from own laundry should be checked prior to leaving the laundry and despatched either to the linen room or direct to the using department. In either case the using department should inspect the linen before use. Linen requiring repair can be despatched from the laundry or using department to the linen room. Linen not meeting the required standard of appearance or cleanliness should be relaundered.
2   Linen from an off-site or group laundry should be checked on receipt against own and laundry despatch notes to ensure all items as specified on the notes are returned. It must also be checked for any damaged items or items not meeting the required standard of appearance. The laundry must be informed immediately of any missing items or defects. In some establishments checking for damaged or poorly laundered linen is carried out by the using department rather than on immediate receipt. This procedure has the disadvantage that action to remedy defects cannot be taken immediately and time is wasted in replacing the defective linen.
3   Hired linen should be checked on receipt against the hire company's despatch note and for any defective items. The hire company must be informed immediately.

Handling of soiled linen   This will depend upon the type of establishment, the type of soilage and where laundering is to be carried out.

In hospitals three basic types of soiled linen are distinguished:

1   *Normally soiled:* includes any non-infectious linen arising from patient areas and staff residential accommodation.
2   *Fouled:* potentially infected linen which has come into contact with blood, vomit, urine or faeces.
3   *Special category:* linen that has been in contact with patients suffering from notifiable diseases, e.g. small pox, typhoid, infectious hepatitis.

Each type may be further subdivided, depending on its source, e.g. linen from operating theatres wards and residential areas will be kept separate from each other. There can therefore be several categories of soiled linen. Each type will be placed into a coloured plastic bag, a different colour being used for each type. When three-quarters full the sacks are sealed and despatched in terylene bags to the laundry. The terylene bags are themselves of particular colours. Normally soiled linen may be placed directly into a terylene bag. Plastic sacks used for special category linen are sealed with water-soluble alginate thread which dissolves in the washing machines. No sorting of linen takes place other than at the laundry.

In hotels the linen will be, for the most part, normally soiled. When laundering is to be carried out on-site the soiled linen arising from a floor or floors is bundled or placed into a linen bag and despatched directly to or via the linen room or store to the laundry. Depending on the system of issuing clean linen, a note indicating the floor and the items included may be attached to the linen.

In the linen room or laundry the linen will be checked. When hire linen is used or own linen is to be laundered off-site, the bundled or bagged linen is despatched to the linen room or store together with a note, if appropriate, where it is checked and sorted. Similar items are bundled together. Own linen, if badly stained or damaged, should be retained for restoration and repair. Fouled linen, whether own or hired, should be sluiced and laundered on site. Linen is usually sent to a laundry in whicker baskets or canvas bags together with a copy laundry list completed in duplicate indicating all the items to be laundered. The other copy will be retained by the hotel.

In residential establishments, soiled linen will include normally soiled and fouled. Normally soiled linen will be laundered on- or off-site. Fouled linen will require sluicing and laundering on-site. The various steps involved and the handling of soiled linen will be similar in most respects to those described for hotels although hire linen is less frequently encountered.

In larger establishments of all types, laundry chutes may be installed to reduce the time spent handling soiled linen. The chute will run from the top of the building to the bottom. Bags or (less satisfactorily) bundles of linen are inserted into the chute at each level in the building and fall into a room at the bottom from where they are despatched either to the laundry or the linen room.

Linen issue   The system employed for linen issue must meet three essential requirements:

1   The supply of linen must be adequate to meet requirements.
2   There should be no unnecessary delay or time spent in the disposal of soiled linen and the collection of clean.
3   It must permit effective stock control to be exercised.

Most methods of issue are derivatives of one or other of two basic systems, new for old and topping up.

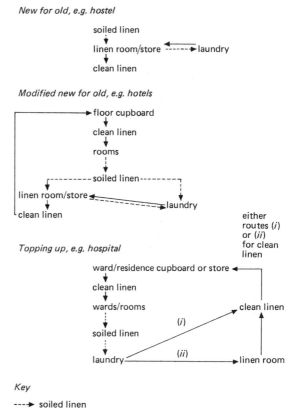

Figure 96   *Systems of linen issue*

New for old essentially involves only issuing clean linen in exchange for soiled. At its simplest soiled linen is handed in at the linen room or store and new linen is issued. Such a system can be employed in smaller establishments or where linen exchange is not required on a daily basis. In larger establishments such a system will be subject to unnecessary delays. Modified new for old systems can be used in larger establishments. In each department, floor, section or ward is located a small linen store, cupboard or trolley. The supply of linen in the store is maintained from a central linen room and is sufficient to meet the daily or any special requirements for clean linen. Access to the store will be restricted to all but authorized staff. Soiled linen despatched to the central linen room or laundry is checked and the same amount of clean linen is issued to restock the floor cupboard. The clean linen may be collected from the central linen room at the time soiled linen is handed in or it may be collected later by domestic staff. Alternatively, each cupboard or trolley will be restocked by linen room staff or porters.

Topping up systems are particularly suitable for very large establishments. A small cupboard, store or trolley is located on each floor or in each section, ward or department. The amount of linen required to meet daily and special requirements is established and the cupboard stocked accordingly. As clean linen is used the cupboard is restocked either direct from the on-site laundry or from a central linen room. However, new linen is not issued on a new for old basis. Clean linen is issued in one of two ways. Stock is replenished in response to a requisition issued by the floor, ward or department supervisor, control being exercised by the laundry, linen, domestic or portering staff determining the difference between the established stock level and a rough count of the stock in hand. The difference should be similar to the stock requisitioned. Alternatively, no requisition is issued and restocking is carried out on the basis of the difference between the established stock levels and a rough count of the stock in hand. The rough count can be made more easily and more accurately by initially establishing the number of items of a particular type per unit of shelf space. Topping up systems are generally less labour-intensive to operate than other methods, but stock control may not be as exact. (See also Volume 2 for a description of linen stock control.)

Manufacture and repair can be undertaken to some extent by most establishments using their own linen. The range of tasks carried out, however, depends very much on the establishment concerned. The types of work undertaken include:

1 Making of new items, e.g. curtains, although it is frequently cheaper to purchase ready-made furnishings.
2 Repair of slightly damaged linen and soft furnishings.

3 Repair of guests' or residents' clothing.
4 Labelling and marking of linen to show establishment, location within establishment and date of issue by embroidering, adhesive labels, tags, tapes, stitch-on labels, indelible ink or colour coding.
5 Reworking of condemned linen, e.g. sheets to pillow cases, cot sheets or dust covers; bath towels to hand and lavatory towels; table cloths to tray cloths.

Guests' and residents' clothes and personal linen   Where the laundering of guests', residents' or staff personal clothing is undertaken, the clothing should be bundled individually in the linen room or store and an identifying label attached to it in order that it can be returned to or collected by its owner. It will then be despatched to the laundry. For hotel guests a typical system would involve collecting the clothing from the guest's room in a purpose-designed bag to which a lable is attached indicating the name of the guest, his room, the type of cleaning required and when required. In the linen room the contents of the label are recorded before despatch to the laundry. When returned to the linen room, reception will be informed of the cost and to whom charged and the clothing then returned to the guest. Services offered to hotel guests can include laundering, dry cleaning, minor repairs and valeting.

Storage

Achieving the maximum possible use from linen and providing an efficient service which lends itself to effective control will depend, with other factors, on well designed storage areas and storing linen correctly and efficiently. Particular factors which must be considered are:

- Shelves should be strong, well fixed and slatted to allow air to circulate.
- Each unit or area of shelf space should be labelled and used to store specific items.
- To permit easier stock control and issuing of items, the various types of linen should be stored in batches or stacked with the folds outwards as appropriate.

Linen storage area

- The total number of items of a particular type which each unit of shelf space can hold should be determined.
- The storage area should be maintained at about 20°C and well ventilated.
- Stock should be stacked to allow air to circulate.
- Stock should be covered with draw sheets or kept behind closed doors to prevent accumulation of dust and to exclude light.
- Stock should be used in rotation.
- Reserve linen stocks must be inspected and turned regularly.

Spoilage of linen

Spoilage can arise in three ways:

Storage Wool and silk can be attacked by moths and cellulosic fabrics by mildew. Poor stacking will result in creasing and poor circulation of air.

Light will cause cotton to yellow and colour changes in other fabrics.

Use As a result of normal use linen may be heavily stained or badly torn as a result of accident or careless use.

Laundering The correct method must be employed for any item to prevent possible shrinkage, physical deterioration, discolouration and staining. Considerations will include dry cleaning or washing, washing temperature, ironing temperature, use of bleach and type of detergent.

Linen rooms

Where linen rooms are required they should be designed in accordance with work study principles and with reference to the range of activities to be carried out. Typical requirements will include some or all of the following;

- Room large enough to allow all activities to be carried out comfortably and with a minimum of unnecessary movement.
- Shelving and storage space sufficient to accommodate all stock to be held in the linen room.
- Room to be secure.
- Floors strong enough to resist the effects of dragging baskets.
- Walls finished with a matt, light coloured, washable covering.
- Lighting which is good and creates no glare.
- A counter where a new for old linen exchange system is employed.
- Coloured work surfaces and chairs sufficient to permit linen repair and other activities to be carried out.
- A wash basin, soap and towel.
- Bags and baskets for soiled linen.
- Steps to gain access to higher shelves.
- Sewing machines.
- Irons and presses.
- Office furniture.
- Suction cleaner or manual sweeper.
- Easy access to a lift or loading bay.

The hours of operation of a linen room should be related to normal work periods, but it should not be open except when supervised by the linen keeper or other authorized staff.

Linen keeper or supervisor

The linen keeper should be responsible for some or all of the following:

- Issue of clean linen.
- Sorting, checking and despatch of soiled linen to the laundry.
- Receipt and checking of new and laundered linen.
- Manufacture and repair of linen.
- Laundering and repair services provided for residents and guests.
- Stock control.
- Correct storage of linen.
- Supervision of staff in the linen room.
- Advising the accommodation services manager of requirements for new linen and laundry services.

Index

in stain removal, 245
resistance of seals, 182–3
resistance of textile fibres, 22–3
use in furniture cleaning, 236
alkyd resin, 28–9
aluminium:
  anodized, 19
  cleaning of, 236
  effect of alkaline cleaning agents, 164, 166
  furniture, 56
  properties and uses, 19
anaglypta, 36
animals:
  as vectors of disease, 86
  see also pests
anionic surfactant:
  definition, 158–9
  in abrasives, 160
  in detergents, 157–9
ant, 97–8
antiseptic, 172
appearance:
  of crockery, 73–4
  of curtains, 69–70
  of floors, 48
  of polish, 193–4
  of sanitary appliances, 49–50
  reasons for polish and seal application, 181, 188
  restoration of seals, 179, 183–5
  retention in carpets, 46
ashtrays, 236
asphalt:
  cleaning of floors, 220–21
  composition, properties and uses of floor, 39
  effect of solvents, 168, 169
  restoration of floors, 220–21
  sealing of floors, 181–5, 216, 220–21
  use of cleaning agents and polish, 216–17, 220–21
autoclave, 178
Axminister, 43

backwashing, 261
backvacs, 122
bacteria:
  characteristics, 85–6
  control, 86–8
  examples, 87
  source and occurence, 86
bactericidal detergent, 158, 164
bactericide, 173, 174–7
bacteriostat, 173, 174–7

bain marie, 256
bamboo, 236
barrier matting, 81–3, 84, 88
basins:
  cleaning of, 249
  description, 52–3
baths:
  cleaning of, 249, 250
  scratch removal, 250
  types, 52–3
bath mat, 67, 249
bathroom, *see* sanitary accommodation
bedbug, 99
bedroom:
  cleaning of, 262–3
  servicing of, 269–70
  see also food service and beverage service
bedding:
  types and characteristics, 65–7
  see also laundering
bed(s):
  cleaning of, 236
  components of, 58–60
  dimensions, 61
  making, 269–70
bedspreads, 65
beeswax, 190
beetling, 26
benzene, 168
beverage service:
  in hospitals, 271, 272
  in hotels, 272–3
bidet, 52
birds, 102
black fluids, 176
blankets, 65
bleach:
  as cleaning agent, 169
  as disinfectant, 174–5
  effect on floors, 38–42
  effect on metals, 19
  effect on sanitary appliance materials, 50
  in cleaning agents, 159
  relevance to sheeting, 66
  resistance of textile fibres, 22–3
  use in kitchens, 253
  use in sanitary accommodation, 249
bleeding, *see* colour fastness
blinds:
  types and construction, 63–4
  cleaning of, 236

mercerization, 26
metal polish, 160, 166, 234, 236
metallized polish, 189, 192–4, 196
metals:
    as surface finish, 37–8
    effect of metal polish, 166
    in furniture, 55
    selection of cleaning methods, etc., 208–9
    types, properties and uses, 19, 50
methylated spirit, 169
methylene chloride, 169, 186
mice, 100
mildew:
    proofing, 27, 63
    resistance of carpets, 46, 47
    resistance of textile fibres and fabric, 20, 22-3
    storage of linen, 285
milk machines, 254–5
millium, 70
mincers, 254
mirrors, 239, 249
mixing machines, 254
mobile platforms, 144
modacrylics:
    composition, 20
    identification of, 24
    in carpets, 44
    properties, 23
montan, 190
mopping:
    applications, 84, 210–11
    damp mopping, 108, 194, 201
    in control of bacteria, 88
    procedures, 210–12
    wet mopping, 108, 201
    see also mops
mops:
    applications, 107–8
    care of, 109
    in control of bacteria, 88
    methods of using, 109
    seal application, 186
    selection criteria, 107–9
    types, 107
mop sweepers:
    care of, 107
    in control of bacteria, 88, 105
    in control of dust, 83, 105
    methods of using, 106–7
    selection criteria, 105–6
    types, 105

moquette, 57
moths:
    description, 96
    proofing, 27, 63, 68
    resistance of carpets, 46–7
    resistance of textile fibres and fabrics, 20, 22–3
    storage of linen, 285
mud, 247
multipurpose detergents, 169
Munsel, 76

nail varnish stains, 246
needle punch carpets, 44
net, 70, 71
neutral detergents, 163
neutralization of floors, 196, 214
nickel plate, 239
noise:
    level of cleaning equipment, 126, 152
    properties of floors, 38–42
non-ionic surfactants:
    definition, 158–9
    in abrasives, 160
    in detergents, 157–9
notice boards, 239
nylon:
    identification in textiles, 20–21, 24
    effect of bleach, 169
    in bedding, 65–7
    in carpets, 44, 46
    in cleaning equipment, 105, 115–16
    in curtains, 70
    in table linen, 67
    in upholstery fabrics, 56–8
    manufacture of fibres, 18
    properties and uses, 16, 23

odours:
    of polishes and seals, 179, 183, 185, 196
    in sanitary accommodation, 249, 252
    see also deodorizers
offices, 258
oils:
    as soil, 80, 81
    effect on floors, 38–42, 48
    effect on polishes and seals, 182–3, 192–3
    effect on sealing process, 185
    emulsification, 156
    relevance to carpets, 48
    removal of stains, 245
    removal by degreasers, 166

upholstery fabrics:
  requirements of, 63
  types and characteristics, 54–8
  see also upholstered furniture
upright suction cleaners, *see* suction cleaners
Urea formaldehyde, 17, 28
urinals:
  cleaning agents, 163–9
  cleaning of, 250
  types, 51
urine stain removal, 247
utensil cleaners, 139, 253
ultrasonic cleaners, 140

vacuum cleaners, *see* suction cleaners
valance, 72
value, 76
varnish, *see* laquer
vehicle cleaning, 139
velour, 57, 71
velvet, 57, 70, 71
velveteen, 71
vending machines, 257
veneer:
  definition, 31
  in furniture, 55, 56, 62
  paper, 36
ventilation:
  environmental requirements, 92
  of kitchens, 54
  of sanitary accommodation, 49
Ventile, 27
Vincel, 22
viscose, 26
vitrification, 30–31
vomit removal, 247

waiting rooms, 257–8
wallpaper:
  cleaning of, 208–9
  types, 35–7
wall(s):
  cleaning agents, 163–9, 203, 208
  cleaning of exterior walls, 203
  cleaning of interior walls, 205–9
  cleaning of kitchen walls, 54, 256
  cleaning of walls in sanitary accommodation, 249
  construction of interior walls, 33
  damage to, 32
  in sanitary accommodation, 49
  materials used in exterior walls, 32

wands, 130. 131, 132, 133, 134
wardrobes:
  cleaning of, 242
  construction of, 55–6
  dimensions, 61
wards, 263
ware washing:
  cleaning agents, 163, 164
  methods, equipment, etc., 252–4
  see also dish washers
Warfarin, 100
warp, 25
washer extractors, 273
washing:
  application, 84, 201
  procedure for furniture, 233
  procedure for kitchen and tableware, 253–4
  procedures for walls, 205–8
wash 'n' wax, 189, 192–3
waste:
  as source of bacteria, 86, 88
  collection of, 267–8
  definitions, 80
  disposal requirements, 266
  disposal equipment, 268–9
  handling of in isolation units, 264
  in kitchens, 55
  types, 266–7
water:
  as cleaning agent, 155–6
  as source of bacteria, 86
  in polish, 190
  in seals, 179–81
  requirement of bacteria, 85
  softening, 159
  solubility of surfactants, 158
  trap, 269
waxes:
  cleaning of wax finishes, 242
  effect on application of water based polish, 196
  effect on sealing, 186
  in polish, 190
  removal of stains, 247
WC pans:
  cleaning agents, 163–9
  cleaning of, 249–50
  description, 50–51
wear:
  of carpets, 46–7
  resistant finishes of textiles, 27
weaves, 25, 43